GUIDE TO

Microsoft®
Office 2003

Getting Started with Word,® Excel,® and PowerPoint®

Utilize

Microsoft's Office

programs to fulfill your

home or business needs

D1247303

Diane Koers and Lois Lowe

ISBN: 1-59200-574-8
Library of Congress Catalog Card Number: 2004108255
Printed in the United States of America
05 06 07 08 BH 10 9 8 7 6 5 4 3 2

Thomson Course Technology PTR, a division of Thomson Course Technology
25 Thomson Place • Boston, MA 02210 • http://www.courseptr.com

In loving memory of Vernon and Rosemary Koers

Acknowledgments

I am deeply grateful to the many people at Course Technology PTR who worked on this book. Thank you for all the time you gave and for your assistance. While I can't name everyone involved, I'd like to especially thank Stacy Hiquet for the opportunity to write this book and her confidence in me; to Greg Perry for his wonderful technical advice; to Dan Foster for his outstanding contributions; and a very special thank you to Jenny Davidson and Estelle Manticas for all their patience and guidance in pulling the project together and making it correct. It takes a lot of both to work with me!

Lastly, a big hug and kiss to my husband, Vern, for his never-ending support. For 35 years we've been a team, and it shows!

—Diane Koers

A big thanks to the top-notch staff at Course Technology PTR for another job well done.

—Lois Lowe

Contents at a Glance

Contents

Introduction

Welcome to the world of Microsoft® Office 2003. This book will help you use the many and varied features of Microsoft's three most popular office suite products—Microsoft Word, Excel, and PowerPoint®.

Microsoft Word 2003 is a powerful word-processing program that will take your documents far beyond what you can produce with a typewriter. Whether you want to create a simple letter to a friend, produce a newsletter for a professional organization, or even write a complicated, multiple-page report containing graphics and tables with numerical data, you will find the information that you need to quickly and easily get the job done in this *Microsoft Office 2003* guide.

Microsoft Excel 2003 is a powerful spreadsheet program with a huge grid designed to display data in rows and columns where you can create calculations to perform mathematical, logical, and other types of operations on the data you enter. You can sort the data, enhance it, and manipulate it a plethora of ways including creating powerful charts and graphs from it. Whether you need a list of names and addresses, or a document to calculate next year's sales revenue based on prior years' performance, Excel is the application you want to use.

Microsoft PowerPoint 2003 is a presentation design program that makes it easy to design a slide show to fit any need so that you can create and deliver informative and effective presentations. It has been popular with users for many years, and new features have been added to each new version of the program to make it more user-friendly and Web-compatible. Anyone can use PowerPoint, not just artists and professional presenters. With PowerPoint, you can create multimedia-rich presentations complete with graphics, sounds, animations, voice-overs, and slide transitions. PowerPoint presentations can be delivered on a computer, through a projector, in a kiosk, or as part of a Web site.

This book uses a step-by-step approach with illustrations of what you will see on your screen in each application, linked with instructions for the next mouse movements or keyboard operations to complete your task. Computer terms and phrases are clearly explained in non-technical language, and expert tips and shortcuts help you produce professional-quality documents, spreadsheets, and presentations.

Microsoft Office 2003: Getting Started with Word, Excel, and PowerPoint provides the tools you need to successfully tackle the potentially overwhelming challenge of learning to use Microsoft Word, Excel, and PowerPoint. Whether you are a novice user or an experienced professional, you will be able to quickly tap into each program's user-friendly integrated design and feature-rich environment.

Through this book you learn *how* to create documents, spreadsheets, and presentations; however *what* you create is totally up to you—your imagination is the only limit! This book cannot begin to teach you everything you can do with Word, Excel, and PowerPoint, nor does it give you all the different ways to accomplish a task. What we *have* tried to do is give you the fastest and easiest way to get started with these fun and exciting programs.

Who Should Read This Book?

This book can be used as a learning tool or as a step-by-step task reference. The easy-to-follow, highly visual nature of this book makes it the perfect learning tool for a beginning computer user as well as those seasoned computer users who are new to Word, Excel, and PowerPoint. No prerequisites are required from you, the reader, except that you know how to turn your computer on and how to use your mouse.

In addition, anyone using software applications always needs an occasional reminder about the steps required to perform a particular task. By using the *Microsoft Office 2003* guide, any level of user can look up steps for a task quickly without having to plow through pages of descriptions.

Added Advice to Make You a Pro

You'll notice that this book uses steps and keeps explanations to a minimum to help you learn faster. Included in the book are a few elements that provide some additional comments to help you master these programs, without encumbering your progress through the steps:

- **Tips** often offer shortcuts when performing an action, or a hint about a feature that might make your work quicker and easier.

- **Notes** give you a bit of background or additional information about a feature, or advice about how to use the feature in your day-to-day activities.

Read and enjoy this book. It certainly is the fastest and easiest way to learn Microsoft Word, Excel, and PowerPoint 2003.

PART I

Word

1

Getting Started with Word

If this is your first opportunity to use Word, you may be a little overwhelmed by the number of buttons and items on the screen. Just remember that although Word is a powerful program, it's also very easy to use, which is why most businesses have adopted it. Don't worry! You'll be creating your first document after just a couple of mouse clicks. In this chapter you'll learn how to:

- Open the Word program
- Explore the Word screen
- Use toolbars, menus, and the task pane
- Enter text and move around the screen
- Search for additional help

Starting Word

There are a number of different methods to access the Word application. One method is from the Start button.

1. **Click** on the **Start button**. The Start menu will appear.

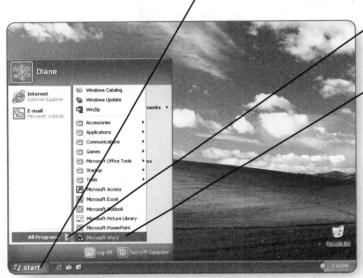

2. **Click** on **All Programs**. A menu of available programs will appear.

3. **Click** on **Microsoft Word**. The Microsoft Word program will open with a blank document screen.

TIP

If you have a Microsoft Word icon on your Windows desktop, you can double-click it to quickly access Word.

Discovering the Word Screen

Many items that you see when you open a new word processing document are standard to most Windows programs. However, the following list illustrates a few elements that are specific to Word:

- **Title bar**. A bar displayed at the top of a document that displays the name of the current document.

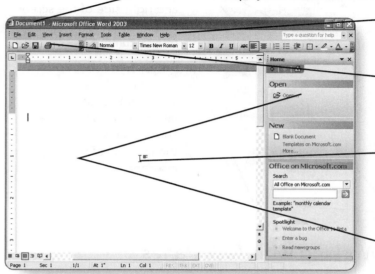

- **Menu bar**. A grouping of most available features in the Microsoft Word program.

- **Toolbar**. A selection of commonly used features. A single click on a toolbar item activates the feature.

- **Mouse pointer**. The shape of the mouse pointer will change as you move it to different locations on the screen.

- **Task pane**. Small windows that assist you when you're working with Word. Task panes store collections of important Word features and present them in ways that that make them much easier to find and use.

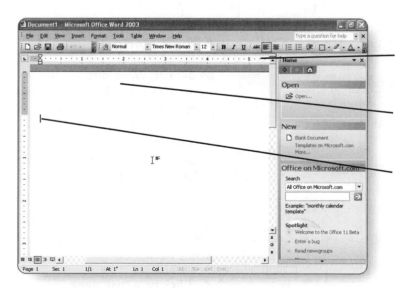

- **Ruler**. Used to measure the document settings within the page margins.

- **Document screen**. The white area of the screen where the actual text will appear.

- **Insertion point**. The blinking vertical line in the document screen that indicates where text will appear when you begin typing.

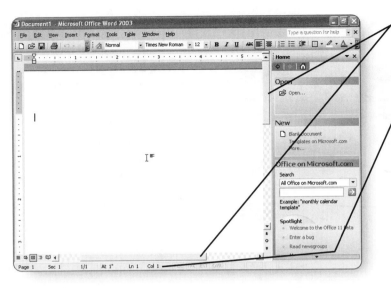

- **Scroll bars**. Horizontal and vertical bars on the bottom and right side of the screen that enable you to see more of a document.

- **Status bar**. A bar at the bottom of the screen indicating document information such as the current page number of the location of the insertion point.

Working with Task Panes

Word contains several different task panes. The task pane that appears depends on what Word task you are performing. One task pane assists you to create a new document while another task pane helps you add clip art to your document.

Selecting a Different Task Pane

By default, Word displays the Home task pane. The Home task pane lists common features associated with opening existing documents or creating a new document. As you select different Word features, the task pane may change.

1. **Click** on the **task pane drop-down arrow**. A list of other task panes will appear.

2. **Click** on a **task pane name**. The selected task pane will appear.

Closing and Redisplaying the Task Pane

While the task pane can be very helpful, it also uses up valuable screen space. You can close the task pane at any time and redisplay it whenever you need it.

1. **Click** on the **task pane Close button**. The task pane will close.

The task pane will reappear automatically when you select a Word feature that uses it. You can, however, redisplay the task pane at any time.

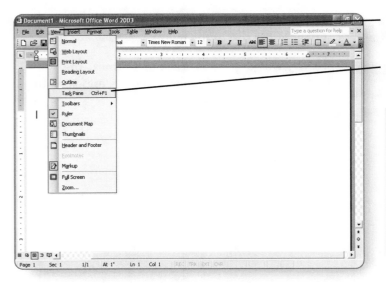

2. **Click** on **View**. The View menu will appear.

3. **Click** on **Task Pane**. The task pane will reopen.

NOTE

For the purposes of this book, most screens will appear without the task pane, unless a feature that uses the task pane is being shown.

Working with Menus

All Windows-based applications use menus to list items appropriate to the program you're using. Word is no different. As you click a menu choice, you'll see the options available under that menu. Some menus have submenus that list additional choices from which you can select. A menu option that appears lighter in color than the other options is said to be "grayed out." When a menu option is grayed out it is unavailable at the moment. Menu options become grayed out when they are not applicable to your current selection.

Personalized Menus

Word includes personalized menus which display the features you use most often at the top of the menu. When you first access a menu, only the most common features are displayed. Notice the down-pointing double arrow at the bottom of the menu. This arrow indicates that additional menu features are available. If you pause the mouse over the top item on the menu bar or move it down to the double arrow, the menu will expand to include all available features for that menu.

As you use the personalized menus, the features you use most often will appear at the top of the menu.

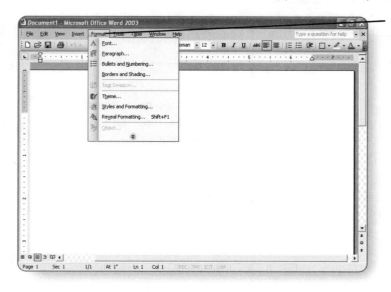

1. Click on **Format**. The Format menu will appear with nine options.

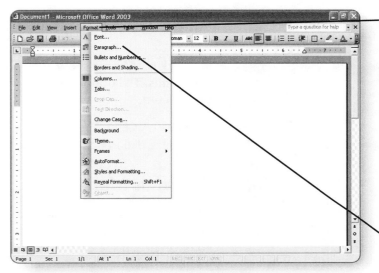

2. Pause the **mouse pointer** over the Format menu. The Format menu will expand to include 16 items.

TIP

Press the Esc key or click on the menu name (such as Format) to close a menu without making any selection.

Many selections in a menu are followed by three periods, called an *ellipsis*. Selections followed by ellipses indicate that if you select one of these items, a dialog box will appear with more options.

If you find that you don't like personalized menus, you can turn the feature off and all of a menu's options will automatically appear when you select the menu.

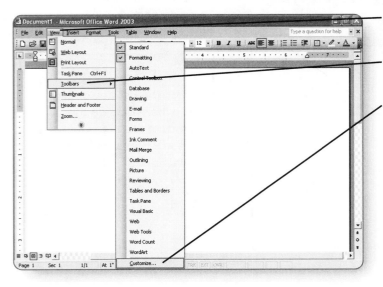

3. Click on **View**. The View menu will appear.

4. Click on **Toolbars**. The Toolbars submenu will appear.

5. Click on **Customize**. The Customize dialog box will open.

6. Click on the **Options tab**. The Options tab will appear in front.

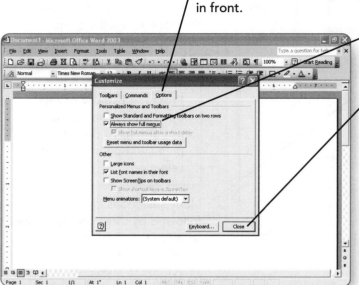

7. Click on **Always show full menus**. The option will be selected.

8. Click on **Close**. The Customize dialog box will close.

Shortcut Menus

Shortcut menus contain a limited number of commands. The commands you see on a shortcut menu are relevant to what you're doing at the time you open the shortcut menu. Click the right mouse button (called a *right-click*) to open a shortcut menu.

1. Right-click anywhere in the **document screen**. A shortcut menu will appear on the screen.

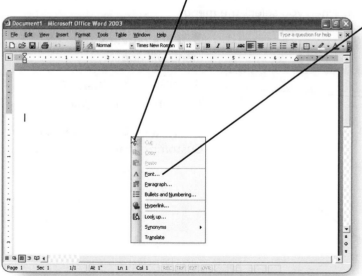

2. Click on a **menu selection**. The menu action will be performed.

TIP

Press the Esc key or click anywhere outside the shortcut menu to close the menu without making a selection.

Using Toolbars

Along the top of the Word screen you see two different toolbars. Toolbars are groups of small icons or buttons that help you access commonly used Word features without digging through the menus. Word includes more than 20 toolbars to assist you but, by default, only the Standard and Formatting toolbars are automatically displayed side-by-side along the top of the Word screen.

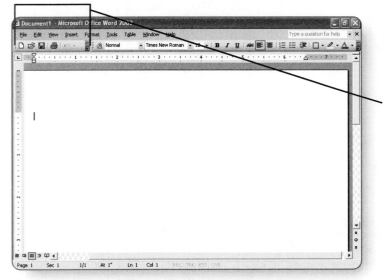

Standard toolbar

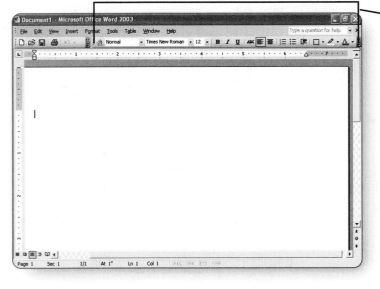

Formatting toolbar

If you look closely, you can see that the toolbar buttons are grouped into related activities. For example, the Alignment buttons (left, center, and right) are grouped together, and options that relate to files, such as saving or opening, are grouped together. You'll learn how to use these buttons in later chapters.

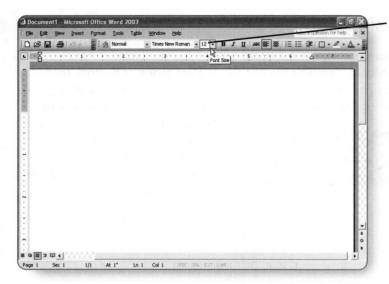

1. Pause the **mouse pointer** over any toolbar item. The description of that feature will appear.

2. Click on a **toolbar button**. The requested action will be performed.

Additional toolbar buttons may be available.

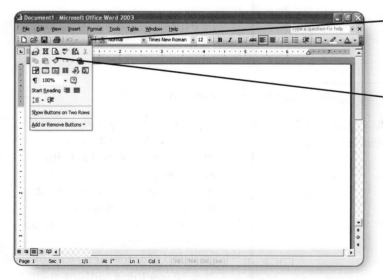

3. Click on the **Toolbar options button**.

A set of additional toolbar buttons will appear from which you can select.

Separating Toolbars

Most people find the Standard and Formatting toolbars difficult to use when displayed side-by-side, so you may want to separate them so that one is on top of the other. Doing so can make all the tools on these bars easier to access.

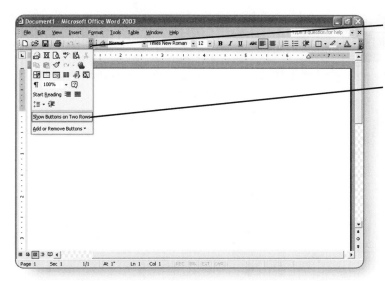

1. **Click** on the **Toolbar options button**. Additional toolbar buttons will appear.

2. **Click** on **Show Buttons on Two Rows**. The Standard and Formatting toolbars will become separated.

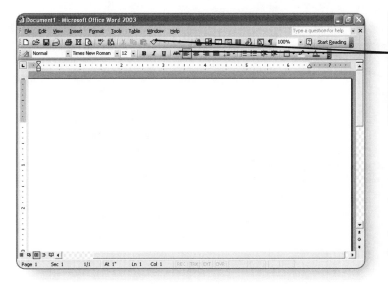

NOTE

For the purposes of this book, most screens will appear with the toolbars separated.

Moving a Toolbar

Most toolbars are docked at the top or bottom of the screen, but if a toolbar is not located in a favorable position for you to access it, or you have accidentally moved a toolbar into the middle of the screen—thereby blocking your view of your document—you can easily move the toolbar into any position you like.

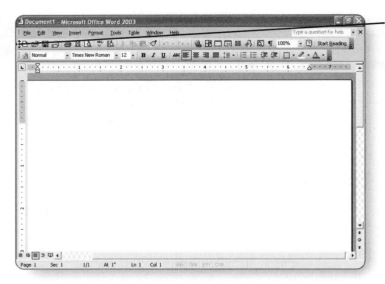

1. Position the **mouse pointer** at the far left side of any toolbar. The mouse pointer will change to a black cross with four arrowheads.

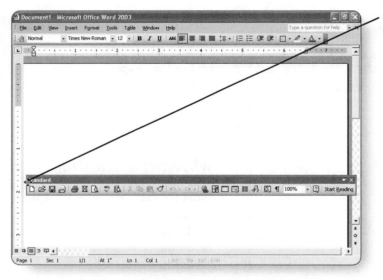

2. Hold down the **mouse button** and **drag** the **toolbar** into the document area. The toolbar may change shape.

NOTE
Although you probably won't want to, you can move the menu bar with the same method.

3. Release the **mouse button**. The toolbar will remain in the new position.

TIP
To return a toolbar to its default position, press and hold the mouse button over the toolbar title bar and drag the toolbar into the default position, which is usually at the top of the screen.

Hiding and Displaying Toolbars

You can hide or display any toolbar. Hiding a particular toolbar can be very helpful if it is using up valuable screen space.

1. **Click** on **View**. The View menu will appear.

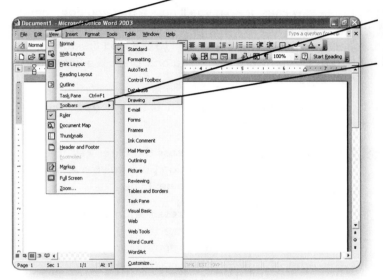

2. **Click** on **Toolbars**. A list of toolbars will appear.

3. **Click** on the **toolbar** you want to turn off or on.

Currently displayed toolbars have a checkmark next to them. Toolbars without a checkmark are not currently displayed.

Entering Text

The small flashing vertical bar on your document screen is called the *insertion point*. It marks the location where text will appear when you type.

If you type a few lines of text, you'll notice that you don't need to press the Enter key at the end of each line. The program automatically moves down (or wraps) to the next line for you. This feature is called *word wrap*. You only press the Enter key to start a new paragraph.

1. Type a small amount of **text,** such as today's date. The text will appear on the screen.

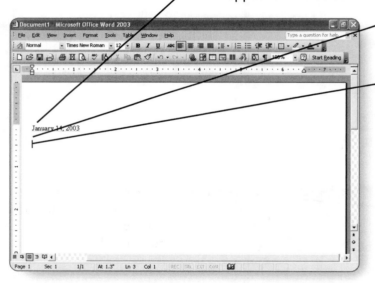

2. Press the **Enter key**. The insertion point will move down to the next line.

3. Press the **Enter key** again. The insertion point will move down another line, creating a blank line between your paragraphs.

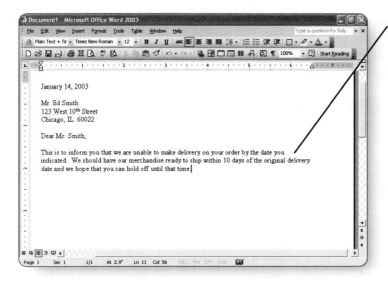

4. Type a **paragraph** of text. Don't press Enter; just keep typing until you have several lines of text.

Word's text wrap feature will move the insertion point down to the next line when necessary.

Moving around the Screen

To make changes to your document, you'll need to move the insertion point around. You can use several methods to move around the Word screen, including a feature called Click and Type.

Using Click and Type

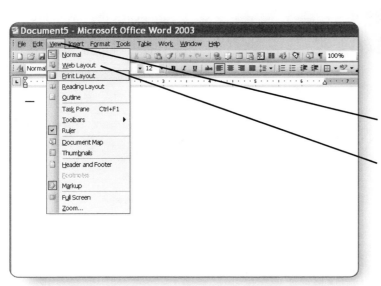

The Click and Type feature works only if you are using Print Layout view or Web Layout view. You'll learn more about using different Word views in Chapter 5, "Working with Pages."

1. Click on **View**. The View menu will appear.

2. Click on **Print Layout**. The document screen will appear in Print Layout view.

You can position the insertion point with the mouse and double-click where you would like to enter text. Word determines and sets any necessary paragraph formatting based on where you double-click the mouse.

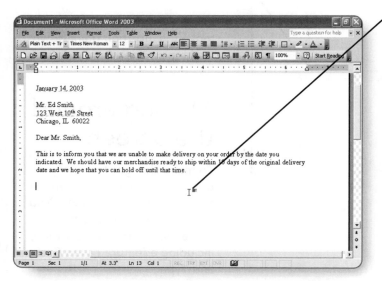

Before double-clicking the mouse, pay close attention to the appearance of the mouse pointer. If there are lines to the right of the I-beam pointer, the text you type will flow to the right of the insertion point. If the lines are to the left, the text will flow to the left of the insertion point, and if the lines are under the I-beam, the text will be centered at the insertion point.

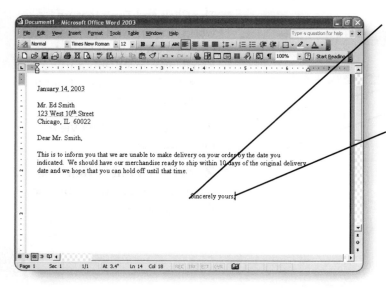

3. Double-click the anywhere on the **document screen**. A blinking insertion point will appear.

4. Type some **text**. The text will appear at the insertion point where you clicked.

Using the Scroll Bars

Word includes two scroll bars, a vertical scroll bar and a horizontal scroll bar, in the document window. Displaying text by using the scroll bars does not move the insertion point. You'll still need to click the mouse wherever you would like to locate the insertion point.

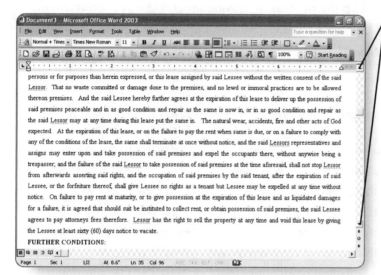

1a. **Click** on the **arrow** at either end of the vertical scroll bar to move the document up or down in the window.

OR

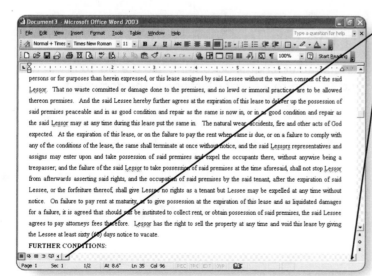

1b. **Click** on the **arrow** at either end of the horizontal scroll bar to move the document left or right.

Using the Keyboard

As you've seen, you can work on any part of the document that appears on your screen simply by clicking the mouse pointer where you want to be. You can also move around in a Word document by pressing the Up, Down, Right, or Left Arrow keys on the keyboard. There are several shortcut keys designed to speed up the process of moving around in a Word document. The following table illustrates these shortcut keys.

To Move	Do This
A word at a time	Press Ctrl+Right Arrow or Ctrl+Left Arrow
A paragraph at a time	Press Ctrl+Up Arrow or Ctrl+Down Arrow
A full screen up at a time	Press the PageUp key
A full screen down at a time	Press the PageDown key
To the beginning of a line	Press the Home key
To the end of a line	Press the End key
To the top of the document	Press Ctrl+Home
To the bottom of the document	Press Ctrl+End
To a specified page number	Press Ctrl+G, and then enter the page number

Using the Go To Command

If you have a rather lengthy document, use the Go To command to jump to a specific location in the document.

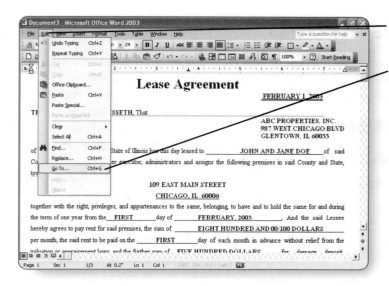

1. Click on **Edit**. The Edit menu will appear.

2. Click on **Go To**. The Go To page of the Find and Replace dialog box will appear.

NOTE

If you are using personalized menus, the Go To command is one of those commands that may not display immediately upon choosing the Edit menu. Hold the mouse over the Edit menu for a few seconds to display the full Edit menu.

TIP

Press Ctrl+G to quickly display the Go To page of the Find and Replace dialog box.

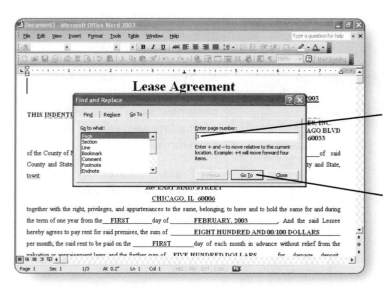

3. Type the **page number** you'd like to display. The number will appear in the Enter page number text box.

4. Click on **Go To**. The specified page will be displayed. The insertion point will be located at the beginning of the specified page.

Using Help

Many of your questions about Word will be answered in this book. But if you can't find the answer to your question here, you can try Word's Help system. Word's Help system is quite extensive, and can include searching the Internet for solutions. The easiest method is to access the very convenient Ask a Question box, wherein you can pose your question in plain English.

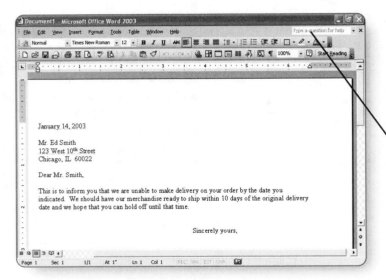

1. **Click** in the **Ask a Question box**. An insertion point will appear in the box.

2. **Type** your **question or words** that describe what you need help with. You can type a complete sentence or just a few words.

3. **Press** the **Enter key**. The Help task pane will appear, displaying a selection of potential help topics.

Word looks for your answer in the Word Help system; however, if you have Internet access, Word will also attempt to contact Microsoft.com for additional options.

4. **Click** on the **topic** that best represents the subject with which you need help. A Help window with instructions will appear.

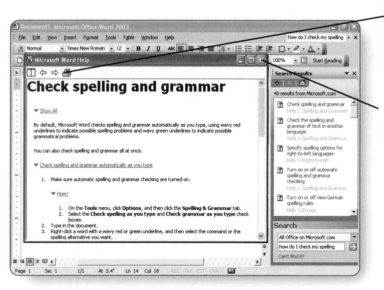

TIP

Click on the Print button to print a hard copy of the Help instructions.

5. **Click** on the **Close button** when you are finished with the Help window.

2
Editing Text

Unless you're a perfect typist, you'll probably make a few mistakes in your document. Or perhaps you'll change your mind about some of the text in the document and want to change it. In a word processing program such as Word, corrections and changes are easy to make. In this chapter you'll learn how to:

- Select, insert, and delete text
- Change the case of text
- Use the Undo and Redo commands
- Move and copy text
- Understand and use Smart Tags
- Display symbols in a document

Inserting, Selecting, and Deleting Text

Editing text with Word is a breeze. Need to insert extra words? Just type them in. Need to delete words? Just highlight them and press the Delete key.

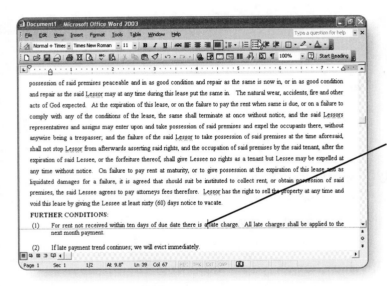

Inserting Text

When you want to add new text to a document, just place the insertion point where you want to locate the new text and begin typing.

1. Click the **mouse pointer** where you want new text to appear. The blinking insertion point will appear.

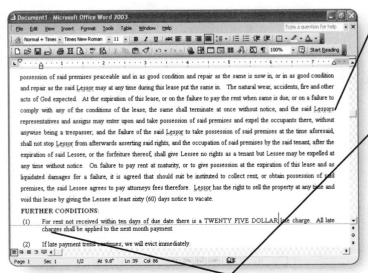

2. Type any **new words**, adding a space before or after as necessary. The new text will be inserted into the document.

Word will push the existing text to the right and keep moving it over or down to make room for the new text.

NOTE

If you notice that the existing text doesn't move over, but seems to disappear, you may have accidentally pressed the Insert key, which takes you out of Insert mode and into Overtype mode. Press the Insert key to return to Insert mode.

Selecting Text

Before you can move, copy, delete, or change the formatting of text, you must first select the text you want to edit. When text is selected (called *highlighted*), it will appear as light type on a dark background on your screen—the reverse of unselected text. You can select sequential or non-sequential text for editing.

The following list shows different selection techniques:

- To select a single word, double-click on the word.

- To select a sentence, hold down the Ctrl key and click anywhere on the sentence.

- To select an entire paragraph, click three times (triple-click) anywhere in the paragraph.

TIP

To select the entire document, press Ctrl+A or choose Edit, Select All.

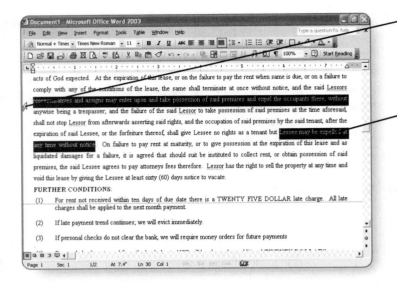

- To select a single line of text, click once in the left margin with the mouse arrow next to the line to be selected.

- To select a block of text, click at the beginning of the text, hold the mouse button down, and drag across the balance of the text you want to select.

- To select a nonsequential block of text, hold down the Ctrl key and use the preceding selection techniques for each additional text block you want to include.

TIP
To deselect text, click once anywhere in the document.

Deleting Text

You can delete unwanted text one character, word, or paragraph at a time, and you can delete any combination of the above.

Two common keys used to delete text are the Backspace and Delete keys. Pressing the Backspace key will delete one character at a time to the left of the insertion point; pressing the Delete key will delete one character at a time to the right of the insertion point.

TIP

An easy way to remember which direction the Backspace key will delete is to look at the arrow printed on the Backspace key. On most keyboards, the arrow points to the left, indicating this is the direction the characters will be deleted.

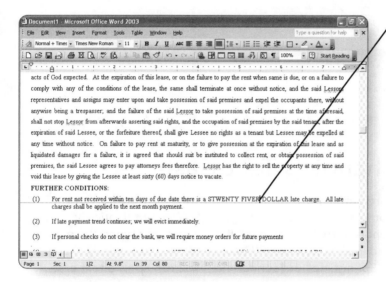

1. Click the **mouse** at the end of a word. The blinking insertion point will appear.

2. Press the **Backspace key**. The last letter of the word will disappear.

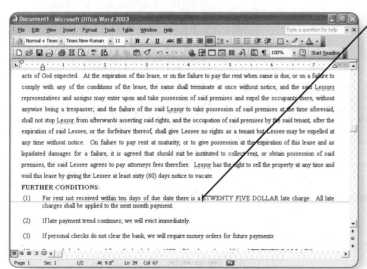

3. Click the **mouse** at the beginning of a word. The blinking insertion point will appear.

4. Press the **Delete key**. The first letter of the word will disappear.

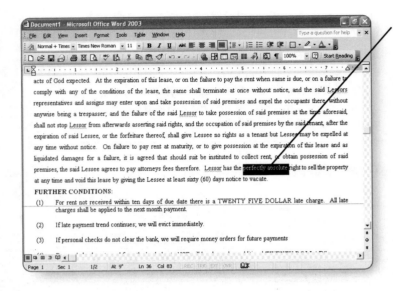

5. Select a **block of text** to delete. The text will be highlighted.

6. Press the **Delete key** or the **Backspace key**. The highlighted block of text will be deleted.

Changing Text Case

Word automatically corrects many text case errors. For example, if you type "SPringtime," Word automatically changes it to "Springtime." If, however, you typed the entire word in all uppercase (SPRINGTIME), you can quickly change it to "Springtime" or "springtime." You can apply a text case change to a word, a phrase, or any amount of selected text.

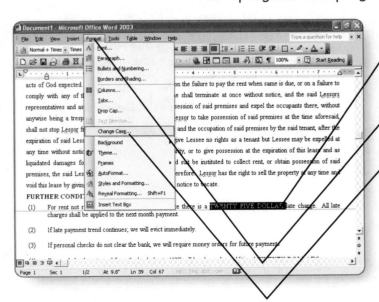

1. Select the **text** you want to change. The text will be highlighted.

2. Click on **Format**. The Format menu will appear.

3. Click on **Change Case**. The Change Case dialog box will open.

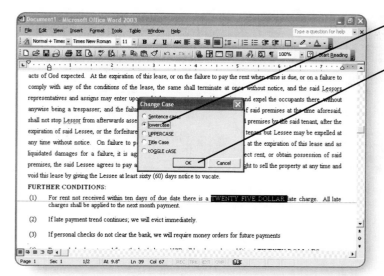

4. **Click** on a **case option**. The option will be selected.

5. **Click** on **OK**. The text will change to the case you selected.

TIP

Optionally, after highlighting your text, press the F3 key. Each time you press F3, the case of the selected text will change to either upper, lower, or title case.

Using Undo and Redo

If you make a change, and then decide you really don't want to make that change after all, use Word's Undo feature. You can use Undo to restore text that you deleted, delete text you just typed, or reverse a recently taken action.

Be aware, however, that if you save your document, you cannot use Undo to "unsave" it. Also, if you close the document, when you reopen it, you cannot undo changes made in the previous editing session.

NOTE

You'll learn more about saving, closing, and opening documents in Chapter 3, "Saving, Opening, Closing, and Printing."

Undoing the Previous Step

You're always one mouse click away from reversing your previous action.

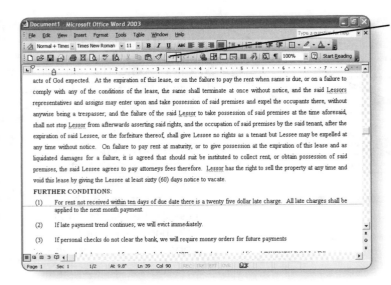

1. **Click** on the **Undo button**. Word will reverse the last action you took with the current document.

TIP

Optionally, choose Undo from the Edit menu.

Redoing the Previous Step

If you undo an action and then decide you prefer the document the original way, use the Redo feature.

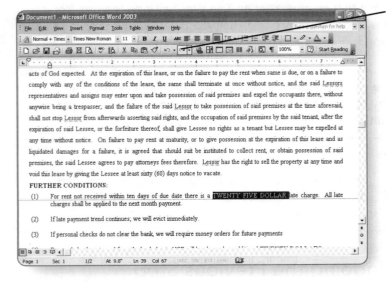

1. **Click** on the **Redo button**. Word will reverse the previous undo action.

Undoing a Series of Actions

Word actually keeps track of several steps you have recently taken. When you undo a previous step, you also automatically undo any actions taken after that step. For example, imagine you changed the case of some text, then bolded the text, then underlined the text. If you undo the Change Case action, Word also reverses the bolding and underlining steps.

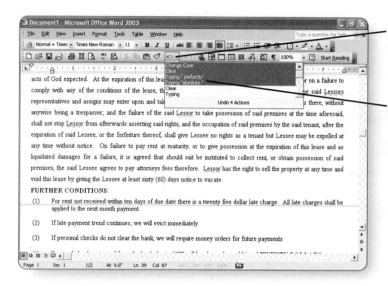

1. Click on the **arrow** next to the Undo button. A list of the most recent actions will be displayed.

2. Click on the **action** you want to undo. Word will reverse the selected action as well as all actions listed above it.

Moving and Copying Text

Word provides a number of different methods with which you can move and copy text, including the *Clipboard*, which temporarily holds text you place on it. You can use the Clipboard feature to move or copy text from one place to another, thereby avoiding the need to retype it.

Moving Text

The features used to move text from one place to another are called *Cut* and *Paste*. With Cut and Paste, Word deletes the selected text, holds it, and then places it into a new location.

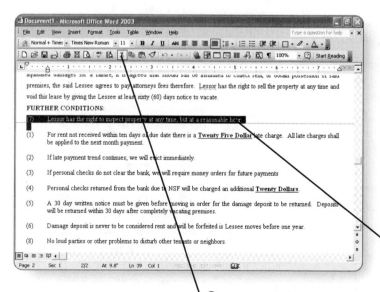

1. Select the **text** you want to move. The text will be highlighted.

2. Click on the **Cut button**. The text will be removed from the document and stored on the Windows Clipboard.

TIP

Optionally, to cut text, press Ctrl+X or select Cut from the Edit menu.

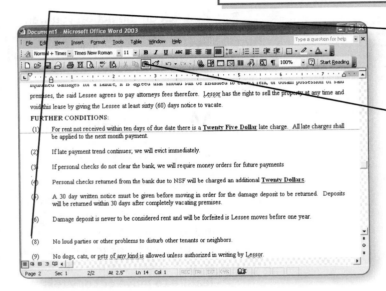

3. Click the **mouse** where you want to place the text. The blinking insertion point will appear.

4. Click on the **Paste button**. The text is placed at the new location.

TIP

Optionally, to paste text, press Ctrl+V or select Paste from the Edit menu.

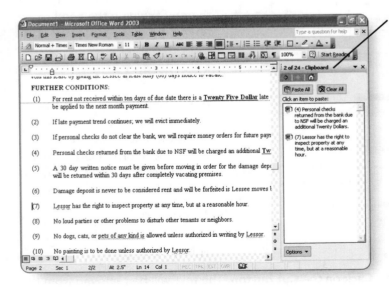

Depending on the number of times you have cut text, the Clipboard task pane may appear when you paste text. You will learn about the Clipboard task pane later in this chapter.

Copying Text

To duplicate text, as when repeating a sentence from an earlier paragraph, Word also uses the Windows Clipboard. Copying text will leave the selected text in its original location but also places a copy of it on the Windows Clipboard.

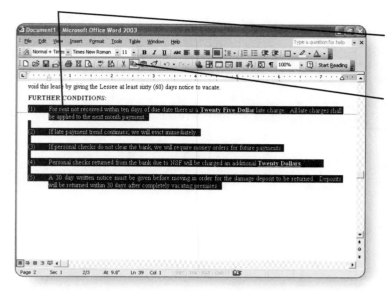

1. Select the **text** you want to copy. The text will be highlighted.

2. Click on the **Copy button**. The text is stored on the Windows Clipboard.

Depending on the number of times you have copied text, the Clipboard task pane may appear. You'll learn more about using the Clipboard task pane later in this chapter.

TIP

Optionally, to copy text, press Ctrl+C or select Copy from the Edit menu.

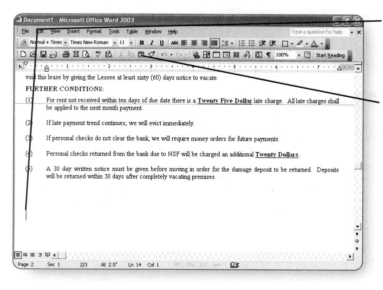

3. Click the **mouse** where you want to place the text. The blinking insertion point will appear.

4. Click on the **Paste button**. The text is placed at the new location.

Notice that the original text is retained in its location and the copy of the text appears in the new location.

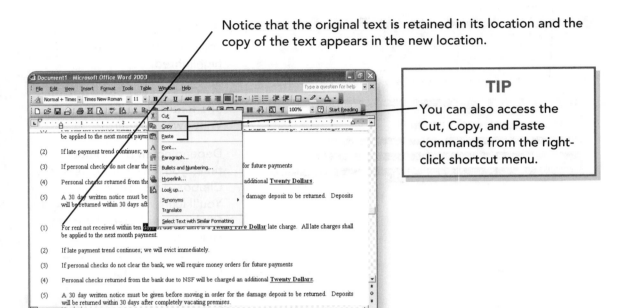

TIP

You can also access the Cut, Copy, and Paste commands from the right-click shortcut menu.

Using Drag and Drop

Another way to move text from one location to another is to use Drag and Drop. The Drag and Drop method works best for moving a small amount of text a short distance.

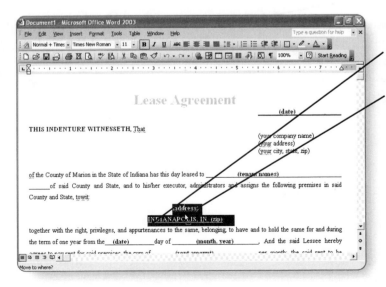

1. Select the **text** to be moved. The text will be highlighted.

2. Position the **mouse pointer** on top of the highlighted text. The mouse arrow will point to the left.

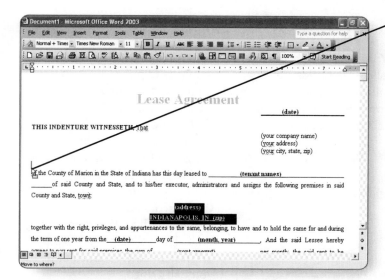

3. **Hold** the **mouse button** down and **drag** the **mouse** to the desired location. A small box will appear at the bottom of the mouse arrow and a gray line will indicate the position of the text.

TIP

To copy text with Drag and Drop, hold down the Ctrl key before dragging the selected text. Release the mouse button before releasing the Ctrl key.

4. **Release** the **mouse button**. The text will be moved.

TIP

If you accidentally move text, or you move it to the wrong position, click on the Undo button to reverse the move.

In some situations, when you paste text you may see a small icon, called a Smart Tag, appear to the right of the pasted text. You'll learn about Smart Tags later in this chapter.

Using the Office Clipboard

Word also uses a special form of the Windows Clipboard, called the Office Clipboard. The Office Clipboard allows you to collect text and other items from any Office document, or even from other programs, then paste them into any Word document. Each item is appended to the Clipboard contents and then inserted as an individual item or as a group in a new location or document. You can copy an item to the Office Clipboard, and then paste it into any Office document at any time. The collected items stay on the Office Clipboard until you exit Office.

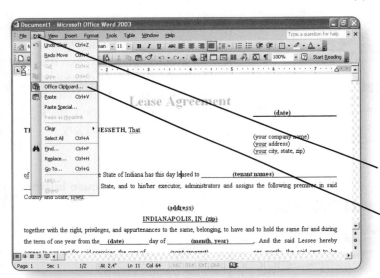

1. Click on **Edit**. The Edit menu will appear.

2. Click on **Office Clipboard**. The Clipboard task pane will appear.

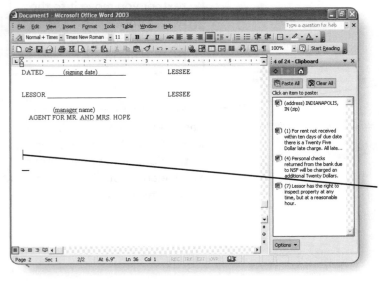

The Office Clipboard stores up to 24 items you have copied or cut, whether you used the Edit menu, the Cut or Copy icons on the toolbar, the shortcut menu, or the shortcut keys.

You can insert all items from the Clipboard or you can insert just one particular item.

3. Click the **mouse** where you want to insert the Clipboard contents. The blinking insertion point will appear.

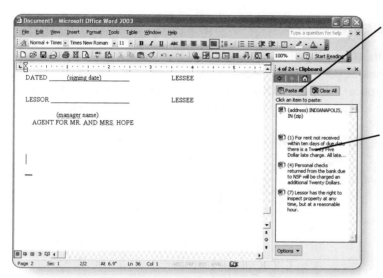

4a. **Click** on the **Paste All button**. The contents of the Clipboard will be placed in the document.

OR

4b. **Click** on the **individual item** you want to insert. The item will be inserted into the document.

TIP

To clear the Clipboard contents, click on the Clear All button.

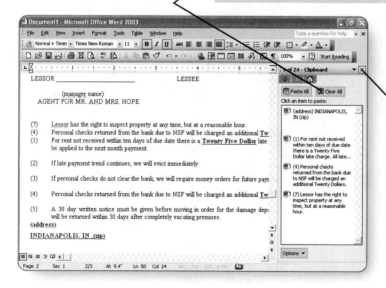

When you are finished with the Clipboard task pane, you may find it helpful to put it away.

5. **Click** the **Close Button**. The Clipboard task pane will disappear.

Understanding Smart Tag Paste Options

Word includes time-saving features called Smart Tags, which look at your text and potentially recognize it as a particular type or format of data. By default, when you paste text from the Clipboard, any formatting the text contained is pasted along with the text. For example, if the original text is underlined, the pasted text will be underlined as well. One Smart Tag provides the option to paste text with or without formatting. (You'll learn how to add formatting in Chapter 6, "Using Fonts Effectively.")

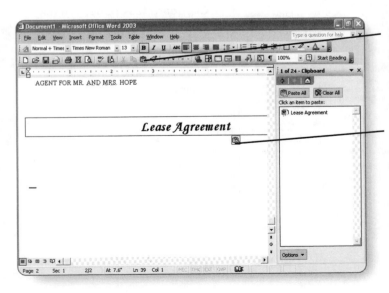

1. Select and cut or copy some **text**. The text and formatting will be stored on the Clipboard.

The Clipboard task pane does not show formatting.

2. Click on the **Paste button** to paste the text into a different location. The pasted text, including any formatting, will appear.

If the pasted text contains different formatting than the text in the current document location, a Smart Tag icon will appear.

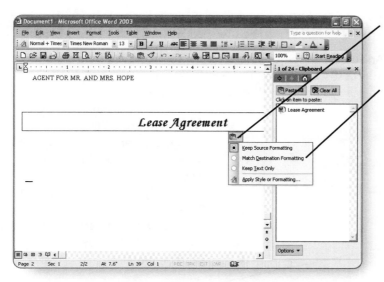

3. Click on the **down arrow** next to the Smart Tag. A list of options will appear.

4. Click on an **option**. The resulting action will depend on the option you select.

- **Keep Source Formatting**. Leaves the pasted text formatted the same as the original text.

- **Match Destination Formatting**. Modifies the pasted test to match the text closest to the pasted text.

- **Keep Text Only**. Modifies the pasted text with the default document font.

- **Apply Style or Formatting**. Displays the Styles and Formatting task pane so you can select different formatting.

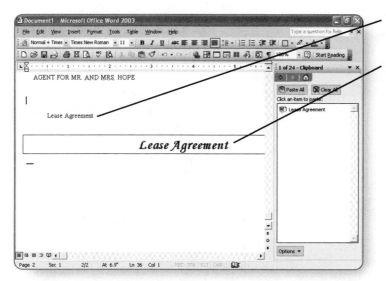

The text pasted with the destination formatting.

The text pasted with the source formatting.

Discovering Other Smart Tags

Another function of Smart Tags is to recognize data as dates, addresses, or names. The type of actions you can take depends on the type of data that Word recognizes and labels with a Smart Tag. For example, if you type an address, Word will display a Smart Tag with options to add the contact information into Microsoft Outlook. Optionally, you can configure the Smart Tag to even recognize a name and offer to schedule a meeting with that person or send an e-mail to him or her.

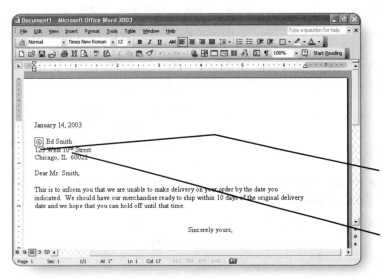

1. Position the **mouse** over a name or an address. A Smart Tag icon will appear.

Smart Tag indicators appear as a series of purple dotted lines beneath your text.

2. Click on the **Smart Tag icon**. A menu of options will appear.

The options that appear depend on which programs are installed on your system. For example, if you also have Microsoft MapPoint installed, a Smart Tag might also offer to display a map or driving directions to the address.

3. Click on **Add to Contacts**. A contact card from Microsoft Outlook will appear with the address and possibly the name already entered.

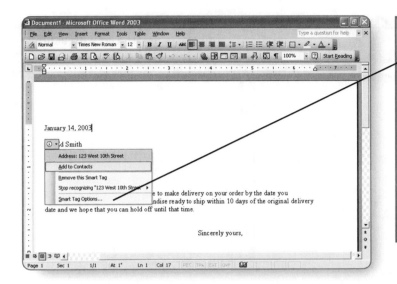

By default, Word's Smart Tags do not automatically recognize text such as a person's name as Smart Tag data. To modify Smart Tag behavior to recognize names, select Smart Tag Options from the Smart Tag, click on Person Name (English), then click on OK.

The Contact card with the address already entered.

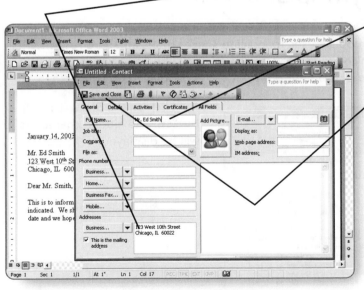

4. Complete any additional **contact data**, if necessary. Refer to your Microsoft Outlook reference guide for instructions.

5. Click on **Save and Close**. The Outlook Contact window will close and you will be returned to your Word document.

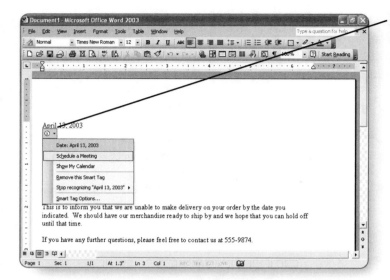

When you type a date, Word will display a Smart Tag with actions you can take, such as scheduling a meeting on that date.

Displaying Nonprinting Symbols

To assist you in editing a document, Word can display hidden symbols it uses to indicate spaces, tabs, and hard returns, which are created when you press the Enter key. These symbols do not print but can be displayed on your screen.

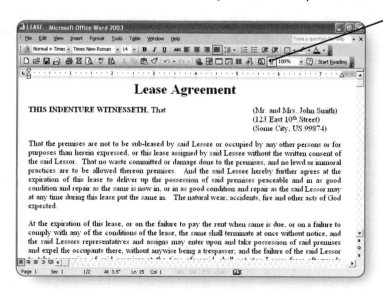

1. Click on the **Show/Hide ¶ button**. The hidden characters will be displayed.

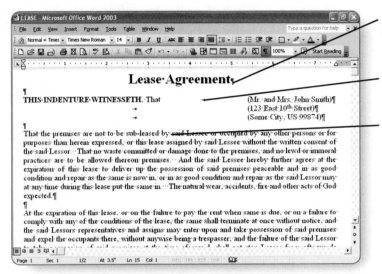

Paragraph hard returns are displayed with the paragraph symbol—¶.

Tabs are displayed with a right-pointing arrow.

Spaces are indicated by a dot.

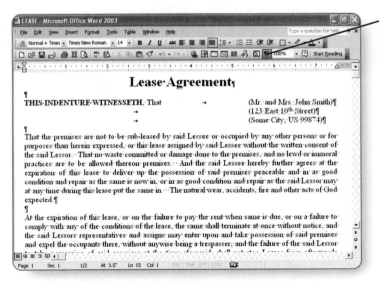

2. **Click** on the **Show/Hide ¶ button.** The displayed special characters will be hidden.

3
Saving, Opening, Closing, and Printing

With the adoption of e-mail within most corporations and homes, many documents today might never be printed on paper—they may only ever exist in an electronic form. Before you send your document into cyberspace, you will probably want to save it for future reference and perhaps editing. And there may even be times when you need a paper copy! In this chapter, you'll learn how to:

- Save a document
- Create a new document
- Open a previously created and saved document
- Print a document on paper
- E-mail a document

Saving a Document

Anyone who uses a computer has probably lost data at one time or another. If you don't save your document regularly, it only takes a second to lose hours of work. Fortunately, Word has a built-in feature called AutoRecover, which you will learn about later in this chapter, to help protect you against such a catastrophe. However, you still need to save your document so that you can refer to it or make changes to it at some future time.

Saving a Document the First Time

When you first open Word, a blank screen appears with the title Document1 in the Word title bar. Word names the next blank document you create Document2, then Document3, and so forth. Those names are temporary names, and they're not very descriptive, so you need to assign your documents names that help you associate them with their contents.

Word asks for a name the first time you save a document, and after that, the name you assign it will appear in the Word title bar.

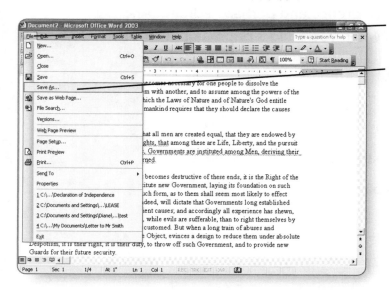

1. Click on **File**. The File menu will appear.

2. Click on **Save As**. The Save As dialog box will open.

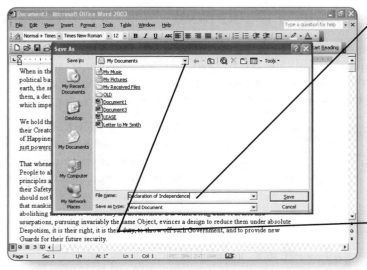

3. **Type** a **name** for your file in the File name text box. The file name will be displayed.

File names can contain spaces, dashes, and many other special characters, but cannot include the asterisk (*), slash (/), backslash (\), or question mark (?) characters.

NOTE

The Save in drop-down list box lists the folders in which you can save the document. The default folder that appears is My Documents. If you don't want to save your document to this folder, or if you want to save it to another disk, you can click on the down arrow to browse for a different location.

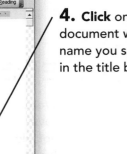

4. **Click** on **Save**. Your document will be saved and the name you specified will appear in the title bar.

Resaving a Document

You should resave your document as you make changes to it. A good rule of thumb is to save your document at least every ten minutes. Word replaces the document copy already saved on the disk with the newly revised document copy.

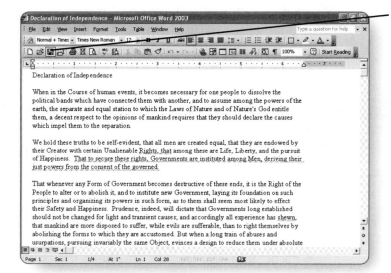

1. **Click** on the **Save button**. The document will be resaved with any changes you made. No dialog box will open because the document is resaved with the same name and in the same folder as previously specified.

TIP

If you want to save the document with a different name or in a different folder, click on File, and then choose Save As. The Save As dialog box will prompt you for the new name or folder. The original document will remain, and a new copy will be created with the name you specified.

Enabling AutoRecover

Word has a feature called AutoRecover that periodically saves a temporary version of your document for you. When you close Word normally, the temporary versions disappear, but if you don't get the chance to exit Word properly (say, due to a computer freeze-up) then when you reopen Word, the program opens recovery versions of the documents you were working on at the time of the crash. You can then choose to save them or not.

You can specify the time intervals at which AutoRecover will save your work.

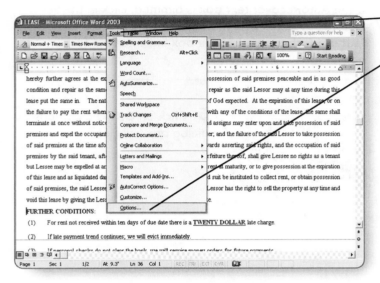

1. Click on **Tools**. The Tools menu will appear.

2. Click on **Options**. The Options dialog box will open.

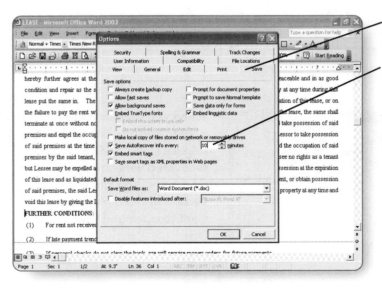

3. Click on the **Save tab**. The Save tab will appear in front.

4. Set the **interval** at which you want AutoRecover to save your work. Click on the down arrow to decrease the time or click on the up arrow to increase the time between AutoRecover saves. The number of minutes you select will appear in the box.

TIP

If the AutoRecover text box is dimmed, click in the Save AutoRecover info every check box to activate the feature. A check mark in the box indicates the feature is activated.

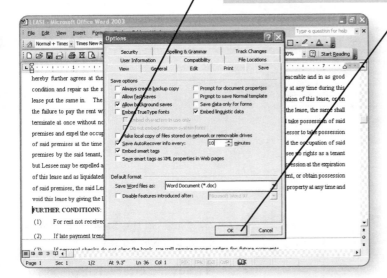

5. Click on **OK**. The Options dialog box will close.

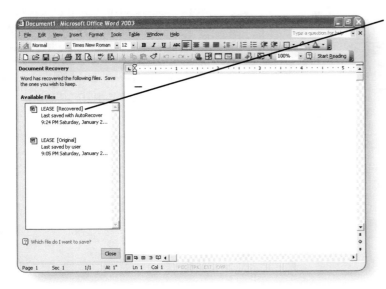

When you reopen Word after a system crash, it lists both the original saved version and the recovered version of your document. You can select which version of the document you want to open and save.

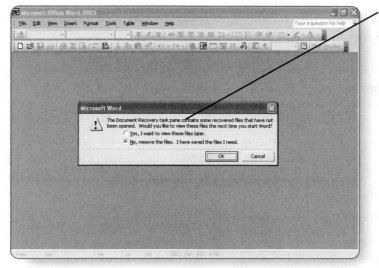

If you opted not to open and save a recovered file, then when you exit Word normally, you can decide to keep the recovered version of the file for later use or let Word go ahead and delete it normally.

Creating a New Document

When a Word session is first started, a blank document appears, ready for you to use. However, during the course of using Word, you may need another blank document. Word includes several methods to access a new document.

Creating a New Document Using the Toolbar

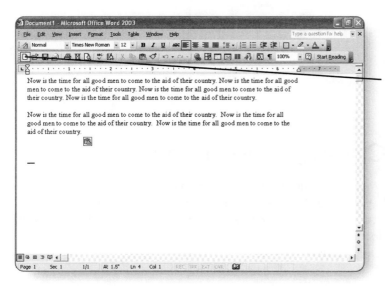

Creating a new document using the standard Word settings is only a mouse click away!

1. Click on the **New Blank Document button**. A new screen will appear with the title Document2 (or Document3, or Document 4, and so on, depending on how many documents you've already created during this session).

Creating a New Document Using the Task Pane

If you choose to create a new document from the task pane, you can select a standard blank document or choose from a variety of templates.

TIP

Click on View, Task Pane if your task pane is not already displayed.

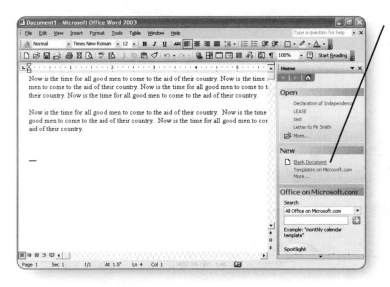

1. Click on **Blank Document**. A standard blank document will appear on the screen.

Closing a Document

When you're finished working on a document, you should close it. Closing a document is the equivalent of putting it away for later use. When you close a document, you are only putting the document away—not the program. Word is still active and ready to work for you.

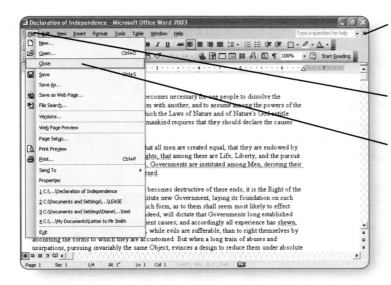

1a. **Click** on the **Close button**. The document will be closed.

OR

1b. **Click** on **File**. The File menu will appear.

2b. **Click** on **Close**. The document will close.

TIP

To save or close all of your open documents in one step, hold down Shift and click on the File menu. Two new options will appear: Close All and Save All.

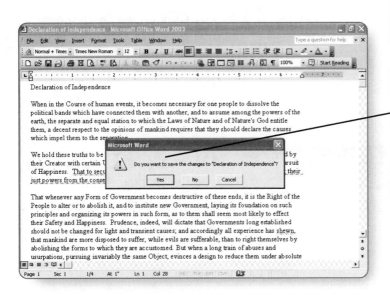

NOTE

If you close a document with changes that have not been saved, Word will prompt you with a dialog box. Choose Yes to save the changes or No to close the file without saving the changes.

Opening an Existing Document

Opening a document is putting a copy of that file into the computer's memory and onto your screen so that you can work on it. If you make any changes, be sure to save the file again. Word provides several different ways to open an existing document.

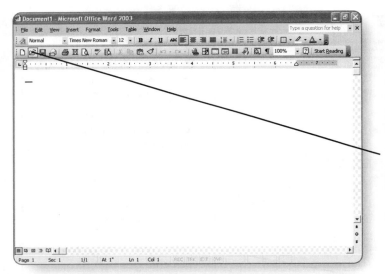

Displaying the Open Dialog Box

Documents you have previously saved can be reopened on your screen through the Open dialog box.

1a. **Click** on the **Open button** to display the Open dialog box. The Open dialog box will open.

OR

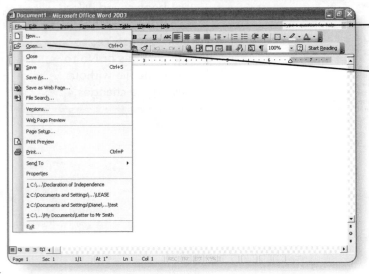

1b. **Click** on **File**. The File menu will appear.

2b. **Click** on **Open**. The Open dialog box will open.

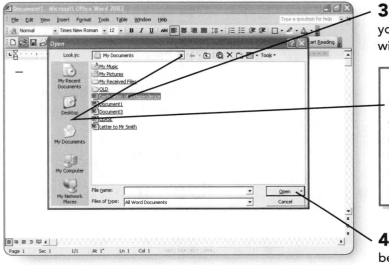

3. Click on the **name of the file** you want to open. The file name will be highlighted.

4. Click on **Open**. The file will be placed on your screen, ready for you to edit.

Opening a Recently Used Document

Both the File menu and the task pane list several of the documents you've recently used, allowing you to quickly locate and open a document.

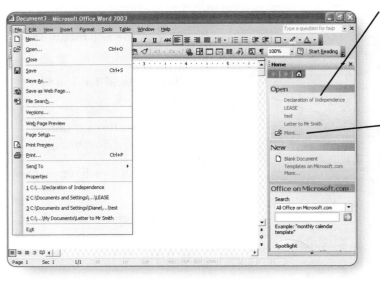

1a. From the task pane, **click** on the **name of the document** you want to open. The document will appear on your screen.

OR

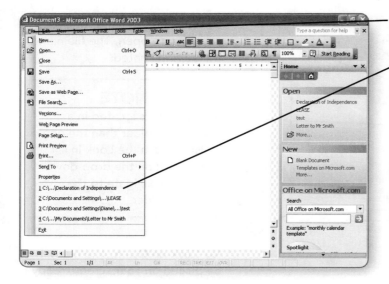

1b. **Click** on **File**. The File menu will open.

2b. **Click** on the **name of the document** you want to open. The document will appear on your screen.

E-Mailing a Document

If you have e-mail access, you can send a document directly to another person. Word copies the content of the document into a blank e-mail message, or sends the document as an attachment to an e-mail message.

NOTE

You must save your document prior to e-mailing it.

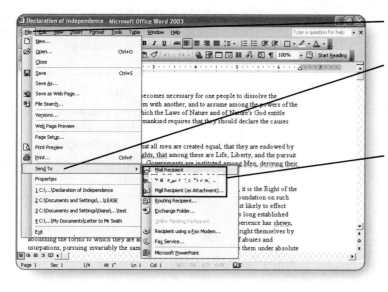

1. **Click** on the **File menu**. The File menu will open.

2. **Click** on **Send To**. The Send To submenu will open.

Word provides three different ways to e-mail a document:

3. **Click** on an e-mail recipient **option**:

- **Mail Recipient**. Sends the document in the body of the e-mail.

- **Mail Recipient (for Review).** The recipient receives either a link, an attachment, or both a link and an attachment to the file, so that they can review it. When a reviewer opens the file, the reviewing tools are enabled and displayed. The files returned from reviewers automatically prompt you to merge changes. You can then use the reviewing tools to accept or reject the changes.

- **Mail Recipient (as Attachment)**. Sends a copy of the document as a file attachment for the recipient to open.

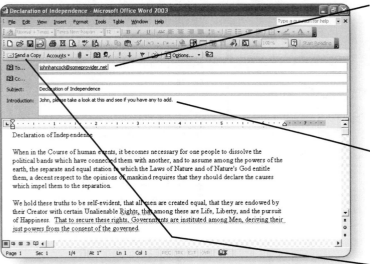

4. Type the **recipient's e-mail address**. The e-mail address will appear in the To box. You can add additional recipients by typing in their e-mail addresses, separated by semicolons.

TIP

Optionally, click in the Introduction text box and type any additional introductory text.

---

5. Click on **Send** or **Send a Copy**. Word will send the document to the e-mail recipients.

Printing a Document

When your document is complete, you may want make a hard copy of it to file away or to share with others.

Using Print Preview

Before you print your document, you may want to preview it on the screen. Previewing a document lets you see how the document layout settings, such as margins, will look in the printed document. In Print Preview, you will only be able to see the document; you won't be able to edit it.

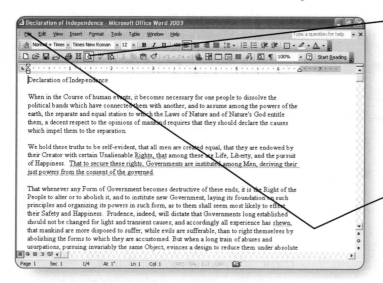

1a. **Click** on the **Print Preview button**. The Print Preview window will open with the document sized so that an entire page is visible on the screen. The mouse pointer will become a magnifying glass with a plus sign on it.

OR

1b. **Click** on **File**. The File menu will open.

2b. **Click** on **Print Preview**. The Print Preview window will open.

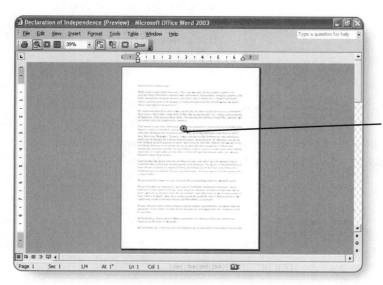

TIP

Press the Page Down or Page Up key on your keyboard to view other pages of the document.

---

2. **Click** anywhere on the **body of the document**. The text will become larger on the screen and the mouse pointer will become a magnifying glass with a minus sign in it.

TIP

Click anywhere on the body of the document again to make the text smaller on the screen.

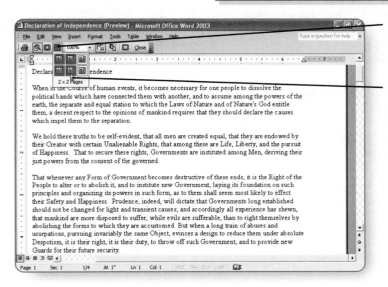

3. Click on the **Multiple Pages button**. A selection of available views will appear.

4. Click on the **number of pages** you'd like to display at the same time. The number of pages you selected will display on the screen.

5. Click on the **One Page button**. The view will return to a single page.

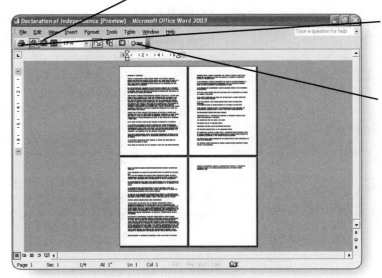

6. Optionally, **click** on the **Print button**. The document will automatically print in its entirety, with standard options.

7. Click on **Close**. The document will be returned to the normal editing view.

Printing with the Print Button

If you need just one copy of the current document, the fastest and easiest way to print is to use the Print button.

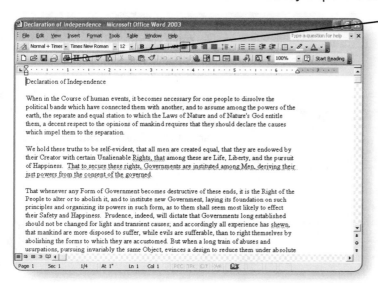

1. Click on the **Print button**. One copy of the entire document is sent to your default printer.

Printing from the Menu

If you need to print multiple copies of the document, or just specific pages, or if you want to change which printer is being used, you must display the Print dialog box.

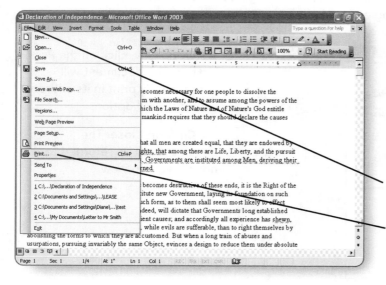

1. Click on **File**. The File menu will appear.

2. Click on **Print**. The Print dialog box will open.

Many options are available from the Print dialog box, including the following:

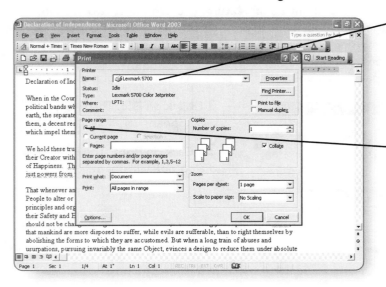

- **Name**. If you are connected to more than one printer, you can select which printer you want to use. Click on the down arrow in the Name drop-down list box and make a selection.

- **Print range**. Determine which pages of your document to print with the Print range options.

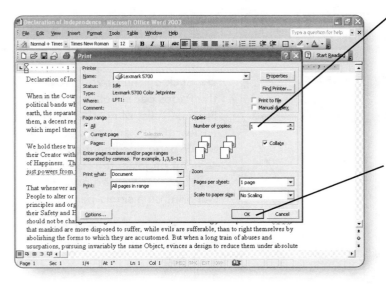

- **Number of copies**. Select the number of copies to be printed by clicking on the up or down arrows at the right of the Number of copies list box.

3. Click on any desired **options**. The options will be activated.

4. Click on **OK**. The document will be sent to the printer.

Scaling a Document for Printing

With Word's Print Zoom feature, you can select two or more pages of a document to print on a single sheet of paper. The formatting and page layout of the document do not change. Word reduces the size of each printed page to fit the number of pages that you select to print on each sheet of paper.

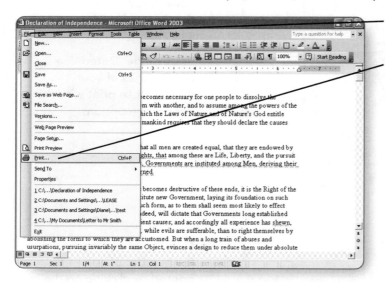

1. Click on **File**. The File menu will appear.

2. Click on **Print**. The Print dialog box will open.

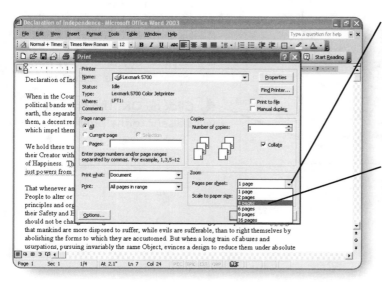

3. Click on the **down arrow** in the Pages per sheet drop-down list box. A list of numbers will appear. For example, if you have a four-page document and you select 4 pages in the Pages per sheet box, the entire document will print on a single page.

4. Click on the **number of pages** you want to print on each page.

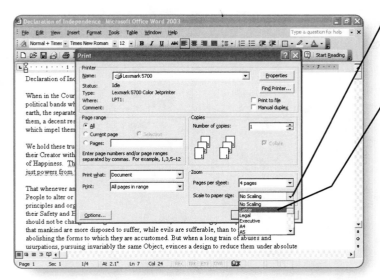

5. Click on the **down arrow** in the Scale to paper size drop-down list box. A list of paper sizes will appear.

6. Click on the **paper size** you'll use for your document. The paper size will appear in the box.

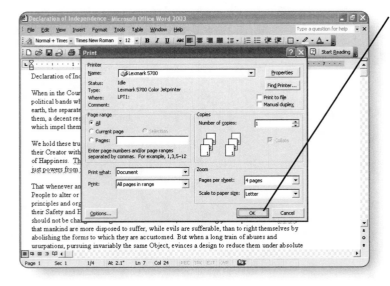

7. Click on **OK**. The document will print to the number of pages you specified.

4

Working with Pages

Balancing *white space*—the amount of blank space on a page—is an important aspect of designing professional-looking pages. You can increase or decrease white space by adjusting margins and the amount of text you place on a page. Also, Word provides the ability to work with multiple documents at the same time, as well as methods for quickly copying information from one document to another. When multiple windows are active, you'll need a way to manage them all. In this chapter, you'll learn how to:

- Set and adjust margins
- Change the document orientation and paper size
- Insert and remove a page break
- Split a document window
- Work with multiple document windows

Working with Split Windows

If you want to see two parts of a document but you can't get them to fit on the screen at the same time, you can split a window. Doing so enables you to view part of a long document in the upper window while you view another part of the document in the lower window.

Adding a Split

When you split a window, each panel of the window will contain its own scroll bar. Click on the up and down arrows of each scroll bar to view other portions of the window.

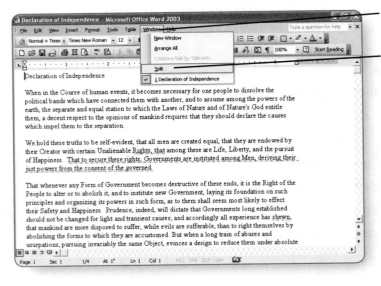

1. **Click** on **Window**. The Window menu will appear.

2. **Click** on **Split**. A gray horizontal line with a double-headed arrow will appear.

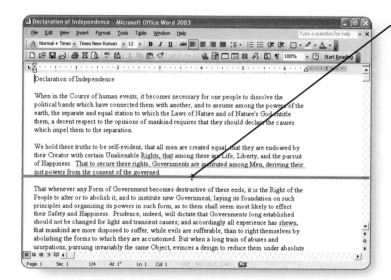

3. Click the **mouse** where you want to divide the window. The gray horizontal line will remain at the location you clicked.

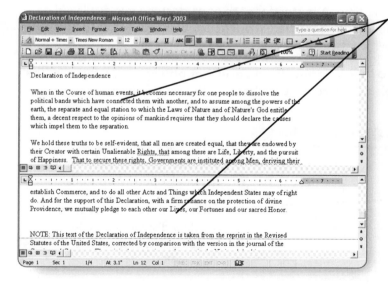

The window will be divided in two, with each section having its own scroll bar.

Removing a Split

When you close the split window, your document will reappear on a single screen.

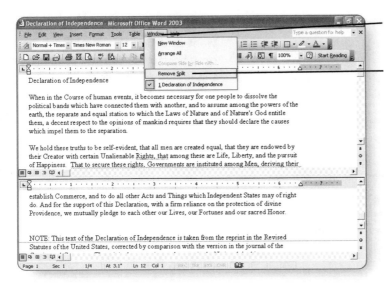

1. **Click** on **Window**. The Window menu will appear.

2. **Click** on **Remove Split**. The split between the windows will disappear.

Moving between Documents

Windows allows you to work with a number of different open documents and applications—whether they be Word documents or documents from other applications such as Excel, PowerPoint, or Solitaire—at the same time. A button for each open document is displayed on the Windows taskbar. Word documents are indicated by a blue "W" on the icon.

1a. **Click** on any **Word document button** on the taskbar. The selected document will become the active document.

OR

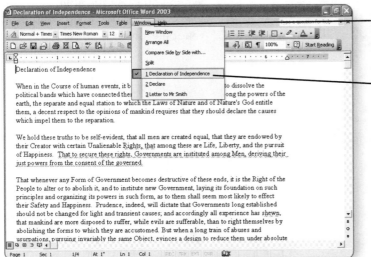

1b. **Click** on **Window**. The Window menu will appear with a list of all open Word documents.

2b. **Click** on the **document** you want to display. The selected document will become the active document.

TIP

Optionally, press Alt+Tab to toggle between open documents and applications.

Viewing Multiple Documents Together

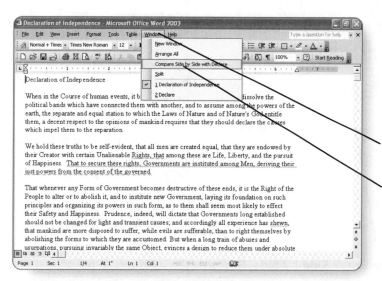

You may occasionally want to view two documents side by side. Word provides you with the ability to view any two open windows next to each other so that you can compare the documents.

1. Click on **Window**. The Window menu will appear.

2. Click on **Compare Side by Side**. The entire work area will be divided between the open documents. If you have more than two Word windows open, Word will first prompt you for which two windows to arrange together.

TIP

To edit a document, click anywhere on the window for that document.

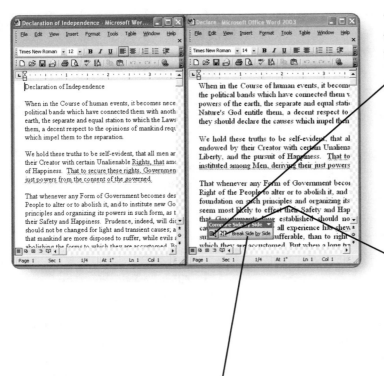

The Compare Side by Side toolbar will also appear. From the toolbar you can select:

- **Synchronous Scrolling**. Scrolls the two documents together. For example, if you scroll down to Page 2 of one document, Page 2 of the second document also appears. Click on the Synchronous Scrolling button to turn the feature on or off.

- **Reset Window Position**. Tiles the two document windows side by side. As they are tiled by default, you won't notice any difference unless you first move or resize the document windows.

- **Break Side by Side**. Restores the windows to full screen and breaks any synchronization between the two windows.

Resizing Word Windows

By default, when you select the Word Compare Side by Side feature, the two windows will be equally sized. You can, however, manually resize a window until it fits your needs. Use the window borders, the small thin edge enclosing a window, to resize it.

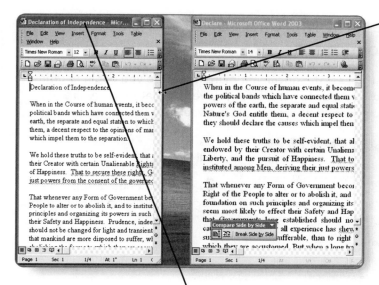

1. Position the **mouse pointer** over a border of the window you want to resize. The mouse pointer will change to a double-headed black arrow.

2. Click and drag the **mouse** to move the border in or out to make the window smaller or larger respectively.

NOTE

You cannot manually resize a maximized window.

3. Release the **mouse button**. The window will remain at the newly created size.

TIP

Click and drag the window title bar to move the entire window to a new position.

Setting Margins

Margins are the spaces between the edges of the paper and where the text actually begins to appear. Word allows you to set margins for any of the four sides of the document and also allows you to mix and match margins for different pages.

Word sets the default margins to 1" on each of the top, bottom, left, and right margins.

Setting Margins for the Entire Document

You can set the document margins before you begin entering text into a document, after you've completed the entire document, or at any time in between.

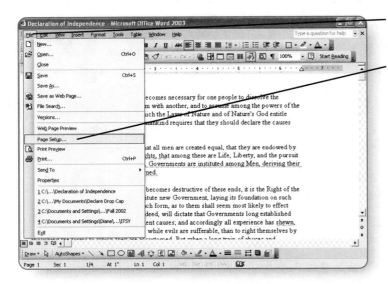

1. Click on **File**. The File menu will appear.

2. Click on **Page Setup**. The Page Setup dialog box will open.

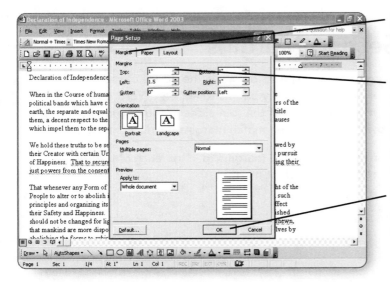

3. If necessary, **click** on the **Margins tab**. The Margins tab will be displayed.

4. Click on the **up or down arrows** to the right of the Top, Bottom, Left, and Right text boxes to increase or decrease the top, bottom, left, or right margin settings.

5. Click on **OK**. The new settings will be applied to the entire document.

Adjusting Margins for Part of a Document

Word can apply different margin settings to selected sections of a document.

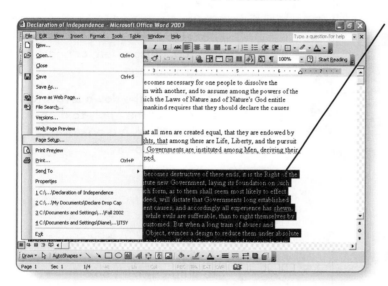

1. Select the **text** in the document that you want to adjust. The text will be highlighted.

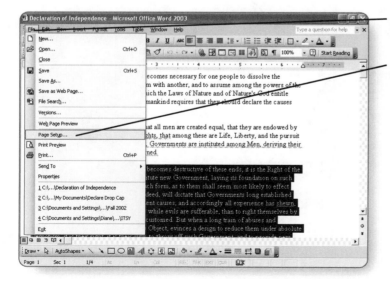

2. Click on **File**. The File menu will appear.

3. Click on **Page Setup**. The Page Setup dialog box will open.

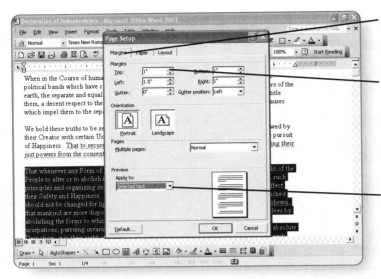

4. If necessary, **click** on the **Margins tab**. The Margins tab will be displayed.

5. **Click** on the **up or down arrows** to the right of the Top, Bottom, Left, and Right text boxes to increase or decrease the top, bottom, left, or right margin settings.

6. **Click** on the **down arrow** to the right of the Apply to drop-down list box. A drop-down menu will appear.

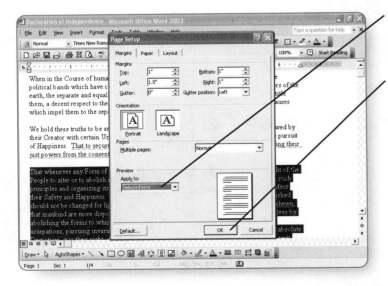

7. **Click** on **Selected text**. The option will appear in the Apply to drop-down list box.

8. **Click** on **OK**. The new margin settings will be applied.

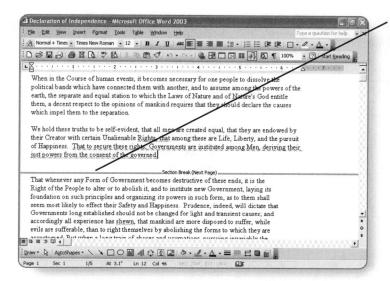

When you apply different margins to a portion of the document, Word creates section breaks to separate the portions of the document with the different margins.

Changing Document Orientation

Use the Page Setup dialog box to change your document to be printed in landscape (along the long edge of the paper) orientation.

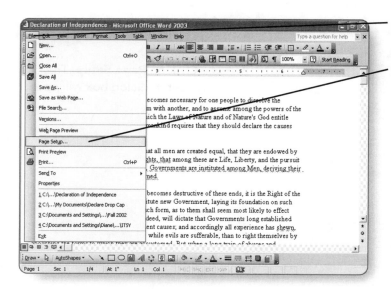

1. **Click** on **File**. The File menu will appear.

2. **Click** on **Page Setup**. The Page Setup dialog box will open.

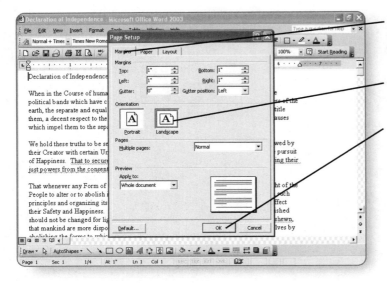

3. If necessary, **click** on the **Margins tab**. The Margins tab will come to the front.

4. Click on **Landscape**. The option will be selected.

5. Click on **OK**. The document will be switched to landscape orientation.

Setting the Paper Size

Although Word can work with many different sizes of paper, the available selections will depend on the type of printer you are using.

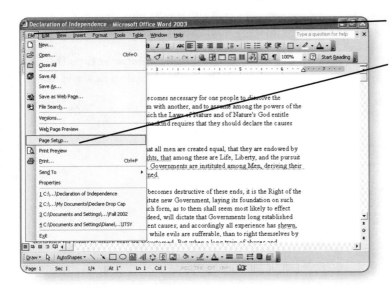

1. Click on **File**. The File menu will appear.

2. Click on **Page Setup**. The Page Setup dialog box will open.

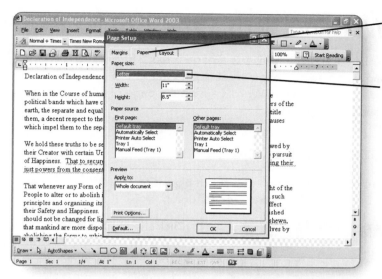

3. Click on the **Paper tab**. The Paper tab will come to the front.

4. Click on the **Paper size down arrow**. A list of available paper sizes will appear.

5. Click on a **paper size**. The selected paper size will appear in the Paper size drop-down list box.

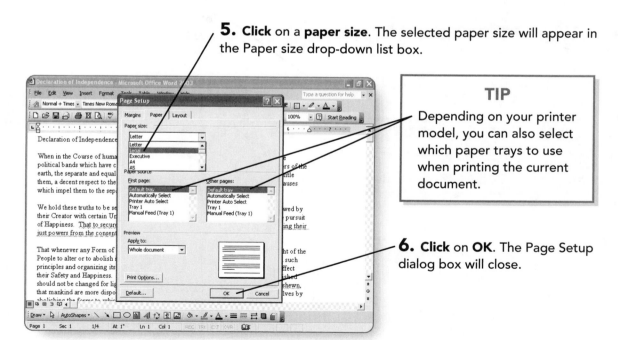

TIP

Depending on your printer model, you can also select which paper trays to use when printing the current document.

6. Click on **OK**. The Page Setup dialog box will close.

Working with Page Breaks

Word automatically inserts a page break when text fills the page. Sometimes page breaks don't fall where you want them to. You can override Word's automatic page break by creating your own page break.

Inserting a Page Break

You can break a page at a shorter position than Word chooses, but you cannot make a page longer.

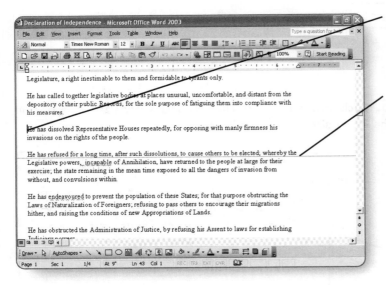

1. **Click** the **mouse** in front of the text where you want the new page to begin. The blinking insertion point will appear.

Notice the location of the normal page break Word would be applying.

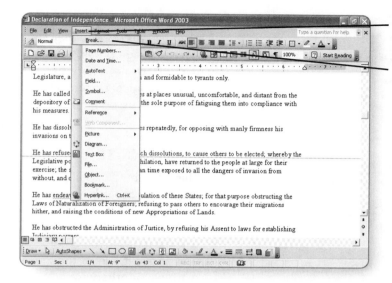

2. Click on **Insert**. The Insert menu will appear.

3. Click on **Break**. The Break dialog box will open.

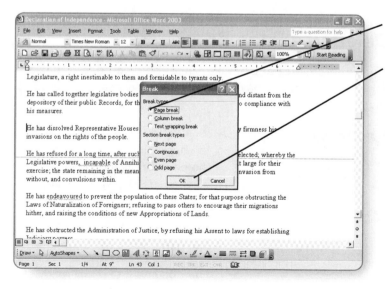

4. Click on **Page break**. The option will be selected.

5. Click on **OK**. The page break will be inserted.

TIP

A faster way to insert a page break is to follow Step 1 and then press Ctrl+Enter.

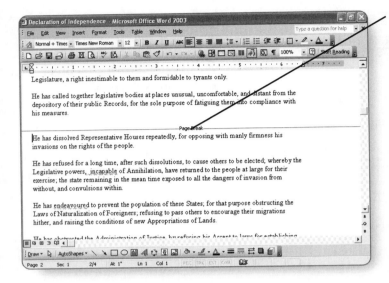

Depending on which document view you are using, you may see the words "Page Break," along with a dotted line, where the new page begins. Document views are discussed later in this chapter.

NOTE

This page break is called a *hard page break* because, unlike the page breaks that Word inserts, this one will not move if you delete text above it, adjust the margins, or otherwise change the amount of text on the page.

Deleting a Page Break

Word's automatic page breaks cannot be deleted, but the hard page breaks that you have inserted manually can be deleted at any time.

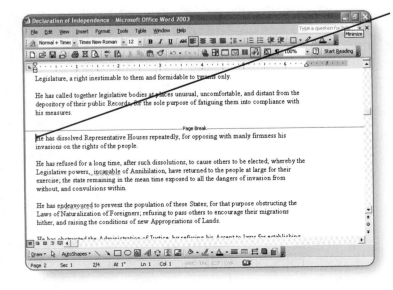

1. Click the **mouse pointer** at the beginning of the text after the page break indication. The blinking insertion point will appear.

2. Press the **Backspace key**. The page break will be deleted.

The document text will readjust to fit on the pages correctly.

Viewing a Document

Word gives you several different view options when displaying a document, including Normal view, Page Layout view, and Reading view. Each view has its own purpose. In Chapter 3, "Saving, Opening, Closing, and Printing," you used the Print Preview view when you were printing your document.

Two other views not covered in this chapter include Outline view and Web Layout view. Chapter 8, "Working with Lists," will teach you about creating outlines.

Viewing in Normal View

Normal view is the default view for Word; it's used for typing, editing, and formatting text. It simplifies the layout of the page so that you can type and edit quickly. Headers, footers, page margins, backgrounds, and some other objects do not appear in Normal view.

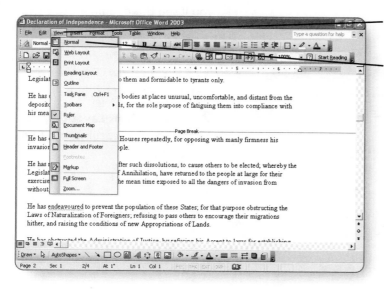

1. Click on **View**. The View menu will appear.

2. Click on **Normal**. Word will display the document in Normal view.

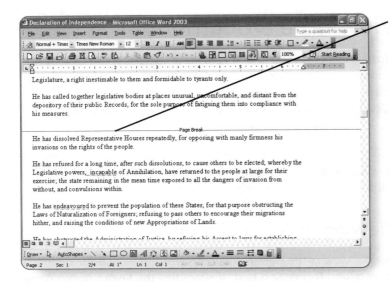

Page breaks are indicated by a dotted line.

Headers, footers, and the top and bottom margins are not displayed.

Viewing in Print Layout View

Use Print Layout view to see how text, graphics, and other elements will be positioned on the printed page. This view is especially helpful if you're working with text columns. Columns are discussed in Chapter 14, "Using Newspaper Columns." In Print Layout view, you'll see the document top and bottom margins, as well as the headers and footers.

1. Click on **View**. The View menu will appear.

2. Click on **Print Layout**. Word will display the document in Print Layout view.

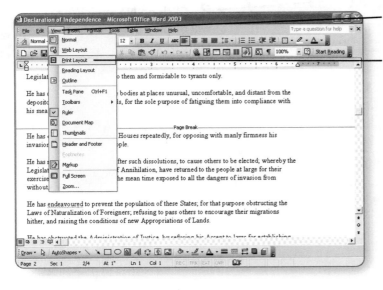

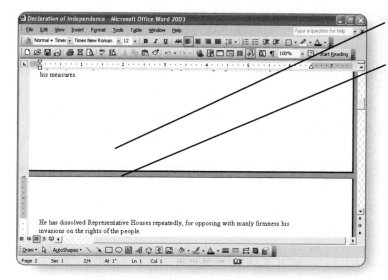

The top and bottom margins appear.

Breaks between pages are indicated by a thick, dark-gray area.

Viewing in Reading Layout

New to this version of Word is a feature called Reading Layout view, which makes it easier to read a document by hiding unnecessary toolbars and scaling the contents of your document to pages that fit comfortably on your screen.

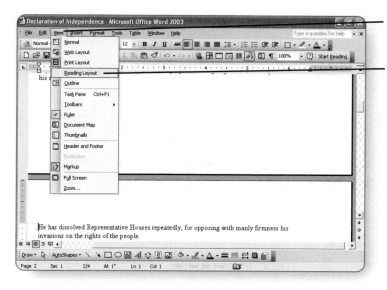

1. **Click** on **View**. The View menu will appear.

2. **Click** on **Reading Layout**. Word will display the document in Reading Layout view.

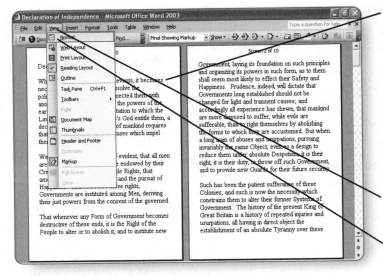

Pages displayed in Reading Layout view are at a larger font size and the page breaks are not necessarily the same page breaks as in the printed document.

When you're finished with the Reading Layout view, use the View menu to select a different view perspective.

3. Click on **View**. The View menu will appear.

4. Click on **Normal**. Word will return to Normal view.

Using the Zoom Feature

Using Word's ability to zoom in on a document allows you to get a close-up view of your text. You can also zoom out to see more of the page, at a reduced rate.

1. Click on **View**. The View menu will appear.

2. Click on **Zoom**. The Zoom dialog box will open.

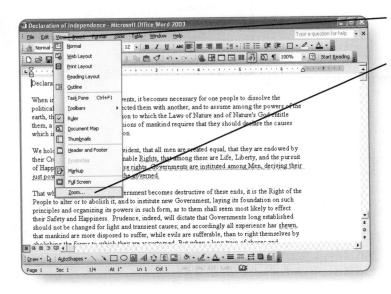

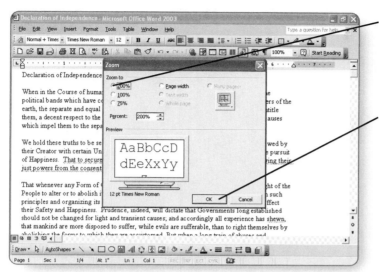

3. Click on **200%**. The document display will enlarge. The text will look larger, but less of the overall page will appear on the screen.

4. Click on **OK**. The Zoom dialog box will close.

NOTE

Using the Zoom feature does not alter the size at which the document will print.

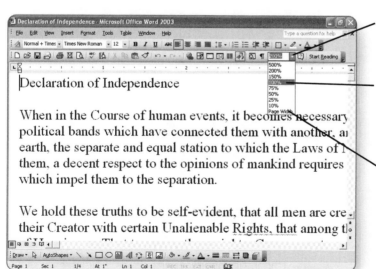

5. Click on the **Zoom drop-down list arrow**. A list of zoom percentages will be displayed.

6. Click on **100%**. The document display will return to normal.

TIP

Setting the zoom to Page Width can be very helpful if your document page is set to landscape.

5

Arranging Text on a Page

Word includes several features to assist you in placing text on the page just the way you want it. You can align text left-to-right using tabs or alignment options, or you can adjust your text vertically using the line spacing options. In this chapter, you'll learn how to:

- Set, move, and delete tabs
- Select line spacing
- Center, justify, left-align, and right-align text

Working with Tabs

If you press the Tab key to move across the page, you'll notice that Word has default stops set every 1/2 inch.

Setting Tabs

You can set tabs at particular points along the ruler so that when you press the Tab key, the cursor moves to that point automatically, instead of stopping every five spaces.

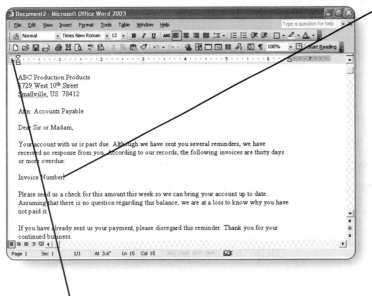

1. Click the **mouse pointer** at the location you want to create a tabbed paragraph. The blinking insertion point will appear.

> **TIP**
>
> If you want to set tabs for multiple previously typed paragraphs, select the paragraphs before proceeding to Step 2.

2. Click the **mouse pointer** on the Tab button at the left end of the ruler to select from the following alignments:

- **Left**. The Tab button is already set to the left tab symbol, an "L." Text will appear with the left edge of the text at the tab.

- **Center**. Click one time to display the center tab symbol. An upside-down "T" will appear. Text will center around a center tab.

- **Right**. Click two times to display the right tab symbol. A backwards "L" will appear. Text will appear with the right edge of the text at the tab.

- **Decimal**. Click three times to display the decimal tab symbol. An upside-down "T" with a dot on the right will appear. Decimal points, used, for example, when writing out dollar and cent amounts, align to the tab. The decimal tab is selected in this example.

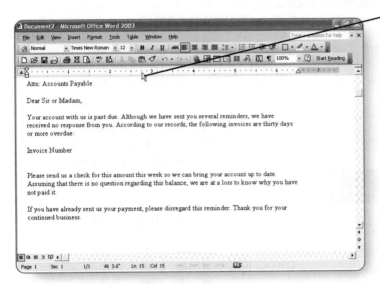

3. Click on the **ruler** to set the tab for the current paragraph or any currently selected text. Depending on the selection you made in Step 2, a left, right, center, or decimal tab symbol will appear in the ruler at the spot you selected.

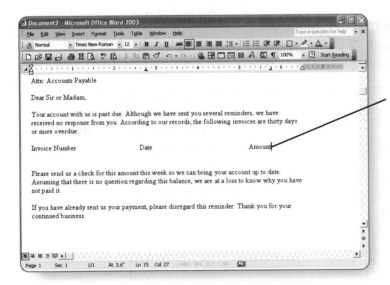

4. Click in the **paragraph** and **press** the **Tab key**. The insertion point will move to the tab where you want the text to appear.

5. Type some **text**. The text you type will appear on the page. In this example, the first tab is a center-aligned tab and the second tab is a right-aligned tab.

Moving a Tab

You can easily move the tab stop if you don't like where you placed it!

1. Select the **paragraphs** that have a tab that needs to be moved. The text will be highlighted.

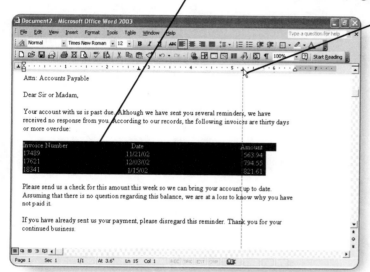

2. Drag the **current tab setting** to the new location on the ruler bar. A vertical, dotted line will mark the new tab position.

3. Release the **mouse button.** The tab will be reset and any text will move to the new tab position.

Deleting a Tab

Deleting an unwanted tab stop is an easy process when you use Word's ruler.

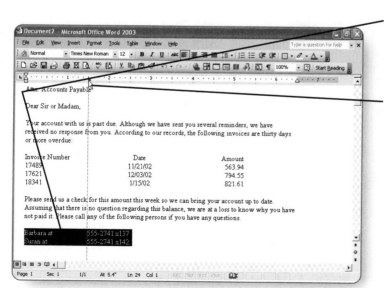

1. Select the **paragraphs** that have a tab that you want to delete. The text will be highlighted.

2. Drag the **current tab setting** off the ruler, into the body of the document. A vertical dotted line will appear.

3. Release the **mouse button.** The tab will be deleted.

Changing Line Spacing

Line spacing is the amount of vertical space between each line of text. You might want to change line spacing when you want to make a document easier to read, for example, or to make room for changes when writing a draft of a document.

1. Select the **text** in which you want to change the line spacing. The text will be highlighted.

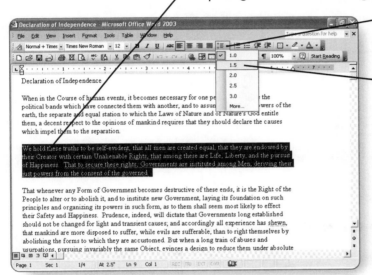

2. Click on the **Line Spacing button down arrow**. The line spacing options will appear.

3. Click on an **option**. The new spacing will be applied to the highlighted text.

TIP

Shortcut keys for set line spacing are: Ctrl+1 for single spacing, Ctrl+2 for double spacing, and Ctrl+5 for 1.5 line spacing.

Aligning Text

Alignment arranges the text to line up at one or both margins or centers it across the page. Like line spacing, alignment is usually applied to an entire paragraph or document.

You can align paragraphs of text to the left, right, or center. You can also justify your text, which means that the text will be evenly spaced across the page from the left edge to the right edge.

1. **Select** the **text** that you want to align. The text will be highlighted.

2. **Click** on the appropriate **alignment button**:

- **Align Left**. The text will be aligned at the left margin. This is the default choice in Word.

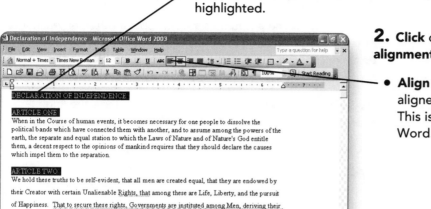

- **Center**. The text will be centered.

- **Align Right**. The text will be aligned at the right margin.

- **Justify**. The text will be evenly spaced across the page.

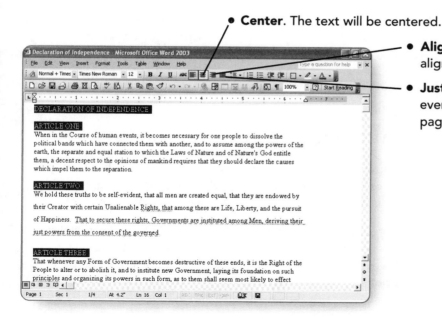

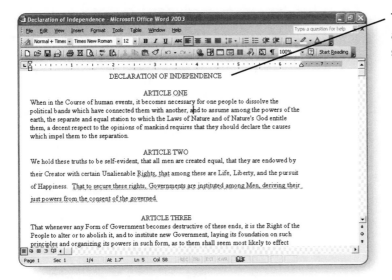

The selected text will realign according to the option you selected.

6
Using Fonts Effectively

When you speak, the tone of your voice conveys how you feel. You can convey your enthusiasm (or lack of it), be friendly, or be sarcastic. In a similar way, *fonts*, which are families of design styles for the numbers, letters, and symbols that make up text, can provide additional information to the reader. Fonts can, for example, make a document appear mature and businesslike or young and casual. In this chapter, you'll learn how to:

- Choose and apply an appropriate font
- Add bold, underline, and italic styles to text
- Use special effects, such as outlining, embossing, subscripts, or animation
- Copy formatting from one selection to another
- Change the default font

Selecting a Font and Font Size

In addition to the fonts you already have on your machine, Word comes with extra fonts. The name of the currently selected font and the font size of the text are displayed on the Font and Font Size drop-down lists on the toolbar.

Choosing a Font

Choose a font such as Times New Roman if you want the text to be modern and businesslike, and choose a font like Monotype Corsiva for a "handwritten" look.

1. **Select** the **text** to be formatted. The text will be highlighted.

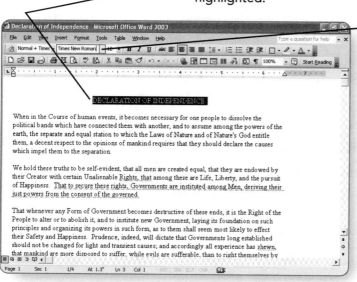

2. **Click** on the **down arrow** to the right of the Font drop-down list. A list of fonts will appear.

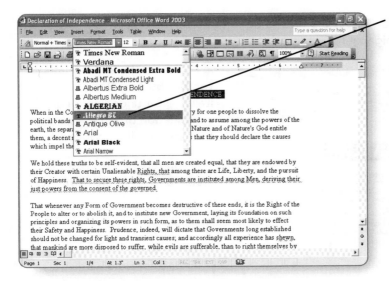

3. Click on a **font**. The new font will be applied to the selected text.

Choosing a Font Size

Each font can be used in different sizes. Font sizes are measured in *points*; a point is approximately 1/72 of an inch. Therefore, a 72-point font is approximately 1 inch tall.

1. Select the **text** to be formatted. The text will be highlighted.

2. Click on the **down arrow** to the right of the Font Size drop-down box. A list of available sizes will appear.

3. Click on a **size**. The new size will be applied to your text.

Applying Bold, Italic, or Underline

Applying formatting attributes like **bold**, *italic,* or <u>underline</u> will call attention to particular parts of your text. You can easily access these choices with the Word toolbar.

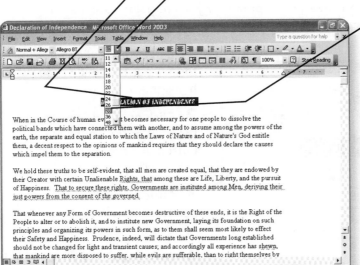

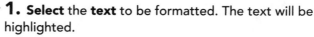

1. **Select** the **text** to be formatted. The text will be highlighted.

2. **Click** on the appropriate **toolbar button**: **B** for bold, *I* for italic, U for underline, or any combination of the three. The formatting will be applied.

You can repeat the previous steps to remove the attribute.

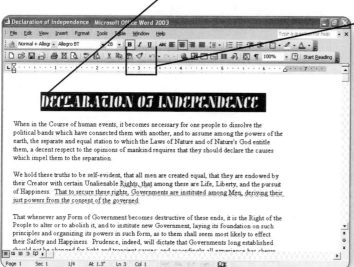

TIP
Shortcut keys include Ctrl+B for bold, Ctrl+I for italic, and Ctrl+U for underline.

Applying Color

If you have a color printer or you are going to share the document electronically, add impact by adding some color.

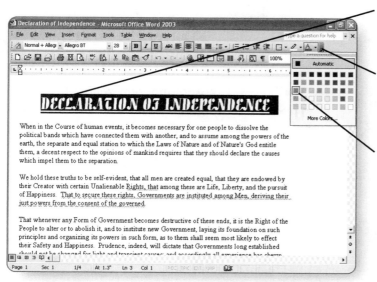

1. **Select** the **text** to be formatted. The text will be highlighted.

2. **Click** on the **down arrow** to the right of the Font Color button. A palette of available colors will appear.

3. **Click** on a **color** in the palette. The Color Palette box will close.

4. **Click anywhere in the document** to deselect the text. The text will appear in the selected color.

Highlighting Text

You can highlight text in your document in the same manner that you highlight text with a marker in a book. You can even choose the color of highlighter you want to use. On a black and white printer, highlighting appears with gray shading over the text. Highlighting text calls attention to specific areas of your document.

1. **Select** the **text** to be formatted with highlighting.

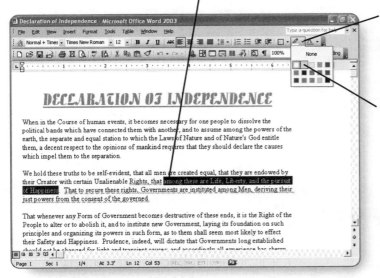

2. **Click** on the **down arrow** to the right of the Highlight button. A list of available colors will appear. The default color is yellow.

3. **Click** on a **color**. The text will become deselected and highlighting color will be applied.

TIP

To remove highlighting, repeat the steps above and select None from the available color selection.

Using Special Effects and Animation

Word has other special effects you can apply to your text. Some are great for printed documents, whereas others are designed for documents being shared electronically.

Applying a Font Special Effect

Font effects can include shadowing, embossing, engraving, and others.

1. Select the **text** to be formatted. The text will be highlighted.

2. Click on **Format**. The Format menu will appear.

3. Click on **Font**. The Font dialog box will open.

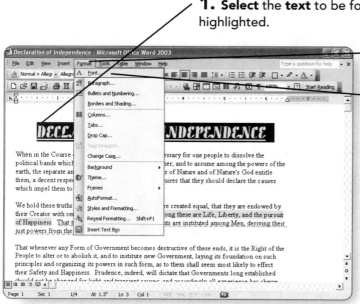

4. If necessary, **click** on the **Font tab**. The Font tab will be on top.

5. Click on any **options** you'd like to use in the Effects boxes. A check mark will appear in any selected effect and a sample of the text with the effect applied will appear in the Preview box.

6. Click on **OK**. The dialog box will close and the effect will be applied to your text.

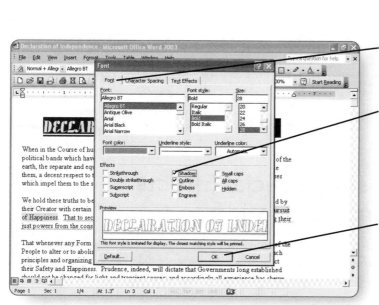

Adding Animation to Text

Word includes six animation effects that can be added to a document. These effects will only display on a document being viewed electronically.

1. Select the **text** to be formatted. The text will be highlighted.

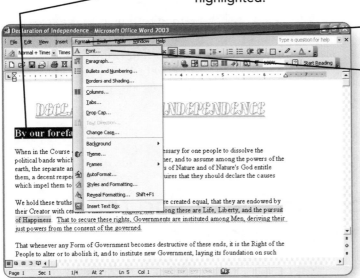

2. Click on **Format**. The Format menu will appear.

3. Click on **Font**. The Font dialog box will open.

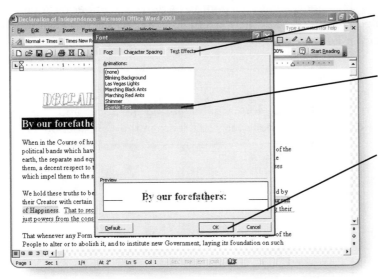

4. If necessary, **click** on the **Text Effects tab**. The Text Effects tab will be on top.

5. Click on the desired **animation** in the Animations list box. A sample of the effect will display in the Preview box.

6. Click on **OK**. The dialog box will close and the animation effect will be applied to your text.

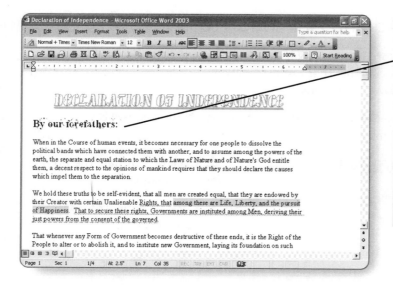

NOTE

Word is sometimes quirky with special effects. If the effect does not display on your screen, try pressing the Page Down and Page Up keys a few times and then returning to the text with the special effect. The effect should be activated.

Copying Formatting to Another Selection

If you spend several minutes setting up just the right formatting for a heading that will appear multiple times in a long document, you don't want to have to remember all your selections and repeat them over and over. Instead, use the Format Painter tool.

TIP

You can also copy formatting by using the Styles and Formatting task pane, as you'll learn in the next section.

1. **Select** some of the **text** that has the formatting you want to use elsewhere. The text will be highlighted.

2. **Click** on the **Format Painter button**. The mouse pointer will change to a paintbrush.

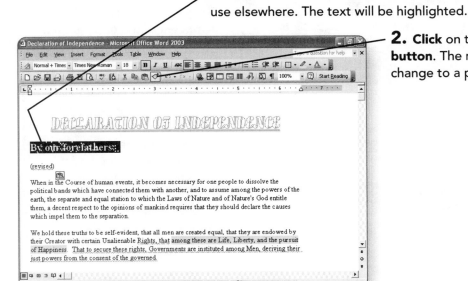

3. **Press and hold** the **mouse button** and **drag** over the **text** to be formatted. The new text will be highlighted.

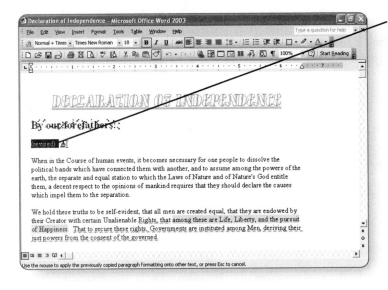

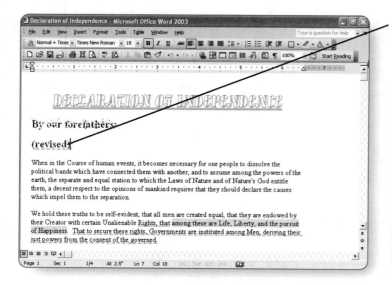

4. **Release** the **mouse button**. The new text will have the attributes of the original text.

TIP

To keep the Format Painter function on for repeated use, click twice on the Format Painter button. When you are finished using the Format Painter function, click on the button again to turn it off.

Using the Styles and Formatting Task Pane

In Chapter 1, "Getting Started with Word," you learned about Word's task panes. One of the task panes, the Styles and Formatting task pane, assists you with formatting.

TIP

If you don't already have the task pane displayed, click on View, Task Pane.

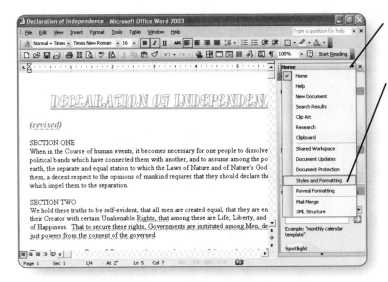

1. **Click** on the **task pane drop down arrow**. A list of other Task Panes will appear.

2. **Click** on **Styles and Formatting**. The Styles and Formatting task pane will appear.

Identifying Text Characteristics

The Styles and Formatting task pane shows you the different character styles you've used in your current document.

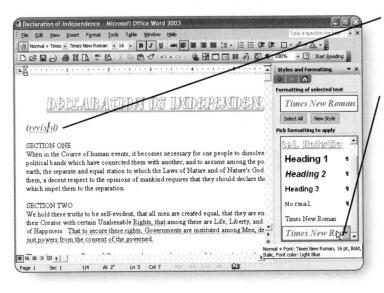

1. **Click** in the **text** you want to identify. A black box will surround the style description of the text.

2. **Pause** the **mouse pointer** over the black style box. A yellow tip will appear listing all style characteristics.

Applying Formatting

Earlier in this chapter you learned how to use the Format Painter tool to copy formatting from one block of text to another. You can also use the Styles and Formatting task pane to apply formatting.

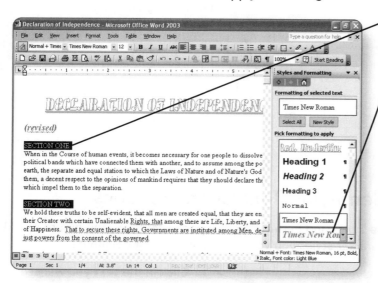

1. Select the **text** to which you want to apply the text characteristics. The text will be highlighted.

2. Click on the **style** you want to use. The new text attributes will be applied to the selected text.

Clearing Formatting

You can also quickly clear all formatting from selected text by using the Styles and Formatting task pane.

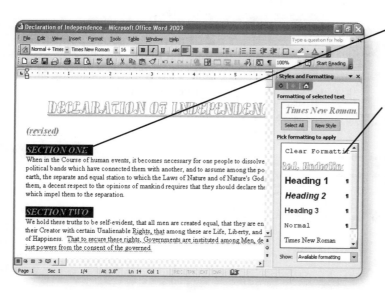

1. Highlight the **text** from which you want to remove formatting. The text will be highlighted.

2. From the Styles and Formatting task pane, **click** on **Clear Formatting**. All formatting will be removed from the selected text.

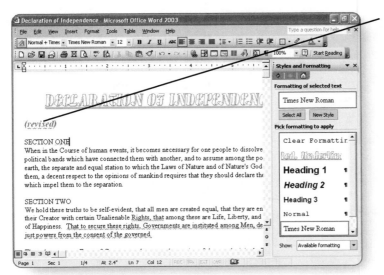

The text will appear in the default font, size, color, and so forth.

Changing the Default Font

The default font, the font used by Word unless you change it, is 12-point Times New Roman. If you'll use a different font for most of your documents, change the default.

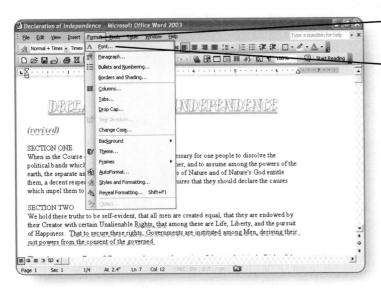

1. **Click** on **Format**. The Format menu will appear.

2. **Click** on **Font**. The Font dialog box will open.

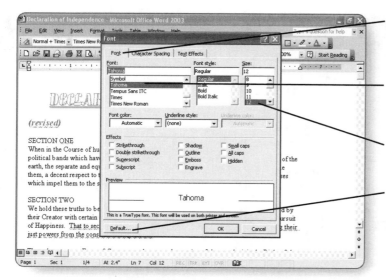

3. If necessary, **click** on the **Font tab**. The Font tab will come to the front.

4. Click on a **font** from the Font box. The font name will be selected.

5. Click on a **size** from the Size box. The size will be selected.

6. Click on **Default**. A dialog box will open.

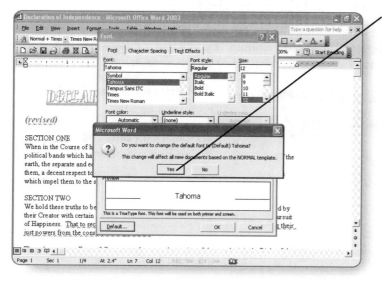

7. Click on **Yes**.

7
Using Special Effects

When you look at all of the keys on the computer keyboard, you may think that you have every character you'd ever need at your fingertips. Occasionally, however, you'll need a special character that isn't on the keyboard. When that happens, Word has several features that can help. You can also add special effects to your document using borders and shading. In this chapter, you'll learn how to:

- Use drop caps
- Insert symbols and special characters
- Add borders to text
- Work with shading

Using Drop Caps

If you're writing a newsletter, preparing a special report, or creating a letterhead, you may want to use a *drop cap*, which is an enlarged first letter. Drop caps provide visual transitions from headings to text.

Creating a Drop Cap

Only the first letter of a paragraph can be formatted as a drop cap. You should set your drop cap significantly larger than the type size of the paragraph it introduces. An undersized drop cap can be more of a distraction than an enhancement.

1. Click anywhere in the **paragraph** for which you want to have a drop cap. The blinking insertion point will appear in the paragraph.

2. Click on **Format**. The Format menu will appear.

3. Click on **Drop Cap**. The Drop Cap dialog box will open.

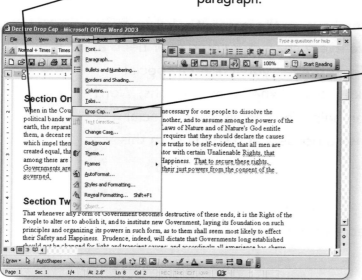

TIP

If Drop Cap does not immediately appear on your Format menu, rest the mouse over the word Format for a couple of seconds. The menu will expand and the Drop Cap option will be displayed.

Word provides two different positions for a drop cap, Dropped or In margin. A Dropped cap position aligns with the left margin and the rest of the paragraph wraps around the cap. With an In margin position, the entire paragraph moves to the right of the drop cap letter.

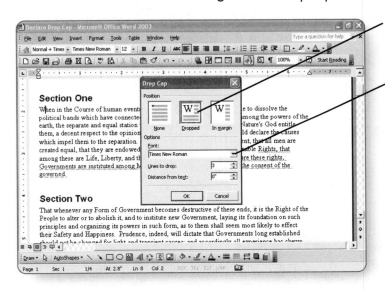

4. **Click** on a **position** for the drop cap character. The selected option will have a box around it.

5. Optionally, **click** on the **Font drop-down arrow**. A list of font choices will appear.

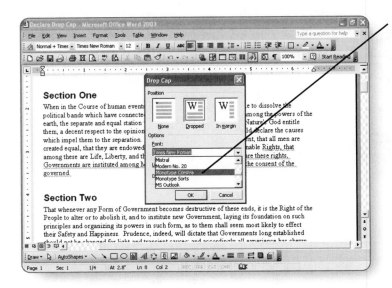

6. **Click** on a **font name**. The selection will appear in the Font drop-down list box.

NOTE

Your font choices may vary from the ones displayed here.

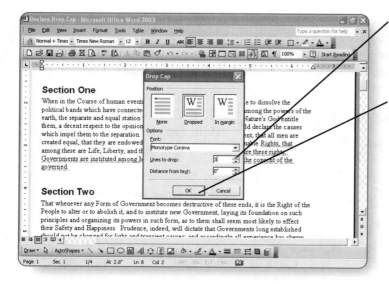

7. Click on the **up or down arrows** in the Lines to drop list box. A higher number indicates a larger drop cap.

8. Click on **OK**. The first character of the paragraph will be changed to a drop cap character.

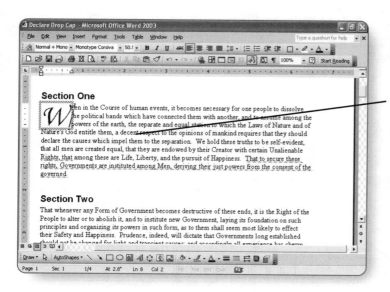

A drop cap character actually appears in a graphic box. You'll learn about graphic images in Part III, "Adding Visual Interest."

9. Click in the **body** of the paragraph. The box surrounding the drop cap will disappear.

A Dropped position drop cap

An In margin position drop cap

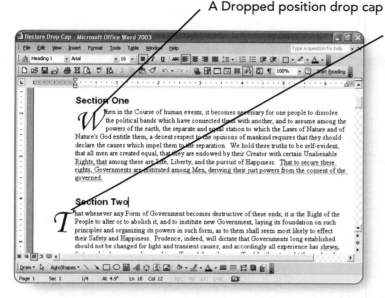

Deleting a Drop Cap

If you decide later that you don't want the first letter of the paragraph to be a drop cap, you can remove it.

1. Click anywhere in the **paragraph** from which you want to remove the drop cap. The blinking insertion point will appear in the paragraph.

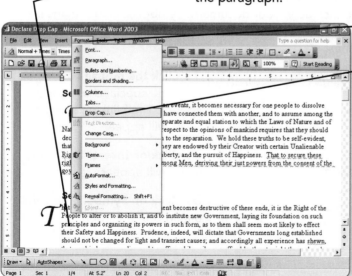

2. Click on **Format**. The Format menu will appear.

3. Click on **Drop Cap**. The Drop Cap dialog box will open.

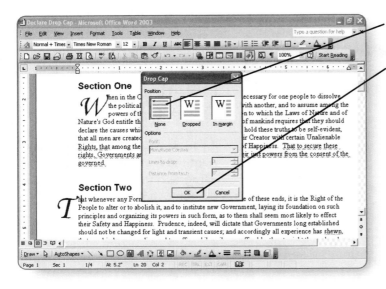

4. **Click** on **None**. The option will have a box around it.

5. **Click** on **OK**. The first character of the paragraph will return to normal.

Inserting Special Characters or Symbols

Word includes hundreds of special characters and symbols for you to include in your document. Symbols include things like copyright or trademark symbols, stars, check marks, or airplanes.

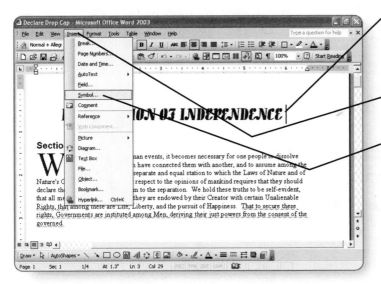

1. **Click** the **mouse** where you want the special character to appear. The blinking insertion point will appear.

2. **Click** on **Insert**. The Insert menu will appear.

3. **Click** on **Symbol**. The Symbol dialog box will open.

NOTE

If you don't see the symbol you want, it may be available in a different font.

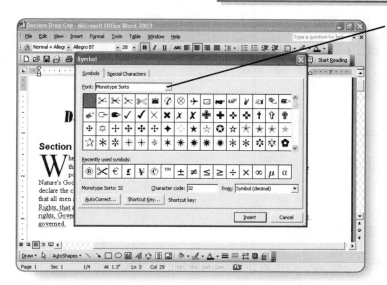

4. Click on the **Font drop-down arrow.** A list of fonts will appear. Your font choices may vary from the ones displayed here.

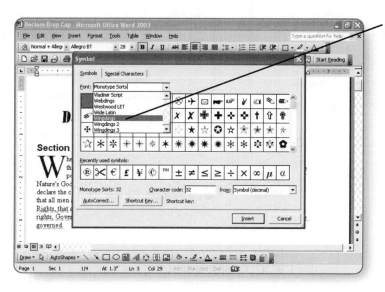

5. Click on a **font.** The symbols available for that font will be displayed.

TIP

For a large variety of unusual characters, look at the Monotype Sorts or Wingdings fonts.

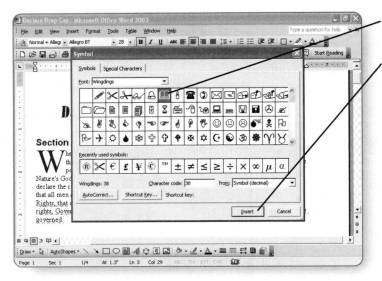

6. Click on a **symbol**. The symbol will appear selected.

7. Click on **Insert**. The symbol or character will be inserted into your document.

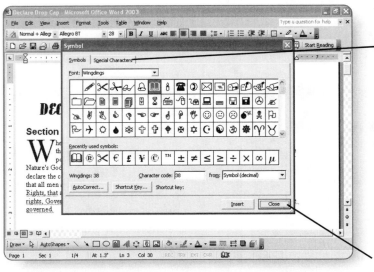

NOTE

Additional special characters are available under the Special Characters tab. To insert one of these special characters, click on the Special Characters tab and then choose the character you want.

8. Click on **Close**. The Symbol dialog box will close.

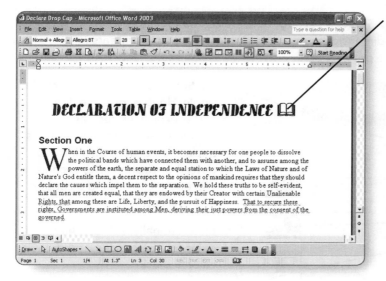

The symbol character will be inserted into your document.

Working with Borders and Shading

Word includes borders and shading that you can apply to any size block of text or even to an entire page of a document. Borders and shading effects bring the reader's eye to specific areas for a "quick read."

Adding Borders

Use borders around a word, phrase, paragraph, or group of paragraphs to frame the text and call specific attention to the area. You can also add a border around an entire page, such as a title page of a document.

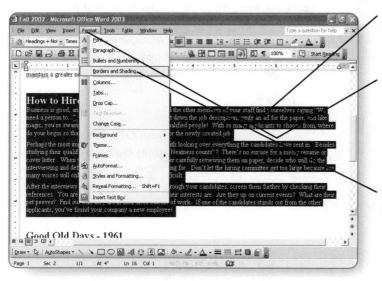

1. Highlight the **text** you want to surround with a border. The text will be highlighted.

2. Click on **Format**. The Format menu will open.

3. Click on **Borders and Shading**. The Borders and Shading dialog box will open.

4. **Select** a **setting**. Borders can be a plain box, 3-dimensional, or with a shadow. A sample appears in the preview box.

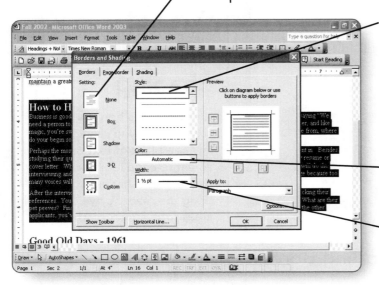

5. **Select** a **style**. Styles include single, double, or triple lines, and special lines such as a double lines where one is side is thicker. Selections also include dotted or dashed lines such as you might use around a coupon in a newsletter.

6. Optionally, **select** a **line color** for the border. The default color is black.

7. **Select** a **line width**. The larger the width, the thicker the border lines around the text will appear.

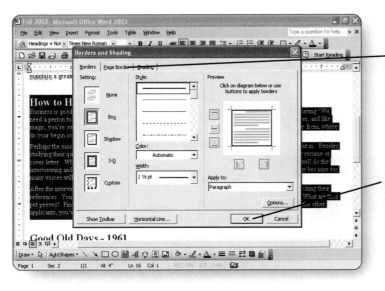

TIP

If you want to apply a border to a page or to the entire document, choose your options from the Page Border tab.

8. **Click** on **OK**. The Borders and Shading dialog box will close.

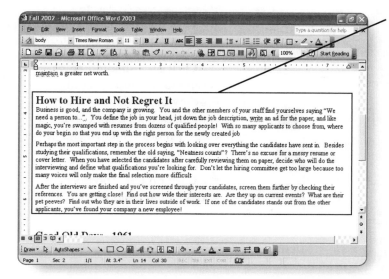

Word will apply the border around the selected text.

Adding Shading to Text

You can distinguish headlines and important passages, such as sidebars, from their surrounding text by creating a *screen*, which is typically light gray shading against the standard black text. Screens can add contrast to and enhance the readability of your document. Shading looks good against text with a border.

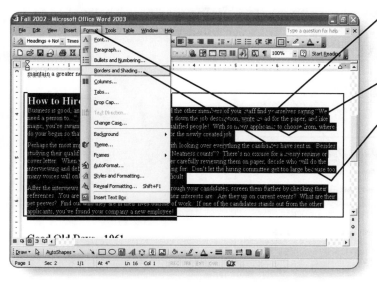

1. Highlight the **text** to which you want to apply shading. The text will be highlighted.

2. Click on **Format**. The Format menu will open.

3. Click on **Borders and Shading**. The Borders and Shading dialog box will open.

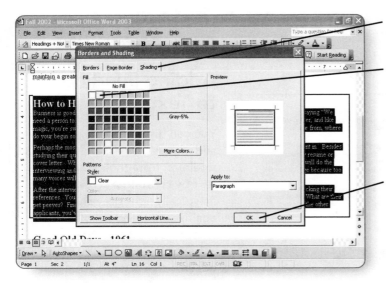

4. Click on the **Shading tab**. The Shading tab will appear in front.

5. Click on a **shading color**. A sample will appear in the Preview box. When working with black text, a light shading color is more effective and easier to read.

6. Click on **OK**. The Borders and Shading dialog box will close.

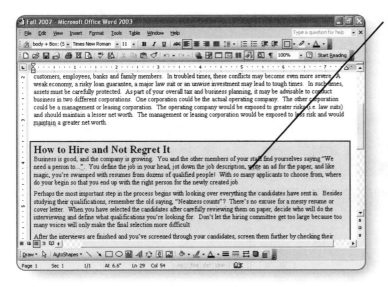

The shading will be applied to the selected text.

Creating Reverse Text

Another effective method to call attention to text in your document is the reverse text effect. Word creates reverse text by using white type against a black background. Reverse text is particularly effective for short lines set in large type, such as headlines or subheadings. Reverse text also adds an illusion of color to text even if printed on a black and white printer.

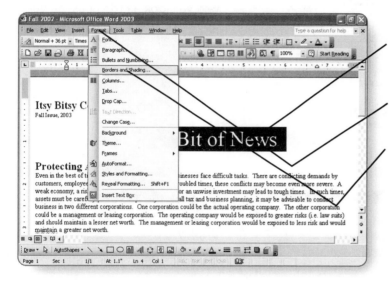

1. Highlight the **text** to which you want to apply shading. The text will be highlighted.

2. Click on **Format**. The Format menu will open.

3. Click on **Borders and Shading**. The Borders and Shading dialog box will open.

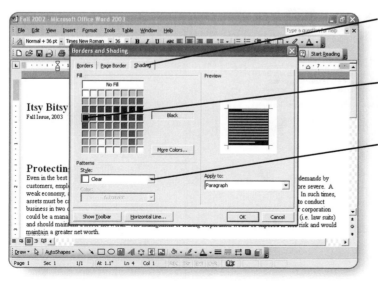

4. Click on the **Shading tab**. The Shading tab will appear in front.

5. Click on the color **black**. A sample will appear in the Preview box.

6. Click on the **Style down arrow**. A list of patterns will appear.

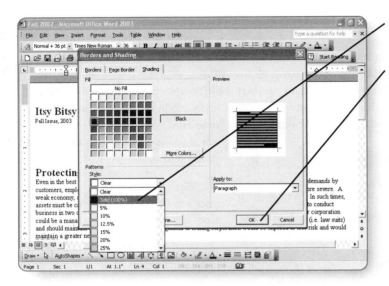

7. **Click** on **Solid (100%)**. The option will be selected.

8. **Click** on **OK**. The Borders and Shading dialog box will close.

The color around the selected text will look a little unusual, but do not deselect the text yet.

9. **Click** the **Text color down arrow**. A list of colors will display.

10. **Click** the color **White**.

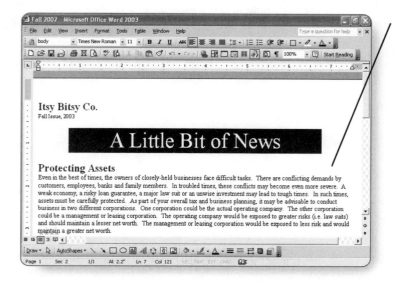

11. **Click** in the **document** to deselect the text.

8
Working with Lists

Everyone uses lists—from shopping lists and check lists to meeting agendas and outlines. We use lists to keep organized. Typically there are two types of lists, bulleted and numbered. You use bulleted lists when you have items with no particular priority, and numbered lists when there is a sequence or priority to the list items. Word can help you format lists in your documents automatically. In this chapter, you'll learn how to:

- Use AutoFormat
- Create a bulleted or numbered list
- Modify the bullet style
- Create a multilevel numbered list
- Remove bullets or numbering
- Work with outlines

Using AutoFormat As You Type

Word includes a feature called AutoFormat As You Type, which guesses what you're trying to do from what you type. This can be a substantial time saver when you're creating lists.

Using AutoFormat to Create a List

If you type the first list item, preceding it with a bullet character or a number, Word continues the list using the same format.

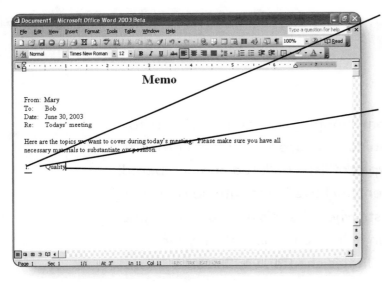

1. **Type** a **number,** then a **closing parenthesis**, a **period**, or a **hyphen.** The number or punctuation will display in your document.

2. **Press** the **spacebar or Tab key.** The insertion point will move accordingly.

3. **Type** the **text** for the first item on your list. The text will display in the document.

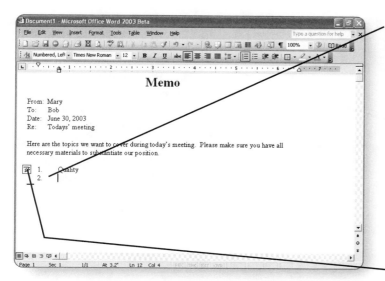

4. Press the **Enter key.** Word will assume that you are trying to create a numbered list and will begin the next line with the next number. Numbered items are also indented.

For example, if you typed a 1 in the first step, then the next line will be a 2; however, if you typed a 6 in the first step, the next line will be a 7.

TIP

A SmartTag appears, from which you can select not to use the automatic numbering, or to discontinue automatic numbering.

5. Type the **text** for the second item on your list.

6. Repeat steps 4 and 5 for each item on your list. Word will automatically number the listed items.

NOTE

If you delete a line that has an automatic number, all steps under that line will be renumbered correspondingly.

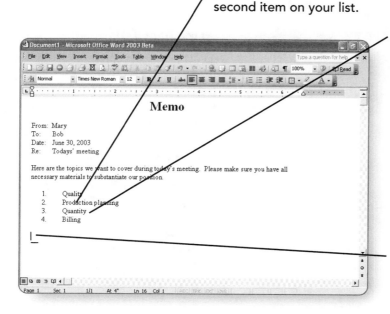

7. Press the **Enter key twice** after the last item in your list. Word will stop automatically entering numbers.

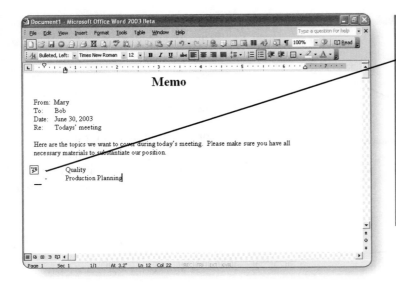

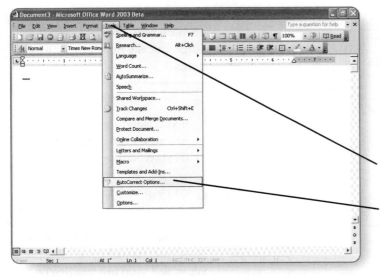

Turning Off AutoFormat

If the AutoFormat As You Type feature is adding numbers or bullets when you don't want numbers or bullets, you can easily turn off the feature.

1. Click on **Tools**. The Tools menu will appear.

2. Click on **AutoCorrect Options**. The AutoCorrect dialog box will open.

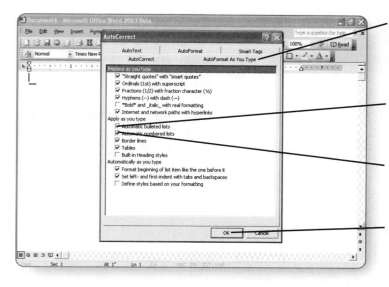

3. Click on the **AutoFormat As You Type tab**. The AutoFormat As You Type tab will come to the front.

4. Click in the **Automatic bulleted lists check box**. The check mark will be removed.

5. Click in the **Automatic numbered lists check box**. The check mark will be removed.

6. Click on **OK**. Word will no longer automatically create bulleted and numbered lists.

Working with Bulleted or Numbered Lists

If you've typed text without bullets or numbering, you can use the toolbar to quickly apply them to your list.

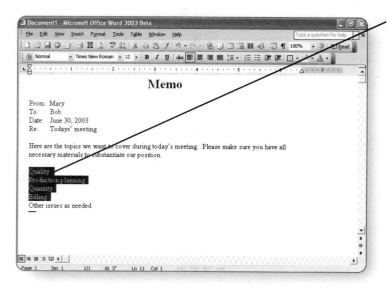

1. Select the **list** of items you want to bullet or number. The text will be highlighted.

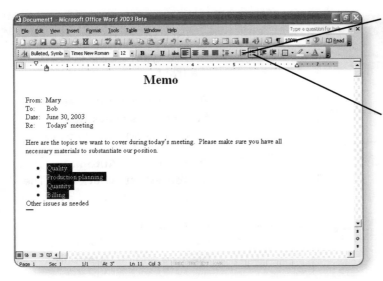

2a. Click on the **Numbering button** on the toolbar. Numbers will be applied to the list.

OR

2b. Click on the **Bullets button** on the toolbar. Bullets will be applied to the list.

Switching between Bulleted and Numbered Lists

If you created a bulleted list and later decide you'd prefer it to be numbered, it's easy to change it. Again, you can use the toolbar to quickly complete the task.

1. Select the **list** of items you want to modify. The list will be highlighted.

2a. Click on the **Bullets button** if the list is currently numbered. The list will change to bulleted.

OR

2b. Click on the **Numbering button** if the list is currently bulleted. The list will change to numbered.

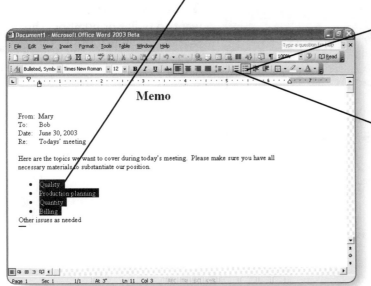

Changing a List Style

By default, Word places a round bullet at the beginning of each item in a bulleted list and uses Arabic numbers for numbered lists. There are many other styles of bullets and numbers from which you can choose.

1. Select the **bulleted** or **numbered list**. The list will be highlighted.

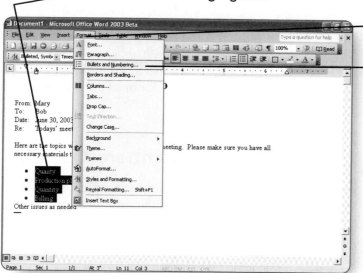

2. Click on **Format**. The Format menu will appear.

3. Click on **Bullets and Numbering**. The Bullets and Numbering dialog box will open.

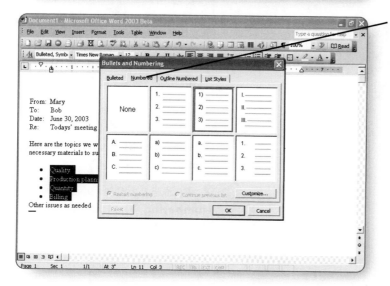

4a. Click on the **Numbered tab** if you want to change the numbering style. The Numbered tab will come to the front.

OR

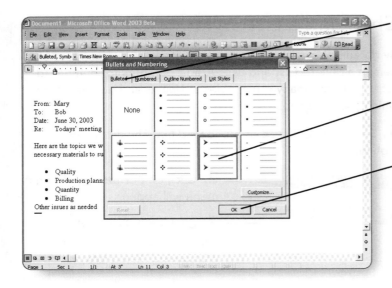

4b. Click on the **Bulleted tab** if you want to change the style of bullet. The Bulleted tab will come to the front.

5. Click on a **style**. A frame will appear around the selected style.

6. Click on **OK**. The dialog box will close.

Word will apply the new style to the existing list and any new lists will be formatted the same way.

Creating Multilevel Numbered Lists

You will occasionally want to have a list within a list. You can tell Word to create different levels within your lists and to choose the style of those levels. Word calls these multilevel lists *outline numbered lists*.

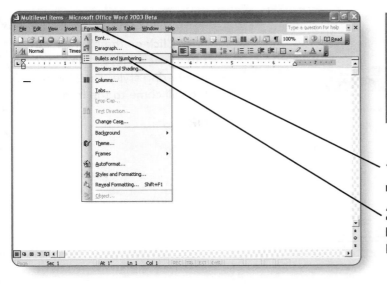

TIP

For an outline numbered list, it's easier if you set the formatting before you actually type the list.

1. Click on **Format**. The Format menu will appear.

2. Click on **Bullets and Numbering**. The Bullets and Numbering dialog box will open.

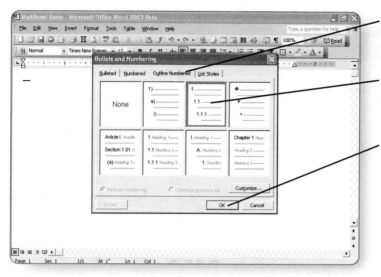

3. Click on the **Outline Numbered tab**. The Outline Numbered tab will be on top.

4. Click on a **style**. A frame will appear around the selected style.

5. Click on **OK**. The dialog box will close and Word will insert a first-level character in your document.

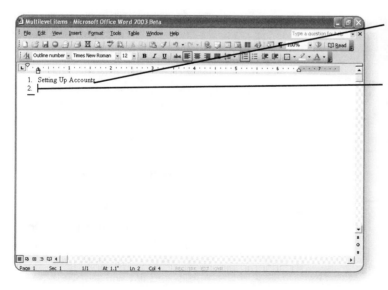

6. Type the **text** of the first-level item. The text will appear in the document.

7. Press the **Enter key**. Word will move to the next line and insert another first-level character.

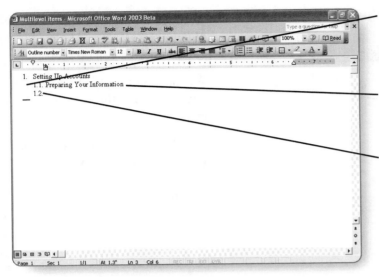

8. Press the **Tab key**. Word will indent the line to the next level and insert the second-level character.

9. Type the **text** for the second-level item. The text will appear in the document.

10. Press the **Enter key**. Word will move to the next line and insert the next second-level character.

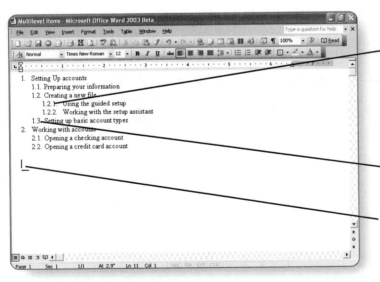

TIP

Each time you want to move another level inward, press the Tab key. Word will shift to the next-level character.

To revert to a higher level, press the Shift and Tab keys.

11. Press the **Enter key twice** after the last item in the list has been added. The outline numbered list will stop.

NOTE

You can learn more about creating and working with outlines later in this chapter in the section titled "Creating an Outline."

Removing Bullet or Number Formatting

If you no longer want the bullet or numbering style applied to your list, it only takes a click to remove it.

1. Select the **list** to be cleared of bullets or numbers. The text will be highlighted.

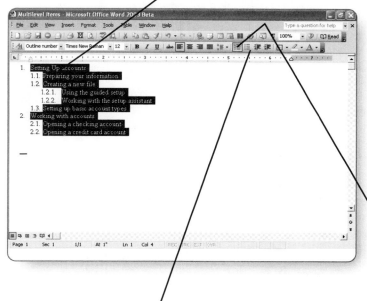

2a. If the highlighted items are numbered, **click** on the **Numbering button** on the toolbar. The numbers will be removed.

OR

2b. If the highlighted items are bulleted, **click** on the **Bullets button** on the toolbar. The bullets will be removed.

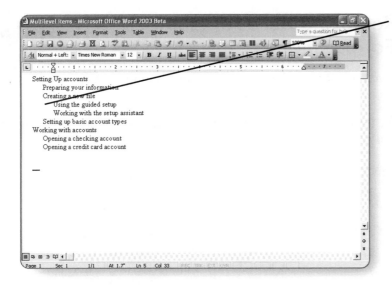

After removing bullets or numbering, any indenting applied will remain.

Creating an Outline

An outline helps you organize the steps needed to accomplish a task. Outlines use headings and subtopics to categorize a process. The best way to create an outline is through the Word Outline view.

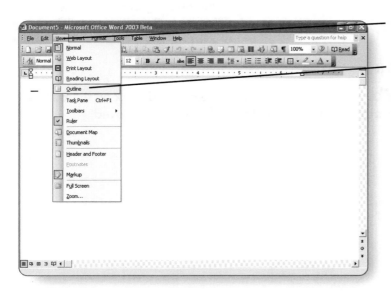

1. Click on **View**. The View menu will appear.

2. Click on **Outline**. The current document view will change to Outline view.

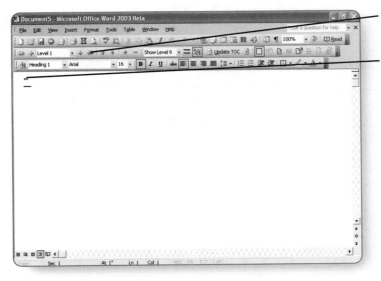

The Outline toolbar will automatically appear.

A small indicator bar will appear next to the blinking insertion point.

Generating Headings

Word considers the first line of text you type in an outline document to be a Level 1 heading, the top-most level. Word uses styles to track outline headings and sub-headings, and a Level 1 heading is a style. You use the Tab key to demote your headings and the Shift+Tab key to promote your headings. A Word outline can contain up to nine different heading levels.

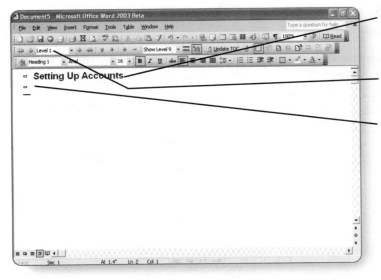

1. Type the **first line** of your outline. The text will appear as a bolded, 16-point Arial font.

Notice the Outline toolbar shows the style as a Level 1 heading.

2. Press the **Enter key**. The insertion point will go to the next line.

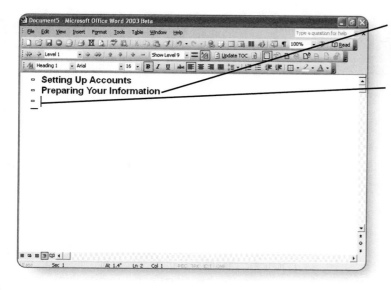

3. Type the **second line** of your outline. Again, the text will appear as a Level 1 heading.

4. Press the **Enter key**. The insertion point will go to the next line.

When you want to create sub-headings, Word uses the Tab key to automatically change level headings.

5. Press the **Tab key**. The insertion point will move to the right.

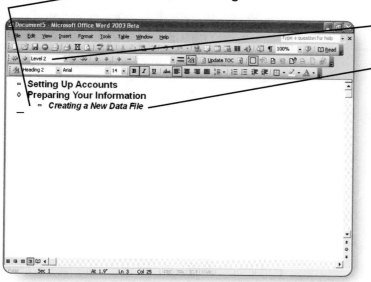

The toolbar shows the style as a Level 2.

6. Type some **text** for the line. The text will appear in an Arial 14-point font, which is the default style for a Level 2 heading.

Each time you press the Tab key, Word creates a lower subheading.

7. Press the **Tab** key. The insertion point will move further to the right.

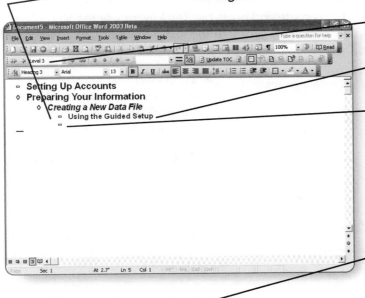

The toolbar shows the style as a Level 3.

8. Type some **text**. The text will appear as a Level 3 heading.

9. Press the **Enter key**. The insertion point will go to the next line.

When you need to return to a higher level, use the combination of the Shift key and the Tab key.

10. Hold down the **Shift key** and **press** the **Tab key**. The insertion point will move back one level to the left. Each press of the Shift and Tab keys moves the insertion point and any text on that line to a level higher.

The toolbar shows the style as a Level 2.

Promoting or Demoting Headings

A Level 1 heading is the highest level in an outline and a Level 9 heading is the lowest. To change the heading level of existing text, place the insertion point anywhere in the line you want to promote and press the Tab key, or use the Shift+Tab keys to demote or promote the text. Optionally, you can use the Outline toolbar to demote or promote your text.

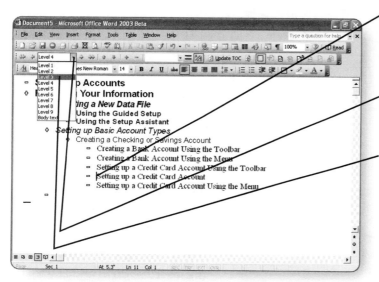

1. **Click** anywhere in the **line** you want to promote or demote. The blinking insertion point will appear in the text line.

2. **Click** on the **down arrow** next to the Outline Level list. A list of outline levels will appear.

3. **Click** on the **level** you want for the current line. The text will be promoted or demoted to the selected level.

You can also use the Promote and Demote buttons on the Outline toolbar.

4. **Click** on the **Promote button.** The current line is promoted to a higher level.

5. **Click** on the **Demote button.** The current line is demoted to a lower level.

6. **Click** on the **Promote to Heading 1 button.** The current line is promoted to the highest level.

Creating Body Text

If you want to add text that isn't really a heading to your outline, you can create body text. Typically, body text elaborates more on the outline level heading directly above it. You create body text by using the Outline toolbar.

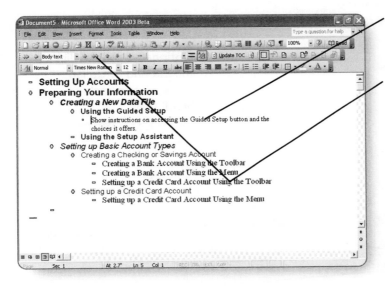

1. Type the **text** you want as body text. The text will appear in the Word document.

2. Click on the **Demote to Body Text button**. The text will appear in a normal Word font.

Viewing the Outline

While in Outline view, you can expand or collapse the various levels to view only the portions you want to see. For example, you can view only the headings in order to get an overview of the entire document. Additionally, you can turn the formatting display on or off.

Word includes five buttons on the Outline toolbar to assist you with viewing your outline.

1. Click on the **Collapse button**. Word will collapse the body text and sub-headings of the first level below the currently selected heading. Each click will collapse an additional sub-heading level.

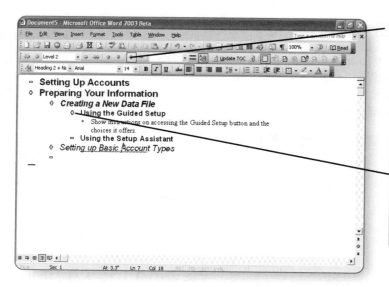

2. Click on the **Expand button**. Word will expand the first heading level below the currently selected heading. Each click will expand additional headings until the body expands.

TIP

Optionally, double-click on the Expand or Collapse icons next to each heading.

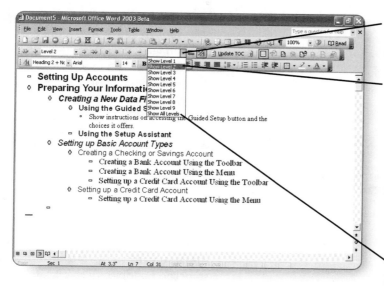

3. Click on the **Show Levels down arrow**. A drop-down list of options will appear.

4. Click on a **level** to display. Word will display only the headings you select and those that are higher than the selected headings. For example, if you select Show Level 2, only Level 1 and 2 headings will be displayed.

TIP

Click on Show All Levels to view the entire outline.

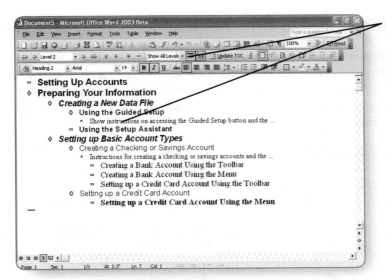

5. Click on the **Show first line only button**. The outline display will toggle between displaying all the body text or only the first line of each paragraph.

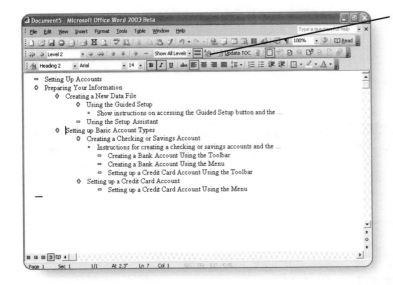

6. Click on the **Show formatting button**. The outline will toggle between displaying the outline with or without character formatting.

NOTE

When you print an outline, Word will print the outline in its entirety and as it displays in Normal view, without the indentation you see in Outline view.

Moving Outline Sections

As you organize your thoughts and ideas in an outline, you might change your mind and want to cover a topic earlier than originally planned. You can move selected headings along with any associated sub-headings and body text up or down to any location in your outline.

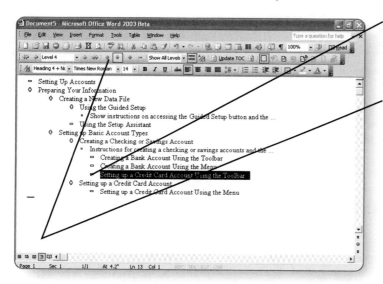

1. **Click** on the **heading icon** of the section you want to move. The heading and all sub-headings will be highlighted.

2a. **Click** on the **Move Up button**. The selected section will move up with each click of the button.

OR

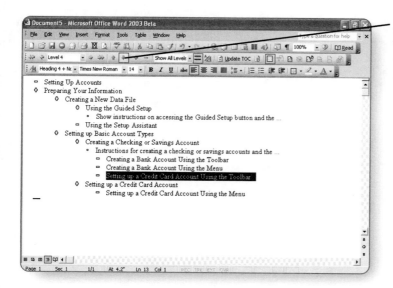

2b. **Click** on the **Move Down button**. The selected section will move down with each click of the button.

9
Communicating Ideas with Art

In a world where everyone is frantically busy, you need to communicate your ideas quickly. Pictures can help you do this. No time to draw? That's not a problem. Word comes with a wide variety of clip art. *Clip art* is simply a collection of computer pictures or graphics that are ready to use. You just select an appropriate picture and insert it in your document. In this chapter, you'll learn how to:

- Insert clip art and other images
- Move and size the art object
- Adjust the contrast and brightness
- Wrap text around an image

Inserting Clip Art

Clip art pictures can be inserted into a document in any Word view, although to view these visual elements you'll need to be in Print Layout or Web Layout view. If you're not already using one of these views, Word will automatically switch you into Print Layout view so that you can see your image.

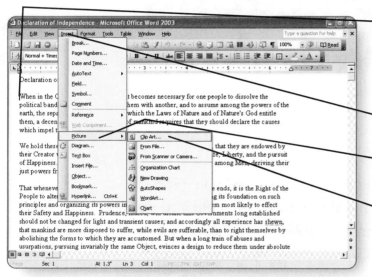

1. Click the **mouse pointer** approximately where you want to insert your image. The blinking insertion point will appear.

2. Click on **Insert**. The Insert menu will appear.

3. Click on **Picture**. The Picture menu will appear.

4. Click on **Clip Art**. The Clip Art task pane will open.

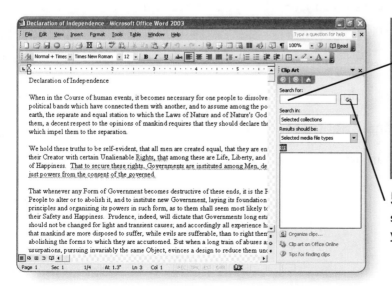

TIP

If you know the specific name of the clip art you want, type it in the Search for box, otherwise leave the Search for box empty and Word will display samples of all clip art.

5. Click on **Go**. Word will search for clip art located on your hard drive.

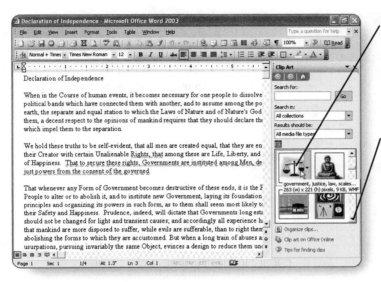

6. Pause the **mouse** over a picture. The selected picture will have a frame around it and an arrow on the right side, and a tip box will describe the selected image.

7. Use the **scroll arrow** when available to preview more images.

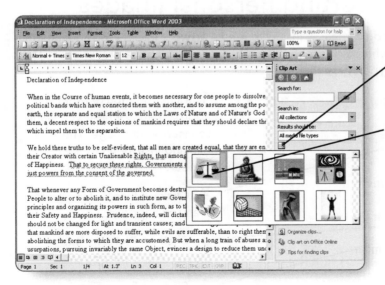

8. Click on the **desired image**. Word will insert the clip into your document.

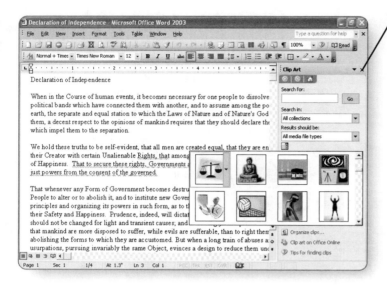

9. **Click** on the **Close button**. The Clip Art task pane will close.

You'll learn in a later section how to move, resize, and adjust any image you insert into your document.

Inserting Personal Images

You can easily insert your own artwork into a Word document, whether it's a photograph, scanned image, a drawing, or other type of artwork.

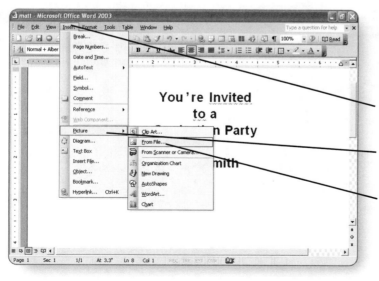

1. **Click** the **mouse pointer** approximately where you want to insert your image. The blinking insertion point will appear.

2. **Click** on **Insert**. The Insert menu will appear.

3. **Click** on **Picture**. The Picture menu will appear.

4. **Click** on **From File**. The Insert Picture dialog box will open.

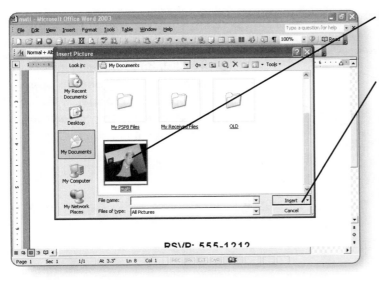

5. Locate and click on the **image** you want to insert. The image will be selected.

6. Click on **Insert**. The image will be inserted into your current document and the Picture toolbar will appear.

You'll learn in a later section how to move, resize, and adjust any image you insert into your document.

Inserting Images from Your Camera

Although you will probably want to use the Windows XP Camera and Scanner Wizard or other software to download a batch of images from your digital camera, you can download images directly from your camera into your Microsoft Word document.

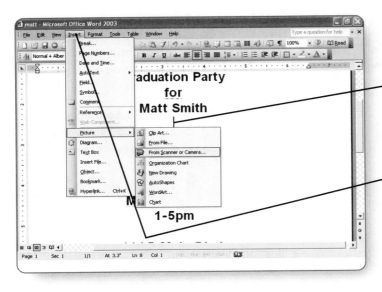

1. Click the **mouse pointer** approximately where you want to insert your image. The blinking insertion point will appear.

2. Click on **Insert**. The Insert menu will appear.

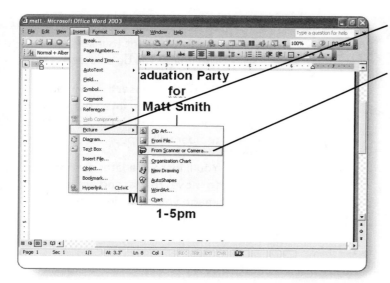

3. Click on **Picture**. The Picture menu will appear.

4. Click on **From Scanner or Camera**. A dialog box will open prompting you to specify the device from which you want to acquire the images.

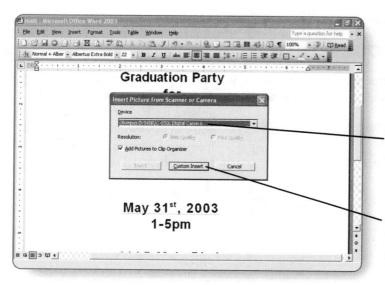

NOTE

Your camera must be installed and properly configured with Windows XP.

5. Click on the **device** you want to use. Your options will depend on the devices you have installed on your system.

6. Click on **Custom Insert**. The Which pictures do you want to copy? dialog box will open.

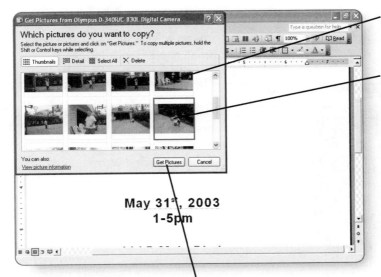

The images stored on your camera will appear as thumbnails.

7. Click on the **image** you want to insert into your document. The selected image will have a border around it.

> **TIP**
>
> If you want to insert multiple images, hold down the CTRL key and select the additional images.

8. Click on **Get Pictures**. Word will insert the selected images into your document.

You'll learn in the next section how to move, resize, and adjust any image you insert into your document.

Customizing Art

After the image is in your document, you can make adjustments to it so that it blends well with your document. You can move an image, change its size, adjust the brightness and contrast, and wrap text around it or over it.

Resizing Images

The image might not fit on the page exactly as you had envisioned it. You can easily make the image smaller or larger.

1. Click on the **image**. The image will be selected and eight small handles will appear.

The Picture toolbar will appear.

2. Position the **mouse pointer** over one of the handles. The mouse pointer will turn into a double-headed arrow.

3. Press and hold your **mouse button** down on one of the selection handles. The pointer will turn into a plus sign.

4. Drag the **selection handle** out to make the picture larger, or inward to make it smaller. A dotted box will indicate the new size.

NOTE

Dragging on any corner handle will resize the height and width of the object at the same time; dragging on any side handle will resize the image in a single direction.

5. Release the mouse **button**. The image will remain at the new size.

Moving Art

The picture you choose might need to be moved. As the image is inserted into the document, surrounding text adjusts to make room for it. When you position an image in a Word document, it automatically aligns (or snaps) to an invisible grid, which helps keep everything lined up.

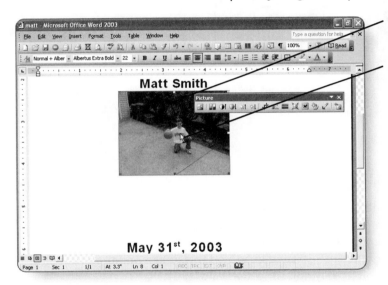

1. **Click** on the **art image**. The image will be selected.

2. **Position** the **mouse pointer** anywhere inside the frame of the graphic. Do not position it over one of the selection handles.

3. **Press and hold** the **mouse button** and **drag** the **insertion point** (in the form of a gray dotted line) to the new location. The mouse pointer will have a small box at the end of it.

TIP

For more exact positioning, you can temporarily override the grid by pressing the ALT key as you drag the object into place.

4. Release the **mouse button**. The graphic will be in the new location. Notice that the text will move to make room for the picture.

TIP

Click anywhere outside of the image to deselect it. The Picture toolbar will also close.

Adjusting the Brightness or Contrast

Controls on the Picture toolbar work in the same way as the controls on your TV that adjust the brightness and contrast of the picture. With a picture in a Word document, adjusting this brightness affects the image on the screen and the printout of the picture by adjusting shades of gray.

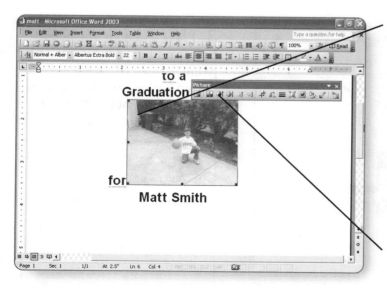

1. Click on the **image**. The image will be selected and the Picture toolbar will be displayed.

TIP

If the Picture toolbar does not appear when you click on the picture object, click on View, and then click on Toolbars. Click on Picture to display the Picture toolbar.

2a. Click on the **More Contrast button**. The image contrast will brighten.

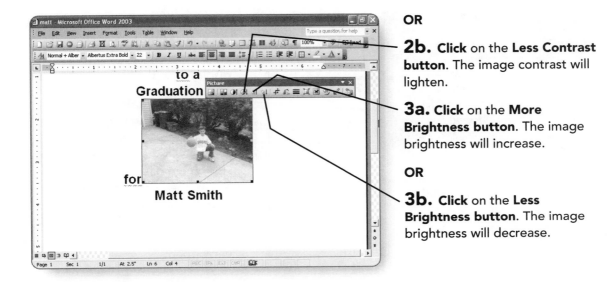

OR

2b. Click on the **Less Contrast button**. The image contrast will lighten.

3a. Click on the **More Brightness button**. The image brightness will increase.

OR

3b. Click on the **Less Brightness button**. The image brightness will decrease.

Cropping the Picture

You might want to use just a portion of the entire picture you've selected. You can easily modify the picture size and content by using the Cropping tool.

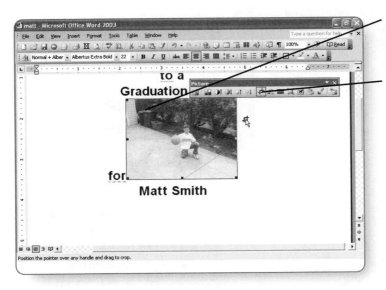

1. Click on the **image**. The image will be selected and the Picture toolbar will display.

2. Click on the **Crop button**. The pointer will change to the Cropping tool.

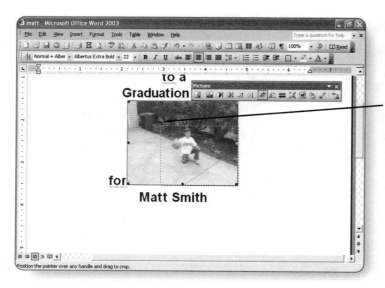

3. Position the **mouse pointer** over one of the selection handles. The Cropping tool will display over the handle.

4. Press and hold the **mouse button** and **drag** toward the **center** of the graphic. The pointer will change to a plus sign, and a dashed line will form a box. The edges of this box form the new edges of the picture, with only the portion inside the box remaining uncropped.

5. Release the **mouse button**. The image will be cropped.

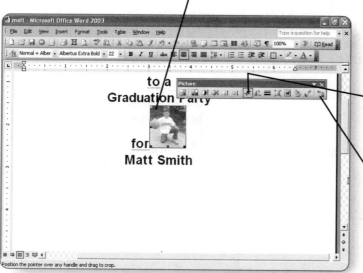

6. Repeat Steps 4 and 5 to crop as many sides as needed until the picture displays only the portion of the image you want.

7. Click on the **Crop button** again. The Cropping tool will be turned off.

TIP

Click on the Reset Picture button on the Picture toolbar if you don't like any of the adjustments that you've made to your image and you would like to start again. The image will return to the way it was originally inserted.

Wrapping Text around Art

When you insert art into a document, lines of text move up or down to accommodate the image. Depending on the size of the image and the length of the lines of text, this effect might not be quite what you want. You might prefer to have the image sit within the lines of text, with the text stopping before the picture and starting again on the other side. This is called *text wrapping*.

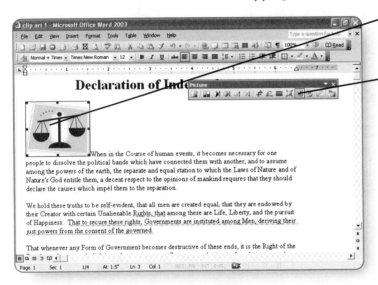

1. Click on the **image**. The image will be selected and the Picture toolbar will display.

2. Click on the **Text Wrapping button**. A list of text wrapping selections will appear.

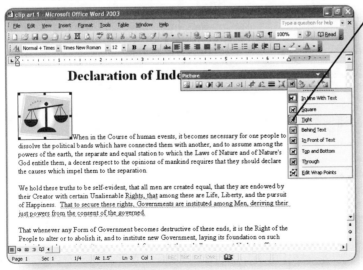

3. Click on one of the following **options**:

- **Square**. Wraps the text around all four sides of the picture boundaries.

- **Tight**. Wraps the text as tightly as possible to the shape of the image.

- **Behind Text**. Places the graphic image under the text so the text will appear on top of the image.

- **In Front of Text**. Places the graphic image on top of the text so the text will appear under the image.

- **Top and Bottom**. Places the text above and below the graphic object but not on either side.

- **Through**. Places text around the perimeter of the graphic object and through any open areas of the object.

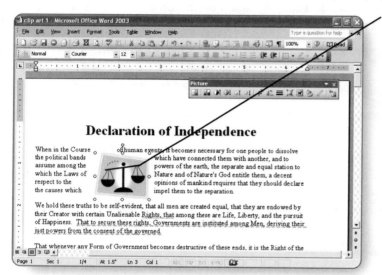

The image here has the text wrapped "tight" around the graphic.

Formatting the Picture

You just learned how to use a variety of the tools on the Picture toolbar to modify your image. Word also allows you to change all of the settings at a single time by using the Format Picture dialog box.

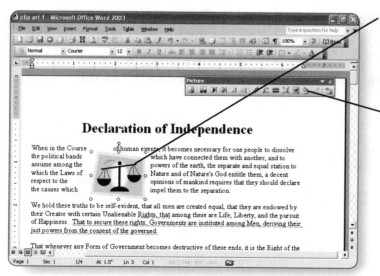

1. Double-click on the **image**. The Format Picture dialog box will open.

TIP

Optionally, click on the Format Picture button.

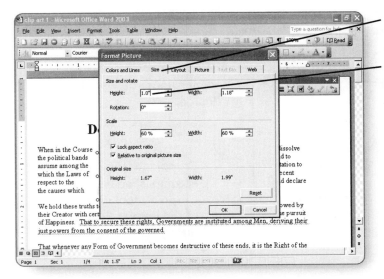

2. Click on the **Size tab**. The Size tab will appear in front.

3. Set the desired image **dimensions** in inches. If you change the image height, the image width will change accordingly to keep the image in proportion.

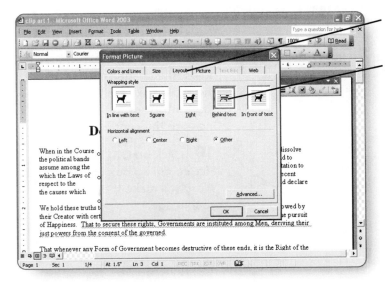

4. Click on the **Layout tab**. The Layout tab will appear in front.

5. Select the type of **text wrap** you want for the image. The option will be selected.

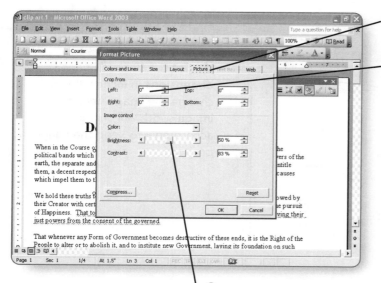

6. Click on the **Picture tab**. The Picture tab will appear in front.

7. Enter any cropping **dimensions** you want for your image.

TIP

Cropping is usually best accomplished with the Cropping tool instead of the Format Picture dialog box.

8. Slide the **Brightness slider** to adjust the image brightness. Slide the slider to the left to decrease the brightness or to the right to increase the brightness.

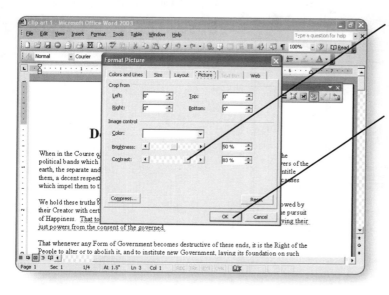

9. Slide the **Contrast slider** to adjust the image contrast. Slide the slider to the left to decrease the contrast or to the right to increase the contrast.

10. Click on **OK**. The Format Picture dialog box will close and Word will make the changes to your image.

Deleting Art

It's easy to delete any unwanted art from your document. Like when deleting Word text, you must first select the item you don't want, then press the Delete key.

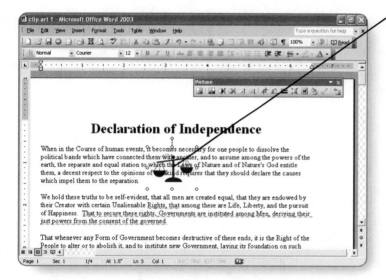

1. **Click** on the **image**.
The image will be selected.

2. **Press** the **Delete key**.
The image will be deleted.

10
Creating WordArt

Adding clip art to a document is one way to add visual excitement, but if you're the creative type, you might want to draw your own pictures using Word's drawing tools. If you want your text to have more impact, WordArt might be your solution. With WordArt, you can take headings or key words and add decorative color schemes, shapes, and special effects. In this chapter, you'll learn how to:

● Create a WordArt object

● Change the object's size and shape

● Rotate and change the direction of a WordArt object

Adding WordArt

Adding WordArt to your document is simply a matter of selecting a predefined style and typing your text. You can create shadowed, skewed, rotated, and stretched text, as well as text that has been fitted to predefined shapes.

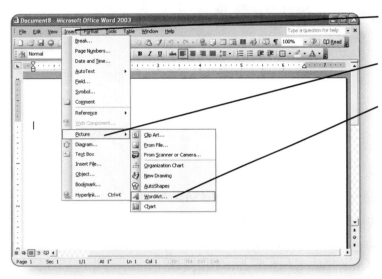

1. Click on **Insert**. The Insert menu will appear.

2. Click on **Picture**. The Picture submenu will appear.

3. Click on **WordArt**. The WordArt Gallery dialog box will open, containing predefined styles in which formats such as shape, color, or shadows are used to enhance text.

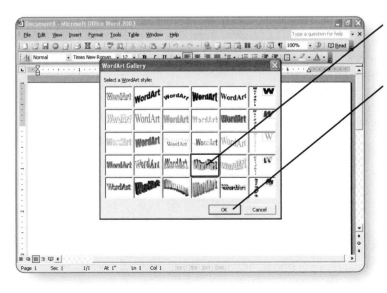

4. Click on a WordArt **style**. The selection will have a box around it.

5. Click on **OK**. The Edit WordArt Text dialog box will open.

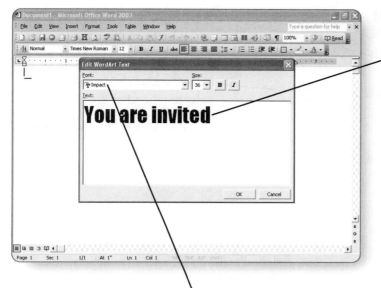

A placeholder in the Text box will say, "Your Text Here."

6. Type the **text** that you want to appear as WordArt. Your text will replace the highlighted text.

NOTE

Limiting WordArt to a single line of text is a good idea; the elaborate formatting can make lengthier text difficult to read.

---

7. Select a **font**. The Text box will display your text in the selected font.

8. Select a **font size**. The Text box will display your text in the selected font size.

9. Click on **OK**. The text that you typed with the WordArt style you selected will be inserted in the document.

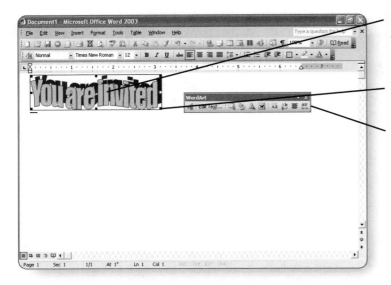

10. **Click** anywhere on the WordArt **text**. The object will be selected.

The WordArt object will have selection handles around it.

The WordArt toolbar will appear.

Making Adjustments to the WordArt

Even though it looks as though you've made a very specific design selection in the WordArt dialog box, you can actually make lots of adjustments to your selection.

Moving WordArt

You can easily move any object, including a WordArt object, around your document. If there is other text in your document, you can move a WordArt object as you learned in Chapter 9, "Communicating Ideas with Art." If, however, no other text exists on the page, you'll need to change the default "in line with text" wrap setting to move or rotate a WordArt object.

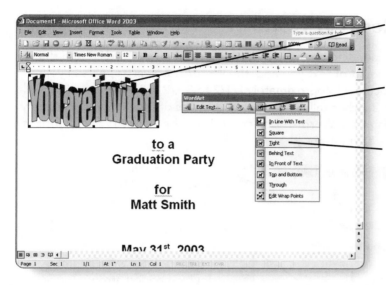

1. Click on the WordArt **object**. The object will be highlighted with selection handles.

2. Click on the **Text Wrapping button**. A list of text wrapping selections will appear.

3. Click on **Tight**. The selected object will appear with a green rotation handle.

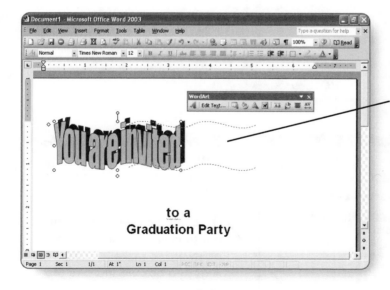

4. Position the **mouse pointer** over the middle of the WordArt object. The mouse pointer will turn into a four-headed arrow.

5. Press and hold the **mouse button** and **drag** the **object** to another position. The new position will be indicated on the screen.

6. Release the **mouse button**. The WordArt object will be in its new position.

Resizing WordArt

Depending on the style you select for your WordArt and the amount of text you add, the WordArt object appears in your document approximately 2 1/2 to 3 1/2 inches long and from 1 to 2 inches tall. Similar to other types of artwork, you can easily resize the WordArt object. Resizing the WordArt object resizes the text letters.

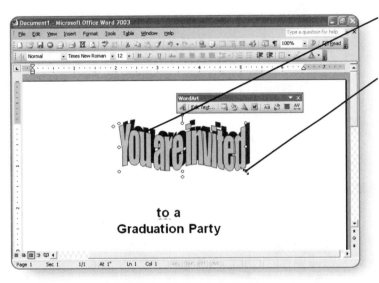

1. **Click** on the WordArt **object**. The object will be highlighted with selection handles.

2. **Position** the **mouse pointer** over one of the handles. The mouse pointer will turn into a double-headed arrow.

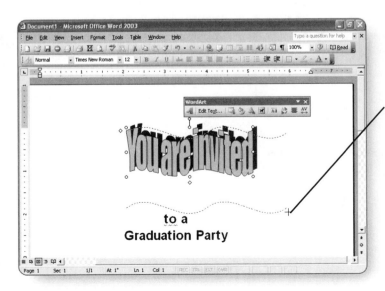

3. **Press and hold** your **mouse button** down on one of the selection handles. The pointer will turn into a plus sign.

4. **Drag** the **selection handle** out to make the picture larger or inward to make it smaller. A dotted box will indicate the new size.

> **NOTE**
>
> Dragging on any corner handle will resize the height and width of the object at the same time; dragging on any side handle will resize the image in a single direction.

5. Release the **mouse button**. The WordArt object will remain at the new size.

Editing WordArt Text

If you made a typing error or you want to adjust the size or font of the text, you can easily open the WordArt feature again.

1. Click on the WordArt **object**. The object will be highlighted with selection handles.

2. From the WordArt toolbar, **click** on the **Edit Text button**. The Edit WordArt Text dialog box will open.

> **TIP**
>
> Optionally, double-click on the WordArt object to display the Edit WordArt Text dialog box.

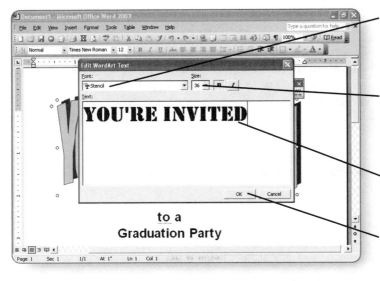

3. Optionally, **select** a new **font**. The Text box will display your text in the newly selected font.

4. Optionally, **select** a new **font size**. The Text box will display your text in the selected font.

5. **Make** any **changes** to your text in the Text box. The Text box will reflect the changes.

6. **Click** on **OK**. The WordArt object will reflect your changes.

Changing WordArt Style

When you created the WordArt object, you selected a style from the WordArt Gallery, which contained various appearance styles such as shape, color, or shadows that were used to enhance your text. If you want a different WordArt style, you can easily access the WordArt Gallery to select a different style.

1. **Click** on the WordArt **object**. The object will be highlighted with selection handles.

2. From the WordArt toolbar, **click** on the **WordArt Gallery button**. The WordArt Gallery dialog box will open.

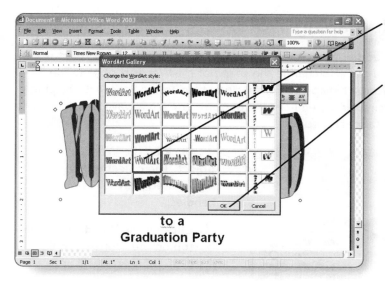

3. Click on a WordArt **style**. The selection will have a box around it.

4. Click on **OK**. The WordArt Gallery dialog box will close.

The existing WordArt object will change to the new style.

Reshaping WordArt

In addition to changing the size and style of the WordArt text, you can also change the shape of the WordArt object. The WordArt shape options include placing the WordArt object in a circular or semi-circular pattern, or even a wave, triangle, or octagonal shape.

1. **Click** on the **WordArt object**. The object will be highlighted with selection handles.

2. **Click** on the **WordArt Shape button** on the WordArt toolbar. A palette of shapes will appear.

3. **Click** on a **shape**. Your WordArt will change to the shape you selected.

NOTE

Some shapes will make your text hard to read, while others will add an exciting or fun tone to your words. You may have to experiment with the different choices to find the shape that best fits your text.

---

4. **Click** anywhere in the **document** outside of the WordArt object. The WordArt object will be deselected.

Making WordArt Text Vertical

Also included on the WordArt toolbar is a button to arrange your text from a horizontal text pattern to a vertical text pattern while retaining its style, shape, and attributes.

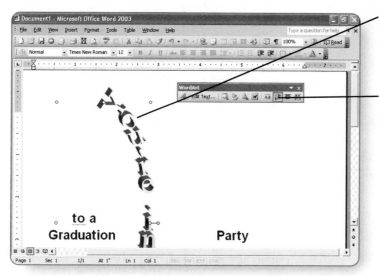

1. **Click** on the **WordArt object**. The object will be highlighted with selection handles.

2. **Click** on the **WordArt Vertical Text button** on the WordArt toolbar. The WordArt object will take the vertical shape.

TIP

Click on the WordArt Vertical Text button again to return the WordArt text to its horizontal shape.

Formatting WordArt

Because a special text effect is a drawing object, you can also use other buttons on the Drawing toolbar to change the effect—for example, to fill a text effect with a picture. Other options available with WordArt include the ability to change colors, level of transparency, size, and rotation. WordArt controls all of these features through a single dialog box, the Format WordArt dialog box.

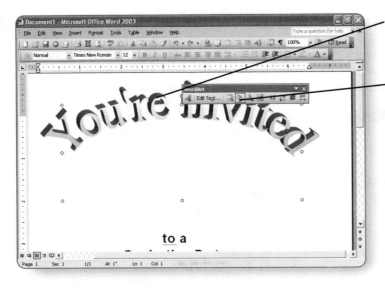

1. Click on the **WordArt object**. The object will be highlighted with selection handles.

2. Click on the **Format WordArt button** on the WordArt toolbar. The Format WordArt dialog box will open.

Changing Colors

The Colors and Lines tab of the Format WordArt dialog box allows you to change the color supplied with the WordArt text. Depending on the WordArt style, you might also be able to change the border color surrounding the text.

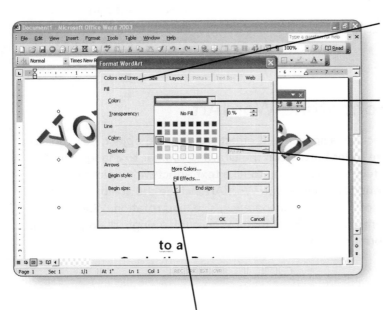

1. If necessary, **click** on the **Colors and Lines tab**. The Colors and Lines tab will come to the front.

2. Click on the **Color down arrow**. A palette of available colors will appear.

3a. Click on a **text color**. The newly selected color will appear in the Fill Color box.

OR

Rather than choosing a solid color, you can specify a gradient, texture, pattern, or even a picture to use as the fill for the WordArt object.

3b. Click on **Fill Effects**. The Fill Effects dialog box will open.

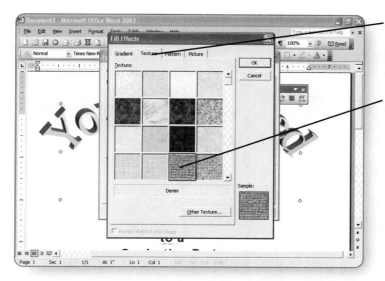

4. Click on the **Gradient**, **Texture**, **Pattern**, or **Picture tab**. The selected tab will come to the front.

5. Select the **fill** you want for your WordArt.

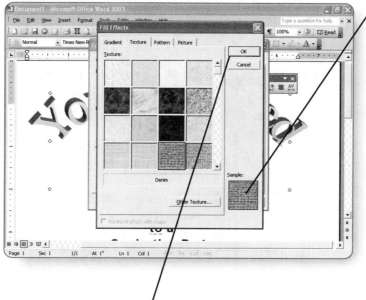

A sample will appear in the Sample box.

6. Click on **OK**. The Fill Effects dialog box will close.

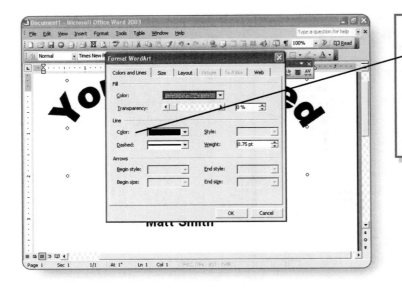

WordArt transparency designates the depth of color, with an object of less transparency containing more vivid colors. Those objects with a higher transparency setting are lighter in shading, becoming sheerer as the transparency setting increases.

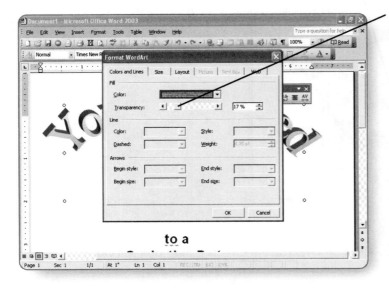

7. Move the **Transparency slider** until the fill color displays the color shading you want.

Editing Size and Rotation

Earlier in this chapter you learned how to resize a WordArt object by dragging the selection handles until the object meets the size you want. You can also specify a specific size for the WordArt object through the Format WordArt dialog box.

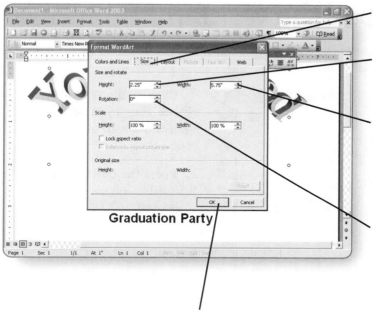

1. Click on the **Size tab**. The Size tab will come to the front.

2. Click on the **height up/down arrows** to select the exact height you want.

3. Click on the **width up/down arrows** to select the exact width you want.

You can also rotate the WordArt object.

4. Click on the **rotation up/down arrows**. The height and width you specified in Steps 2 and 3 are for an non-rotated object.

5. Click on **OK**. The Format WordArt dialog box will close.

The WordArt object will display the newly selected formatting.

Deleting WordArt

Since anything you create in WordArt is an object, you can easily delete it.

1. **Click** on the **WordArt object**. The object will be highlighted with selection handles.

2. **Press** the **Delete key**. the WordArt object will be deleted.

11

Using the Drawing Toolbar

In the previous chapter, you learned how WordArt can be used to create interesting graphics by applying predefined text effects. Many of those same effects, such as shadows, can be added to objects that you create in your Word document using the Drawing toolbar. This toolbar offers predefined drawing shapes, called *AutoShapes*, as well as tools to draw and format lines, boxes, circles, and more. In this chapter, you'll learn how to:

- Display the Drawing toolbar
- Draw AutoShapes
- Add text to a drawing
- Make a shape three-dimensional
- Create relationship diagrams

Displaying the Drawing Toolbar

Word provides the drawing tools through the Drawing toolbar. Each button on the Drawing toolbar corresponds to a tool that performs a specific function. Some tools draw lines or shapes, some tools help position the drawn objects on the screen, and some drawing tools can change the color or appearance of a drawn shape or line.

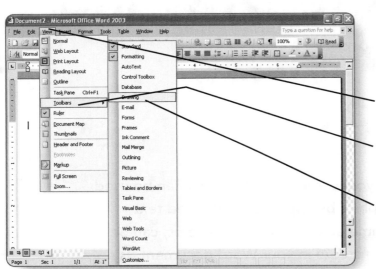

1. Click on **View**. The View menu will appear.

2. Click on **Toolbars**. A list of available toolbars will be displayed.

3. Click on **Drawing**. The Drawing toolbar will be displayed at the bottom of your screen.

The Drawing toolbar

Working with AutoShapes

Word includes built-in images called AutoShapes that make it easy to click and drag to draw anything on your document page. AutoShapes are a group of ready-made shapes including arrows, lines, stars, and banners, as well as basic shapes such as rectangles or pyramids.

Drawing AutoShapes

Drawing an AutoShape is as easy as selecting a shape and then using your mouse to click and draw the shape in your document.

> ### TIP
> Drawing must be done in the Print Layout view. If you are not already in Print Layout view, then as soon as you select an AutoShape, Word will change to Print Layout view for you.

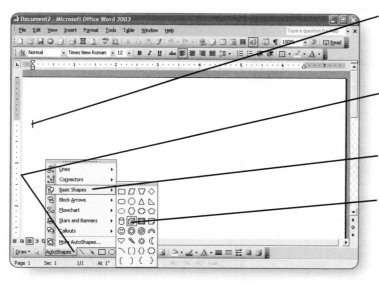

1. **Click** in the **document** where you want to locate the shape. The blinking insertion point will appear.

2. **Click** on **AutoShapes**. A list of AutoShapes categories will appear.

3. **Click** on a **category**. A selection of shapes will appear.

4. **Click** on a **shape**. The palette will close, and a large blank canvas with the words "Create your drawing here" will appear on your screen. Word calls this the Drawing canvas.

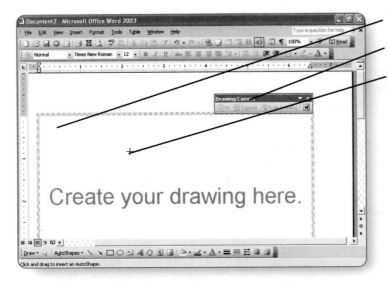

The Drawing canvas

The Drawing Canvas toolbar

The pointer will change to a large crosshair

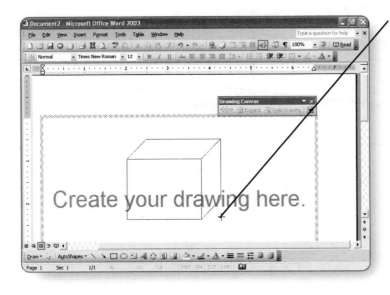

5. In the Drawing canvas, **click and drag** the **mouse**. A shaped object will appear.

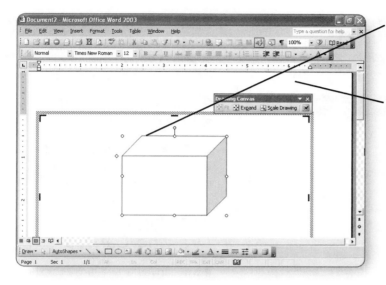

6. Release the **mouse button**. The new drawing shape will display with selection handles surrounding it.

7. Click anywhere outside the **Drawing canvas**. The drawn image will be deselected.

Resizing the Drawing

When you originally create the drawn object, it might not end up the exact size you need, or the canvas might be too large or too small to fully represent the drawn object. You can resize a drawing quite easily.

Resizing the Drawing Image

The drawn object can be resized by selecting the object and dragging any of the selection handles. Selection handles on a drawn object are indicated by small white circles.

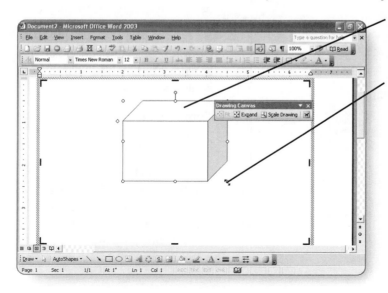

1. Click on the drawn **object**. The object and the Drawing canvas will be selected.

2. Position the **mouse pointer** over any of the selection handles. The mouse pointer will turn into a double-headed arrow.

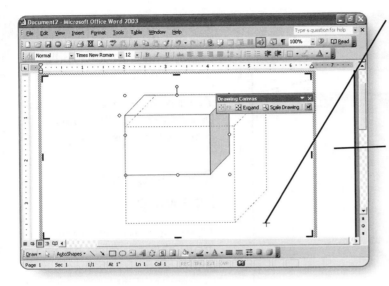

3. Click and drag any of the **drawing handles** to resize the object. A dotted outline will indicate the new object size.

4. Release the **mouse**. The object will be resized.

5. Click anywhere outside the **Drawing canvas**. The drawn image will be deselected.

Resizing the Drawing Canvas

If the canvas is too large for the object, you can resize the canvas so it better fits into your document. Canvas resizing is accomplished by resizing each corner of the canvas until it meets your needs.

1. Click next to the drawn **object**. The Drawing canvas will be selected, but not the actual drawn object.

Drawing canvas selection handles are indicated by black corner angles and small black bars.

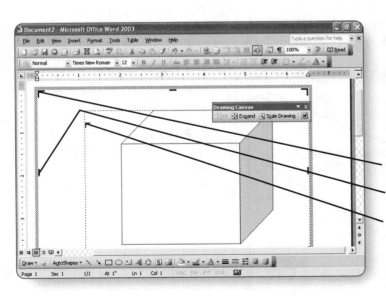

Corner resizing handle

Side resizing handle

2. Click and drag as many **handles** as needed until the canvas is the desired size. As you drag the handles, a dotted line will indicate the new size.

Deleting a Drawn Object

If you no longer want an object, you can delete only the object, or the object and the Drawing canvas.

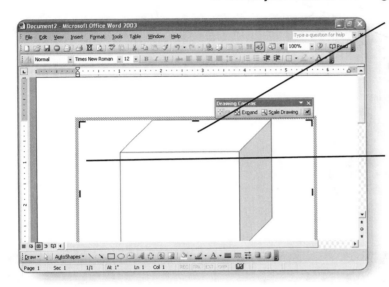

1a. **Click** on the **object**. The object will be selected.

2a. **Press** the **Delete key**. The object will be deleted, but the Drawing canvas will remain.

OR

1b. **Click** in the **Drawing canvas**. The Drawing canvas will be selected.

2b. **Press** the **Delete key.** Both the object and the canvas will be deleted.

Adding Text to AutoShapes

When you create an AutoShape object, you can add text to it, making it more informative and useful. If you selected an AutoShape from the Callouts category, the shape will be ready for text to be entered. You can skip Steps 1 and 2.

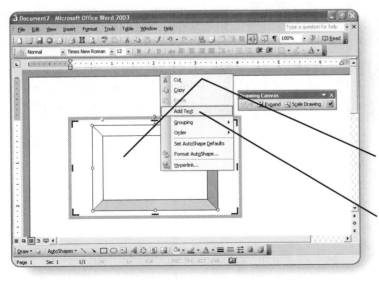

1. **Right-click** on the **drawn shape**. A shortcut menu will appear.

2. **Click** on **Add Text**. The blinking insertion point will appear inside the AutoShape.

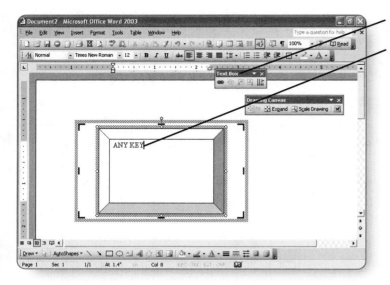

The Text Box toolbar will appear.

3. Type some **text**. The text will appear in the AutoShape object.

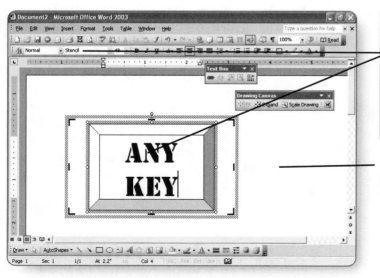

TIP

You can select and format the text font, size, color, or alignment in the same manner as any other document text.

4. Click outside the **shape**. The blinking insertion point and the Text Box toolbar will disappear.

Making Shapes Three-Dimensional

Make objects come alive by adding three-dimensional effects! Some objects won't work with three-dimensional shapes, so the feature will not be available.

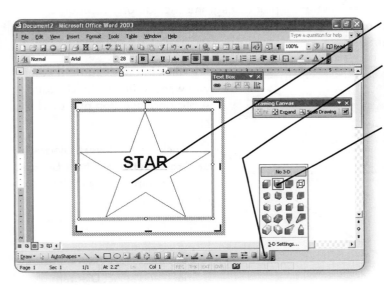

1. Click on the **shape object**. The object will be selected.

2. Click on the **3-D Style button**. A palette with selections of 3-D settings will appear.

3. Click on a **3-D option**. The object will take on the added dimension.

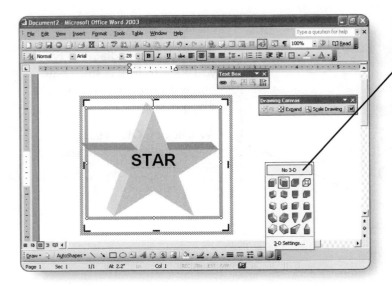

TIP

Remove 3-D settings by choosing No 3-D from the 3-D pallette.

Creating Relationship Diagrams

When creating reports, you may want to add a diagram to further illustrate a point. Diagrams include organization charts or other charts that show a relationship between two or more entities.

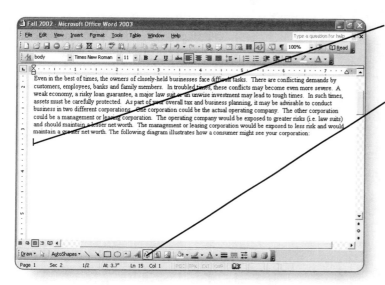

1. Click in the **document** where you want to insert the diagram. A blinking insertion point will appear.

2. Click on the **Insert Diagram or Organizational Chart button**. The Diagram Gallery dialog box will appear.

TIP

Optionally, click on the Insert menu and select Diagram.

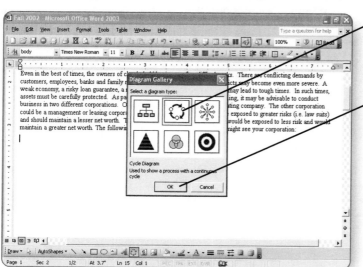

3. Click on the **diagram type** you want to use. A small blue box will surround the selected diagram type.

4. Click on **OK**. A sample diagram will appear in your document.

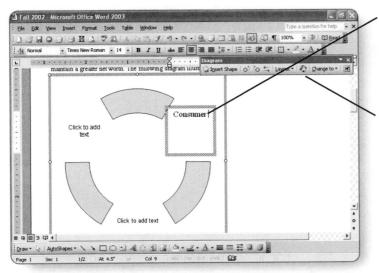

5. **Click** on any desired **Click to add text box** and **replace it** with your own text. Your text will replace the Click to add text box.

A toolbar applicable to the selected diagram type will also appear. From the toolbar, you can add elements to the diagram or change the diagram type without losing any text data you might have already entered. The available toolbar options will vary according to the type of diagram you are using.

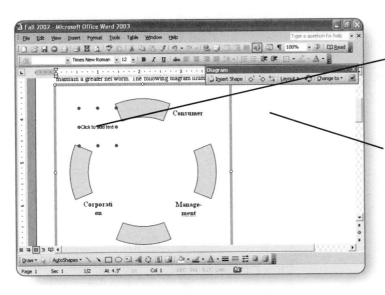

TIP

Click on any diagram element and press the Delete key to delete that element.

6. **Click** anywhere outside the **diagram**. The diagram will be deselected.

TIP

You can resize a diagram in the same way you would resize other drawn objects.

12
Working with Tables

Tables are great for organizing information. When you need to compare data or follow information across several columns, it's easier if the information is displayed in a table. Tables can be used to place pieces of data side-by-side in a document; for example, in the various sections of an invoice or address list. If you have used Microsoft Excel or another spreadsheet program, you will find working with tables in Word very similar. In this chapter, you'll learn how to:

- Create a simple table
- Use the AutoSum feature
- Format a table
- Add and delete rows and columns
- Add borders around cells

Creating a Simple Table

A table is a grid of columns and rows. The intersection of a column and row is called a *cell*. You can insert a table in a number of different ways. You can insert it from a menu selection, create it from the toolbar, or draw it manually. You can even type on your keyboard and Word will create a table from your typed text.

Inserting a Table Using the Menu

To create a simple table, all you need to do is estimate the number of rows and columns that you want to start working with, and you're ready to go.

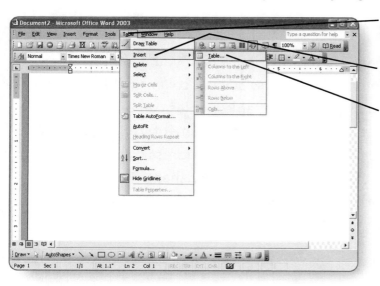

1. Click on **Table**. The Table menu will appear.

2. Click on **Insert**. The Insert submenu will appear.

3. Click on **Table**. The Insert Table dialog box will open.

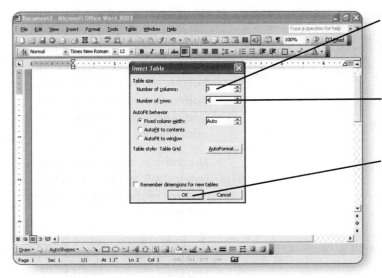

4. Enter the **number of columns** in the Number of columns text box. The number will be displayed.

5. Enter the **number of rows** in the Number of rows text box. The number will be displayed.

6. Click on **OK**. The table will be created.

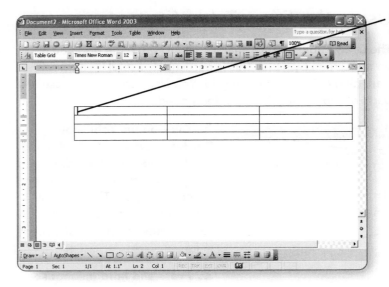

The table will appear in the Word document with the blinking insertion point ready for you to enter table information.

Creating a Table Using the Toolbar

A button is located on the Word standard toolbar to help you quickly create a table.

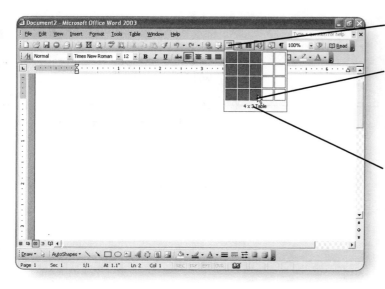

1. **Click** on the **Insert Table button**. A small grid will appear.

2. **Press and hold** the **mouse button** and **move** your **mouse pointer** down and across this grid. The selected squares of the grid will turn black.

Numbers at the bottom of the palette will appear, showing you the size of the table in columns and rows.

3. **Release** the **mouse button** when the table is the size that you want. The table grid will appear in the document.

Using the Draw Table Feature

The Draw Table feature enables you to draw the grid you need on the screen by hand. This is particularly useful if you don't want all the lines inside the grid. You also can quickly erase any parts of those lines that you don't need.

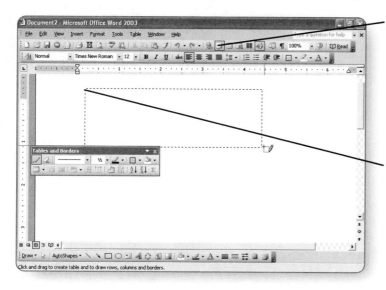

1. **Click** on the **Tables and Borders button**. The Tables and Borders toolbar will be displayed and the pointer will immediately change to a pen. The view will automatically change to Print Layout view, if you're not already in it.

2. **Press and hold** the **mouse button** to anchor the upper-left corner of the table. The mouse pointer will turn into an arrow with a small box at the tip of it.

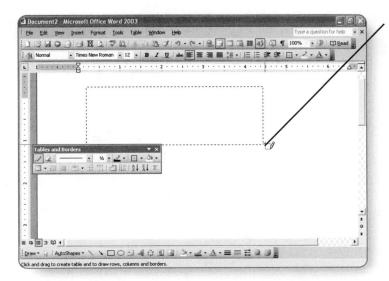

3. Press the **mouse button** and **drag** to draw a box that is the approximate size you need for your table. A dotted box will represent the table size.

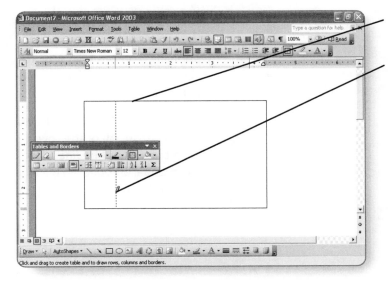

4. Release the **mouse button**. The table border will appear.

5. Press and hold the **mouse button** and **drag** to draw as many vertical lines as you need to create columns. The lines will appear as you draw them.

NOTE

Don't be too concerned with exact placement and spacing of drawn lines. You'll learn how to space or move them later in this chapter.

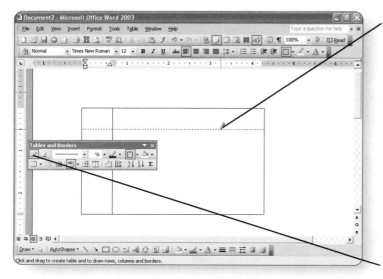

6. Press and hold the **mouse button** and **drag** to draw as many horizontal lines as you need to create rows. The lines will appear as you draw them.

NOTE

You'll notice as you draw these lines that they complete themselves when you reach a particular point.

7. Click on the **Draw Table button**. The feature will be deactivated.

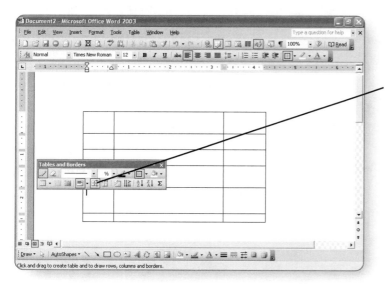

Optionally, you can tell Word to make the rows and columns an equal size.

8. Click on the **Distribute Rows Evenly button**. All of the rows you've created will be lined up with an equal amount of space between them.

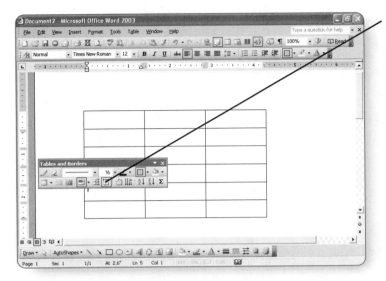

9. Click on the **Distribute Columns Evenly button**. The table columns will have an equal amount of space between them.

Typing Out a Table

You can create tables in Microsoft Word by simply typing out a string of plus signs (+) and minus signs (−). Word uses its AutoCorrect feature to interpret your typing and convert it into a table.

1. Type a **plus sign (+)**. The plus sign will appear in your document.

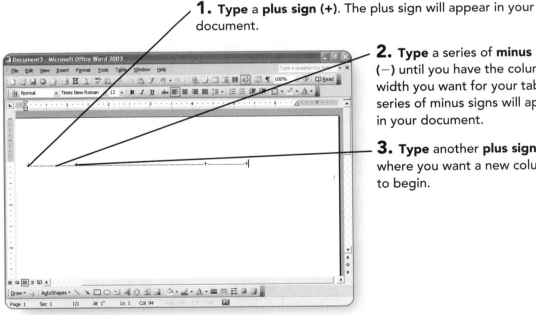

2. Type a series of **minus signs** (−) until you have the column width you want for your table. A series of minus signs will appear in your document.

3. Type another **plus sign (+)** where you want a new column to begin.

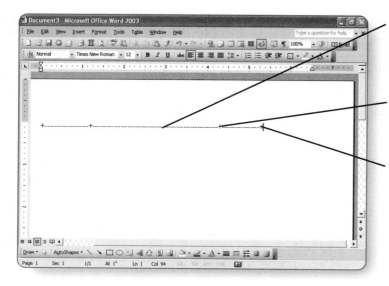

4. Type another series of **minus signs (−)** until you have the column width you want for the second column of your table.

5. Repeat Steps 3 and 4 until you have the number of columns you want in your table.

6. Type a **plus sign (+)** at the end of the row.

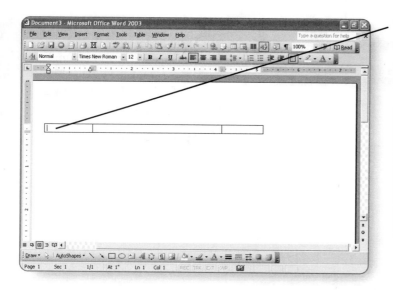

7. Press the **Enter key**. Word will create a table, making columns where you placed the plus signs (+).

NOTE

The table will have a single row, but you can add additional rows by pressing the Tab key in the last cell of the table.

Entering Text

Each intersection of a column and row is called a *cell*. Text is typed into the individual cells. As you enter text in the cells, if you have more characters than will fit horizontally, the text automatically wraps to the next line, and the cell and the row will expand vertically to hold it.

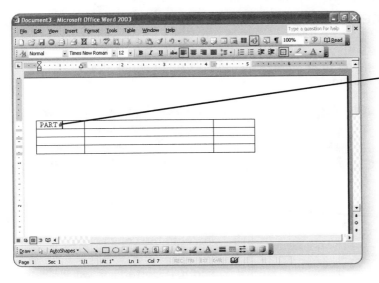

1. Click the **mouse pointer** in a cell. The blinking insertion point will appear.

2. Type some **text**. The text will display in a single cell.

You can use your keyboard or mouse to move around in a table. To use the mouse, simply click in the cell you want to work with. Use the following keys to move around the table with your keyboard:

- **Tab key.** The insertion point will move to the cell to the right.

- **Down Arrow key.** The insertion point will move down to the next row.

- **Shift+Tab key.** The insertion point will move to the cell to the left.

- **Up Arrow key.** The insertion point will move up a row.

Adjusting Column Width

The text-wrapping feature sometimes causes words to break oddly in the middle. When the text does not break in the position you expect, you might want to widen the column.

Changing Column Width Using the Mouse

You can easily modify any column width by clicking and dragging the mouse. You can enlarge or shrink the width of any column.

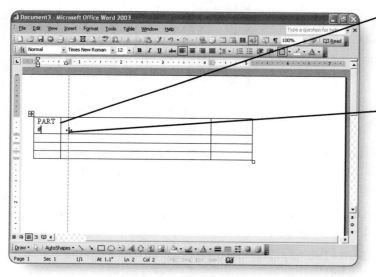

1. Place the **mouse pointer** over the border line of the column. The mouse pointer will change to a double-headed arrow.

2. Press and hold the **mouse button** and **drag** to the right to increase the column width or to the left to decrease the column width. A dotted line will indicate the new border line position.

3. Release the **mouse button** when the column is at the width you want. The column width will change. Any text that was wrapped in the cell will adjust to fit the new column width.

NOTE
Widening one column might make an adjacent column shrink so that the table will fit the document width.

Using AutoFit

The Table AutoFit feature will automatically adjust all columns to fit your text or the width of the document. This saves you the time of adjusting each column individually.

1. Click the **mouse** anywhere inside the table. The blinking insertion point will appear.

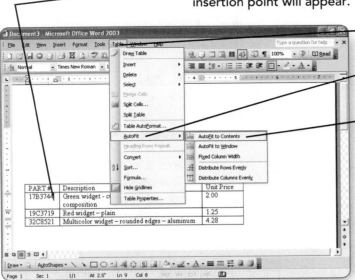

2. Click on **Table**. The Table menu will appear.

3. Click on **AutoFit**. The AutoFit submenu will appear.

4. Click on **AutoFit to Contents**. The columns will widen or shrink according to the cell contents.

Formatting Cell Contents

You can perform a variety of formatting effects on the contents of a cell, just as you can with any text in Word. However, you also can apply some unique formatting to cells themselves.

Aligning Cell Contents

The entries you make in cells are, by default, all aligned at the top of the cells, along the left side. You can go in and align the contents of each cell separately.

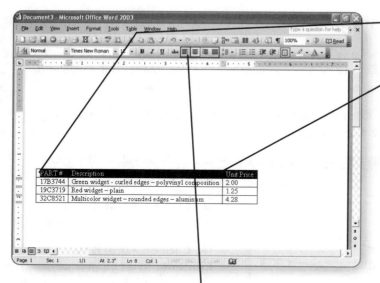

1. **Click** in the **first cell** you want to format. The blinking insertion point will appear.

2. **Press and hold** your **mouse button** and **drag** across any adjacent **cells** that you want to format. The selected cells will be highlighted.

TIP

You also can select a whole row at a time by moving your insertion point to the left of the row until it becomes a white arrow, and then clicking. This works the same way for selecting a column— move the insertion point to the top of the column until you see the same arrow.

---

3. **Click** on an **alignment button**. The alignment option will be applied to the selected cells.

Formatting Text in Cells

Text inside tables is formatted exactly the same way any other text in the document is formatted.

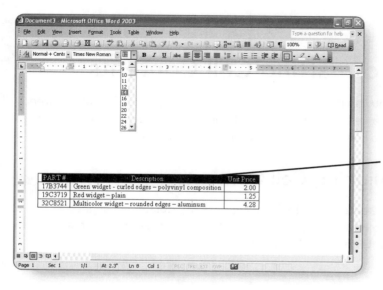

1. **Press and hold** the **mouse button** and **drag** across any **cells** that you want to format. The selected cells will be highlighted.

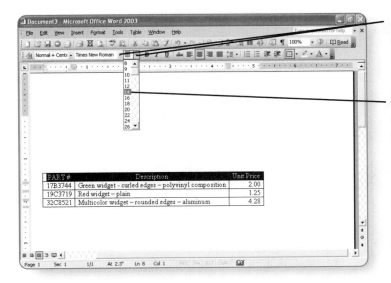

2. Click on the appropriate **down arrow** to the right of the Font or Font Size text box. A list of options will appear.

3. Click on the **option** you want. The option will be applied to the selected cells.

Using AutoFormat

You can add formatting to the lines that divide your rows and columns, and even add color or patterns to the interior of the cells. Of course, you don't want to spend hours trying different line sizes, colors, and patterns. Instead, you can use AutoFormat.

1. Click in any table **cell**. The blinking insertion point will appear.

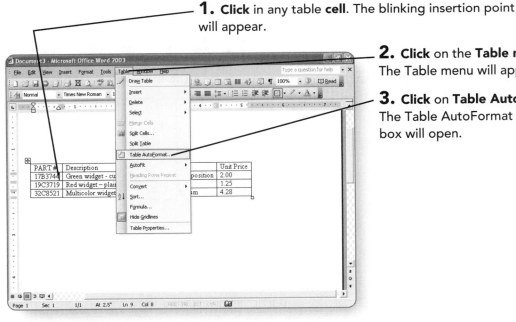

2. Click on the **Table menu**. The Table menu will appear.

3. Click on **Table AutoFormat**. The Table AutoFormat dialog box will open.

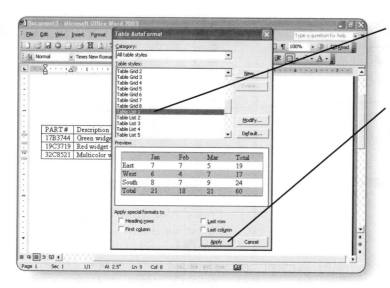

4. **Click** on a **format** in the Table styles scroll box. A sample of the format will appear in the Preview window.

5. **Click** on **Apply**. The selected format will be applied to your data.

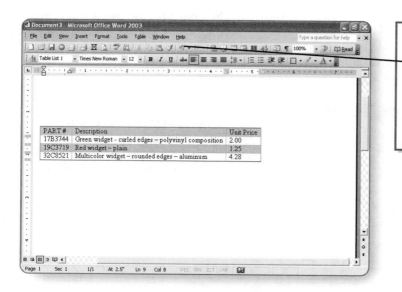

TIP

If you're not pleased with the AutoFormat you selected, click on the Undo button to reverse the AutoFormat settings.

Using AutoSum

Frequently, tables contain numbers that must be added up. For this reason, Word includes an AutoSum button on the Tables and Borders toolbar. Automatically add table cell values together by using the Word AutoSum feature.

TIP

If you do not already have the Tables and Borders toolbar displayed, click on the Tables and Borders button.

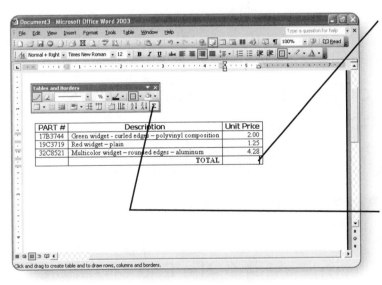

1. Click in the **cell** where you want the total to appear. The blinking insertion point will appear.

The AutoSum feature will first add the cells directly above the selected cell. If no values are available above the selected cell, the AutoSum feature will add the cells directly to the right of it.

2. Click on **AutoSum**. The total will be calculated and will be displayed in the selected cell.

Updating AutoSum Totals

If you change any of the values in the cells that are totaled, the cell that holds the total does not automatically update. You must update it manually.

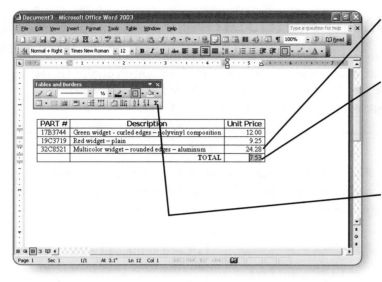

1. Make a **change** to a cell value. The cell will reflect the new number.

2. Click in the **cell** with the current total. Depending on exactly where you click in the cell, either a blinking insertion point will appear or a gray highlight will surround the total.

3. Click on **AutoSum**. The new total will be displayed.

Adding and Deleting Rows and Columns

When you're designing a table, it's easy to forget an essential row or column. However, Word makes it easy to add new rows and columns or delete ones you don't need.

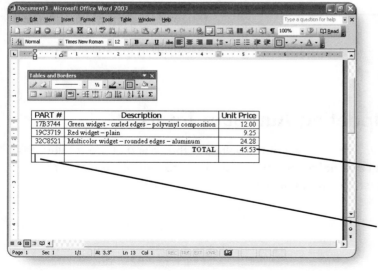

Adding a Row to the End of a Table

You can easily add a row to the bottom of the table you originally created.

1. Click in the **last cell** of the last row. The blinking insertion point will appear.

2. Press the **Tab key**. A new row will automatically appear.

Inserting a Row between Existing Rows

You might want to add a row at the beginning or in the middle of a table.

1. Click in the **row** where you want to insert a new row. The blinking insertion point will appear.

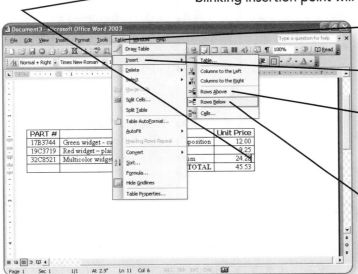

2. Click on **Table**. The Table menu will appear.

3. Click on **Insert**. The Insert submenu will appear.

4a. Click on **Rows Above**. The new row will be inserted above the insertion point row.

OR

4b. Click on **Rows Below**. The new row will be inserted below the insertion point row.

Inserting a Column

Again, you can easily add a column between two existing columns or add one to the end of a set of existing columns.

1. **Click** in the **cell** where you want the new column. The blinking insertion point will appear.

2. **Click** on **Table**. The Table menu will appear.

3. **Click** on **Insert**. The Insert submenu will appear.

4a. **Click** on **Columns to the Left**. The new column will be inserted to the left of the insertion point column.

OR

4b. **Click** on **Columns to the Right**. The new column will be inserted to the right of the insertion point column.

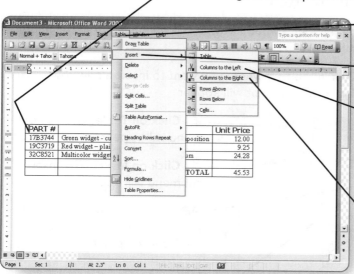

Deleting Rows or Columns

Deleting a row will delete an entire row across a table while deleting a column will delete an entire column. Word also deletes any data in the deleted rows or columns.

1. **Click** the **mouse pointer** in the row or column that you want to delete. The blinking insertion point will appear.

2. **Click** on **Table**. The Table menu will appear.

3. **Click** on **Delete**. The Delete submenu will appear.

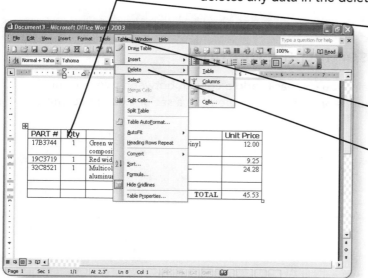

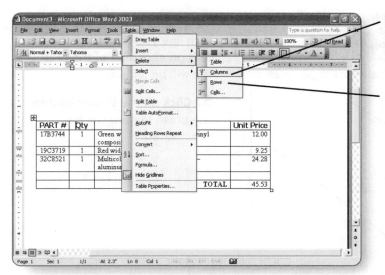

4a. Click on **Columns**. The current column will be deleted.

OR

4b. Click on **Rows**. The current row will be deleted.

Erasing Cell Partitions

When you work with tables, you often find that you don't want all of the lines that divide cells. Erasing lines will combine connecting cells. You need the Tables and Borders toolbar displayed to easily erase cell partitions.

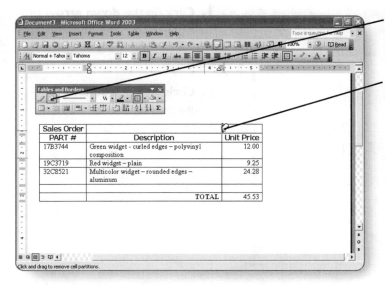

1. Click on the **Eraser button**. The pointer will change shape to look like an eraser.

2. **Press and hold** the **mouse button** and **drag** the **eraser** over the lines you don't need.

3. **Release** the **mouse button**. The lines will change color and then disappear.

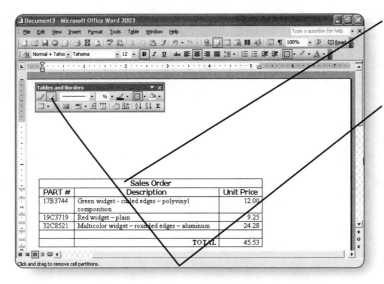

4. Repeat Steps 2 and 3 for each line you want to erase. The cells on each side of the erased line will be joined.

5. Click on the **Eraser button**. The erase feature will be deactivated.

Modifying Table Cell Borders

By default, the table cells have a single-line grid around each cell. You can modify the style of the lines that surround your table cells by selecting a style and drawing around the area you want bordered.

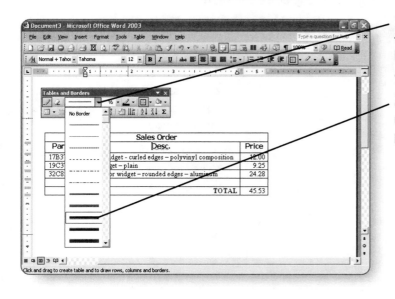

1. Click on the **down arrow** to the right of the Line Style text box. A list of line styles will appear.

2. Click on a **line style**. The mouse pointer will turn into a pencil.

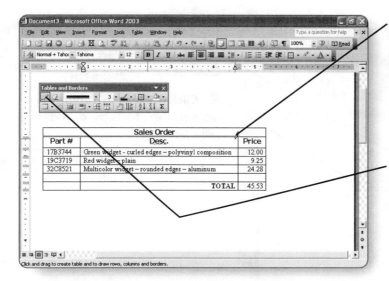

3. Press and drag the **mouse** across the lines that you want to have the new border line style. A gray line will appear.

4. Release the **mouse button**. The style will be applied to the selected cells.

5. Click on the **Draw button**. The feature will be deactivated.

Converting Tables

If you type some text and then later decide it would be better in a table (or vice versa), let Word convert the text directly into a table or the table into text for you.

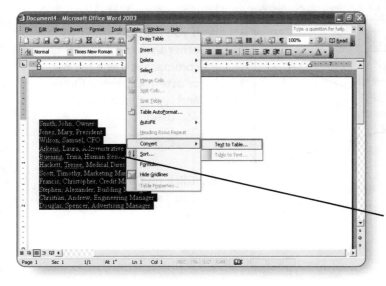

Converting Text into a Table

Word uses commas, tabs, or other separator characters within text to decide where to begin a new column. Word also uses the paragraph mark (created when you press Enter to begin a new paragraph) to begin each new row.

1. Select the **text** you want to convert. The text will be highlighted.

2. Click on **Table**. The Table menu will appear.

3. Click on **Convert**. The Convert submenu will appear.

4. Click on **Text to Table**. The Convert Text to Table dialog box will open.

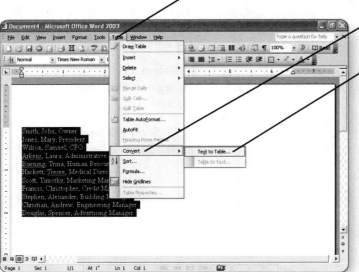

5. Select the **character** you used to separate your columns.

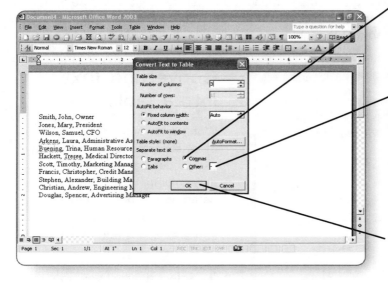

TIP

If you used something other than the Tab key or comma, such as a hyphen or asterisk, choose Other and type the character you used.

6. Click on **OK**. The Convert Text to Table dialog box will close.

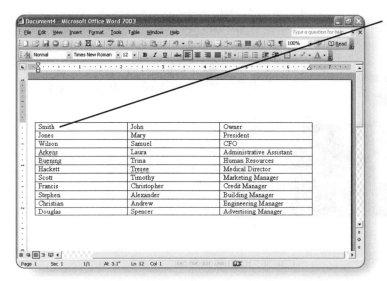

Word will convert the selected text into a table.

Converting a Table into Text

Once a table is created, you can easily convert it to regular document text. Word can separate the columns with a comma, a tab, or any other special character you specify. Each row will appear on a new line in the document.

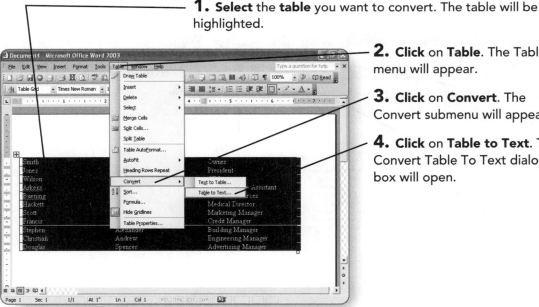

1. Select the **table** you want to convert. The table will be highlighted.

2. Click on **Table**. The Table menu will appear.

3. Click on **Convert**. The Convert submenu will appear.

4. Click on **Table to Text**. The Convert Table To Text dialog box will open.

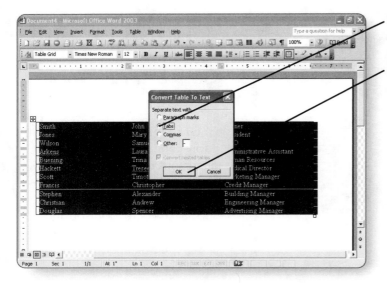

5. **Select** the **character** you want to separate your columns.

6. **Click** on **OK**. The Convert Table to Text dialog box will close.

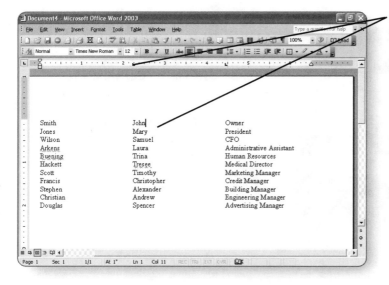

Word will convert the selected table into text. In this example, each column is separated by a tab.

13
Creating Graphs and Charts

Charts summarize data and make it easy for the reader to compare results. They also add color and interest to what otherwise might be a dull document. In this chapter you'll learn how to:

- Create a column chart from the data in a table
- Add a chart title
- Adjust the size of your chart and format elements
- Edit chart data

Creating a Chart from a Table

You can make a column chart from a table you've already created. Column charts are easy for readers to understand and are often used for comparing data from one year to another, one quarter to another, or for comparing estimated budget data against actual data.

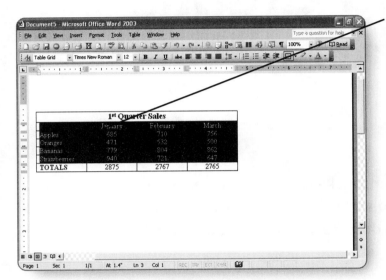

1. Select the **data, column heads,** and **row labels** of your table. The data will be highlighted.

TIP

When selecting data for your chart, be careful not to include data that you don't want to chart. For example, including totals can distort the overall chart picture.

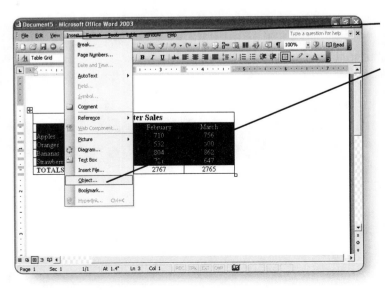

2. Click on **Insert**. The Insert menu will appear.

3. Click on **Object**. The Object dialog box will open.

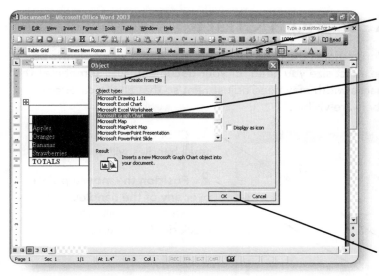

4. If necessary, **click** on the **Create New tab**. The Create New tab will come to the front.

5. Click on **Microsoft Graph Chart**. The selection will be highlighted.

> ## NOTE
> Your selections might vary from the choices shown here.

6. Click on **OK**. A datasheet and chart with all of the data that you selected in the table will appear.

If you work with spreadsheet software such as Excel, the datasheet will look familiar. Notice the following differences in the window, though:

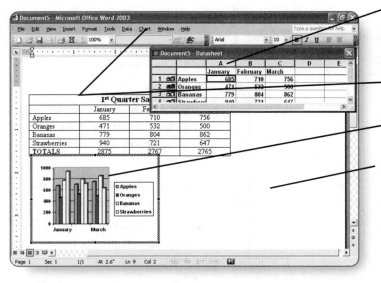

• The datasheet is set up with letters labeling the columns and numbers labeling the rows.

• The menu bar changes to include options for charts.

• The chart is complete with legend and category labels.

7. Click anywhere in the document **body**. The datasheet will close and your Word document will return with a chart inserted.

Resizing a Chart

Word creates the chart automatically, and it won't always be the exact size you need for your document. And sometimes the chart's width may need adjustment so that all the category labels are visible.

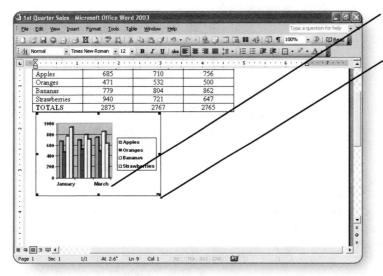

1. Click on the **chart**. Eight small handles will appear.

2. Position the **mouse pointer** over any of the handles. The mouse pointer will turn into a black double-headed arrow.

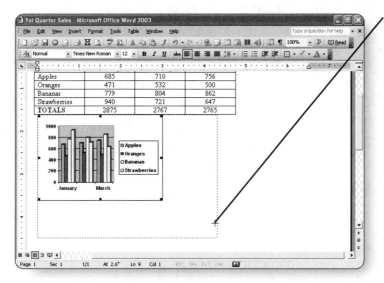

3. Press and drag the **handle**. A dotted line will indicate the chart's new size.

- Dragging corner handles will enlarge or shrink the window in both height and width in proportion to its original size.

- Dragging a side handle will modify the width only.

- Dragging a top or bottom handle will modify the height only.

4. Release the **mouse button**. The chart will be resized.

Editing a Chart

There are many options you can modify on a chart. You can add a title, modify a font, select colors, and even totally change the type of chart you're using.

Hiding the Datasheet

Frequently the datasheet is lying on top of the chart, making it difficult to work with the elements of the chart. You can hide the datasheet and then redisplay it if necessary.

1. Double-click on the **chart**. The datasheet will reappear and the chart menu will be reactivated.

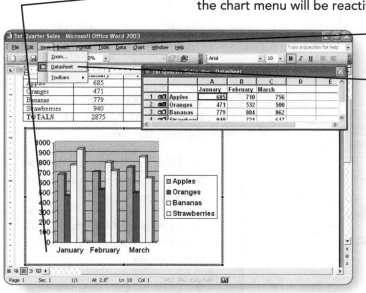

2. Click on **View**. The View menu will appear.

3. Click on **Datasheet**. The datasheet will close.

Repeat Steps 2 and 3 to redisplay the datasheet.

Adding a Chart Title

A chart title helps your reader quickly interpret the information displayed in the chart. You can type a title for the chart in general, for the x-axis (the categories), or the y-axis (the values).

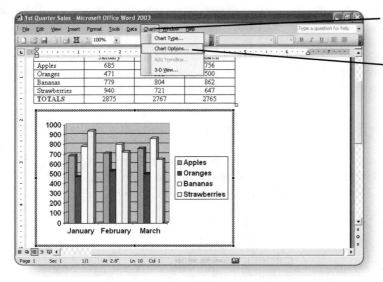

1. Click on **Chart**. The Chart menu will appear.

2. Click on **Chart Options**. The Chart Options dialog box will open.

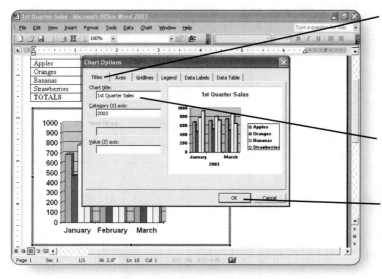

3. If necessary, **click** on the **Titles tab**. The Titles tab will come to the front.

4. Click in the **Chart title text box**. A blinking insertion point will appear.

5. Type a **title** for your chart. The title will display in the chart preview box.

6. Click on **OK**. The new title will be added to your chart.

Formatting Chart Text

Like with standard Word documents, you can change the font, size, style, color, and other attributes for text on a chart.

1. Double-click on the **text element** of the chart that you want to format. The Format dialog box will open.

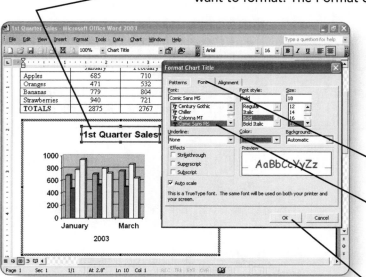

2. Click on **Font**. The Font tab will come to the front.

3. Click on the **font, font style, or font size** you want for the selected object. The choices will be highlighted.

4. Click on **OK**. The Format dialog box will close.

Modifying Chart Colors and Patterns

Each series in the chart can be of any color or fill pattern you specify. You can even make the series fill with a picture you select.

1. Double-click on the **bar** of the series in the chart you want to change. The Format Data Series dialog box will open.

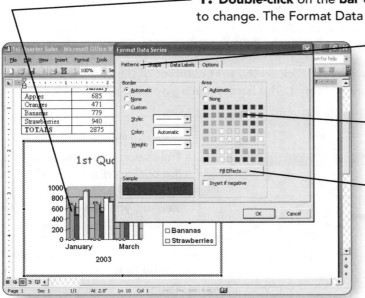

2. If you want the bar to have a filled pattern, **click** on **Patterns**. The Patterns tab will come to the front.

3. Click on a **color** for the selected series. A preview will display in the Sample box.

4. Click on the **Fill Effects button**. The Fill Effects dialog box will open.

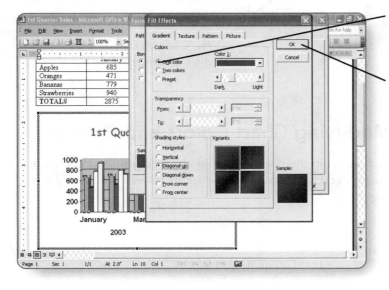

5. Click on a **fill choice** for the selected bar series. A sample will be displayed.

6. Click on **OK**. The Fill Effects dialog box will close.

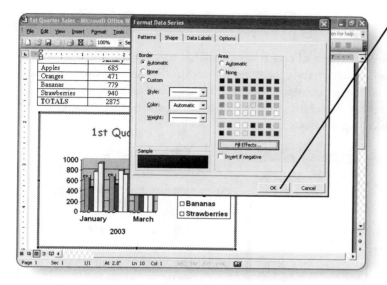

7. Click on **OK**. The Format dialog box will close and the series, including the legend, will change to the new color.

8. Repeat Steps 1-7 for each series you want to modify.

Selecting Bar Shapes

Word includes several fun shapes you can use for column charts instead of the default rectangular bars. You can select from conical shapes, round bar shapes, or even pyramid shapes.

1. Double-click on the **first bar** of any series in the chart. The Format Data Series dialog box will open.

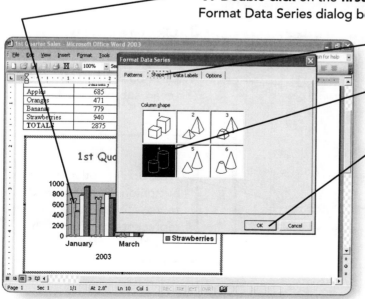

2. Click on the **Shape tab**. The Shape tab will come to the front.

3. Click on a **shape** for the selected series. The option will be selected.

4. Click on **OK**. The selected series on the chart will change to the new shape.

5. Repeat Steps 1-4 for each series you want to modify.

Changing the Chart Type

Several types of charts are available to you. Column charts, the default chart style, are fine for comparing sets of data, and line charts are useful for showing trends, such as population growth. Pie charts, on the other hand, show percentages that make up a whole.

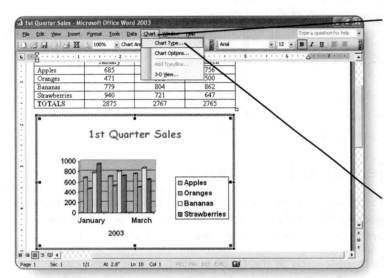

1. Click on **Chart**. The Chart menu will appear.

TIP

If the Chart menu is not displayed on the menu bar, double-click on the chart.

2. Click on **Chart Type**. The Chart Type dialog box will open.

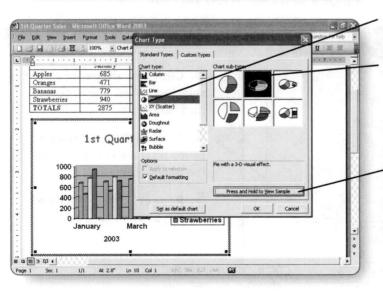

3. Click on a **chart type**. A selection of options will appear.

4. Click on a chart **sub-type**. The chart sub-type will be selected.

TIP

Press and hold the mouse button on Press and Hold to View Sample to see a representative chart with your "live" data.

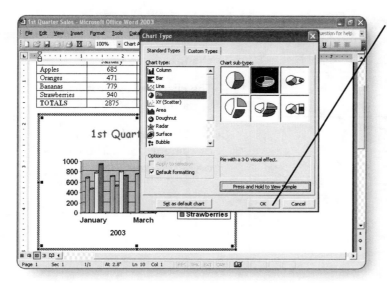

5. Click on **OK**. The Chart Type dialog box will close and the chart will change to the new type.

Editing Chart Data

Data that you change in a table is not automatically reflected in a chart. If, after you've inserted the chart into your document, you need to make changes to the data, you can do so by modifying the datasheet.

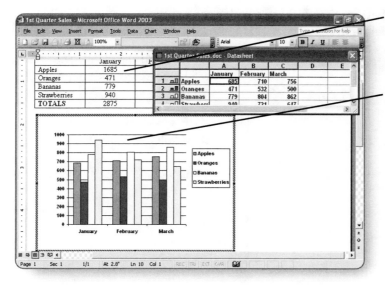

In this example, the first value is changed in the Word table. Neither the chart nor the datasheet reflect the change.

1. Double-click on the **chart**. The chart options will be reactivated.

TIP

If the datasheet is not displayed, display it by clicking on the View menu and selecting Datasheet.

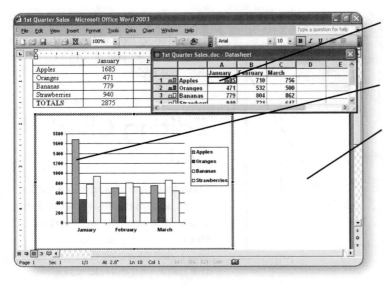

2. Click in any **cell** of the datasheet and **type** any desired **changes**.

The chart will automatically update to reflect the changes.

3. Click anywhere in the **document body**. The chart will be deselected.

Deleting a Chart

If at any time a chart is no longer necessary, you can easily delete it.

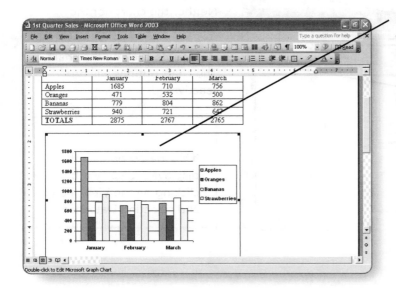

1. Click on the **chart**. The chart will be selected with eight black handles.

2. Press the **Delete key.** The chart will be deleted.

14
Using Newspaper Columns

When you think of columns you probably think of newspapers or newsletters, the kind that arrive through the mail from hospitals, schools, insurance companies, and other local businesses. These documents use columns to break up stories, with the text flowing from the bottom of one column to the top of the next. Of course, columns can be used for many other things, such as creating attractive forms or marketing materials. In this chapter, you'll learn how to:

- Create newspaper columns
- Change the number and width of columns
- Add vertical lines between columns
- Remove newspaper columns

Creating Newspaper Columns

Newspaper columns will apply to the entire document unless you select a portion of the document before creating the columns.

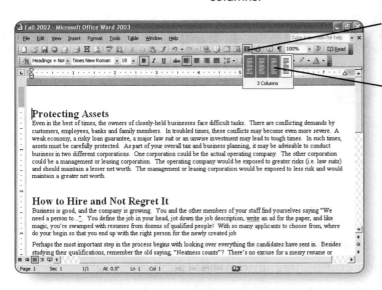

1. Click on the **Columns button.** A palette of column choices will appear.

2. Press and hold the **mouse button** and **drag across** the **palette** to select the number of columns. The number at the bottom of the palette will change as you drag over the selections.

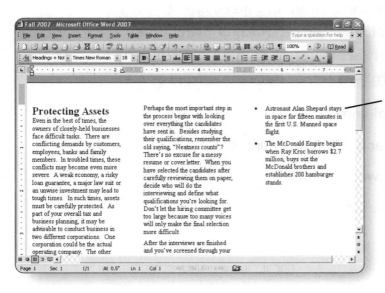

3. Release the **mouse button** on the number of columns that you want to use. The Columns palette will close.

The selected text will flow into the number of columns that you chose, from the top to the bottom of the left-most column, and then up to the top of the column to its right, and so on.

> **NOTE**
>
> Multiple columns are not displayed side-by-side in Normal view. If you are using Normal view, Word will automatically switch you to Print Layout view when you create multiple columns.

Changing the Number of Columns

Perhaps you decide after formatting your text in columns that you want one more column or one less column. Word enables you to change the number of columns easily.

Again, if you want to make this change to only a portion of the document, you must select that portion before continuing with these steps.

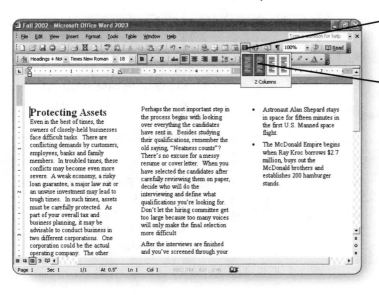

1. **Click** on the **Columns button.** The palette of column choices will appear.

2. **Press and hold** the **mouse button** and **drag across** the **palette** to make your new selection. The number at the bottom of the palette will change as you drag over the selections.

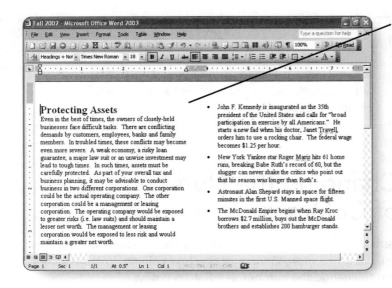

3. Release the **mouse button** on your new column choice. The selected text will flow into the new number of columns that you chose.

Changing Column Width

When you select the number of columns to be created, Word divides the text into columns of equal width. However, you can modify column width, and you can also adjust the space between columns, called the *gutter*.

Changing the Width of Columns

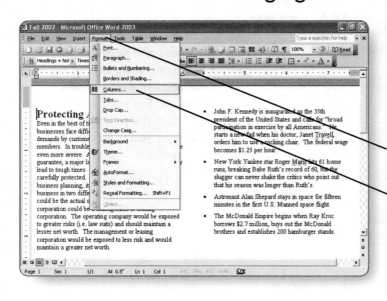

Word enables you to set the width of each column individually, in case you don't want your columns to be of equal width. Column width is controlled through the Columns dialog box.

1. Click on **Format**. The Format menu will appear.

2. Click on **Columns**. The Columns dialog box will open.

3. Click on the **up/down arrows** for the width and spacing of each column you want to modify. The remaining columns will adjust accordingly.

4. Click on **OK**. The Columns dialog box will close.

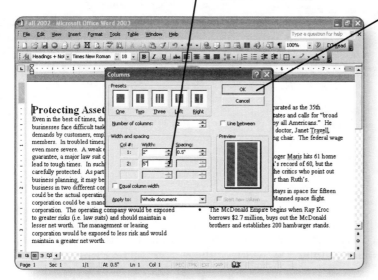

Word will adjust the column widths per your selections.

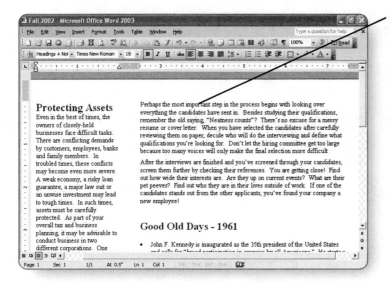

Changing the Width of Space between Columns

The space between each column is called the gutter. You can individually adjust the gutter between any two columns. Column spacing is also controlled through the Columns dialog box.

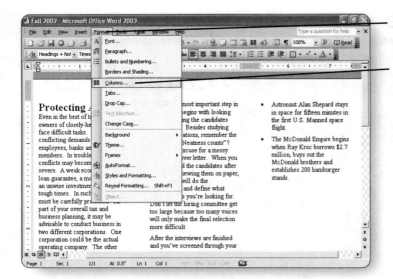

1. Click on **Format**. The Format menu will appear.

2. Click on **Columns**. The Columns dialog box will open.

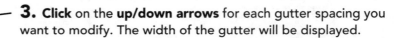

3. Click on the **up/down arrows** for each gutter spacing you want to modify. The width of the gutter will be displayed.

4. Click on **OK**. The gutter widths will be modified.

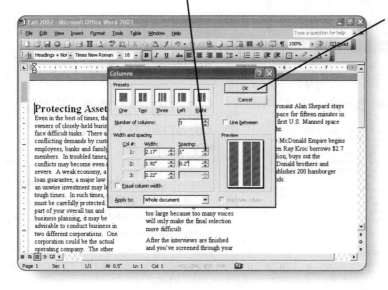

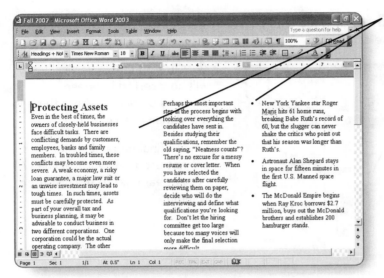

In this example, the gutter between Columns 1 and 2 is increased and the gutter between Columns 2 and 3 is decreased.

Creating Vertical Lines between Columns

Newspapers and magazines often add vertical lines between columns to make it easier to separate the columns when reading the text.

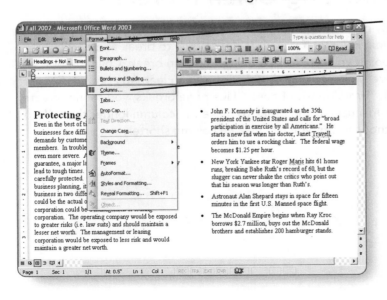

1. **Click** on **Format**. The Format menu will appear.

2. **Click** on **Columns**. The Columns dialog box will open.

3. **Click** in the **Line between check box**. The option will be selected.

4. **Click** on **OK**. A vertical line will be inserted between columns on pages where there is more than one column.

On the final page, if all columns are not used, the vertical line will not appear next to the last-used column.

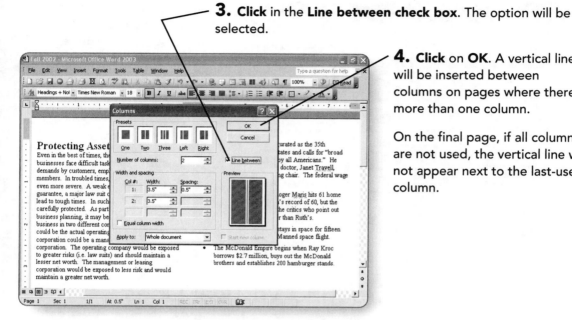

Creating Column Breaks

By default, text will flow down one column, then over to the next column. If you want the column to break at a particular point, you can insert a manual column break. Column breaks are similar to page breaks, which you learned about in Chapter 4, "Working with Pages." Like page breaks, you cannot create a manual column break to make the column longer than Word chooses, but you can make a column shorter.

1. Click the **mouse** where you want the new column to begin. A blinking insertion point will appear.

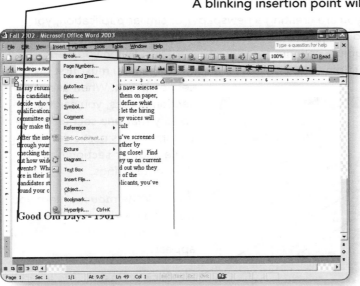

2. Click on **Insert**. The Insert menu will appear.

3. Click on **Break**. The Break dialog box will appear.

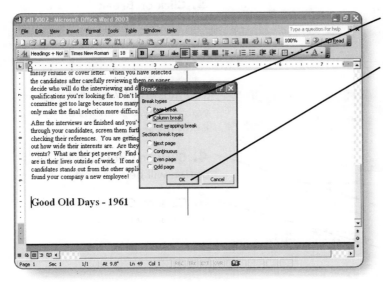

4. Click on **Column break**. The option will be selected.

5. Click on **OK**. The Break dialog box will close and the next column will begin at the position of the insertion point.

Working with Sections

If you are creating a newspaper or similar publication, you probably want a headline spanning the top of the page and multiple columns for the actual articles. When you want multiple column types on a single page, you must first insert a section break. When using section breaks, you can then specify that one section of the document has particular settings, while another section has different settings.

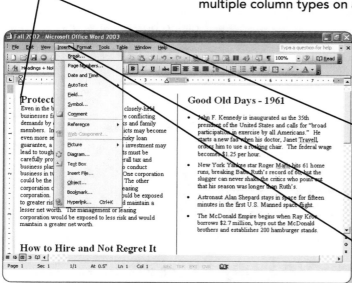

1. Click the **mouse** where you want the new section to begin. The blinking insertion point will appear.

2. Click on **Insert**. The Insert menu will appear.

3. Click on **Break**. The Break dialog box will open.

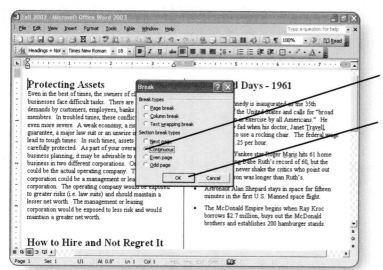

You must tell Word that you want the two sections on the same page.

4. Click on **Continuous**. The option will be selected.

5. Click on **OK**. The Break dialog box will close.

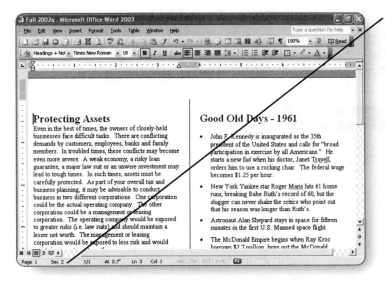

Look at the Status bar. It will indicate which section the insertion point is in.

By default, the new section will take the same column layout as the original section. However you can change either section to take the column layout you want.

6. Position the **insertion point** anywhere in the section you want to modify. The status bar will indicate your section.

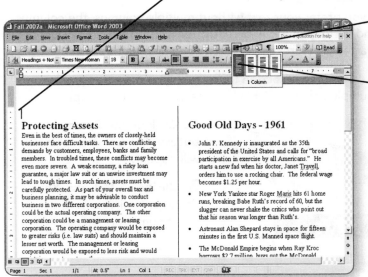

7. Click on the **Columns button.** The palette of column choices will appear.

8. Press and hold the **mouse button** and **drag across** the **palette** to make your new column selection.

9. Release the **mouse button**. The current section will take the new options.

10. Type and format your **headline** as desired.

> **TIP**
>
> Section breaks are useful if you want different margins, orientation, or paper sizes for particular areas of your document.

Removing Newspaper Columns

If you prefer your text without multiple columns, the columns and vertical lines can be easily removed. This is really just a matter of returning the text to a one-column format.

1. Click in the **section** from which you want to remove the multiple columns. A blinking insertion point will appear.

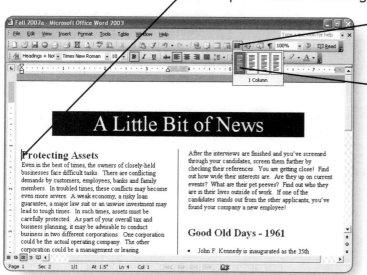

2. Click on the **Columns button**. The Columns palette will appear.

3. Click on **1 Column**. Your document will return to a one-column format.

PART II

Excel

15

Exploring the Excel Screen

Previously, you may have used a paper, pencil, and calculator to track information, whether to figure a simple calculation or track a list of items in alphabetical order. Excel handles those tasks and many more, including very complex calculations. At first glance, however, the Excel opening screen can feel very intimidating with all of its buttons, options, rows, and columns. Once you understand the purpose for all those options, you will feel much more comfortable with the Excel screen.

In this chapter, you'll learn how to:

- Open the Excel program
- Explore and move around the Excel screen
- Understand cell addresses
- Work with the task pane
- Use Excel menus
- Use Excel Help

Starting Excel

There are a number of different methods to access the Excel application. One method is from the Start button.

1. **Click** on the **Start button**. The Start menu will appear.

2. **Click** on **All Programs**. A menu of available programs will appear.

3. **Click** on **Microsoft Excel**. The Microsoft Excel program will open with a blank worksheet screen.

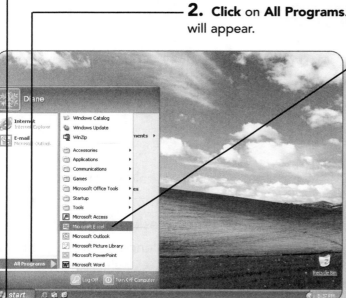

TIP

If you have a Microsoft Excel icon on your Windows desktop, you can double-click it to quickly access Excel.

Exploring the Worksheet Screen

Many items that you see when you open a new worksheet (also known as a spreadsheet) are standard to most Microsoft Office programs. However, the following list illustrates a few elements that are specific to a spreadsheet program. These include:

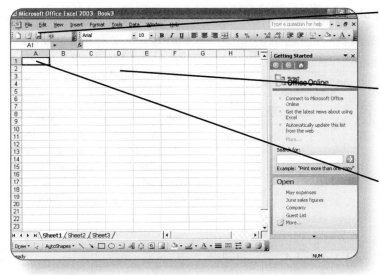

- **Toolbars**. A selection of commonly used Excel features. A single click on a toolbar item activates the feature.

- **Worksheet area**. A rectangular grid, consisting of rows and columns. Columns are labels with letters across the top, and rows are indicated by numbers.

- **Cell**. The intersection of a row and a column. Also known as a cell address. When referring to a cell address, Excel references the column letter first then the row number. For example, Excel refers to a cell address as B6 not 6B. A selected cell has a heavy border around it.

NOTE

Each worksheet has 256 columns and 65,536 rows, for a total of 16,777,216 cells in each worksheet.

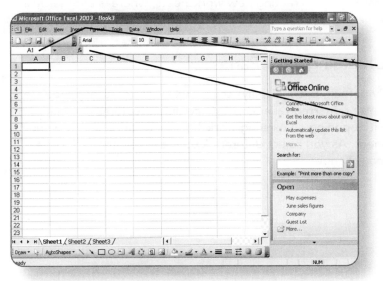

- **Edit line**. The edit line consists of two parts:

- **Selection Indicator**. Shows the address or name of the currently selected cell.

- **Contents Box**. Displays the contents of the currently selected cell.

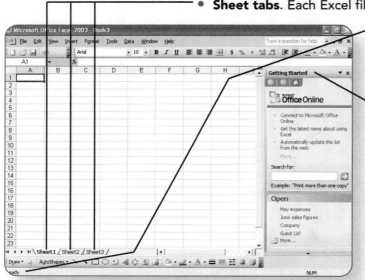

- **Sheet tabs**. Each Excel file can contain 256 worksheets.

- **Status Bar**. Displays information about the current selection and what Excel is doing.

- **Task pane**. Small windows that assist you when working with Excel. Task panes store collections of important Excel features and present them in ways that are easy to find and use.

Working with the Task Pane

Excel contains several different task panes, each of which appears when you use various Excel tasks. One task pane assists you in creating new worksheets, whereas another task pane helps you add clip art to your worksheet.

Changing Task Panes

By default, Excel displays the Getting Started task pane. The Getting Started task pane lists common features associated with opening an existing worksheet or creating a new worksheet. As you select different Excel features, the task pane may change.

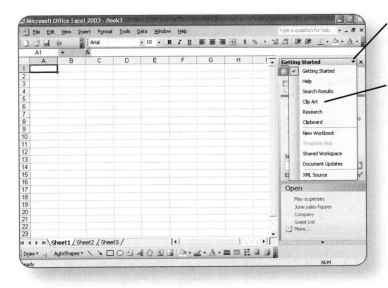

1. **Click** on the **task pane drop-down menu**. A list of other task panes will appear.

2. **Click** on a **task pane name**. The selected task pane will appear.

Closing and Redisplaying the Task Pane

While the task pane can be very helpful, it also uses up valuable screen space. You can close the task pane at any time and redisplay it whenever you want it back.

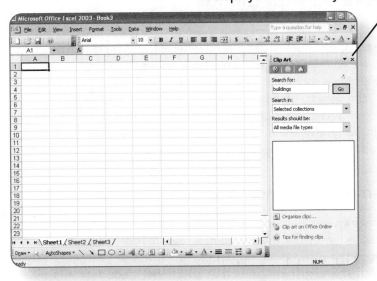

1. **Click** the **task pane close button**. The task pane will close.

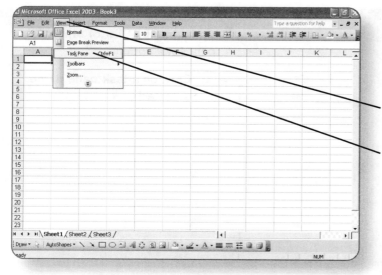

The task pane will reappear automatically when you select an Excel feature that uses the task pane. You can, however, redisplay the task pane at any time.

2. **Click** on **View**. The View menu will appear.

3. **Click** on **Task Pane**. The task pane will reopen.

NOTE

For the purposes of this book, most screens will appear without the task pane, unless a feature that uses the task pane is being shown.

Working with Menus

All Windows-based applications use menus to list items appropriate to your program. Excel is no different. As you click a menu choice, you see the options available under that menu. Some menus have submenus which list additional choices from which you can select. A menu option lighter in color than the other options is said to be grayed out and means that particular choice is unavailable at the moment. Menu options become grayed out when they are not applicable to your current selection.

Personalized Menus

Excel includes personalized menus. When the menu is first accessed, only the most common features are displayed. Notice the down-pointing double arrow at the bottom of the menu. This arrow indicates that additional menu features are available. If you pause the mouse over the top item on the menu bar or move it down to the double arrow, the menu will expand to include all available features for that menu.

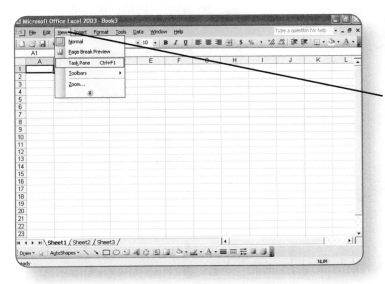

As you use the personalized menus, the features you use most often will appear at the top of the menu.

1. Click on **View**. The View menu will appear with five options.

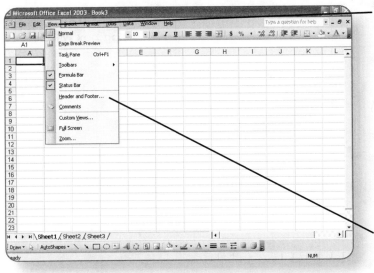

2. Pause the **mouse pointer** over the View menu. The View menu will expand to include 11 items.

TIP

Click on the menu name (such as View) to close a menu without making any selection.

Many selections in a menu are followed by three periods, called an *ellipsis*. Selections followed by ellipses indicate that, if you select one of these items, a dialog box will appear with more options.

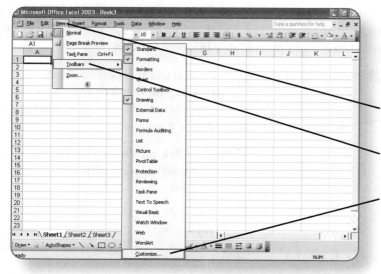

If you find you don't like the personalized menus, you can turn the feature off and all options will automatically appear when you select a menu.

3. **Click** on **View**. The View menu will appear.

4. **Click** on **Toolbars**. The Toolbars submenu will appear.

5. **Click** on **Customize**. The Customize dialog box will open.

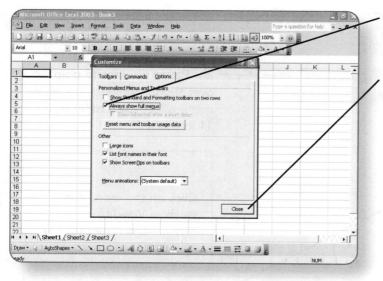

6. **Click** on **Always show full menus**. The option will be selected.

7. **Click** on **Close**. The Customize dialog box will close.

Shortcut Menus

Shortcut menus contain a limited number of commands. The commands you see on a shortcut menu are relevant to what you are doing at the time you open the shortcut menu. Click the right mouse button (called a *right-click*) to open a shortcut menu. Be sure the mouse pointer is in the shape of a white cross before right-clicking to open a shortcut menu.

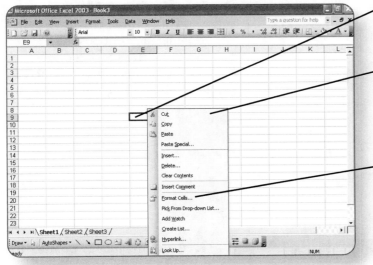

1. Click on any **cell** of the worksheet. The cell will be selected.

2. Press the **right mouse button**. The mouse pointer will change to an arrow and a shortcut menu will appear on the screen.

3. Click on a **menu selection**. The menu action will occur.

TIP

Press the Esc key or click anywhere outside the shortcut menu to close the menu without making a selection.

Using Toolbars

Along the top and bottom of the Excel screen, you see several different toolbars. Toolbars are small icons or buttons that help you access commonly used Excel features without digging through the menus. Excel includes over 20 toolbars to assist you.

When you first use Excel, you see three toolbars displayed by default. The Standard and Formatting toolbars display side-by-side along the top of the Excel screen, and the Drawing toolbar displays along the bottom of the screen.

Standard toolbar

Formatting toolbar

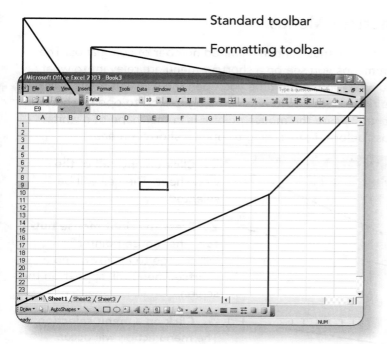

Drawing toolbar

If you look closely, you can see that the toolbar buttons are grouped into related activities. For example, the Alignment buttons (left, center, and right) are together, and options that relate to files, such as saving or opening, are grouped together. You'll learn about using these buttons in later chapters.

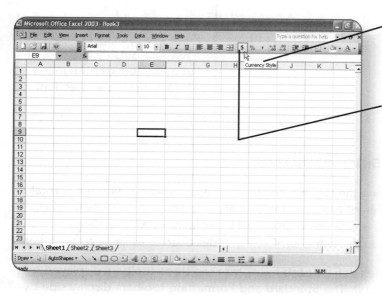

1. Pause the **mouse pointer** over any toolbar item. The description of that feature will appear.

2. Click on a **toolbar button**. The requested action will occur.

Additional toolbar buttons may be available.

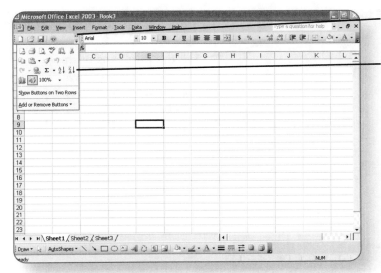

3. Click on the **Toolbar options button**.

Additional toolbar buttons appear from which you can select.

Separating Toolbars

Most people find the Standard and Formatting toolbars difficult to use when displayed side-by-side, so you may want to separate them so one is on top of the other, which makes all the tools on these bars much easier to access.

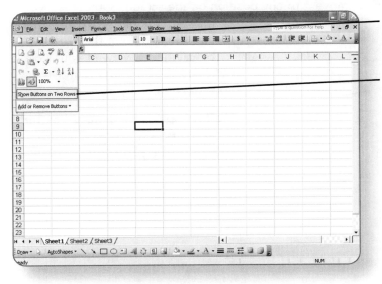

1. Click on the **Toolbar options button**. Additional toolbar buttons appear.

2. Click on **Show Buttons on Two Rows**. The Standard and Formatting toolbars become separated.

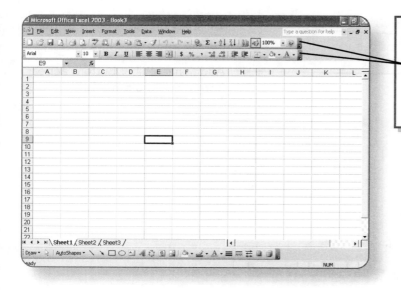

Moving a Toolbar

Most toolbars are docked at the top or bottom of the screen, but if a toolbar is not located in a favorable position for you to access, move it to any position on the screen. Sometimes, you may accidentally move a toolbar into the middle of the screen, blocking your view of your worksheet. It's very easy to move a toolbar into any position.

1. Position the **mouse pointer** at the far-left side of any toolbar. The mouse pointer changes to a black cross with four arrowheads.

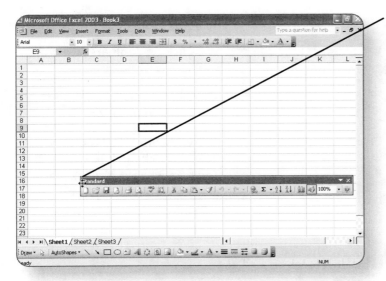

2. **Hold down** the **mouse button and drag** the mouse into the worksheet area. The toolbar may change shape.

NOTE

Although you probably won't want to, you can move the menu bar with the same method.

---

3. **Release** the **mouse button**. The toolbar will remain in the

---

TIP

To put a toolbar back to the normal position, press and hold the mouse button over the toolbar title bar and drag it into the desired position, usually at the top of the screen.

Hiding and Displaying Toolbars

You can hide or display any toolbar. This can be very helpful if a particular toolbar is using valuable screen space. For example, if you are not doing any drawing, you may want to hide the drawing toolbar.

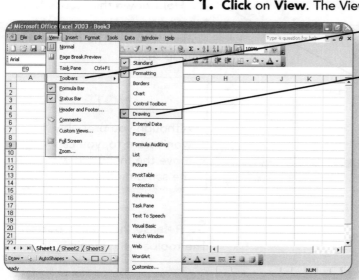

1. **Click** on **View**. The View menu will appear.

2. **Click** on **Toolbars**. A list of toolbars will appear.

3. **Click** on the **toolbar** you want to turn off or on.

Currently displayed toolbars have a check mark next to them. Toolbars without a check mark are not currently displayed.

Moving around the Worksheet Screen

You can use your mouse or keyboard to move around a worksheet. Because of the large size of an Excel worksheet, you need ways to move around quickly.

For illustration purposes, in the following two figures you see a worksheet with a lot of information stored in it. You will learn how to enter information into your worksheets in Chapter 16, "Creating a Simple Worksheet."

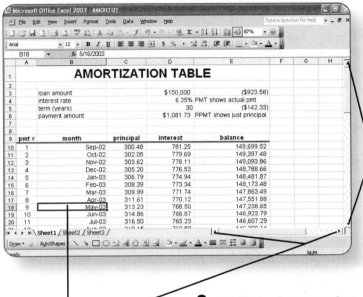

Using the Mouse

Because there are over 16 million possible cells in a single worksheet, you may find that using the mouse is an easy way to move around in the worksheet.

1. Click the **vertical scroll arrows** until the row you want is visible.

2. Click the **horizontal scroll arrows** until the column you want is visible.

3. Click on the desired **cell**. The cell becomes the currently selected cell.

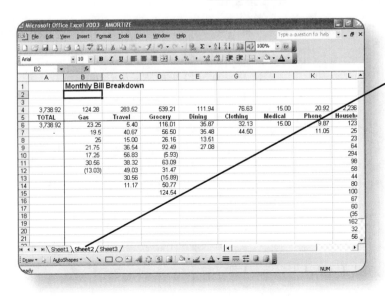

By default, Excel displays three worksheets, labeled Sheet1, Sheet2, and Sheet3.

4. Click a **worksheet tab**. The selected worksheet appears on top of the stack.

You'll learn more about working with multiple worksheets in Chapter 22, "Working with Larger Workbooks."

Keystroke	Result
Arrow keys	Moves one cell at a time up, down, left, or right
Page Down	Moves one screen down
Page Up	Moves one screen up
Home	Moves to column A of the current row
Ctrl+Home	Moves to cell A1
Ctrl+Arrow key	Moves to the beginning or end of a row or column
Ctrl+Page Down	Moves to the next worksheet
Ctrl+Page Up	Moves to the previous worksheet
F5	Displays the Go To dialog box which enables you to specify a cell address

Using the Keyboard

As you have just discovered, you can use your mouse to move around an Excel worksheet; however, you may find using the keyboard faster and easier. The table shown here describes keyboard methods for moving around a worksheet.

Accessing the Go To Command

If you have a rather large worksheet, you can use the Go To command to jump to a specific cell or area of the worksheet.

1. Click on **Edit**. The Edit menu will appear.

2. Click on **Go To**. The Go To dialog box will appear.

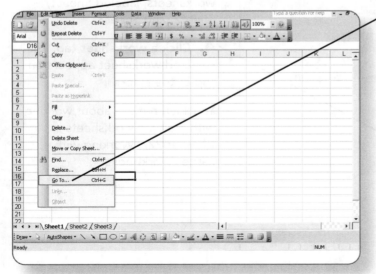

NOTE

If you are using personalized menus, you may not immediately see the Go To command. Pause the mouse over the Edit menu to display the additional options.

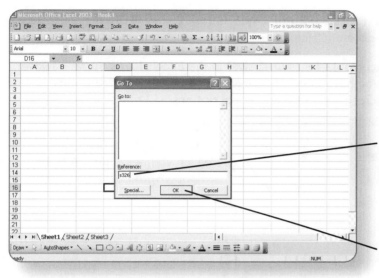

3. In the Reference box, **type** the **cell address** you want to locate. Remember to enter the column letter first, then the row number. In this example, we are looking for column S and row 326.

4. Click on **OK**. The specified

Using Excel Help

Many of your questions about Excel can be answered in this book. However, Excel includes an extensive Help system which can include searching the Internet for solutions. The easiest method is to access the very convenient Ask a Question box where you can pose your question or enter a term in plain English.

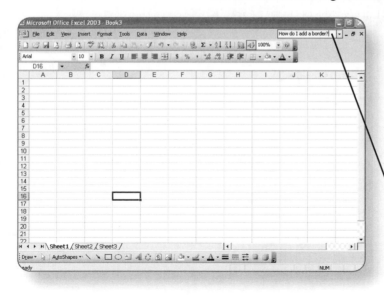

1. Click in the **Ask a Question box** located in the upper-right corner of the screen. An insertion point will appear in the box.

2. Type your **question or words** that describe what you need help with. You can type a complete sentence or just a few words.

3. Press the **Enter key**. The task pane will display a selection of potential Help topics.

Excel looks for your answer in the Excel Help system; however, if you have Internet access, Excel will attempt to contact Microsoft.com for additional options.

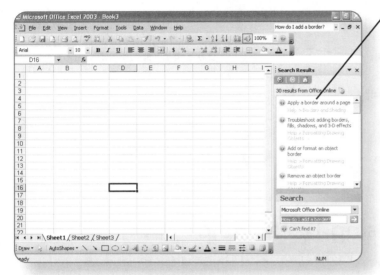

4. Click on the **topic** that best represents the subject with which you need help. A Help window with instructions will appear.

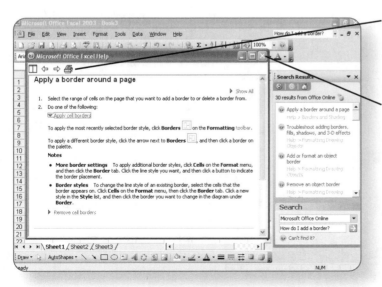

5. Click the **Print button** to print a hard copy of the Help instructions.

6. Click the **Close button** when you are finished with the Help window.

16

Creating a Simple Worksheet

There's an old adage that "you have to crawl before you can walk." That saying applies to Excel worksheets as well. You need to learn the basics before you learn the more complex features of Excel. That's what this chapter is about—the basics.

In this chapter, you'll learn how to:

- Enter labels, values, and dates
- Save, close, and open worksheet files
- E-mail your worksheet
- Create a new worksheet

Entering Data

Worksheet data is made up of three components: labels, values, and formulas. This section discusses entering labels and values, and you'll learn about creating and entering formulas in Chapter 20, "Working with Formulas." When you are ready to enter data into a worksheet cell, you must first click on the cell in which you want the information.

Entering Labels

Labels are traditionally descriptive pieces of information, such as names, months, or other identifying information. Excel automatically recognizes information as a label if it contains alphabetic characters. Don't worry if the entire label does not appear to fit into a cell width. If needed, Excel automatically extends the data past the cell width.

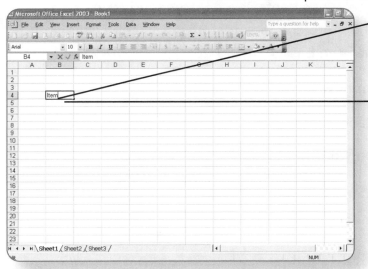

1. **Click** on the **cell** in which you want to place the label. A border will appear around the selected cell.

2. **Type** some **text**. A blinking insertion point will appear.

TIP

If you make a mistake and have not yet pressed the Enter key, press the Backspace key to delete characters and type a correction, or press the Escape key to cancel typing in the selected cell.

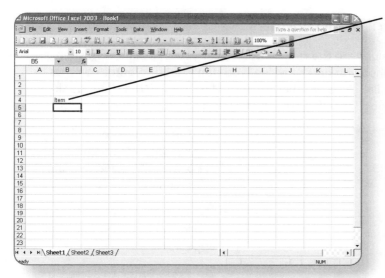

3. Press the **Enter key**. Excel accepts the label and aligns the data along the left edge of the cell. The cell below the one in which you just entered data will then be selected.

TIP

Optionally, instead of pressing the Enter key, press the Tab key and Excel will move to the right of the current cell instead of below it.

4. Repeat steps 1-3 for each label you want to enter. Data will appear in the multiple cells.

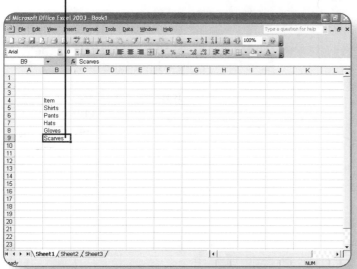

Excel also displays the contents of the current cell in the Formula bar.

NOTE

Optionally, you can press an arrow key instead of the Enter key. This will accept the cell content you were typing and move to the next cell in the direction of the arrow key.

Entering Values

Values are the raw numbers that you track in a worksheet. When you enter a value, you don't need to enter commas or dollar signs. In Chapter 18, "Making the Worksheet Look Good," you'll learn how to let Excel do that for you.

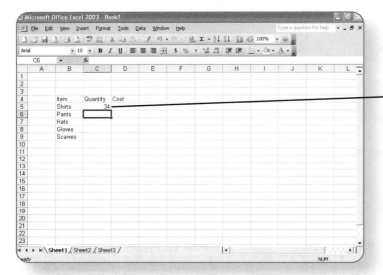

1. Click on the **cell** in which you want to place the value. A border will appear around the selected cell.

2. Type the numerical **value**. A blinking insertion point will appear.

3. Press Enter to accept the value. The number will be entered into the cell and the cell below will then be selected.

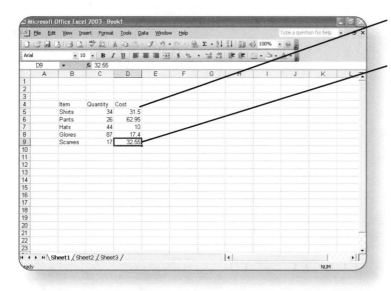

Excel aligns values along the right edge of the cell.

4. Repeat steps 1-3 for each value you want to enter.

TIP

To enter a value as a label, type an apostrophe (') character before the number. The apostrophe character tells Excel to treat the information as a label instead of a value.

If your value is too large to fit into the cell width, Excel may display a series of number signs (####) or it may round the value display. Don't worry about the appearance that displays in Excel. Remember that you'll discover how to change the display of your data in Chapter 18. The following table illustrates some of the ways Excel, by default, displays numeric data:

You enter	Excel may display
1074	1074
0174	174
'0174	0174
39.95	39.95
39.50	39.5
39.501	39.501
4789547.365	4789547.37

Entering Dates

Although dates contain characters and look like a label, Excel technically considers them values, because Excel can calculate the time between dates, which you will learn about in Chapter 20, "Working with Formulas." For example, day 1 is January 1st, 1900, day 2 is January 2nd, 1900, and so forth.

When you enter a date, Excel may not display it on the screen in the same way that you type it. You will discover how to format dates in different perspectives in Chapter 18. The following table shows how Excel automatically displays dates:

You type	Excel displays
January 23, 2003	23-Jan-2003
January 23	23-Jan
Jan 23	23-Jan
1/23	23-Jan
1-23	23-Jan
1-23-03	1/23/2003
1/23/03	1/23/2003

NOTE

Depending on the Regional and International settings of your computer, your system may display differently, such as displaying only the last two digits of a year.

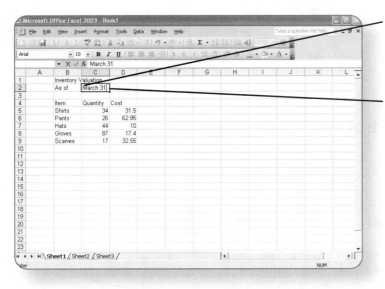

1. **Click** on the **cell** in which you want to enter the date. A border will appear around the selected cell.

2. **Type** the **date**. A blinking insertion point will appear.

3. Press Enter to accept the date. Excel will enter the date into the cell and display it in the default date format.

In the Formula bar, Excel displays the date in numeric *mm/dd/yyyy* format.

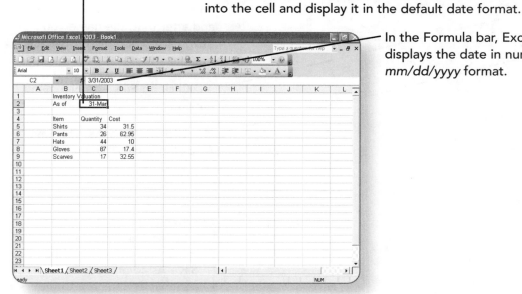

Saving a Worksheet File

Anyone who uses a computer has probably lost data at one time or another. If you don't save your worksheet regularly, it only takes a second to lose hours of work. Fortunately, Excel has a built-in feature to help protect you against this eventuality. However, you still need to save your worksheet so you can refer to it or make changes to it at some future time.

Saving a File the First Time

When you first open Excel, a blank screen appears with the title Worksheet1 in the Excel title bar. The next blank worksheet you create is named Worksheet2, then Worksheet3, and so forth. Those names are temporary names and are not very descriptive, so you need to assign a name that is associated with the worksheet contents.

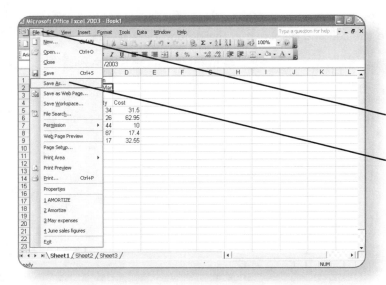

Excel asks for a name the first time you save the worksheet, and after that, the name you assign it will appear in the Excel title bar.

1. **Click** on **File**. The File menu appears.

2. **Click** on **Save As**. The Save As dialog box will open.

> ## NOTE
>
> When you first save an unnamed file, you can use the Save command or the Save As command. Both commands take you to the Save As dialog box.

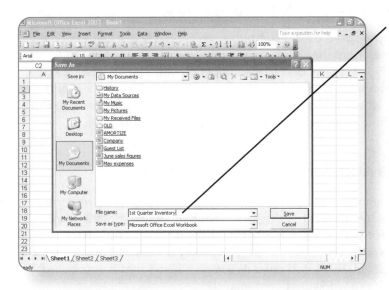

3. **Type** a **name** for your file in the File Name text box. The file name will be displayed.

File names can contain spaces, dashes, and many other special characters, but cannot include the asterisk (*), slash (/), backslash (\), or question mark (?) characters.

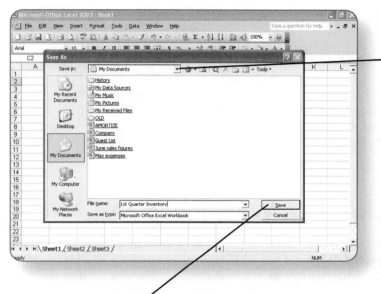

4. Click on **Save**. Your worksheet is saved and the name you specified will appear in the title bar.

Resaving a Worksheet

As you make changes to your worksheet, you should resave it. A good rule is to save your worksheet at least every ten minutes. Excel replaces the worksheet copy already saved on the disk with the newly revised worksheet copy.

1. Click on the **Save button**. The worksheet will be resaved with any changes you made. No dialog box will open because the worksheet is resaved with the same name and in the same folder as previously specified.

TIP

If you want to save the worksheet with a different name or in a different folder, click on File, then choose Save As. The Save As dialog box will prompt you for the new name or folder. The original worksheet will remain, as well as the new one.

Closing a Worksheet

When you are finished working on a worksheet, you should close it. Closing is the equivalent of putting it away for later use. When you close a worksheet, you are only putting the worksheet away—not the program. Excel is still active and ready to work for you.

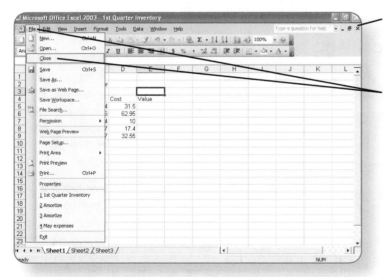

1a. **Click** on the **Close Button**. The worksheet will be closed.

OR

1b. **Click** on **File**. The File menu will appear. **Click** on **Close**. The worksheet will close.

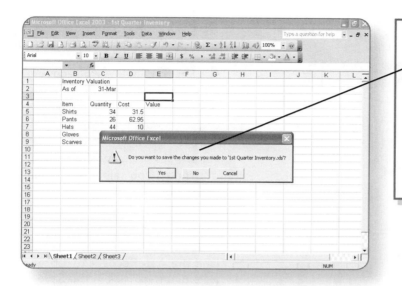

NOTE

If you close a worksheet with changes that have not been saved, Excel will prompt you with a dialog box. Choose Yes to save the changes or No to close the file without saving the changes.

Enabling AutoRecover

Excel has a feature called AutoRecover, which periodically saves a temporary version of your worksheet for you. When you close Excel normally, the temporary versions disappear, but if you don't get the chance to exit Excel (say, due to a computer freeze up), when you reopen Excel, the program opens a recovery version of the worksheets you were working on at the time of the crash. You can then choose to save them or not.

You can specify the time intervals for the AutoRecover to save your work.

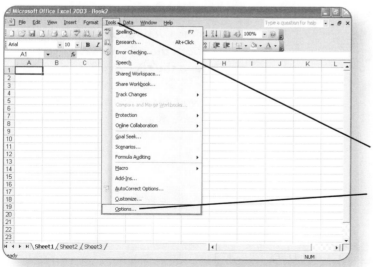

1. Click on **Tools**. The Tools menu will appear.

2. Click on **Options**. The Options dialog box will open.

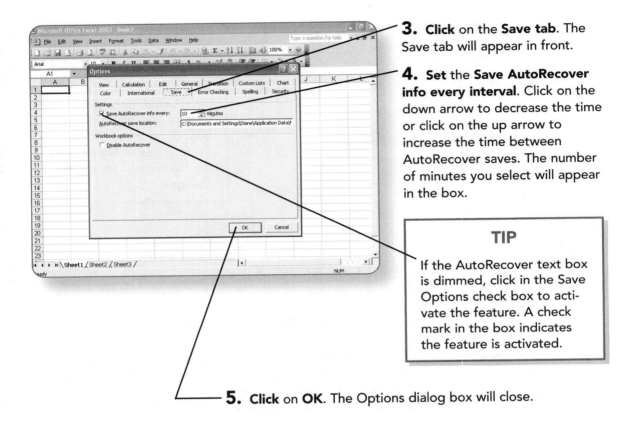

3. Click on the **Save tab**. The Save tab will appear in front.

4. Set the **Save AutoRecover info every interval**. Click on the down arrow to decrease the time or click on the up arrow to increase the time between AutoRecover saves. The number of minutes you select will appear in the box.

TIP

If the AutoRecover text box is dimmed, click in the Save Options check box to activate the feature. A check mark in the box indicates the feature is activated.

5. Click on **OK**. The Options dialog box will close.

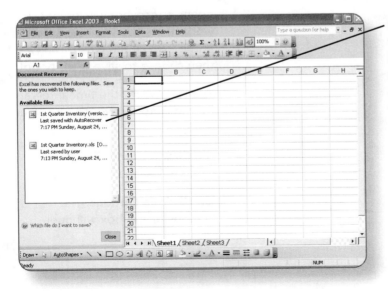

In the event of a system crash, when you reopen Excel, it lists both the original saved version and the recovered version. You can select which version of the worksheet you want to open and save.

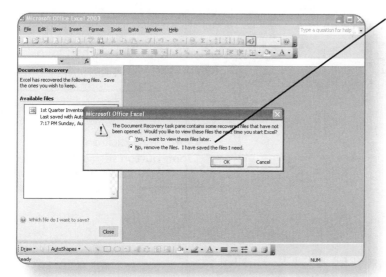

If you opted not to open and save a recovered file, when you exit Excel normally, you can decide to keep the recovered version of the file for later use or let Excel go ahead and delete it normally.

Opening an Existing File

Opening a worksheet is putting a copy of that file into the computer's memory and onto your screen so that you can work on it. If you make any changes, be sure to save the file again. Excel provides several different ways to open a worksheet.

Displaying the Open Dialog Box

Worksheets you have previously saved can be reopened on your screen through the Open dialog box.

1. **Click** on **File**. The File menu will appear.

2. **Click** on **Open**. The Open dialog box will appear.

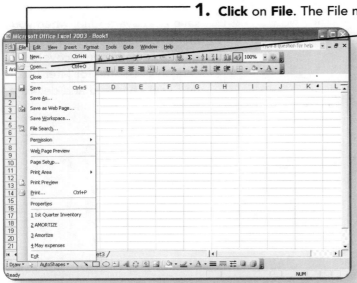

TIP

Optionally, click on the Open button to display the Open dialog box.

3. **Click** on the **file name** you want to open. The file name will be highlighted.

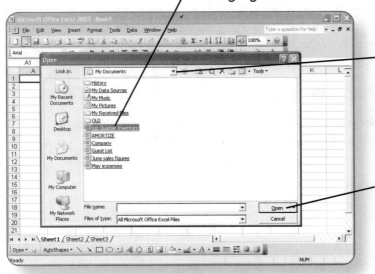

NOTE

If your file is located in a different folder than the one displayed in the Look in list box, click on the drop-down menu to navigate to the proper folder.

4. **Click** on **Open**. The file will be placed on your screen, ready for you to edit.

Opening a Recently Used Worksheet

Both the File menu and the task pane list several of the worksheets you've recently used, allowing you to quickly locate and open a worksheet.

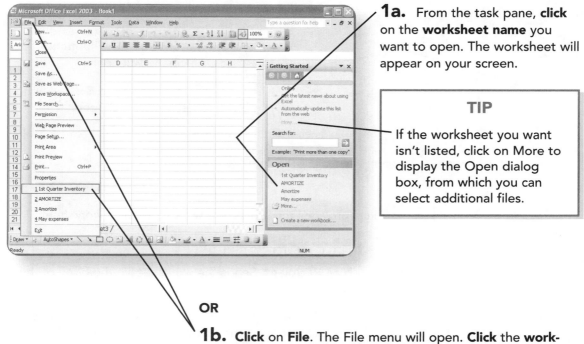

1a. From the task pane, **click** on the **worksheet name** you want to open. The worksheet will appear on your screen.

> **TIP**
>
> If the worksheet you want isn't listed, click on More to display the Open dialog box, from which you can select additional files.

OR

1b. **Click** on **File**. The File menu will open. **Click** the **worksheet name** you want to open. The worksheet will appear on your screen.

E-Mailing a Worksheet

If you have e-mail access, you can send a worksheet directly to another person. Excel either copies the content of the worksheet into a blank e-mail message or sends the worksheet as an attachment to an e-mail message.

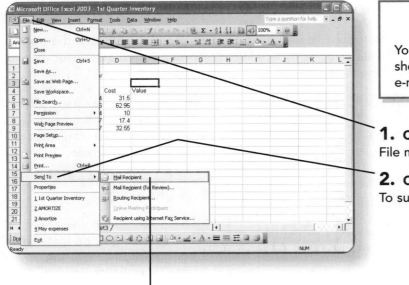

NOTE

You must save your worksheet prior to e-mailing it to someone.

1. **Click** on the **File menu**. The File menu will open.

2. **Click** on **Send To**. The Send To submenu will open.

Excel provides three different ways to e-mail a worksheet:

3. **Click** on the **appropriate option**:

- **Mail Recipient**. Sends the worksheet in the body of the e-mail.

- **Mail Recipient (for Review)**. The recipient will receive a link or an attachment, or both a link and an attachment to the file so they can review the file. When a reviewer opens the file, the reviewing tools are enabled and displayed. The files returned from reviewers automatically prompt you to merge changes. You can then use the reviewing tools to accept or reject the changes.

- **Mail Recipient (as Attachment)**. Sends a copy of the worksheet as a file attachment for the recipient to open.

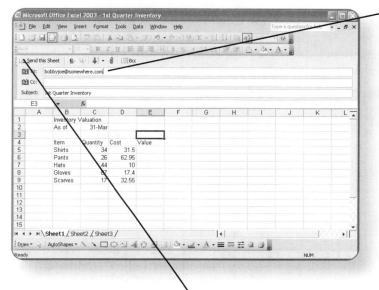

4. Type the **recipient's e-mail address**. The e-mail address will appear in the To box. You can add additional recipients by separating their e-mail addresses with a semicolon.

> **TIP**
>
> Some mail programs also allow you to add additional introductory text.

5. Click on **Send** or **Send this sheet**. Excel will send the worksheet to the e-mail recipients.

Starting a New Worksheet

When an Excel session is first started, a blank worksheet appears ready for you to use. However, during the course of using Excel, you may need another blank worksheet. Excel includes several methods to access a new worksheet.

By using the toolbar, creating a new worksheet using the standard Excel settings is only a mouse click away!

1a. **Click** on the **New Blank Worksheet button**. A new screen will appear with the title Worksheet2, Worksheet3, Worksheet4, and so on, depending on how many worksheets you've created during this session.

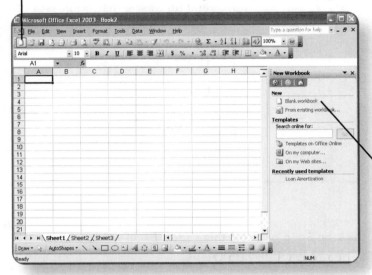

OR

> **TIP**
>
> Click on View, Task Pane if your task pane is not already displayed.

1b. **Click** on **Blank Workbook**. A standard blank worksheet will appear on the screen.

17

Editing a Worksheet

When you create a worksheet, a lot of data entry is usually involved. Excel has features to assist you with some of the repetitive work, but, unfortunately, you'll probably still make mistakes. You may need to edit the entries you made in some cells and you may want to make changes to the construction of your worksheet. Excel includes the ability to reorganize your worksheet without having to reenter any data.

In this chapter, you'll learn how to:

- Edit cell data
- Select cells
- Insert and delete rows, columns, and cells
- Use Undo and Redo
- Use the Clipboard task pane
- Use the Fill feature
- Transpose data

Editing Data

You can edit your data in a variety of ways. You might need to change the contents of a cell or you might want to move the data to a different area of the worksheet.

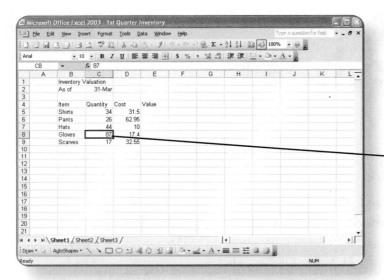

Replacing the Contents of a Cell

You can make changes to the contents of a cell in two ways. One method is by typing over the existing cell contents.

1. Click on an occupied **cell**. The cell and its contents will be selected.

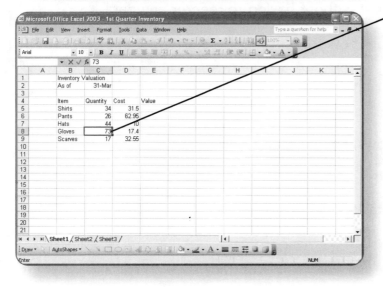

2. Type a new **label or value**. The new data will appear in the cell.

3. Press the **Enter key**. The new data will be accepted in the selected cell.

Editing the Contents of a Cell

The other method in which you can make changes to the contents of a cell is to use the Edit feature.

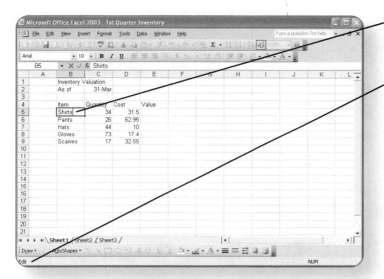

1. **Double-click** on the **cell** you want to edit. The insertion point will blink within the cell.

The status bar indicates that you are in Edit mode.

TIP

You can also press the F2 key to edit the contents of a cell.

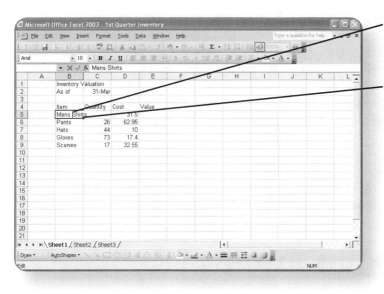

2. **Press** the **left arrow key**. The insertion point will move within the current cell.

3. **Type** the **changes**. The changes will appear in the current cell.

4. **Press** the **Enter key**. The changes will be entered into the current cell.

Clearing Cell Contents

If you enter data into a cell then later decide you do not want the information in the worksheet, you can quickly clear the contents.

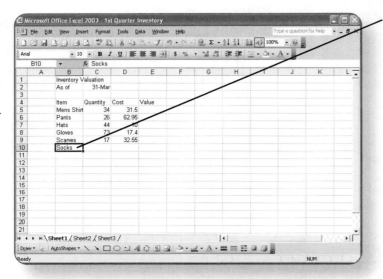

1. **Click** on the **cell** you want to clear. The cell is selected.

2. **Press** the **Delete key**. The content of the cell is cleared and the cell becomes empty.

Learning Selection Techniques

To move, copy, delete, or change the formatting of data in a worksheet, you must first select the cells you want to modify. Selected cells appear darker on screen—just the reverse of unselected text, with the exception of the first cell. The first cell does not appear darker; it just has a dark border around it.

TIP

Make sure the mouse pointer is a white cross before attempting to select cells.

The following table describes some of the different selection techniques:

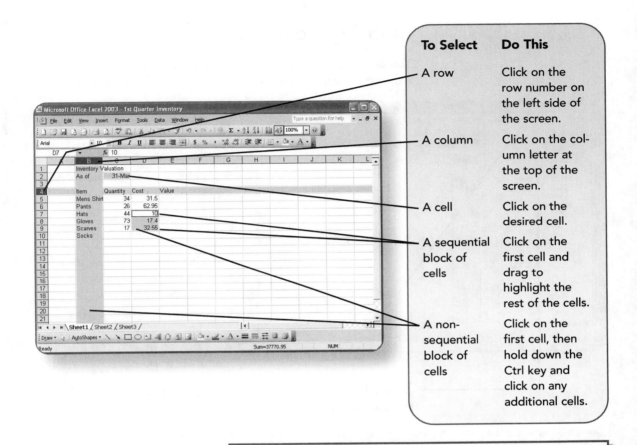

To Select	Do This
A row	Click on the row number on the left side of the screen.
A column	Click on the column letter at the top of the screen.
A cell	Click on the desired cell.
A sequential block of cells	Click on the first cell and drag to highlight the rest of the cells.
A non-sequential block of cells	Click on the first cell, then hold down the Ctrl key and click on any additional cells.

TIP

To deselect a block of cells, click the mouse in any single cell.

Inserting Areas

Occasionally you need to insert a column, row, or a single cell in the middle of existing information. Inserting rows, columns, or cells moves data to make room for new rows or columns.

Inserting Columns

You can insert a column anywhere you need it. Excel moves the existing columns to the right to make room for the new column.

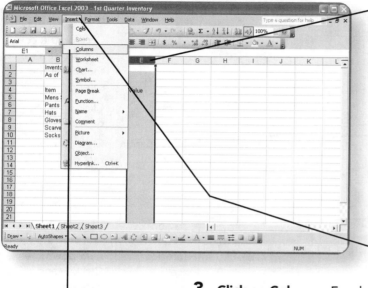

1. Click the heading letter of the **column** *after* which you want to insert the new column. (Excel will insert the new column in front of the selected one.) The entire column is selected.

TIP

To insert multiple columns, select headings across multiple columns.

2. Click on **Insert**. The Insert menu will appear.

3. Click on **Columns**. Excel will insert a new column in the selected area.

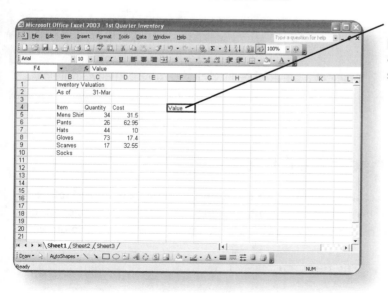

Excel moves information in the previously selected column and all columns to the right of the selected column to the right.

Inserting Rows

You can insert a row anywhere you need it. Excel will move the existing rows down to make room for the new ones.

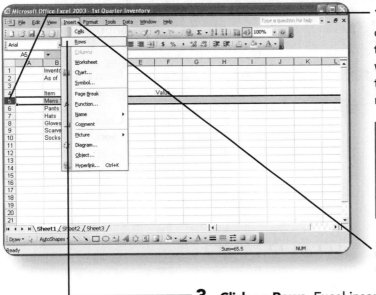

1. **Click** on the row number of the **row** *after* which you want to insert the new row. (Excel will insert the new row above the selected one.) The entire row is selected.

> ### TIP
> To insert multiple rows, select cells across multiple rows.

2. **Click** on **Insert**. The Insert menu will appear.

3. **Click** on **Rows**. Excel inserts a new row in the selected area.

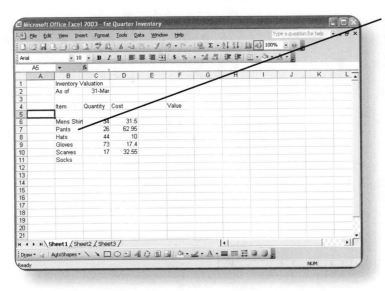

Excel moves information in the previously selected row and all rows below the selected row down.

Inserting Cells

Instead of inserting an entire column or an entire row, you can insert a single cell or even a group of cells. Excel then moves existing data down or to the right, depending on the option you specify.

1. Select the **cells** currently where you want the new cells. The cells will be selected.

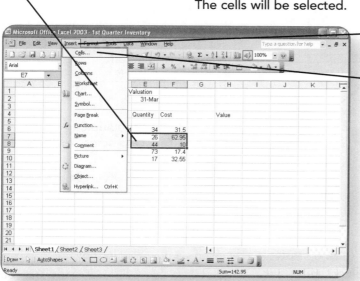

2. Click on **Insert**. The Insert menu will appear.

3. Click on **Cells**. The Insert dialog box will open.

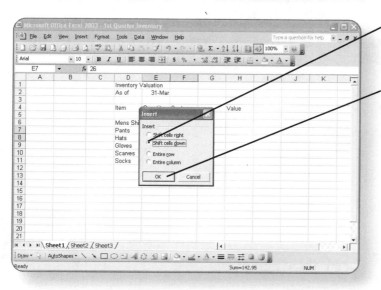

4. Click on **Shift Cells Right or Shift Cells Down**. A dot appears next to the selection.

5. Click on **OK**. The Insert dialog box will close and the new cells will be inserted.

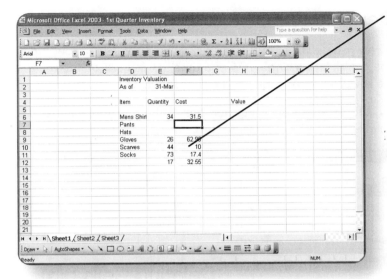

Existing data is moved down or to the right.

Deleting Areas

Use caution when deleting rows or columns. Excel will delete the entire row of 256 columns or the entire column of 65,536 rows. Any data in the selected row or column is deleted as well.

Deleting Columns

When you delete a column, Excel will pull the remaining columns to the left. You can delete a single column at a time, or you can delete multiple columns, whether sequential or non-sequential columns.

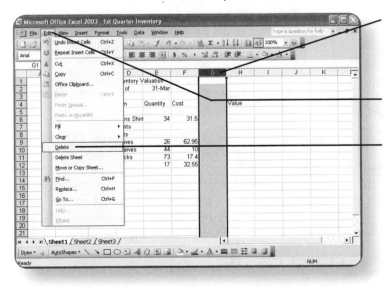

1. **Click** the **column heading letter** of the column you want to delete. The entire column is selected.

2. **Click** on **Edit**. The Edit menu will appear.

3. **Click** on **Delete**. The selected column is deleted.

Deleting Rows

When you delete a row, Excel will pull the remaining rows up. You can delete a single row at a time, or you can delete multiple rows, whether sequential or nonsequential.

1. **Click** the **row heading number** of the row you want to delete. The entire row is selected.

2. **Click** on **Edit**. The Edit menu will appear.

3. **Click** on **Delete**. The selected row is deleted.

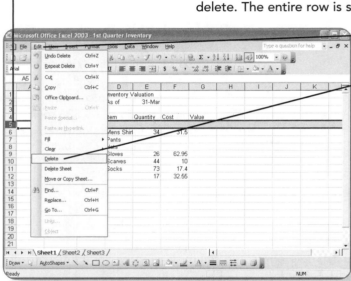

Deleting Cells

When clearing the contents of a cell, the cell remains in its current location, whereas deleting a cell eliminates not only the contents of the cell but also the actual cell. Other cells move into the deleted cell position.

1. **Select** the **cells** you want to delete. The cells will be selected.

2. **Click** on **Edit**. The Edit menu will appear.

3. **Click** on **Delete**. The Delete dialog box will open.

Unlike when a column or row is selected, the Delete menu option has an ellipsis, which indicates a dialog box will open.

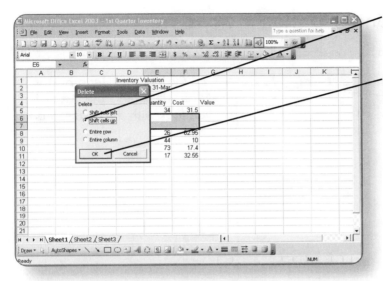

4. **Click** on **Shift Cells Left or Shift Cells Up**. A dot appears next to the selection.

5. **Click** on **OK**. The Delete dialog box will close and the selected cells will be deleted.

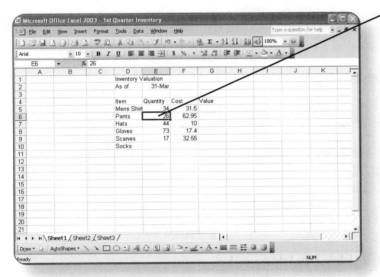

Existing data is moved up or to the left.

Using Undo and Redo

If you make a change, then determine you really didn't want to make that change, Excel provides an Undo feature. You can use Undo to restore text that you deleted, delete text you just typed, or reverse a recently taken action.

An exception to the Undo function is if you save your worksheet—you cannot "unsave" it. Also, if you close the worksheet, you cannot undo changes made in the previous editing session when you reopen the worksheet.

Undoing the Previous Step

You are one mouse click away from reversing your previous action.

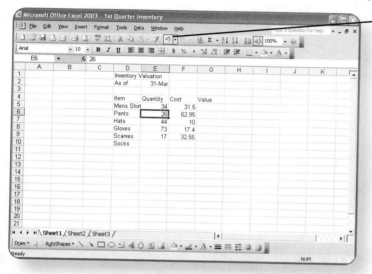

1. Click on the **Undo button**. Excel will reverse the last action you took with the current worksheet.

TIP

Optionally, choose Undo from the Edit menu.

Redoing the Previous Step

If you undo an action and then decide you prefer the worksheet the original way, use the Redo feature.

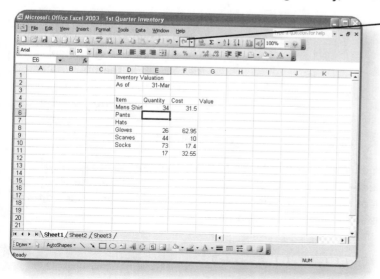

1. Click on the **Redo button**. Excel will reverse the previous undo action.

Undoing a Series of Actions

Excel actually keeps track of several steps you have recently taken. When you Undo a previous step, you also undo any actions taken after that step. For example, imagine you changed the value in a cell then bolded the cell contents. If you undo the typing, Excel also reverses the bolding step.

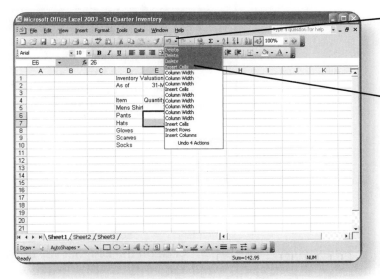

1. Click on the **arrow** next to the Undo button. A list of the most recent actions will be displayed.

2. Click on the **action** you want to undo. Excel will reverse the selected action as well as all actions listed above it.

Moving Data Around

If you're not happy with the placement of data, you don't have to delete it and retype it. Excel makes it easy for you to move it around. In fact, Excel provides several ways to move data.

Cutting and Pasting Data

Excel uses the Windows copy and paste features to assist you with moving data.

1. Select the **cells** you want to move. The cells will be highlighted.

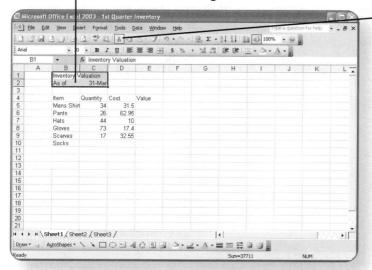

2. Click on the **Cut button**. Moving dashes, called a *marquee*, will appear around your selection.

TIP

Optionally, press Ctrl + X or choose Cut from the Edit menu.

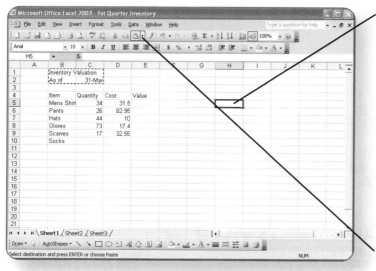

3. Click on the **cell** that will be the upper-left corner of the new location of the range. The cell will be selected.

NOTE

There must be enough empty cells in the new location to accommodate the cut data or existing data will be overwritten.

---

4. Click on the **Paste button**.

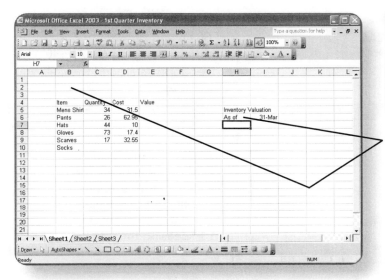

TIP

Optionally, press Ctrl + V or choose Paste from the Edit menu.

The data is pasted into the new location and removed from the previous location.

Using Drag and Drop to Move Cells

Drag and drop is another method used to move data from one location to another. The drag and drop method works best for moving a few cells of data a short distance.

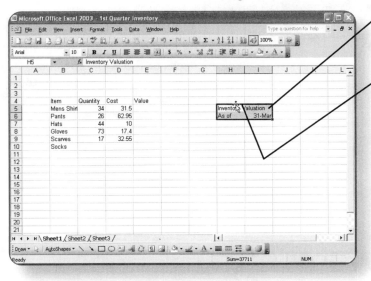

1. **Select** the **cells** you want to move. The cells will be highlighted.

2. **Position** the **mouse pointer** on the border edge of the highlighted cells. The mouse pointer will appear as a white arrow pointed to the left with four black arrow heads.

NOTE

Make sure the mouse pointer is a white arrow and not a black cross, which accomplishes a different function.

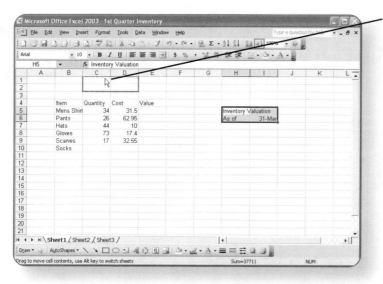

3. Hold the **mouse button** down **and drag** the mouse to the desired location. A gray border appears around the cells you point to.

TIP

To copy text with drag and drop, hold down the Ctrl key before dragging the selected text. Release the mouse button before releasing the Ctrl key.

4. Release the **mouse button**. The cells will move to the new location.

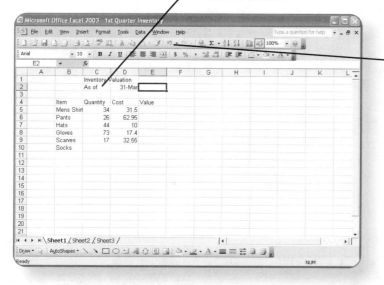

TIP

If you accidentally move cells to the wrong position, click on the Undo button to reverse the move.

Copying Data

If you want to duplicate cell data, again, you don't have to retype it. You can use the Copy command to replicate information.

1. Select the **cells** you want to duplicate. The cells will be highlighted.

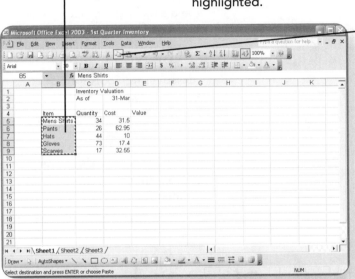

2. Click on the **Copy button**. The marquee, sometimes called "marching ants," will appear around the selected cells.

TIP

Optionally, press Ctrl + C or choose Copy from the Edit menu.

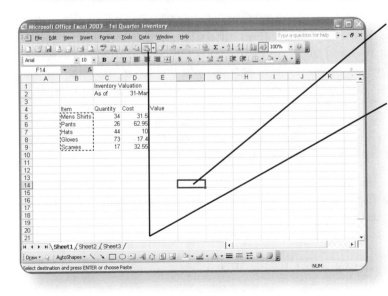

3. Click on the beginning **cell** where you want to paste the duplicated information. The cell will be highlighted.

4. Click on the **Paste** button.

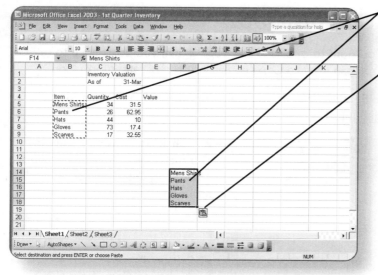

The pasted text will appear in both the original and new location.

In some situations, when you paste information or perform other Excel functions, you may see a small icon, called a Smart Tag, appear to the right of the pasted text. You'll learn about Smart Tags in Chapter 14, "Discovering Tools for Speed and Quality."

TIP

If the marquee does not stop marching, press the Enter key.

Using the Office Clipboard

Excel also uses a special form of the Windows clipboard, called the Office Clipboard. The Office Clipboard allows you to collect text and other items from any Office document or even other programs, then past them into any Excel worksheet. Each item is appended to the clipboard contents and then inserted as individuals or as a group in a new location or worksheet. You copy an item to the Office Clipboard, then paste it into any Office worksheet at any time. The collected items stay on the Office Clipboard until you exit Office.

Depending on the number of times you have copied text, the Clipboard task pane may appear automatically when you paste text.

1. Click on **Edit**. The Edit menu will appear.

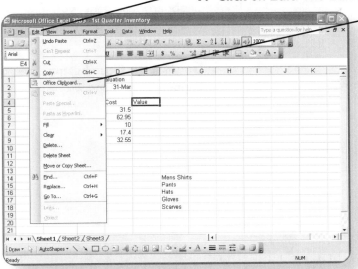

2. Click on **Office Clipboard**. The Clipboard task pane will appear.

The Office Clipboard stores up to 24 items you copied or cut. It doesn't matter whether you used the Edit menu, the cut or copy icons on the toolbar, the shortcut menu, or the shortcut keys.

You can insert any desired item from the clipboard or you can insert all items.

3. Click the **mouse** where you want to insert the Clipboard contents. The blinking insertion point will appear.

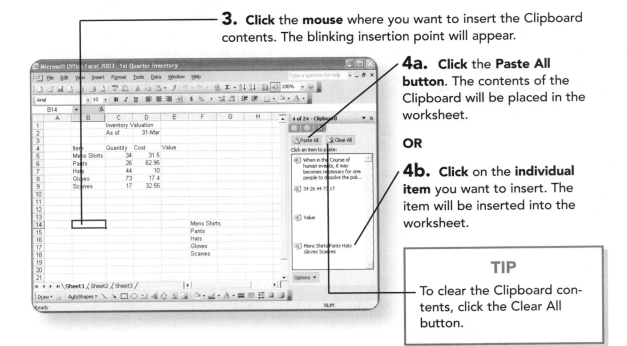

4a. Click the **Paste All button**. The contents of the Clipboard will be placed in the worksheet.

OR

4b. Click on the **individual item** you want to insert. The item will be inserted into the worksheet.

TIP

To clear the Clipboard contents, click the Clear All button.

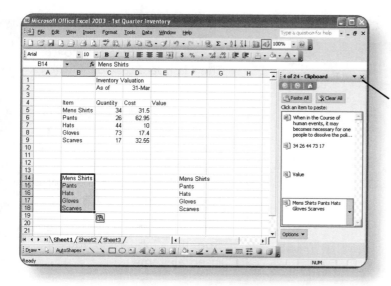

If you are finished with the Clipboard task pane, you may find it helpful to put the task pane away.

5. **Click** the **Close button**. The Clipboard task pane will disappear.

Using the Fill Feature

Excel includes a great built-in, time-saving feature called *Fill*. If you provide Excel the beginning pattern, such as a Month, Day, or numbers, Excel can fill in the rest of the pattern for you. For example, if you type January, Excel fills in February, March, April, and so on.

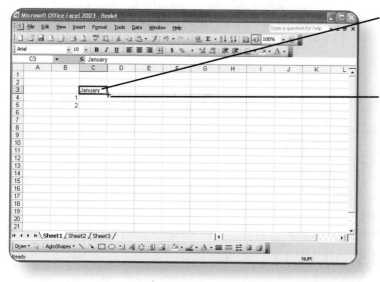

1. **Type** the beginning **month, day, or number** in the beginning cell. The text will be displayed in the cell.

2. **Position** the **mouse pointer** on the lower-right corner of the beginning cell. The mouse pointer will become a small black cross.

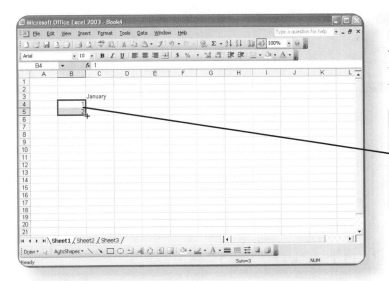

If you want Excel to fill in numbers, you must first give it a pattern. For example, enter the value of **1** in the first cell, and then enter **2** in the second cell.

TIP

For numbers, select both the first and second cells before proceeding to step 3.

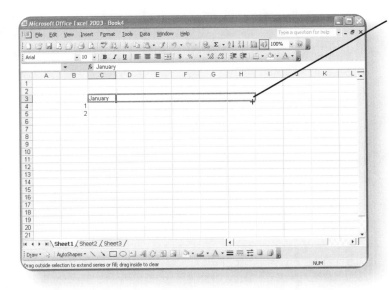

3. Press and hold the **mouse button and drag** to select the next cells to be filled in. The cells will have a gray border surrounding them.

4. Release the **mouse button**. The pattern will be repeated.

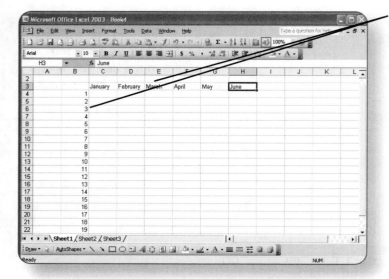

You can fill a series up, down, left, or right in your worksheet.

18

Making the Worksheet Look Good

You can make your worksheets more interesting and easier to read by formatting the worksheet cells. Change the fonts, font sizes, and styles or make the numbers easier to read by adding numeric formatting. Liven up the worksheet with effective use of borders, lines, and colors.

In this chapter, you'll learn how to:

- Use AutoFormat
- Format numbers and dates
- Use fonts and font attributes
- Modify column width and row height
- Adjust cell alignment
- Add cell borders and patterns
- Copy cell formatting

Using AutoFormat

AutoFormat is a quick, easy method to format your worksheet. It allows you to select from a number of professionally designed formats that automatically add colors, fonts, lines, borders, and more to your worksheets. Excel provides 16 different predefined AutoFormat patterns, some color and some black and white.

1. **Click and drag** the **mouse** across the cells you want to format. The cells will be highlighted.

2. **Click** on **Format**. The Format menu will appear.

3. **Click** on **AutoFormat**. The AutoFormat dialog box will open.

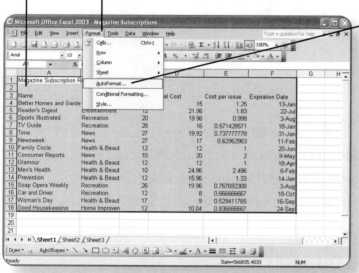

4. Click on a sample **format**. A border appears around the selected format.

Click on the Options button to specify additional preferences.

5. Click on **OK**. The effect will be applied to the selected cells.

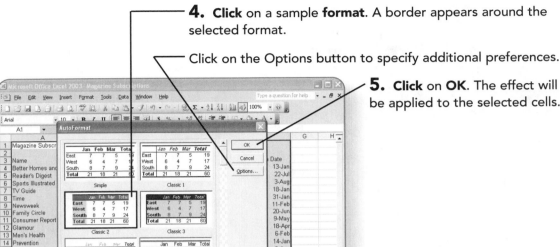

6. Deselect the highlighted **cells** to see the full effect of the AutoFormat. Depending on your selection, AutoFormat may have added color, changed the fonts, applied italics or bolding, and adjusted row heights.

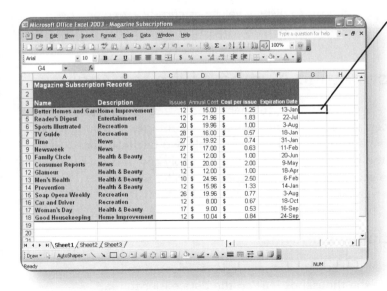

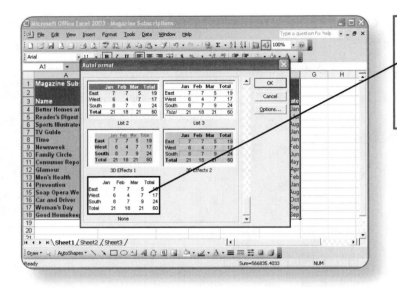

TIP

Apply the AutoFormat option "None" to remove the formatting from any selected cells.

Formatting Numbers

By default, values are displayed as general numbers; however, you can choose to display values as currency, percentages, fractions, dates, and many other formats.

Formatting Numbers with the Toolbar

The Excel formatting toolbar includes three popular number styles: commas, accounting, and percentages. Accounting and comma formats automatically apply two decimal places, whereas the percentage format doesn't apply any decimal points. The accounting style also applies a dollar sign to the number.

Adding Commas

When you apply a comma style to selected values, Excel separates the thousands making the data easier to read.

1. **Select** the **cells** you want to format. The cells will be highlighted.

2. **Click** on the **Comma button**. The cells will be formatted with two decimal places and a comma to separate numbers greater than 999.

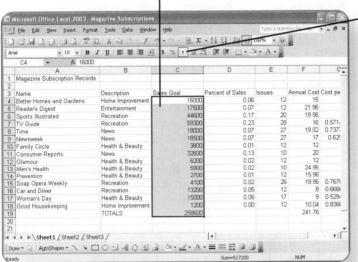

Cells formatted with a comma.

Formatting for Currency

Excel has a little quirk that appears when choosing the Currency button on the toolbar. The Excel tooltip calls this button the currency style; however, it actually applies an accounting style. The difference is in the placement of the dollar sign.

In currency style, the dollar sign is right next to the numbers, but in accounting style, the dollar sign is on the left edge of the cell

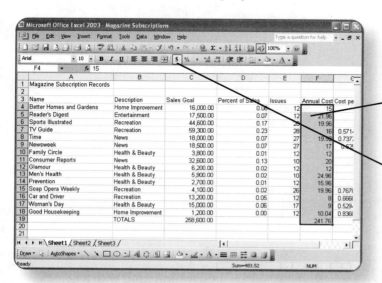

1. Select the **cells** you want to format. The cells will be highlighted.

2. Click on the **Currency button**. The cells will be formatted with a dollar sign and two decimal places.

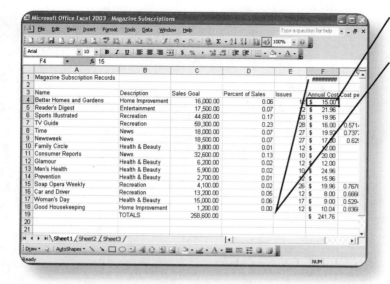

Cells formatted with currency and two decimal places.

If a formatted value cannot fit within the width of a cell, Excel may display a series of ###. You will discover how to widen a column later in this chapter.

Formatting Percentages

Excel provides a button on the toolbar for quick access when changing numbers to display as a percentage. Excel automatically multiplies the cell value by 100 and displays the result with a percent symbol. For example, if the cell has a value of 15, Excel will display 1500%; however, if the cell has a value of 0.15, Excel will display 15%.

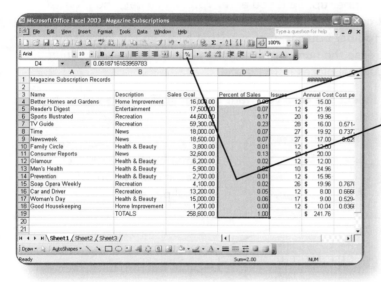

1. Select the **cells** you want to format. The cells will be highlighted.

2. Click on the **Percent button**. The cells will be formatted with a percent sign and no decimal places.

Cells formatted with the percent symbol.

Changing the Decimal Point Values

As mentioned earlier, by default, the comma and currency styles include two decimal places, and percentages don't include decimal points. If you have a number in a formatted cell with more than the two decimal points, Excel will round the number up. So if you enter 75.257 in a cell, then format that cell to comma or currency, Excel will display $75.26. There are toolbar buttons, however, that allow you to increase or decrease the number of decimal places. The maximum number of decimal places is 15 places.

1. **Select** the **cells** you want to format. The cells will be highlighted.

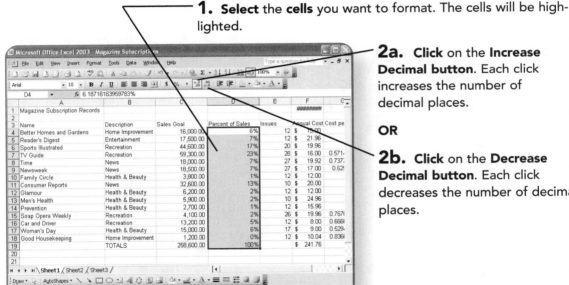

2a. **Click** on the **Increase Decimal button**. Each click increases the number of decimal places.

OR

2b. **Click** on the **Decrease Decimal button**. Each click decreases the number of decimal places.

Formatting Numbers through the Menu

Excel includes a dialog box where you can change all the formatting options in one step.

Formatting Numbers

The Format Cells dialog box allows you to select from several different number formatting styles, including whether to display negative numbers in red, choosing the number of decimal points, and even selecting the desired type of currency symbol. There is also a "Special" category where you can format numbers to match the pattern for telephone numbers or social security numbers.

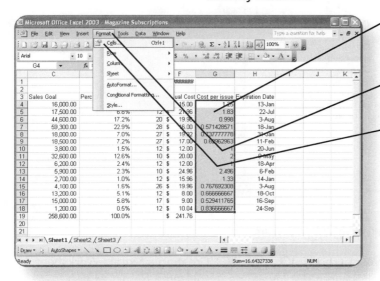

1. Select the **cells** you want to format. The cells will be highlighted.

2. Click on **Format**. The Format menu will appear.

3. Click on **Cells**. The Format Cells dialog box will open.

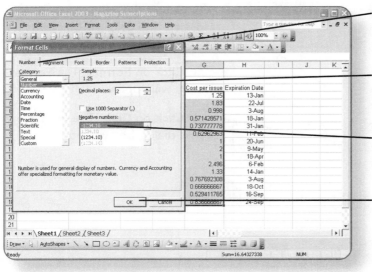

4. If necessary, **click** the **Number tab**. A list of number formats will display.

5. Click on a **category**. Available options for the selected category will appear.

6. Click on any desired **options**. A sample will appear in the sample box.

7. Click on **OK**. The Format Cells dialog box will close and Excel will apply the selected format.

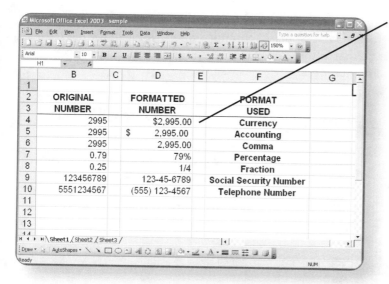

A sample of different number formats.

Formatting Dates

As you learned in Chapter 16, "Creating a Simple Worksheet," Excel may not display a date in the same format as you entered the data. Through the Format Cells dialog box you can select the format you want for cells containing dates.

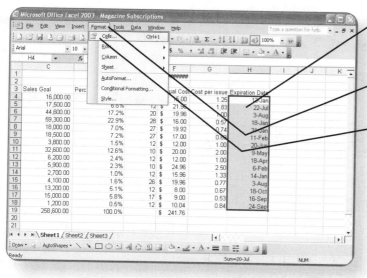

1. Select the **cells** you want to format. The cells will be highlighted.

2. Click on **Format**. The Format menu will appear.

3. Click on **Cells**. The Format Cells dialog box will open.

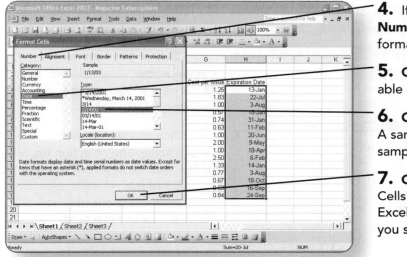

4. If necessary, **click** the **Number tab**. A list of number formats will display.

5. **Click** on **Date**. A list of available date formats will appear.

6. **Click** on a **date style**. A sample will appear in the sample box.

7. **Click** on **OK**. The Format Cells dialog box will close and Excel will apply the date style you selected.

Formatting with Fonts

Excel uses a default font of Arial 10 points, but from the toolbar you can easily change the font typeface, size, style, and color.

Selecting a Typeface

Fonts are typefaces in different styles that give your text character and impact. Your selection of fonts will vary depending on the software installed on your computer.

1. **Select** the **cells** you want to format. The cells will be highlighted.

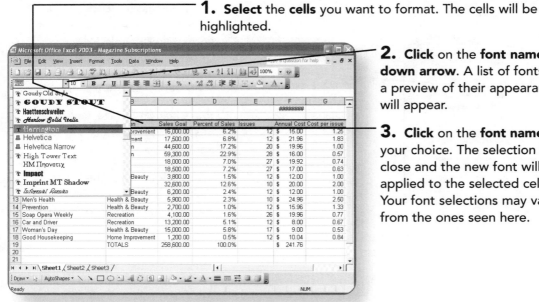

2. **Click** on the **font name down arrow**. A list of fonts and a preview of their appearance will appear.

3. **Click** on the **font name** of your choice. The selection list will close and the new font will be applied to the selected cells. Your font selections may vary from the ones seen here.

Selecting a Font Size

The default font size in an Excel worksheet is 10 points. There are approximately 72 points in an inch, so a 10 point font is slightly less than one-seventh of an inch tall.

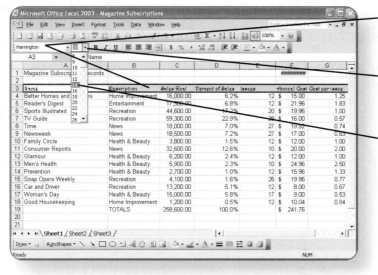

1. **Select** the **cells** you want to format. The cells will be highlighted.

2. **Click** on the **font size down arrow**. A list of available sizes will appear.

3. **Click** on the **font size** of your choice. The selection list will close and the new font size will be applied to the selected cells.

Adding Bold, Underline, or Italics

Excel includes three different font styles you can select from the toolbar. Font styles include **bold**, <u>underline</u>, and *italics*.

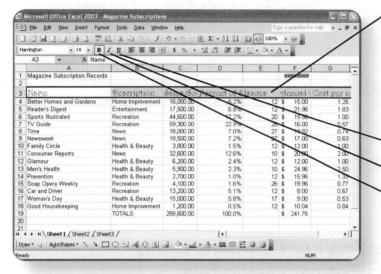

1. Select the **cells** you want to format. The cells will be highlighted.

2. Click on any of the following **options**. The attributes will be applied to the selected cells.

- Underline button
- Italics button
- Bold button

The Bold, Italics, and Underline buttons are like toggle switches. Click on them a second time to turn the attribute off.

NOTE

Underlining is not the same as a cell border. Cell borders are discussed later in this chapter.

Working with Font Colors

If you want to add color to your worksheet, try changing the font color.

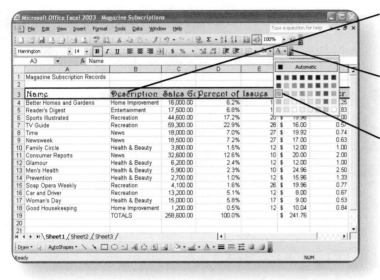

1. **Select** the **cells** you want to format. The cells will be highlighted.

2. **Click** the **font color down arrow**. A color palette will appear.

3. **Click** on a **color**. The color palette will close and the font color will be applied to the selected cells.

Setting Font Options Using the Format Dialog Box

Setting formatting from the toolbar is easy, but Excel also provides a dialog box that offers font choices plus a few extras.

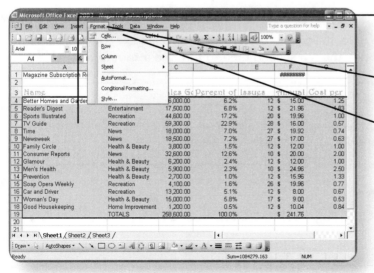

1. **Select** the **cells** you want to format. The cells will be highlighted.

2. **Click** on **Format**. The Format menu will appear.

3. **Click** on **Cells**. The Format Cells dialog box will open.

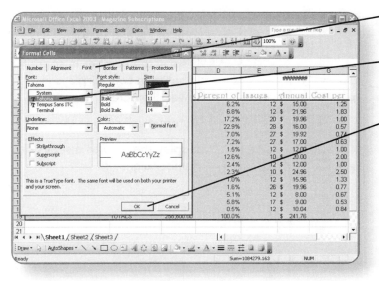

4. **Click** on the **Font tab**. The Font tab will appear in front.

5. **Select** any desired **font options** including typeface, size, color, and other options.

6. **Click** on **OK**. Excel will apply all the font options at once.

Adjusting Column Width

By default, Excel columns are 8.43 points wide. When the content of a cell is too long to fit into its cell, depending on the type of data, Excel may automatically widen the column or display the information in a different format. You can manually resize a column so all data displays correctly.

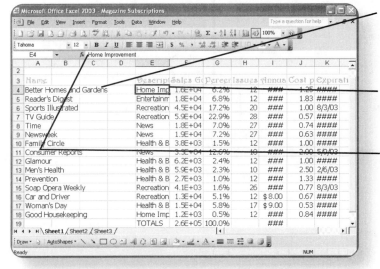

If a label does not fit into the cell, the contents will spill into the next cell to the right, if the next cell is empty.

If the next cell is not empty, Excel displays only the amount of text that will fit into the cell.

The extra text is not cut off, just not displayed.

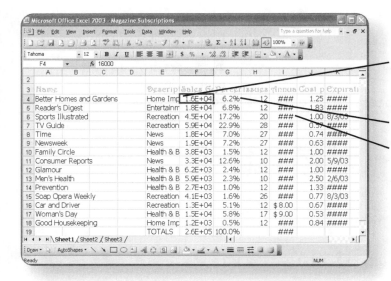

If a value is too wide, Excel may do one of several things:

- Display the number in scientific notation so it displays in fewer characters.

- Automatically widen the cell.

- Display the data as a series of number signs (#).

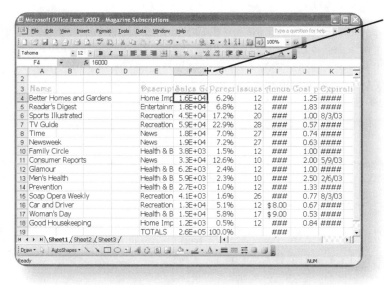

1a. **Double-click** on the **dividing line** to the right of the column heading letters. The column will automatically expand to fit the column contents.

TIP

To resize multiple columns at the same time, select the columns you want to modify.

OR

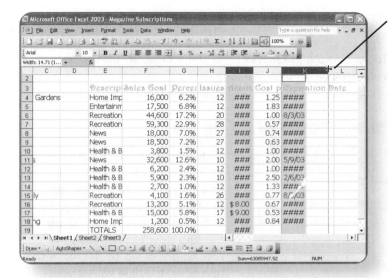

1b. **Position** the **mouse pointer** on the dividing line between the column heading letters until the mouse pointer becomes a double-headed arrow. **Drag** the **line** to the right to widen the column or to the left to make the column narrower. A line will appear showing the new column width. **Release** the **mouse button**. The new column width will apply to the selected column.

TIP

To manually set the column width, click the Format menu, select Column, then Width. Enter the desired column width in points.

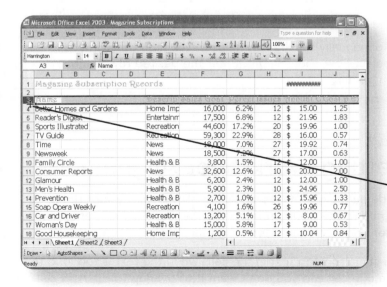

Adjusting Row Height

When you change to a larger font, Excel usually enlarges the row height to accommodate the larger font size. You can also manually resize the row height.

1a. **Double-click** on the **dividing line** below the row that needs to be resized. The row will automatically expand to fit the row contents.

TIP

To resize multiple rows at the same time, select the rows you want to modify.

OR

1b. **Position** the **mouse pointer** on the dividing line below the row that needs to be resized until the mouse pointer becomes a double-headed arrow. **Drag** the **line** down to increase the row height or up to decrease the row height. A line will appear showing the new row height. **Release** the **mouse button**. The new row height will apply to the selected column.

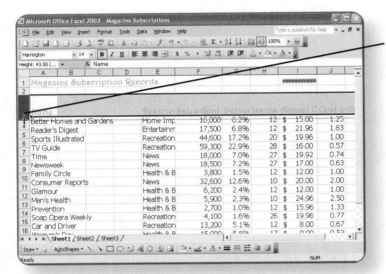

TIP

To manually set the row height, click the Format menu, select Row, then Height. Enter the desired row height in points.

Setting Worksheet Alignment

By default, Excel makes labels left-aligned and values right-aligned to their cells. You can change the alignment of either to left, right, centered, or full justified.

You can also wrap text in the cells when the text is too long to fit in one cell and you don't want it to overlap to the next cell.

Adjusting Cell Alignment

You can adjust cells individually or adjust a block of cells.

1. **Select** the **cells** you want to format. The cells will be highlighted.

2. **Click** on **Format**. The Format menu will appear.

3. **Click** on **Cells**. The Format Cells dialog box will open.

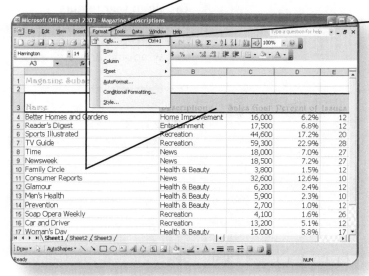

4. If necessary, **click** on the **Alignment tab**. The Alignment tab will come to the top.

5. **Click** the **Horizontal drop-down menu**. A list of options will appear.

6. **Click** an alignment **option**. The option will be selected.

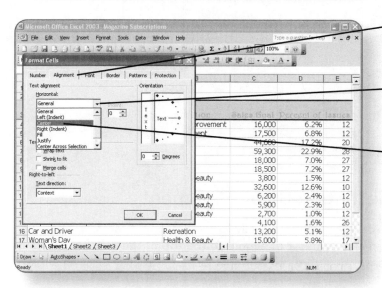

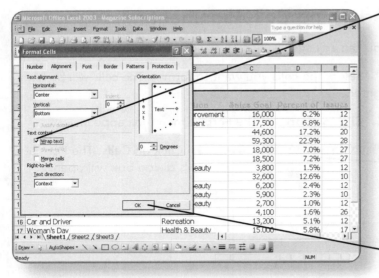

7. Optionally, **click** on a **Text control option** to activate any desired feature. A check mark will appear in the selection box.

TIP

The Wrap text feature treats each cell like a miniature word processor, with text wrapping around in the cell.

8. **Click** on **OK**. The selections will be applied to the highlighted cells.

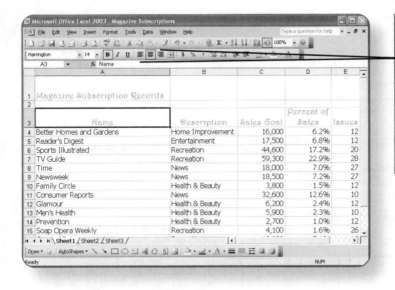

TIP

Optionally, you can quickly align text with the toolbar. Select the text you want to align, then click on one of the three alignment buttons on the toolbar: Left, Center, or Right.

Setting Vertical Alignment

Excel aligns text vertically to the bottom of the row, but you can also center it or align it to the top of the cell. You can also make the entire cell contents display vertically or at an angle.

1. Select the **cells** you want to format. The cells will be highlighted.

2. Click on **Format**. The Format menu will appear.

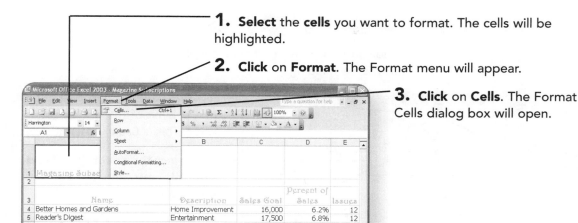

3. Click on **Cells**. The Format Cells dialog box will open.

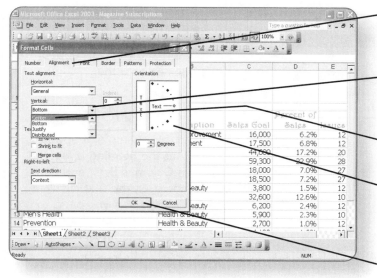

4. If necessary, **click** on the **Alignment tab**. The Alignment tab will come to the top.

5. Click the **Vertical drop-down menu**. A list of options will appear.

6. Click an alignment **option**. The option will be selected.

7. Optionally, **select** an **orientation**, and if you want the text to be displayed at an angle, select the angle degrees.

8. Click on **OK**. The selections will be applied to the highlighted cells.

Centering Headings

You can also center text across a group of columns to create attractive headings.

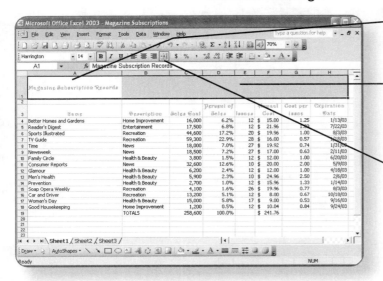

1. Type the heading **text** in the first column of the worksheet body. This is usually column A.

2. Select the **heading cell and the cells** you want to include in the heading. The cells will be highlighted.

3. Click on the **Merge and Center button**. The title will be centered.

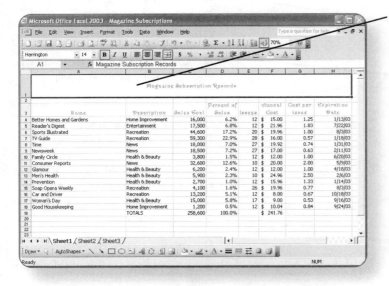

Notice the gridlines have disappeared and the cells appear to be joined together.

NOTE

In this example, it appears that the heading is located in Columns B, C, and D; however, the text is still in Column A. If you need to change the text, be sure to select Column A, not Column B, C, or D.

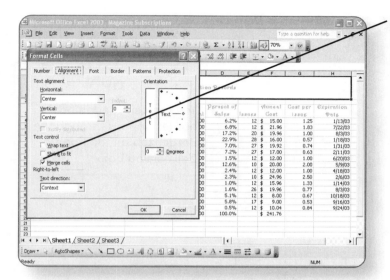

Remove the Merge and Center option through the Format Cells dialog box.

Adding Cell Borders

You can add border lines to individual cells and groups of cells. A border can appear around all sides of the cell or only on certain sides, such as the top or bottom. Unlike an underline, which runs directly under letters and numbers, a border includes the entire width or height of a cell.

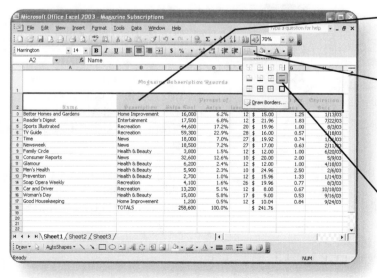

1. **Select** the **cells** you want to format. The cells will be highlighted.

2. **Click** on the **down arrow** next to the Borders button. The Borders palette will appear with icons displaying how the borders will be applied to a selected range.

3. **Click** on the desired **format**. The Borders palette will close.

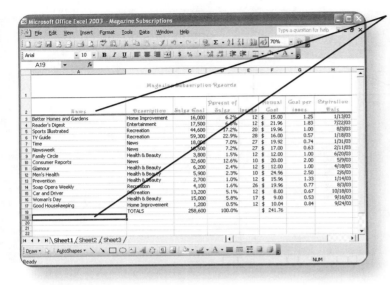

4. Deselect the **cells** to easily see the border.

Adding Background Color

Adding a background color to a cell or group of cells can make your worksheet more interesting and can call attention to specific areas of the worksheet. Excel calls the background color the Fill color.

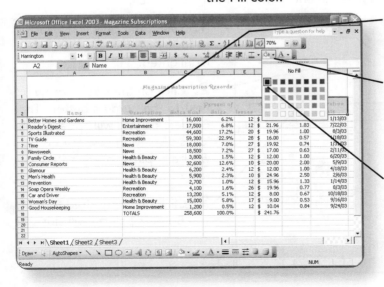

1. Select the **cells** you want to format. The cells will be highlighted.

2. Click on the **down arrow** next to the Fill Color button. The Fill Color palette will appear with icons displaying a selection of colors.

3. Click on the desired **color**. The Fill Color palette will close and the color will be applied to the selected cells.

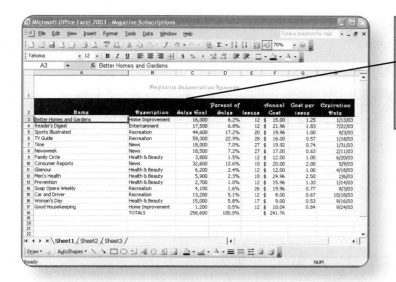

TIP

For a nice effect, use a dark background in combination with a light font color.

Using Cell Patterns

You can use a pattern instead of a single color as a background to your cells. A pattern uses two colors, arranged in some design, such as stripes or dots. Each pattern has both a background and a foreground color. The background color is the base color, whereas the foreground color is the color of the stripes or dots. Be careful using patterns because they can be distracting to the reader.

1. **Select** the **cells** you want to format. The cells will be highlighted.

2. **Click** on **Format**. The Format menu will appear.

3. **Click** on **Cells**. The Format Cells dialog box will open.

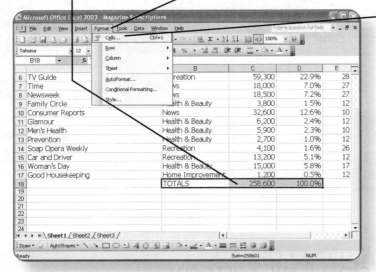

4. **Click** on the **Patterns tab**. The Patterns tab will appear in front.

5. **Click** on the Pattern **drop-down menu**. A palette of patterns and colors will appear.

6. **Click** on a **pattern** at the top of the list. The pattern and color palette will close.

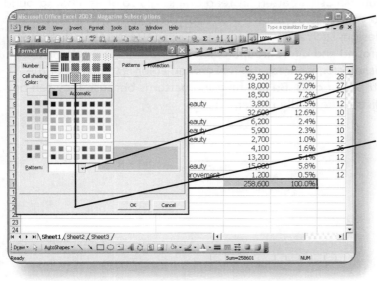

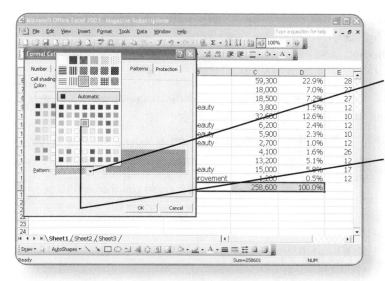

By default, the patterns are black and white, but you can change the colors.

7. Optionally, **click** on the Pattern **drop-down menu** again. A palette of patterns and colors will appear.

8. **Click** on a **color**. The pattern and color palette will close.

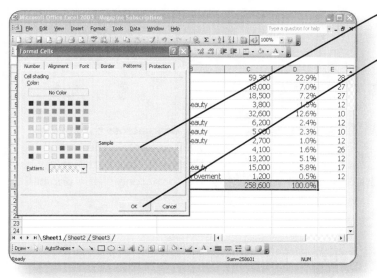

A sample will appear in the sample box.

9. **Click** on **OK**. The Format Cells dialog box will close and the selected cells will have the pattern selection.

Copying Cell Formatting

Sometimes it takes a lot of time and effort to get the formatting of a cell just the way you want it. Rather than duplicate all those steps for another cell, Excel includes a Format Painter feature which copies formatting from one cell to another. Copied formatting includes font size, color, style attributes, shading, and alignment. When you copy the formatting, the values in the cells are not affected.

1. **Select** a **cell** containing the formatting you want to copy. The cell will be highlighted.

2. **Click** on the **Format Painter button**.

The mouse pointer will turn into a paintbrush with a plus sign.

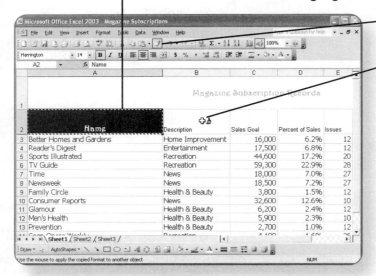

3. **Drag across** the **cells** you want to contain the formatting. Excel will "paint" the cells with the formatting of the original cell.

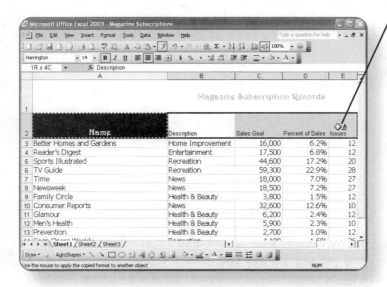

19

Selecting Printing Options

Before you print your worksheet, you can adjust the printing options. In addition, Excel can save you time and money by letting you see exactly what you're going to print before you use any paper.

In this chapter, you'll learn how to:

- Set up page margins
- Specify page orientation and size
- Create a header or footer
- Adjust printing size
- Use Print Preview
- Print the worksheet

Setting Up the Pages

With a single click, you can print your worksheet. But before you print your worksheet, you might want to specify what paper size to use, how large to make the margins, and whether to print the gridlines. You also might want to specify to print only a portion of the worksheet instead of printing it in its entirety.

Setting Up Margins

By default, Excel uses a top and bottom margin of 1 inch and left and right margins of .75 inch. You can change these margins to meet your needs.

1. **Click** on **File**. The File menu will appear.

2. **Click** on **Page Setup**. The Page Setup dialog box will open.

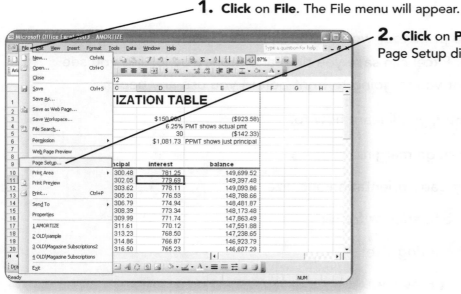

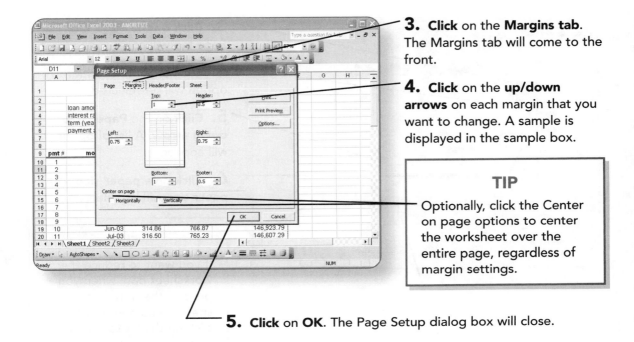

3. Click on the **Margins tab**. The Margins tab will come to the front.

4. Click on the **up/down arrows** on each margin that you want to change. A sample is displayed in the sample box.

TIP

Optionally, click the Center on page options to center the worksheet over the entire page, regardless of margin settings.

5. Click on **OK**. The Page Setup dialog box will close.

Setting Page Orientation and Size

If your worksheet uses quite a few columns, you might want to change the orientation or paper size. The default size is $8\frac{1}{2}$ x 11-inch paper in portrait orientation—the short side at the top and bottom. Changing to landscape orientation will print with the long edge of the paper at the top and bottom.

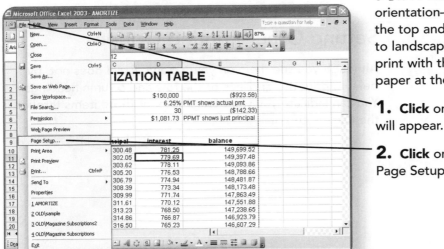

1. Click on **File**. The File menu will appear.

2. Click on **Page Setup**. The Page Setup dialog box will open.

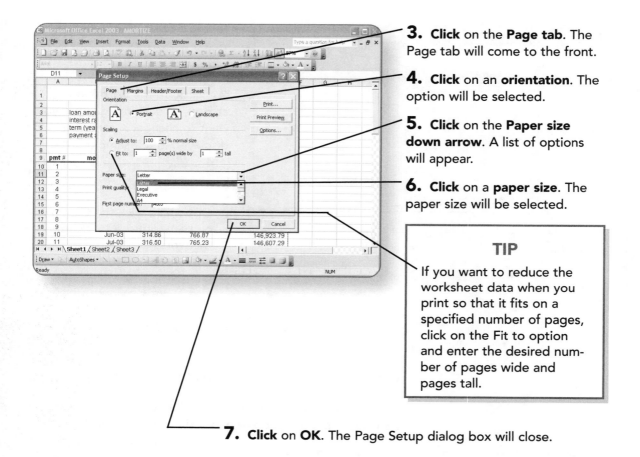

3. **Click** on the **Page tab**. The Page tab will come to the front.

4. **Click** on an **orientation**. The option will be selected.

5. **Click** on the **Paper size down arrow**. A list of options will appear.

6. **Click** on a **paper size**. The paper size will be selected.

TIP

If you want to reduce the worksheet data when you print so that it fits on a specified number of pages, click on the Fit to option and enter the desired number of pages wide and pages tall.

7. **Click** on **OK**. The Page Setup dialog box will close.

Setting Other Printing Options

Although you see them on your screen, Excel does not, by default, print the gridlines or the row and column headings. You can indicate you want Excel to print those items through the Page Setup dialog box.

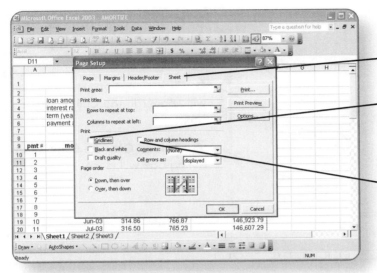

1. **Open** the **Page Setup** dialog box.

2. **Click** on the **Sheet tab**. The Sheet tab will come to the front.

3. **Click** on **Gridlines** if you want Excel to print the gridlines. A check mark will appear in the selection box.

4. **Click** on **Row and column headings** if you want Excel to include the headings when printing. A check mark will appear in the selection box.

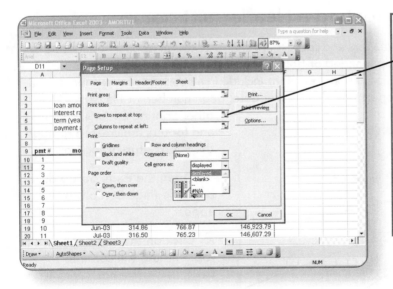

TIP

If your worksheet will be more than one printed page in height or width, you may want to print a particular column or row on each page, sort of as a title for each page. Click on the worksheet icon on the Rows or Columns to select which rows or columns to repeat.

In some worksheets, especially those that include formulas, you may see an error message. An example might be when a formula divides a cell by zero; the resulting answer displays as #DIV/0! in the worksheet cell. You can tell Excel to print the error messages as displayed, print N/A, print two dashes (--), or print nothing at all, leaving the cell blank when printing. (You will learn more about formulas in Chapter 20, "Working with Formulas.")

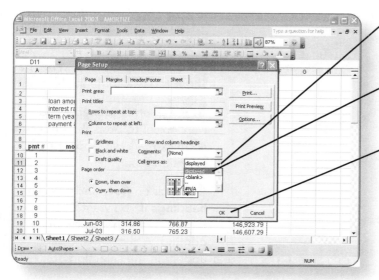

5. Click the **Cell errors as drop-down menu**. A list of options will appear.

6. Click an **option**. The selection will appear in the Cell errors as box.

7. Click on **OK**. The Page Setup dialog box will close.

Creating a Header or Footer

Headers and *footers* are simply text that appears either at the top (header) or bottom (footer) of every page. The types of information you might include in a header or footer might be a report title, the current date, page number, or file name. Like other printing options, headers and footers are created through the Page Setup dialog box.

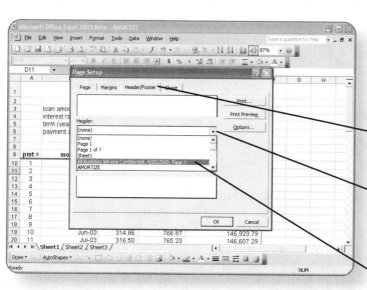

1. Open the **Page Setup** dialog box. The Page Setup box will appear.

2. Click on the **Header/Footer tab**. The tab will come to the front.

3. Click on the **Header** or **Footer drop-down menu**. A list of predefined headers or footers will appear.

4. Click a predefined **header or footer**. The header or footer will appear in the sample box.

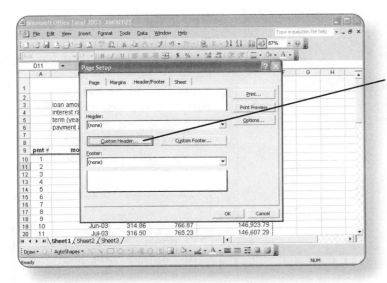

If none of the predefined headers or footers meets your needs, you can create your own.

5. **Click** on **Custom Header** or **Custom Footer**. The Header or Footer dialog box will open.

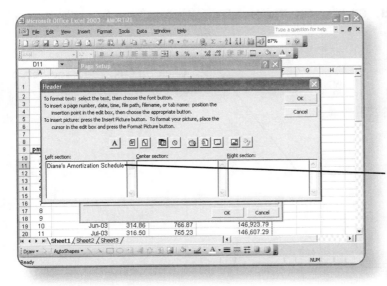

Headers and Footers are divided into three areas of the page: the left side, the center, or the right side.

6. **Click** in the Left, Center, or Right section **text box**. A blinking insertion point will appear in the section you selected.

7a. **Type** any **text** you want to appear in the header or footer. The text you type will appear in the section box.

AND/OR

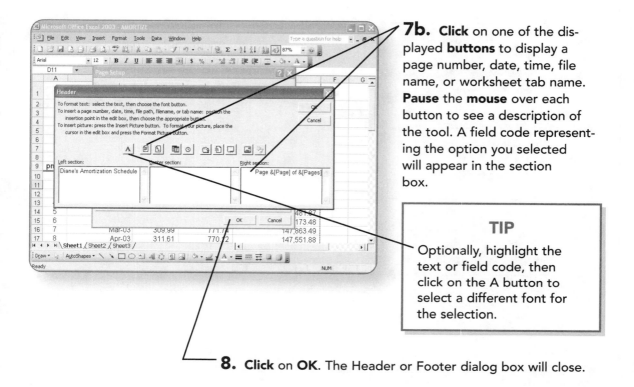

7b. Click on one of the displayed **buttons** to display a page number, date, time, file name, or worksheet tab name. **Pause** the **mouse** over each button to see a description of the tool. A field code representing the option you selected will appear in the section box.

TIP

Optionally, highlight the text or field code, then click on the A button to select a different font for the selection.

8. Click on **OK**. The Header or Footer dialog box will close.

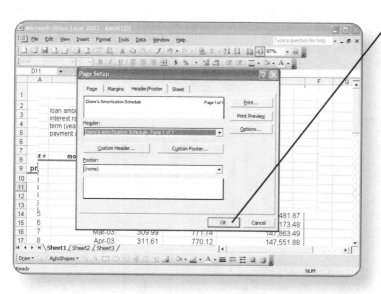

9. Click on **OK**. The Page Setup dialog box will close.

Selecting a Print Area

Excel assumes you want to print the entire worksheet, but you may only want to print a portion of the sheet. You can specify a specific print range for Excel to print.

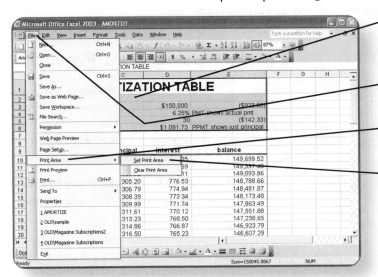

1. **Select** the **cells** you want to print. The cells will be highlighted.

2. **Click** on **File**. The File menu will appear.

3. **Click** on **Print Area**. The Print Area submenu will appear.

4. **Click** on **Set Print Area**. Excel will display a dotted line around the area you selected.

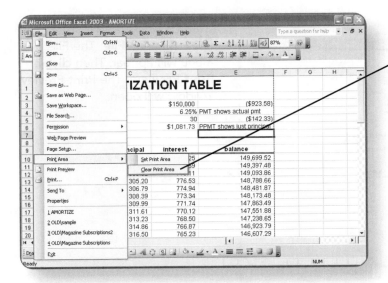

TIP

To clear the print area so Excel will print the entire worksheet or so you can define a different print area, select Clear Print Area from the File, Print Area menu.

Printing a Worksheet

Once you have specified any print specifications and options, you can print the worksheet. You may want to preview the worksheet on the screen before you print, just to make sure you have all the options set correctly.

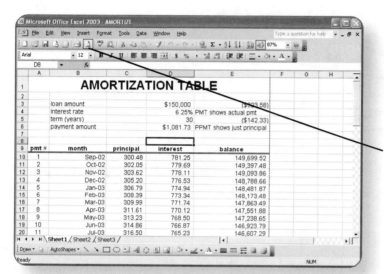

Using Print Preview

Using the Print Preview feature can save lots of paper by allowing you to see the worksheet on your screen before actually printing it to paper.

1a. **Click** on the **Print Preview button**. The Print Preview window will open.

OR

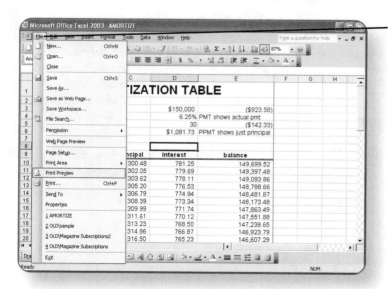

1b. **Click** on **File**. The File menu will appear. Then **click** on **Print Preview**. The Print Preview window will open.

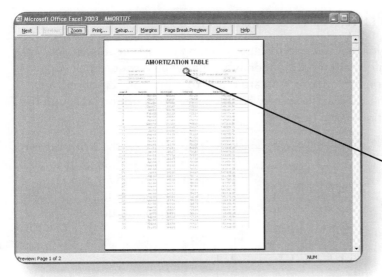

Don't strain your eyes trying to read the text in the Preview window. You are looking at the overall perspective here, not necessarily the individual cell contents. You cannot edit the worksheet cell contents while in Preview mode.

Your mouse pointer is a magnifying glass while in Print Preview.

2. Click on the **worksheet** to zoom in on a specific area. The worksheet will be magnified.

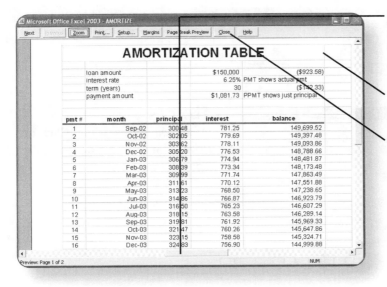

While zoomed in on the worksheet, you can use the scroll bars to view different areas of the worksheet.

3. Click on the **worksheet** again. The worksheet will shrink.

4. Click on the **Close button**. The view will return to the actual worksheet.

Printing the Worksheet

Typically, the end result of creating a worksheet is to get the information onto paper. Now that you've checked all your printing options, you are ready to print. You can print from the toolbar, or specify additional printing options through the Print dialog box.

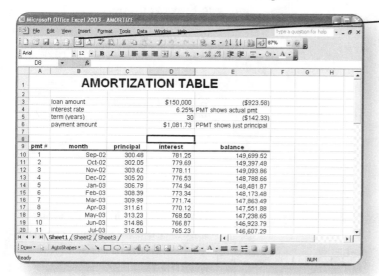

1a. Click on the **Print button**. The worksheet will print to your default printer with the options you specified in the Page Setup box. No dialog box will appear.

OR

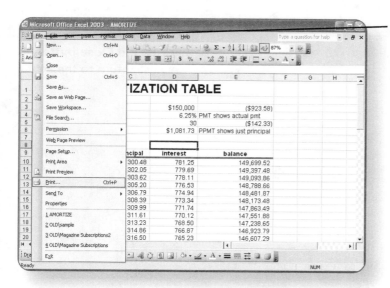

1b. Click on **File**. The File menu will appear. Then **Click** on **Print**. The Print dialog box will open.

2. **Click** on any desired **options** from the Print dialog box, including:

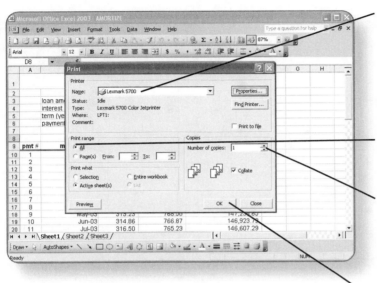

- **Printer name**. If you have access to more than one printer, you can choose which printer to use for this print job. Click on the Name drop-down menu and select the printer you want to use.

- **Print range**. Choose which pages of your document you want to print.

- **Number of copies**. Select the number of copies you want to print by clicking on the up/down arrows in the Number of copies list box.

3. **Click** on **OK**. The document will print.

20

Working with Formulas

Many people use a worksheet to perform mathematical calculations. By using formulas, if a value in a referenced cell changes, any formula based on the cell automatically adjusts to accommodate the new value. Excel can accommodate both simple formulas, such as adding two values together, and complex formulas, such as adding two values together and multiplying the result by another number. In addition, Excel can include the values from many different worksheet cells.

In this chapter, you'll learn how to:

● Create simple and compound formulas

● Edit formulas

● Copy formulas

● Create an absolute reference in a formula

● View formulas in the worksheet

● Understand common formula error messages

Creating Formulas

All formulas must begin with the equal (=) sign, regardless of whether the formula consists of adding, subtracting, multiplying, or dividing. Formulas can reference either a static value or the value in a referenced cell.

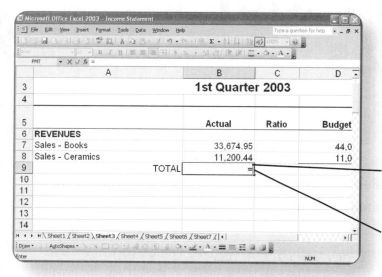

Creating a Simple Formula

An example of a simple formula is to add two cell values together. For example, you could elect to add the values of B7 and B8.

1. Click on the **cell** in which you want to place the result. The cell will be selected.

2. Type an **equal (=) sign** to begin the formula. The symbol will display in the cell.

3. Type the **cell address** of the first cell to be included in the formula. This is called the cell reference.

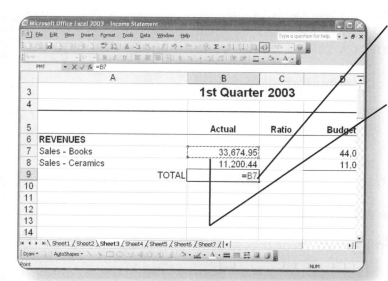

Excel references the cell address in color and places a matching color box around the referenced address.

NOTE

Worksheet formulas are not case sensitive. For example, B7 is the same as b7.

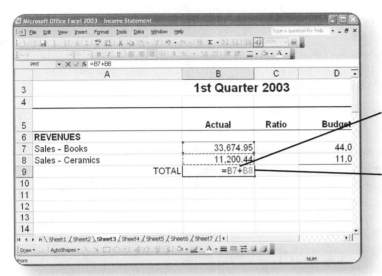

A formula needs an operator to suggest the next action to be performed. Operators are plus (+), minus (-), multiply (*), or divide (/) symbols.

4. **Type** the **operator**. The operator will display in the formula.

5. **Type** the **reference** to the second cell of the formula. The reference will display in the cell.

Excel references the second cell address in a different color and places a matching color box around the referenced address.

6. **Press** the **Enter key**. The result of the calculation will appear in the cell.

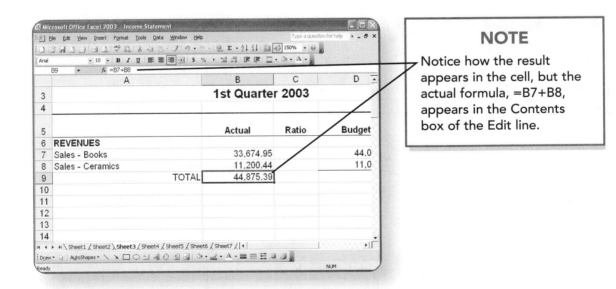

NOTE

Notice how the result appears in the cell, but the actual formula, =B7+B8, appears in the Contents box of the Edit line.

Creating a Compound Formula

You use compound formulas when you need more than one operator. Examples of a compound formula might be =B7+B8+B9+B10 or =B11-B19*A23.

NOTE

When you have a compound formula, Excel will do the multiplication and division first, then the addition and subtraction. If you want a certain portion of the formula to be calculated first, put it in parentheses. Excel will do whatever is in the parentheses before the rest of the formula. For example, the formula =B11-B19*A23 will give a totally different answer than =(B11-B19)*A23.

---

1. **Click** on the **cell** in which you want to place the formula answer. The cell will be selected.

2. **Type** an **equal sign (=)** to begin the formula. The symbol will display in the cell.

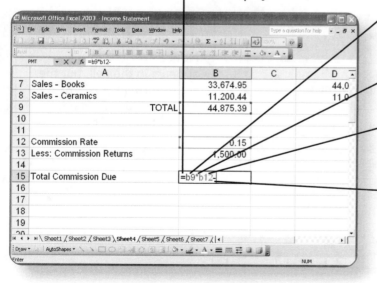

3. **Type** the **reference** to the first cell of the formula. The reference will display in the cell.

4. **Type** the **operator**. The operator will display in the cell.

5. **Type** the **reference** to the second cell of the formula. The reference will display in the cell.

6. **Type** the next **operator**. The operator will display in the cell.

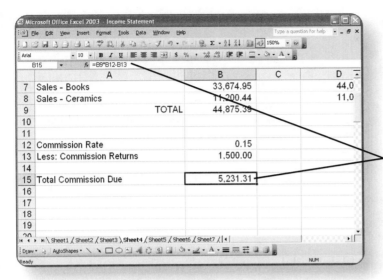

7. **Type** the **reference** to the third cell of the formula. The reference will display in the cell.

8. **Repeat steps 6 and 7** until the formula is complete, adding the parentheses wherever necessary.

9. **Press** the **Enter key** to accept the formula. The calculation answer will be displayed in the cell and the formula will be displayed in the content bar.

Try changing one of the values you originally typed in the worksheet and watch the answer to the formula change.

NOTE

Excel also provides more complex formulas, called Functions, that can perform statistical, financial, mathematical, and many other types of calculations. You'll learn about Functions in Chapter 21, "Using Excel Functions."

Editing Formulas

Excel provides several methods for editing an incorrect cell, whether it's a label, a value, or a formula. One method involves simply retyping the desired data in the correct cell. When you press Enter, the new data replaces the old data.
If, however, the data is complex or lengthy, you might want to edit only a portion of the existing information. You can make changes to a cell entry directly in the cell.

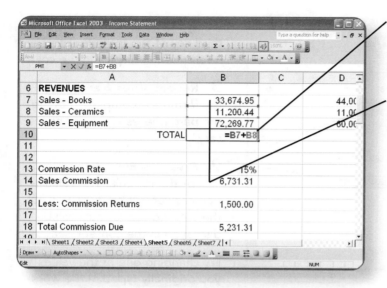

1. Double-click on the **cell** you want to modify. The blinking insertion point will appear in the cell.

When editing formulas, Excel color codes each cell address to its corresponding cell.

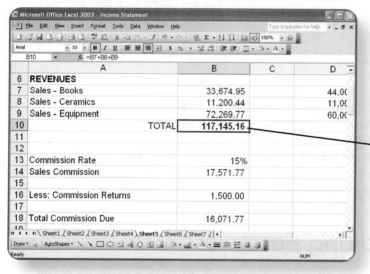

2. Type any **corrections**. You may need to use the keyboard arrow keys to move the insertion point to the position of the incorrect data. The changes will appear in the cell and on the Formula line.

3. Press the **Enter key**. The change will be accepted and if the data was a formula, the answer will be recalculated.

Copying Formulas

Now that you've created a formula, there's no reason to type it repeatedly for subsequent cells. Let Excel copy the formula for you! When you copy a formula, the formula changes depending on where you put it. It is said, therefore, to be *relative*—relative to the position of the original formula.

Copying Using the Fill Feature

If you're going to copy a formula to a surrounding cell, you can use the Fill method. You first learned about the Fill command in Chapter 17, "Editing a Worksheet."

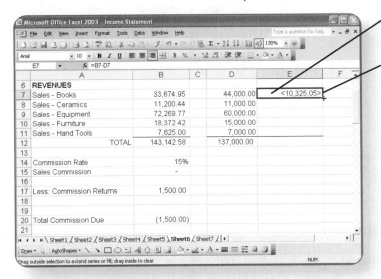

1. **Click** on the **cell** that has the formula. The cell will be selected.

2. **Position** the **mouse pointer** on the lower-right corner of the beginning cell. The mouse pointer will become a black cross.

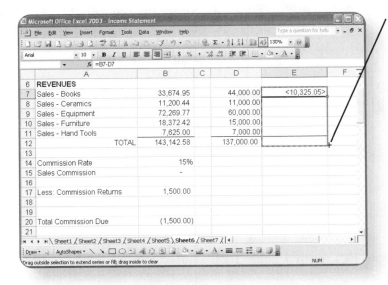

3. **Press and hold** the **mouse button and drag** to select the next cells to be filled in. The cells will be selected.

4. **Release** the **mouse button**. The formula will be copied.

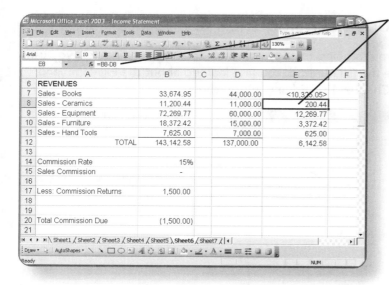

When Excel copies a formula, the references change as the formula is copied. If the original formula was =B7-D7 and you copied it to the next cell down, the formula would read =B8-D8. Then, if you copied it down again it would be =B9-D9, and so on.

Copying with Copy and Paste

If the originating cells and the recipient cells are not sequential, you can use copy and paste. You first learned about copy and paste in Chapter 17, "Editing a Worksheet."

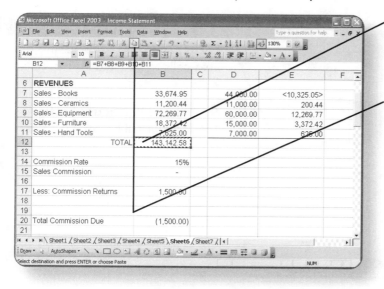

1. Select the **cell** with the formula that you want to duplicate. The cell will be selected.

2. Click on the **Copy button.** Marching ants will appear around the copied cells.

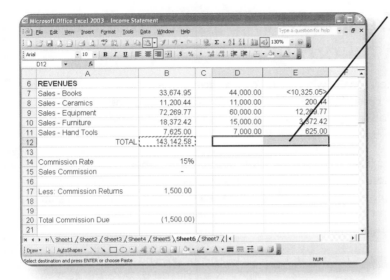

3. Highlight the **cells** in which you want to place the duplicated formula. The cells will be selected.

4. Press the **Enter key**. The formula will be copied to the new location.

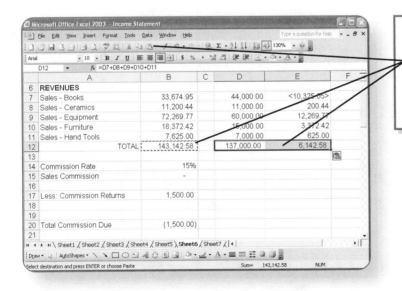

TIP

Optionally, click on the Paste button and then press Esc to cancel the marching ants.

Creating an Absolute Reference in a Formula

Occasionally when you copy a formula, you do not want one of the cell references to change. That's when you need to create an *absolute reference*. To indicate an absolute reference, use the dollar sign ($).

It's called an absolute reference because when you copy it, it absolutely and positively stays that cell reference and never changes. An example of a formula with an absolute reference might be =B22*B24. The reference to cell B24 will not change when copied.

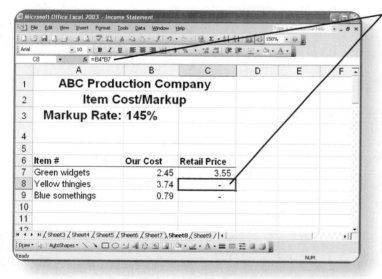

This figure shows a formula that is supposed to take the cost of an item and multiply it to the mark up rate. The result is the retail cost of the item. The first formula is fine, but as you can see, when the formula is copied or filled down, the other products display an erroneous cost. The original formula was B3*B6, where B3 is the mark up percentage rate. When the formula is copied down to the next cell, it becomes B4*B7, and the cell in B4 is not the mark up percentage rate cell.

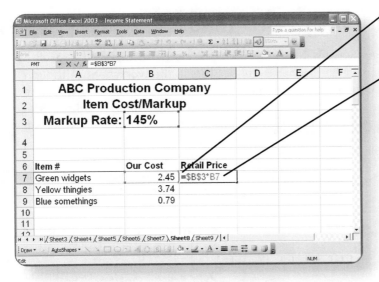

1. Click on the **cell** in which you want to place the formula answer. The cell will be selected.

2. Type the **formula.** If any references are to be an absolute reference, add dollar signs ($) in front of both the column reference and the row reference.

3. Press the **Enter key**. The answer will display in the cell.

NOTE

Compound formulas can also have absolute references.

---

4. Copy the **formula** to the adjacent cells using one of the methods in the preceding section.

Viewing Formulas

As you've already seen, when you create formulas, the result of the formulas is what Excel displays in the worksheet. Although the Edit bar displays the actual formula, you can only view one formula at a time. Excel provides a method to view the formulas in the cells. Having the formulas display is a wonderful tool for proofing and troubleshooting formula errors in your worksheet.

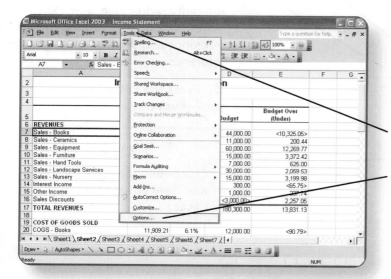

1. Click on **Tools**. The Tools menu will appear.

2. Click on **Options**. The Options dialog box will open.

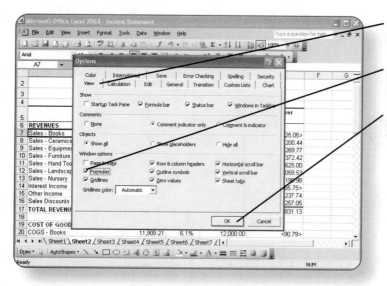

3. Click on the **View tab**. The View tab will come to the front.

4. Click on **Formulas**. A check mark will display in the option.

5. Click on **OK**. The dialog box will close.

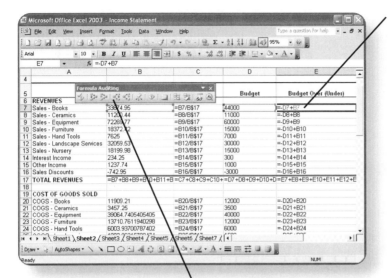

The formulas will be displayed in each cell instead of the formula result. Each cell reference in a formula is assigned a color and a corresponding colored box surrounds the referenced cell.

The Formula Auditing toolbar may appear to assist you in tracing through formulas. You may find the Auditing toolbar handy when resolving worksheet errors. The Formula Auditing toolbar can display tracer arrows, which are arrows that show the relationship between the active cell and its related cells. It traces Dependents, which are cells that contain formulas that refer to other cells, and Precedents, which are cells that are referred to by a formula in another cell.

6. **Repeat steps 1-5** to turn off the formula display.

Understanding Common Formula Error Messages

There are a number of error messages that may appear when you type a formula. Some are typing mistakes and some may be a result of a cell value.

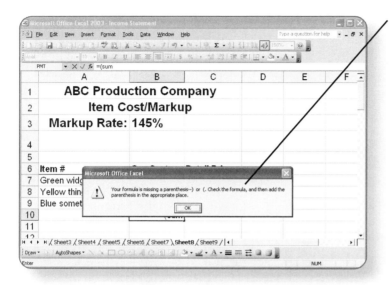

Often when you enter a formula with an error, Excel notifies you of the error and attempts to correct the error for you or offers suggestions on correcting the error.

Other errors may appear in the formula result cell. Following are a few of the more common error messages:

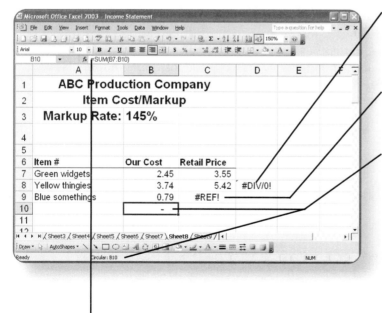

#DIV/0!. This means that the formula is trying to divide by either an empty cell or one with a value of zero.

#REF!. This may mean that the formula includes an invalid cell reference.

Circular. This means that a formula in a cell refers to the same cell. Excel displays a circular reference notation in the status bar. Excel may also display an error box and display a Circular Reference toolbar to assist you in locating the erroneous formula.

In this example, the formula in B10 is trying to add itself to the total, thereby creating the circular reference.

21

Using Excel Functions

While creating a formula provides mathematical calculations, Excel includes a much more powerful feature called functions. Functions are basically a fast way to enter a complex formula. Excel has over 230 different functions you can use, and it groups them together by categories such as mathematical, statistical, logical, or date and time. Using functions can save considerable room in the Formula bar and cuts down on typographical errors that are so easy to make when typing formulas.

In this chapter, you'll learn how to:

- Understand function requirements
- Use the SUM function and AutoSum button
- Work with numerical functions
- Create statistical, date, and logical functions

Understanding Function Syntax

Functions consist of several different parts. Like a formula, a function begins with an equal (=) sign. The next part is the function name, which might be abbreviated to indicate what the function does. Examples of a function name might be SUM, AVERAGE, or COUNT. After the name, you enter a set of parentheses and enter *arguments* within those parentheses. Arguments are additional pieces of information that clarify how you want the function to behave. Arguments can consist of one or more components, ranging from cell addresses such as D13 or a range of cell addresses like D13:D25, to other variables such as a number of digits you want Excel to do something to. With only a few exceptions, all functions in Excel must follow that pattern. This function structure is called the *syntax*. Here are a few examples of function syntax. You'll learn throughout this chapter what these functions do.

> **NOTE**
> Function names are not case sensitive.

- =SUM(B3:B21)

- =AVERAGE(F1:G6)

- =IF(B3>B4,"yes", "no")

Creating a Total with the SUM Function

The most commonly used function in Excel is the SUM function, which adds two or more values together and displays the total in the current cell. If any of the values change, the SUM total will automatically update. There are a number of different methods to enter the SUM function, but the following section describes two of the most common ways. The syntax for the SUM function is =SUM(*range of values to total*).

Entering a SUM Function

One way to enter a SUM function is to type the function in its syntax directly into a cell where you want the answer. Like other formulas, Excel will display the answer in the current cell, but display the actual function in the Formula bar.

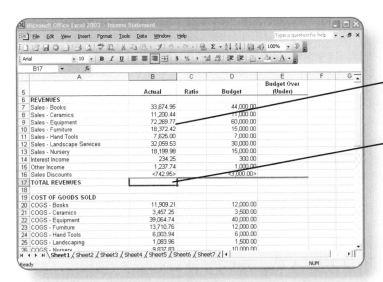

1. **Enter** some **values** in two or more cells. The values display in the cells.

2. **Click** in the **cell** where you want the total of the values to display. The cell will be selected.

3. **Type** an **equal sign (=)**. The blinking insertion point will appear after the equal sign. (Do not press the Enter key until the function is complete.)

4. **Type** the word **SUM**. The word SUM will appear after the equal sign.

5. **Type** an **opening parenthesis**. The (character will appear after the function name.

The arguments for a SUM function require that you enter the cell addresses you want to add. You can enter the cell addresses using the keyboard or the mouse. The next two sections will show you both methods.

Entering an Argument with the Keyboard

When you enter function arguments with the keyboard, you type the cell addresses you want to add. If the cell addresses are adjacent to each other, you separate them with a colon (:). For example, typing B2:B5 will add the values in B2 plus B3 plus B4 plus B5. If the cell addresses you want to add are not adjacent, you separate them with a comma. For example, B2, B5, B13 will add the values in cells B2 and B5 and B13 but not the value of any cells in between. You can also combine adjacent and non-adjacent cells, such as B2, B5, B13:B15 which would add the values in the cells B2 and B5 and B13, B14, and B15.

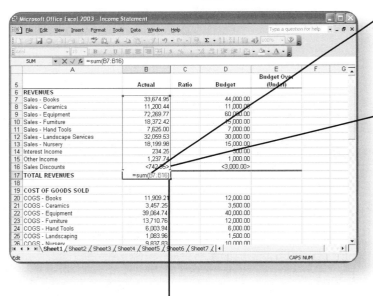

1. After you type the opening parenthesis, **type** the **cell addresses** you want to add together, using the colon or comma to separate the addresses.

As you type the cell addresses, Excel puts a border around the cells so you can quickly see if you typed the correct cell address.

NOTE

When typing a cell address, the address is not case-sensitive, but you must remember to type the column letter first, followed by the row number.

2. **Type** a **closing parenthesis**. A) character will appear after the cell addresses.

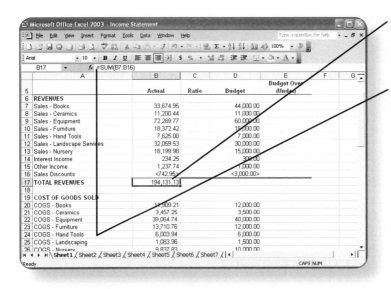

3. Press the **Enter key**. The resulting value will appear in the cell.

The Formula bar still reflects the function and its options.

Entering an Argument with the Mouse

Instead of typing cell addresses, you can use your mouse to highlight the desired cells. Highlighting the cells instead of typing them makes it easier to see that you have selected the correct cells.

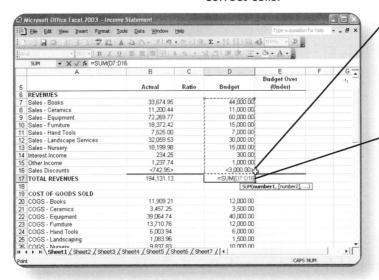

1. After you type the opening parenthesis, **click and drag** the **mouse** around the cells you want to add. A marquee of marching ants will appear around the selected cells.

The cell addresses appear in the function cell.

TIP

If you have a non-adjacent range to select, separate them with a comma so Excel will let you continue to the next selection.

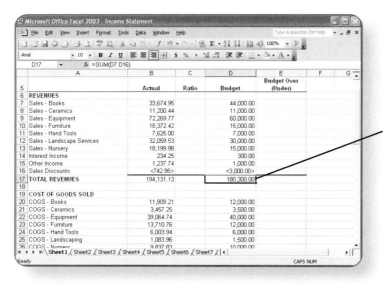

2. Type a **closing parenthesis**. A) character will appear after the cell addresses, and the selected cells will have a temporary border surrounding them.

3. Press the **Enter key**. The resulting value will appear in the cell.

Using the AutoSum Button

Since the SUM function is the function used most, Microsoft includes a button for it on the standard Excel toolbar. This makes creating a simple addition formula a mouse click away!

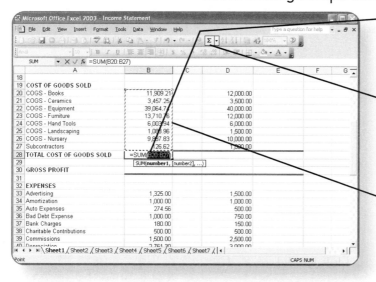

1. Click on the **cell** below or to the right of the values you want to total. The cell will be selected.

2. Click on the **AutoSum button**. The cells to be totaled are highlighted.

NOTE

Excel will suggest the values above it first. If no values are directly above the current cell, Excel will look for values in the cells to the left.

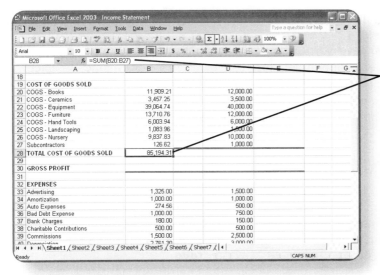

If you want to total different cells than Excel has highlighted, select them with your mouse.

3. Click the **AutoSum button** again **or press** the **Enter key**. Excel will enter the total value of the selected cells.

Using Other Functions

As mentioned at the beginning of this chapter, Excel includes over 230 different built-in functions that are divided into categories according to the function's purpose. The SUM function, for example, is considered a mathematical function.

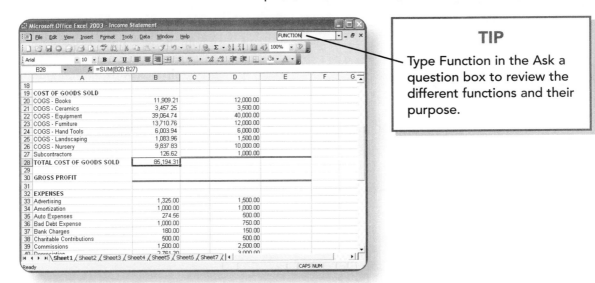

TIP

Type Function in the Ask a question box to review the different functions and their purpose.

Calculating with Mathematical Functions

You have learned how to create a mathematical function to add a series of numbers together by using the SUM function. Excel includes many other mathematical functions, including some for complex trigonometry calculations. The next section illustrates a couple of other commonly used mathematical functions.

Using the INT Function

The INT function rounds a number down to the nearest integer. The number can be a specific number you type or, more commonly, the reference to a specific cell. The syntax is =INT(*cell address or number*). For example, to find the integer of cell B3, you would enter =INT(B3).

TIP

Functions can be nested. For example, to find the integer of the SUM of a range of cells, you might type =INT(=SUM(B3:B10)). Excel will add each cell and round down the total.

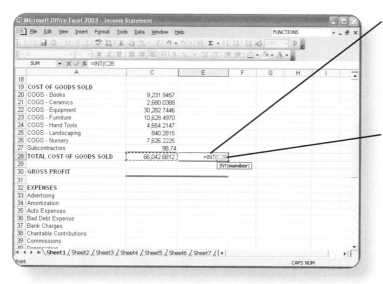

1. Type **=INT(** in the cell you want to place the integer. Excel will immediately identify the entry as a function and will display a tip box with the function syntax.

2. Type or click on the **cell** you want to reference. The referenced cell will have a border surrounding it.

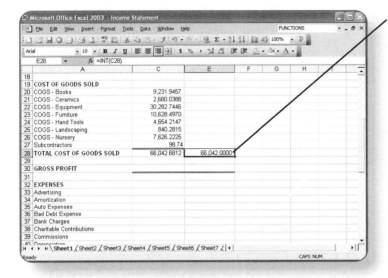

3. Type a **closing parenthesis**. The symbol will display in the cell.

4. Press the **Enter key**. The integer value of the referenced cell will display. The result will contain the same number of decimal points as the referenced cell.

Using the ROUND Function

Whereas the INT function displays whole numbers for you, the ROUND function takes a value and rounds it to a specified number of digits. The ROUND function contains two different arguments; one to specify which cell you want to round and the second to tell Excel how many decimal places you want to display. The syntax is =ROUND(*number,num of digits*). For example, if cell B10 has a value of 79.3264 and you want it rounded to two decimal places, you would enter =ROUND(B10,2); then Excel would display the answer of 79.3300.

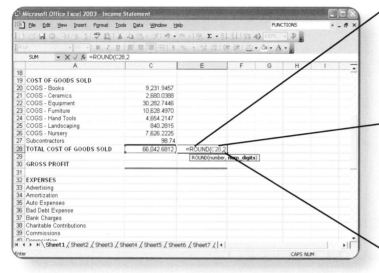

1. **Type =ROUND(** in the cell you want to place the integer. Excel will immediately identify the entry as a function and display a tip box with the function syntax.

2. **Type or click** on the **cell** you want to reference. The referenced cell will have a border surrounding it.

3. **Type** a **comma**. The comma divides the arguments.

4. **Type** the number of **decimal places** you want in the result. You can enter from 0 to 15 as the number of decimal places.

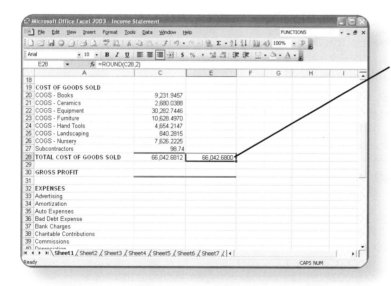

5. **Type** a **closing parenthesis**. The symbol will display in the cell.

6. **Press** the **Enter key**. The rounded value of the referenced cell will display.

Analyzing with Statistical Functions

Statistical-based functions provide a means for analysis of data. Statistical analysis helps you explore, understand and visualize your data.

Using the AVERAGE Function

The AVERAGE function finds an average of a range of values. The syntax for this function is =AVERAGE(*range of values to average).* An example might be =AVERAGE(B7:D7), which would add the values in the three cells B7, C7, and D7, then divide that total by three to get the average value.

1. Type =AVERAGE(in the cell you want to place the averaged result. Excel will immediately identify the entry as a function and display a tip box with the function syntax.

2. Type or highlight the **cells** you want to add together and average. A colored border will appear around the selected cells.

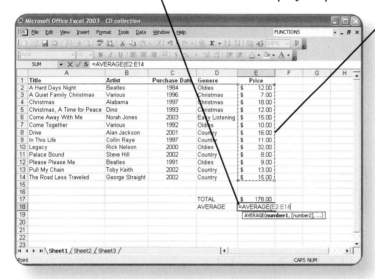

3. Type a **closing parenthesis**. The symbol will display in the cell.

4. Press the **Enter key**. Excel will add the referenced cells and display an average of those numbers.

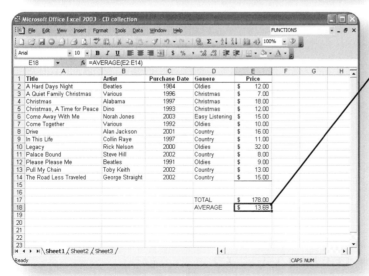

Using the MAX and MIN Functions

Two other common statistical functions are the MAX and MIN functions. The MAX function will display the largest value in a range of cells, whereas the MIN function will display the smallest value in a range of cells. The syntax is =MAX(*range of values*) or =MIN(*range of values*).

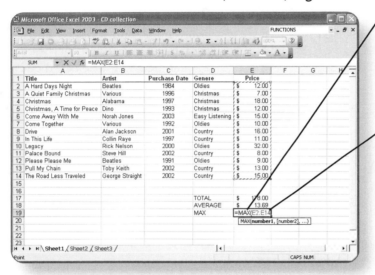

1. Type =MAX(or **=MIN(** in the cell where you want the result to be displayed. Excel will immediately identify the entry as a function and display a tip box with the function syntax.

2. Type or highlight the **cells** you want to analyze. A colored border will appear around the selected cells.

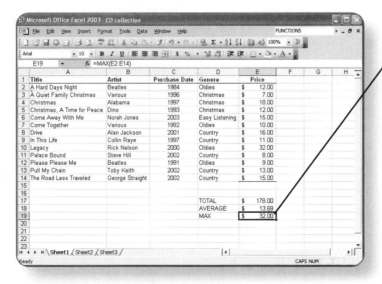

3. Type a **closing parenthesis**. The symbol will display in the cell.

4. Press the **Enter key**. If you typed =MAX in step 1, the largest number in the referenced area will display.

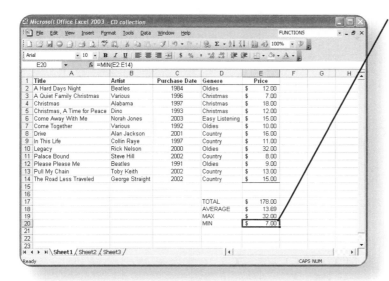

If you typed =MIN in step 1, the smallest number in the referenced area will display.

Using the COUNT and COUNTA Functions

The COUNT function is handy to find out how many numerical entries are in a specified area. The COUNTA function is similar except it is not limited to numerical entries; it will count any non-blank cell, no matter what type of information the cell contains. The syntax of these functions is very similar: =COUNT(*range of cells to count*) and =COUNTA(*range of cells to count*).

1. Type =COUNT(or **=COUNTA(** in the cell where you want the result to be displayed. Excel will immediately identify the entry as a function and display a tip box with the function syntax.

2. Type or highlight the **cells** you want to count. A colored border will appear around the selected cells.

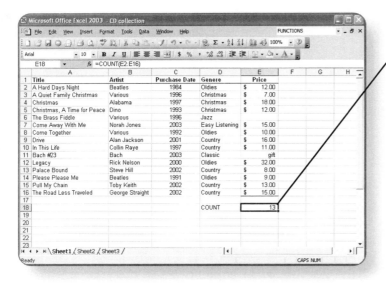

3. Type a **closing parenthesis**. The symbol will display in the cell.

4. Press the **Enter key**. If you typed =COUNT in step 1, the number of cells containing numerical entries in the referenced area will display.

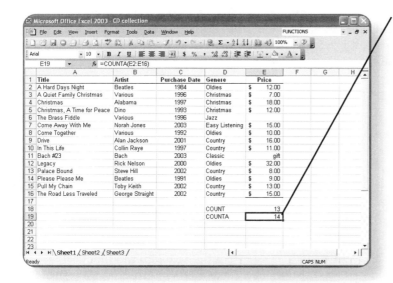

If you typed =COUNTA in step 1, Excel will count all the non-blank entries in the referenced area.

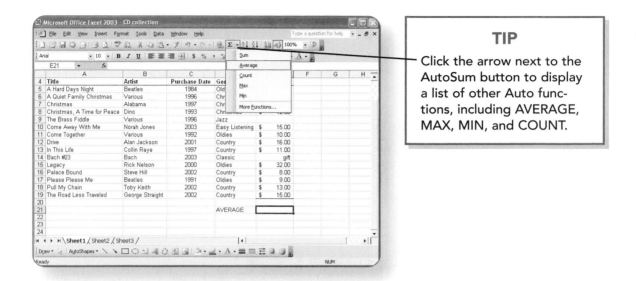

TIP

Click the arrow next to the AutoSum button to display a list of other Auto functions, including AVERAGE, MAX, MIN, and COUNT.

Using Date Functions

Date functions are commonly used to enter the current date into a worksheet, or to calculate the difference between two or more dates. Excel stores dates as sequential serial numbers so they can be used in calculations. By default, January 1, 1900 is serial number 1, and September 16, 2003 is serial number 37880, because it is 37,880 days after January 1, 1900. When you type a date in Excel, it will display the date in a regular date format, such as 9/16/2003, but behind the scenes Excel still considers that date a serial number.

Because dates and times are values, they can be added, subtracted, and included in other calculations.

Using the NOW Function

If you enter the NOW function in a cell, Excel will display the current date and time. The date and time are dynamic in that the current date and time will change whenever you recalculate anything in the worksheet. By default, Excel recalculates the worksheet whenever any changes, additions, or deletions are made. The NOW function does not contain any arguments, so the syntax is =NOW().

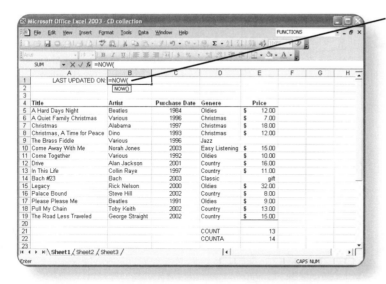

1. Type =NOW(in the cell where you want the current date and time to display. Excel will immediately identify the entry as a function and display a tip box with the function syntax.

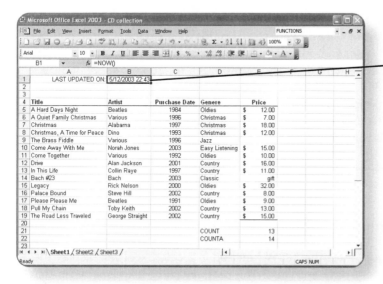

2. Type a **closing parenthesis**. The symbol will display in the cell.

3. Press the **Enter key**. The cell will display the current date and time.

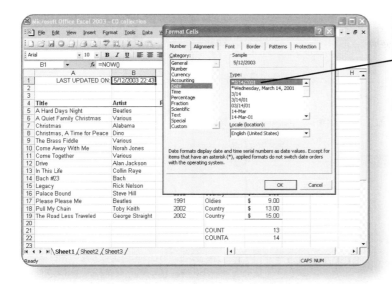

TIP

You can change the date and time display through the Format Cells dialog box.

Finding the Difference between Two Dates

A very popular use for entering dates in an Excel worksheet is to find the number of days between two dates. Since Excel stores dates as serial numbers, you can create a simple mathematical function to figure the number of days between two dates. While this is more of a formula instead of an Excel function, the mathematical calculation can include a cell with a date function, such as =NOW.

1. **Enter** a **date** in a cell. Excel will display the date you entered. In the example you see here, the current date was entered in cell A1 with the =NOW function.

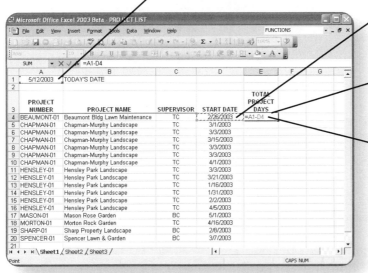

2. **Enter** another **date** in a different cell. Excel will display the date you entered.

3. **Click** in the **cell** where you want the difference stored. The cell will be selected.

4. **Enter** a **formula** to subtract the older date from the newer date.

The example you see here is a formula to subtract the project start date from today's date, so the formula is A1-D4.

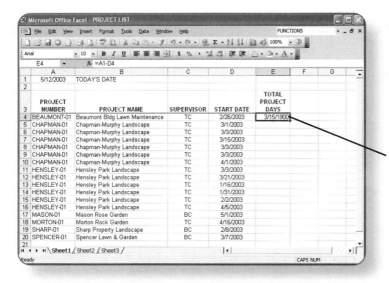

NOTE

You cannot subtract a date that is later than another date, or the error #### appears in the cell.

5. Press the **Enter key**. Excel will calculate the difference.

Since both of the original dates are in a date format, Excel will display the difference in a date format. You will need to tell Excel to display that value as a number.

6. Click on the **Comma style button**. The value is displayed in numeric format with two decimal points. The decimal points represent the portion of the day.

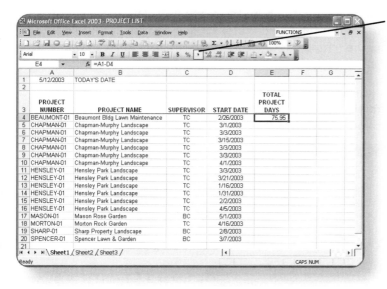

TIP

Unfortunately, there is no *easy* method to calculate the exact difference in years. While you can change the mathematical formula to divide the total by 365, this calculation does not take into account leap years. It will, however, give a pretty close calculation of years.

Figuring with Financial Functions

Financial functions perform elaborate calculations such as returns on investments or cumulative principal or interest on loans. Functions exist to calculate future values or net present values on investments or to calculate amortization.

Using the PMT Function

The PMT function calculates the payment for a loan based on a constant interest rate. You will need to enter the interest rate, the number of payments, and the amount of the loan. The syntax is =PMT(*rate,nper,pv,fv,type*) where *rate* is the interest rate, *nper* is the number of payments and *pv* is the loan amount. There are two other optional arguments, including *fv*, (future value),which Excel assumes to be zero unless you enter an *fv*. The other optional argument is for *type*, which refers to when the payment is due.

TIP

Be uniform about the units you use for specifying *rate* and *nper*. If you make monthly payments on a six-year loan at an annual interest rate of 8 percent, use 8%/12 for *rate* and 6*12 for *nper*. If you make annual payments on the same loan, use 8 percent for *rate* and 6 for *nper*.

---

1. Enter a **loan amount** in a worksheet cell. The value will appear in the cell.

2. Enter an **interest rate** in a worksheet cell. The value will appear in the cell.

3. Enter the **number of payments** you intend to make. The value will appear in a cell.

4. Type **=PMT(** in the cell where you want to display the payment amount. Excel will immediately identify the entry as a function and display a tip box with the function syntax.

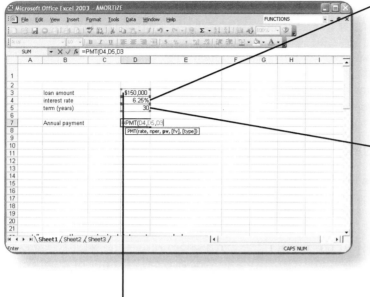

5. **Click on or type** the **cell address** you entered in step 2, which is the interest rate. The referenced cell will have a border around it.

6. **Type** a **comma**. Excel uses a comma to separate arguments

7. **Click on or type** the **cell address** you entered in step 3, which is the number of payments. The referenced cell will have a border around it.

8. **Type** another **comma**. The comma will precede the next argument.

9. **Click on or type** the **cell address** you entered in step 1, which is the value of the loan. The referenced cell will have a border around it.

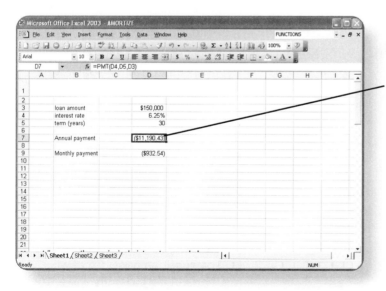

10. **Type** the **closing parenthesis**. The symbol will display in the cell.

11. **Press** the **Enter key**. Excel will calculate and display the payment amount.

NOTE

The payment amount returned by PMT includes principal and interest only

Understanding Logical Functions

You have seen that most functions work in basically the same way. You enter the equal sign, enter the function name, and then tell the function which data to use. Most functions involve some sort of mathematical calculation. Logical functions are different in that they use operators such as equal to (=), greater than (>), less than (<), greater than or equal to (>=), less than or equal to (<=), and not equal to (<>).

Using the IF Function

The IF function is a logical function that evaluates a condition and returns one of two answers, depending on the result of the evaluation. The IF function has three parts. The first part determines if a situation is true or false; the second part determines the result to display if the first part is true; and the third part determines the result to display if the first part is false. It's really not as confusing as it may sound. The syntax is =IF(*item to test, value if true, value if false*).

For example, in cell C1 you want to find out if the value in cell B5 is greater than the value in cell B6. If B5 *is* larger than B6 (true), you want to enter "Yes" in cell C1; if B5 is not larger than B6 (false), you want the answer "No" in cell C1. You would enter the function as =IF(B5>B6,"Yes","No").

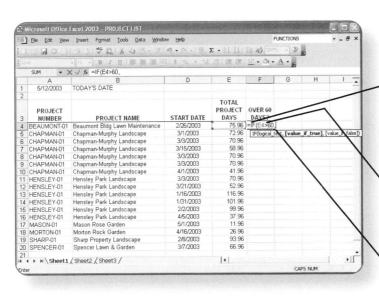

1. Type =IF(in the cell in which you want to display the answer. Excel will immediately identify the entry as a function and display a tip box with the function syntax.

2. Type the **first argument** including an operator. This is the condition you want Excel to evaluate.

3. Type a **comma**. This will begin the second argument.

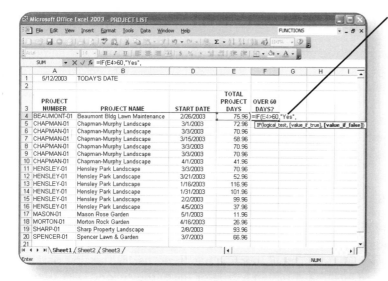

4. Type the **result** you want if the evaluation is true. The true result can be a value, a calculation, or text.

5. Type a **comma**. This will begin the third argument.

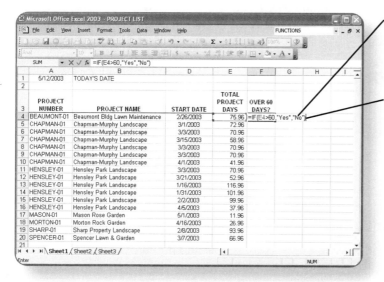

6. Type the **result** you want if the evaluation is false. The false result can also be a value, a calculation, or text.

7. Type the **closing parenthesis**. The symbol will display in the cell.

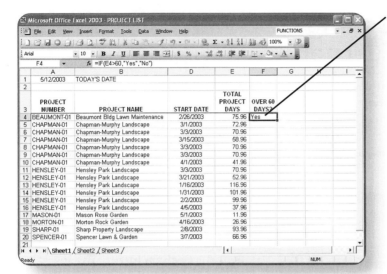

8. Press the **Enter key**. Excel will calculate and display the evaluation result.

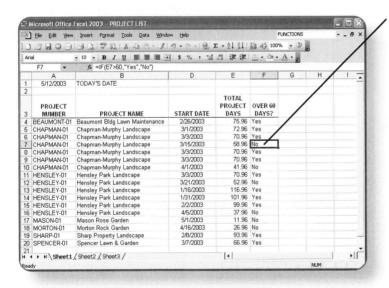

In this example, the IF function checks if the total job days is greater than 60 days. If it is, Yes is displayed; if not, No is displayed.

Getting Help with Excel Functions

With each Excel function having a different syntax, it becomes almost impossible to remember the syntax of each function. You've already seen that when you begin typing the function and the open parenthesis, Excel displays a tooltip to help you, but you can get even more help with functions by using the Insert Function dialog box.

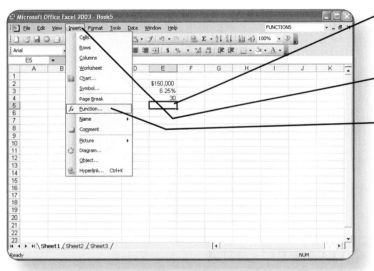

1. **Click** in the **cell** where you want to enter a function. The cell will be selected.

2. **Click** on **Insert**. The Insert menu will appear.

3. **Click** on **Function**. The Insert Function dialog box will open.

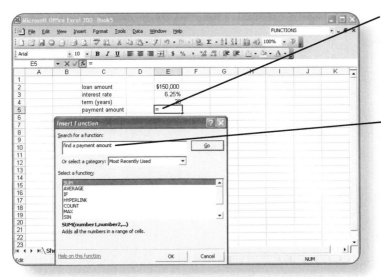

Excel will automatically insert the equal (=) sign in your selected cell.

TIP

If you don't know the name of the function you want, type a description of what you want to do, then click Go. Excel will display a list of possible functions to meet your needs.

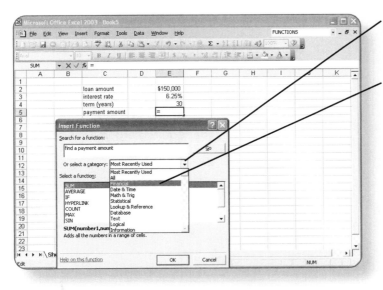

4. **Click** on the **Or select a category down arrow**. A list of function categories will appear.

5. **Click** on the **function category** you want to use. A list of available functions under that category will appear in the Select a function list.

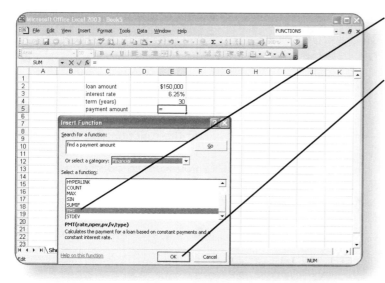

6. **Click** on a **function**. The function syntax and a description of the function will display.

7. **Click** on **OK**. The Function Arguments dialog box will open.

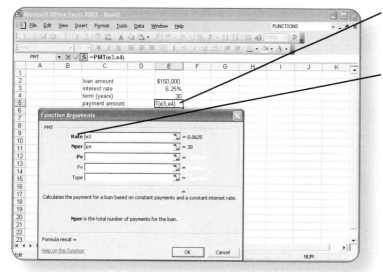

Excel will insert the Function name and the parentheses in the selected cell.

Some function arguments are optional. In the Function Arguments dialog box, Excel lists the required arguments in bold.

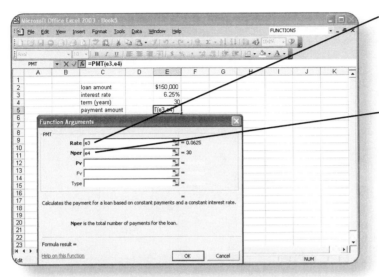

8. **Type** the **cell address, actual value, or click on the cell** that contains the argument. The argument box will contain the cell reference or value.

9. **Click** in the **next argument and repeat** step 8. The argument box will contain the cell reference or value.

As you click in each argument, a description will appear.

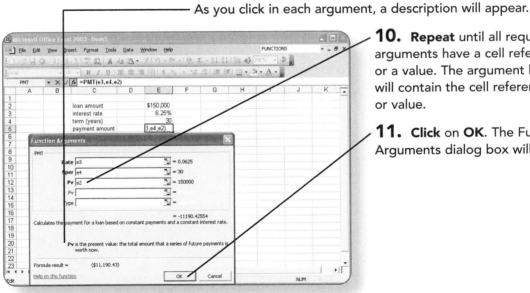

10. **Repeat** until all required arguments have a cell reference or a value. The argument box will contain the cell reference or value.

11. **Click** on **OK**. The Function Arguments dialog box will close.

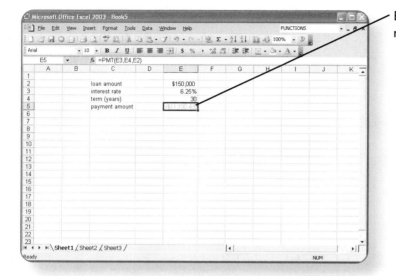

Excel will display the function result in the selected cell.

22

Working with Larger Workbooks

A single Excel file can have multiple worksheets—up to 256—in a single file. And since each worksheet has 256 columns and 65,536 rows, that's a potential for 4,294,967,296 cells of information in a single Excel file! Technically, Excel calls files with multiple sheets *workbooks*.

In this chapter, you'll learn how to:

- ⬤ Move between worksheets
- ⬤ Insert and name a worksheet
- ⬤ Hide a worksheet
- ⬤ Delete a worksheet
- ⬤ Create a reference to another worksheet
- ⬤ Link to other workbooks

Moving from Worksheet to Worksheet

By default, a new blank worksheet includes three worksheets named Sheet1, Sheet2, and Sheet3. You can move from worksheet to worksheet using the mouse or the keyboard.

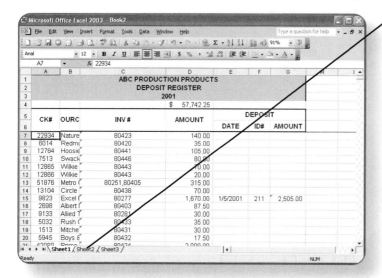

1. **Click** on the desired **worksheet tab**. That worksheet will come into view.

TIP

If you cannot see the tab for the desired worksheet, click on the sheet navigation arrows to move other sheets into view.

You also can use the keyboard to move from worksheet to worksheet.

2. **Press** either **Ctrl + Page Up** or **Ctrl + Page Down**. The cell pointer will move to the preceding or next sheet.

Inserting Worksheets

If you need extra worksheets in your workbook, you can easily add them through the Insert menu. Whenever you save your Excel file, all worksheets in the workbook are saved.

1. **Click** on **Insert**. The Insert menu will open.

2. **Click** on **Worksheet**. Excel will insert another worksheet.

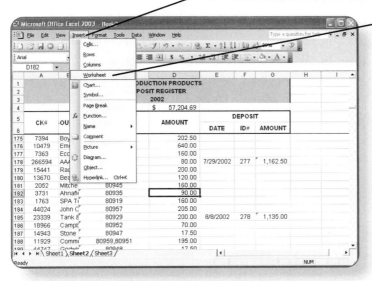

The new sheet is named with the next sequential number, such as Sheet4.

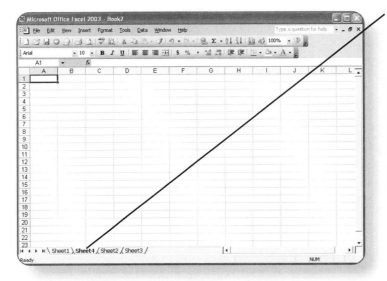

TIP

You can rearrange the order of the tabs on the screen by dragging the tab to the desired position.

Naming Worksheets

Since Excel uses the rather generic name scheme of Sheet1 or Sheet2, you can more easily identify the type of data each worksheet contains if you give the worksheets more descriptive names. Names for sheets can be up to 31 characters long and are not case sensitive; however, a worksheet name cannot be left blank and cannot include a few special characters— namely * / \ ? : [ ]

1. Double-click on the **tab** of the sheet you want to rename. The sheet name will become highlighted and a blinking insertion point will appear.

2. Type a new **name** for the sheet. The name you type will replace the default Excel name.

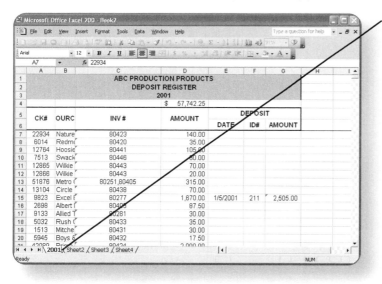

> ### TIP
> Optionally, right-click on a worksheet tab and select Rename.

3. Press the **Enter** key. The worksheet will be renamed.

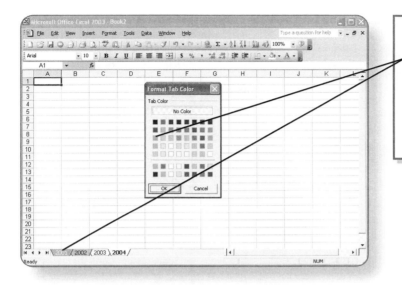

TIP

Color-code sheet tabs for easier identification by clicking on the sheet you want to color code and clicking Format, Sheet, then Tab Color.

Hiding a Worksheet

A worksheet can be hidden from view but still contain active working formulas and data.

1. Click anywhere on the **worksheet** you want to hide.

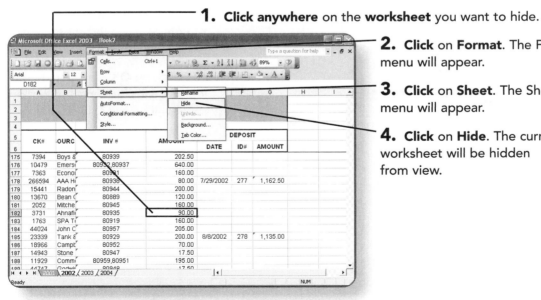

2. Click on **Format**. The Format menu will appear.

3. Click on **Sheet**. The Sheet menu will appear.

4. Click on **Hide**. The current worksheet will be hidden from view.

Notice in this example, the sheet named 2002 is not visible.

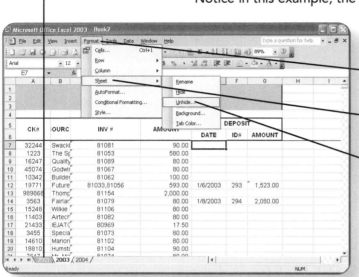

You can just as easily redisplay any hidden worksheets.

5. Click on **Format**. The Format menu will appear.

6. Click on **Sheet**. The Sheet menu will appear

7. Click on **Unhide**. The Unhide dialog box will appear showing a list of all hidden worksheets.

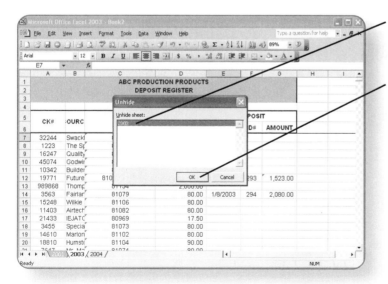

8. Click on the **sheet you want to unhide**. The worksheet name will be highlighted.

9. Click on **OK**. The Unhide dialog box will close and the worksheet will be redisplayed.

Deleting Worksheets

If you have created a worksheet in an Excel file that you no longer need, you can delete it. Deleting unnecessary worksheets can save on file size and make the file quicker to open and close.

1. **Click anywhere** on the **worksheet** you want to delete.

2. **Click** on **Edit**. The Edit menu will appear.

3. **Click** on **Delete Sheet**. If there is data anywhere on the sheet, a confirmation box will appear. If there is no data on the sheet, the current sheet will be deleted and no confirmation box will appear.

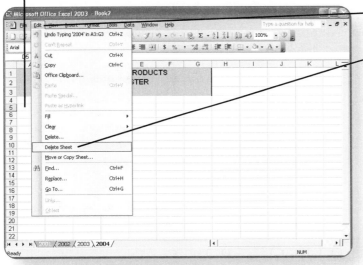

4. **Click** on **Delete**. The current worksheet will be deleted.

CAUTION

Use extreme caution here! When you choose to delete a sheet, the sheet is deleted permanently. You will not be able to undo the deletion.

Creating a Reference to Another Worksheet

Sometimes you need to refer to information stored in another worksheet. For example, if you have a workbook with sheets for each month's sales information, along with a worksheet that totals the monthly worksheets, you can create a reference in the Totals worksheet that instructs Excel to reference the data in the various monthly worksheets. When you create a reference to a different sheet, Excel will use the name of the sheet first, then the cell location.

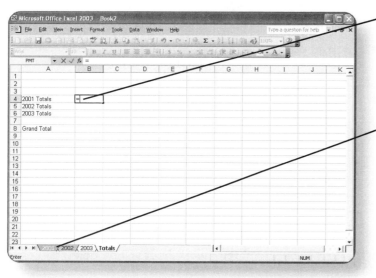

1. Type the **equal sign** in the cell where you want the cross reference (the destination cell). This will instruct Excel to take the value of whatever you type or click on next.

2. Click on the **worksheet tab** that contains the cell you want to reference.

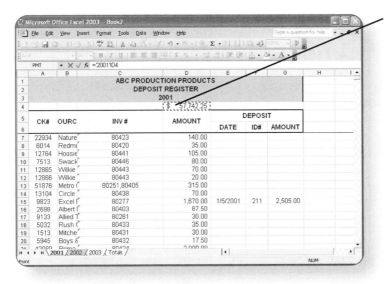

3. Click on the **cell** you want to reference. A marquee will surround the selected cell.

4. Press the **Enter key**. The reference is complete.

Excel will return you to the original worksheet with the value displayed.

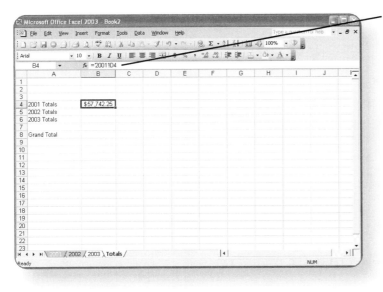

The answer is displayed in the worksheet, but on the Edit line, the originating cell location is displayed. The linked reference is the sheet name followed by an exclamation point and the cell location.

If the value in the originating cell changes, the value in the cross reference cell will also change.

Creating Links to Other Workbooks

Similar to creating a link to a different worksheet in the current workbook, you can also create links to specific locations in other workbooks. The easiest method to create a workbook link is to have both the origination and the destination workbooks open.

1. Type the **equal sign** in the cell where you want the cross reference (the destination cell). This will instruct Excel to take the value of whatever you type or click on next.

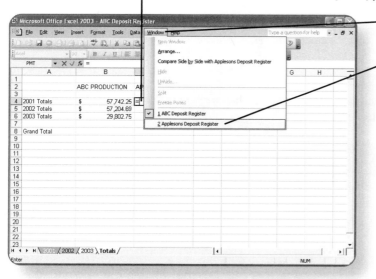

2. Click on the **Window menu**. The Window menu will appear.

3. Click on the **file** that contains the data you want to reference. Excel will switch to the selected file.

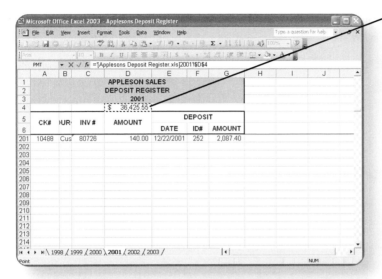

4. Click on the **cell** you want to reference. A marquee will surround the selected cell.

5. Press the **Enter key**. The reference is complete.

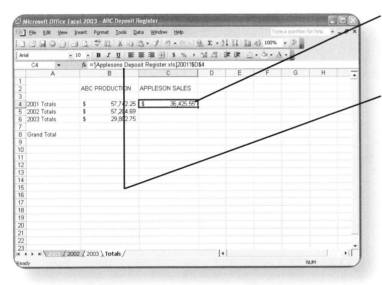

Excel will return you to the destination worksheet with the cross-referenced value displayed.

Excel will display the result in the worksheet, but on the Edit line, the originating cell location is displayed. The linked reference is the data path, the Excel file name (in brackets), then the sheet name, an exclamation point, and the cell location.

When you reopen the current workbook, Excel will prompt you whether to check for changes in the linked workbook.

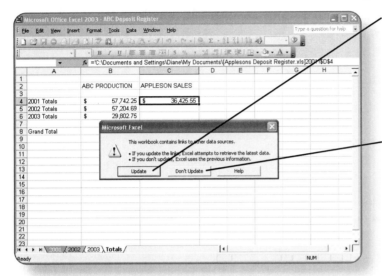

6a. **Click** on **Update**. Excel will check the linked workbook for changes in the cross-referenced cell, and if needed, update the current workbook.

OR

6b. **Click** on **Don't update**. Excel will display the data that was in the cell the last time the workbook was saved.

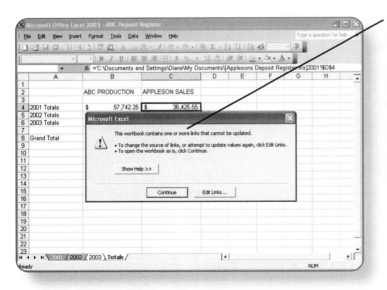

If, when updating links, the originating workbook was renamed, deleted, or moved, an information dialog box will appear notifying you it could not update the link. You have the option of continuing, leaving the data as it was last saved, or clicking an Edit Links button to change the link references.

23

Managing Larger Worksheets

Because workbooks can get very large, it sometimes becomes difficult to maneuver around the workbook efficiently. You may find yourself bouncing from one part of the worksheet to another. Excel contains several tools to aid navigation and viewing of worksheets.

In this chapter, you'll learn how to:

- Hide and display parts of a worksheet
- Split a window
- Freeze window panes
- Zoom in and out of a worksheet
- Work with ranges
- Use the Find and Replace feature

Modifying Worksheet Views

When working with a larger worksheet, it can become difficult to see the entire worksheet on the screen. As you scroll down or across the worksheet, you may lose track of which column or row of data you are entering. Excel contains several tools to help you view your worksheet from different perspectives.

Hiding Rows and Columns

If you have rows or columns you don't really need to see, or that you don't want to print, you can hide them from view. Hiding them doesn't delete them or make their data inaccessible; it only keeps them out of view. When you hide rows or columns, Excel is actually changing the row height or column width to zero.

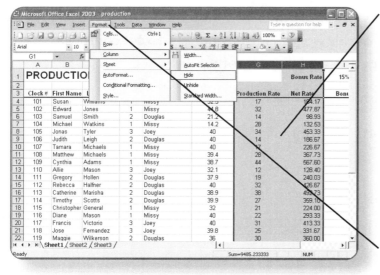

1. **Select** the **columns or rows** you want to hide. The columns or rows will be highlighted.

NOTE

You can hide multiple columns at one time or multiple rows at one time, but do not try to hide both columns and rows in a single step.

2. **Click** on **Format**. The Format menu will appear.

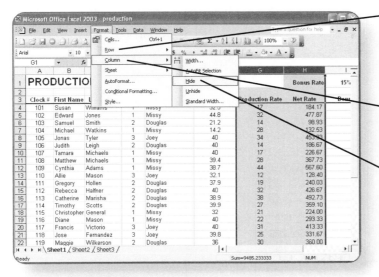

3a. **Click** on **Row** if you want to hide rows. The Row menu will appear.

OR

3b. **Click** on **Column** if you want to hide columns. The Column menu will appear.

4. **Click** on **Hide**. The selected columns or rows will be hidden from view.

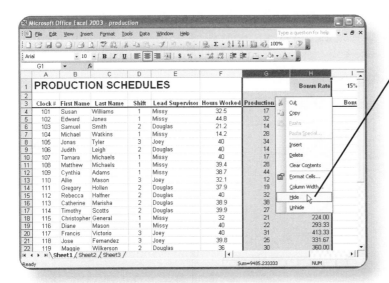

TIP

Optionally, right-click over a selected column or row and choose Hide.

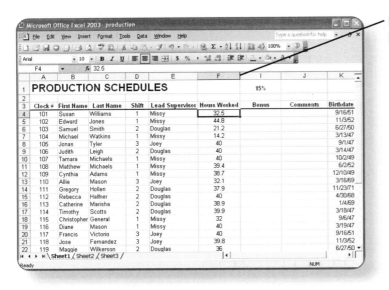

In this example, columns G and H are hidden.

If you need to see the hidden rows or columns, you can easily make them redisplay in the worksheet.

5. Select the **rows or columns** on both sides of the hidden rows or columns. The rows or columns will be highlighted.

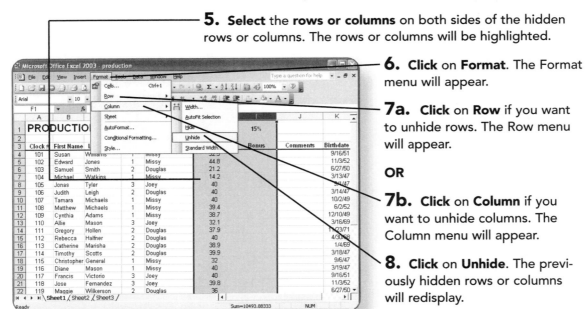

6. Click on **Format**. The Format menu will appear.

7a. Click on **Row** if you want to unhide rows. The Row menu will appear.

OR

7b. Click on **Column** if you want to unhide columns. The Column menu will appear.

8. Click on **Unhide**. The previously hidden rows or columns will redisplay.

TIP

Optionally, right-click over a selected column or row and choose Unhide.

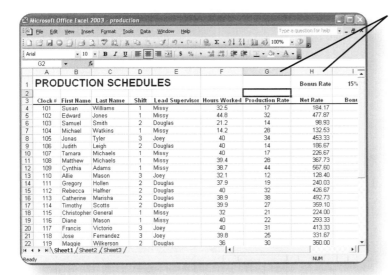

In this example, columns G and H are redisplayed.

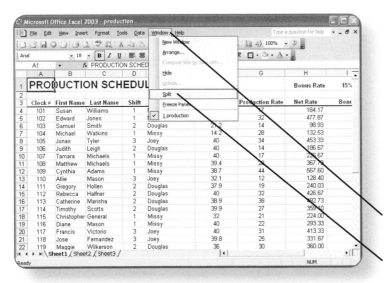

Splitting a Window

Sometimes you need to see two or more different sections of your worksheet at the same time, but your worksheet is too large to view both sections. Excel includes a feature which allows you to split a window into four sections which you can move independently of each other.

1. Click on **Window**. The Window menu will appear.

2. Click on **Split**. Split bars will appear on the worksheet.

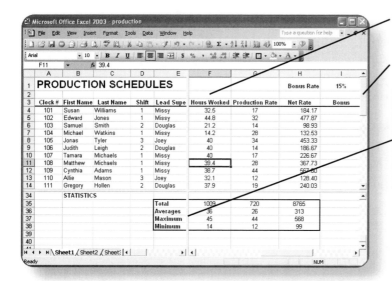

The current worksheet will be divided into four panes.

Each section has its own scroll bar.

TIP

Click and drag the split bars until the panes are the size you want.

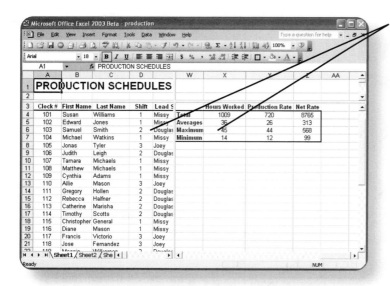

3. Scroll through the different **panes** until you see the sections of the worksheet you want to compare.

When you are finished working in the split view, you can easily return the worksheet to a single panel.

4. **Click** on **Window**. The Window menu will appear.

5. **Click** on **Remove Split**. The split bars will disappear.

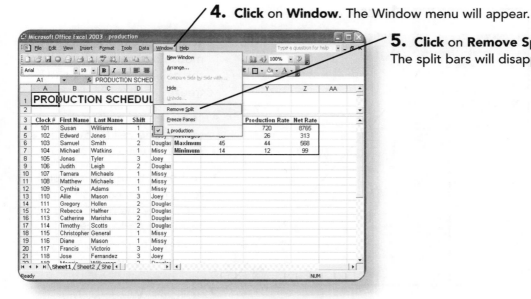

Freezing Panes

When working with a long or wide list, as you add more data, you might lose track of which column or row you are entering data into. It would be helpful if you could see which column or row label you are working with. You can freeze the column headings and row labels so they remain visible no matter where you are working in your worksheet.

1. Click on the desired **cell**:

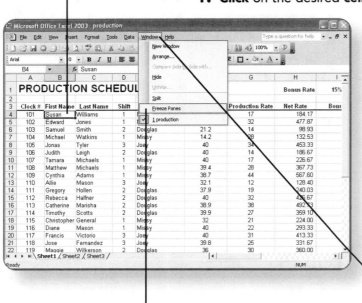

- To freeze columns, click the mouse one cell to the right of the columns you want to freeze.

- To freeze rows, click the mouse one cell below the rows you want to freeze.

- To freeze both columns and rows, click the mouse in the cell below the rows, hold down the Ctrl key, and click to the right of the columns you want to freeze.

2. Click on **Window**. The Window menu will appear.

3. Click on **Freeze Panes**. A black line will appear below the column labels and to the right of the row labels.

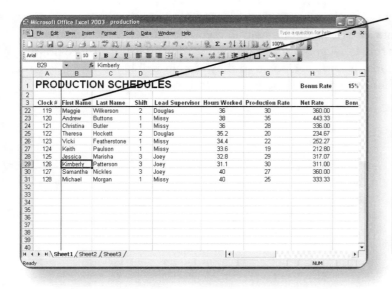

As you scroll through your worksheet, the column and row headings will remain visible.

NOTE

Typically, when you press the Home key, Excel takes you to cell A1, but when you have the Freeze Panes feature active, Excel will take you to the cell just below and to the left of the frozen headings.

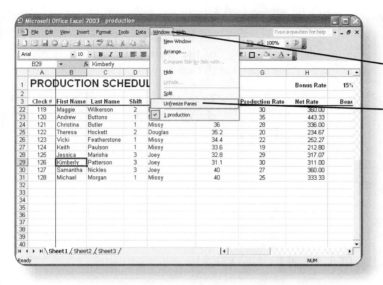

You can easily remove the freeze from row and column headings.

4. Click on **Window**. The Window menu will appear.

5. Click on **Unfreeze Panes**. The black divider lines will disappear and the heading columns and rows will scroll with the rest of the worksheet.

Using Zoom

The Zoom feature enlarges or shrinks the display of your worksheet to allow you to see more or less of it. Excel can zoom your worksheet in percentages, with the normal display of your worksheet being 100%. Zooming in or out does not affect printing.

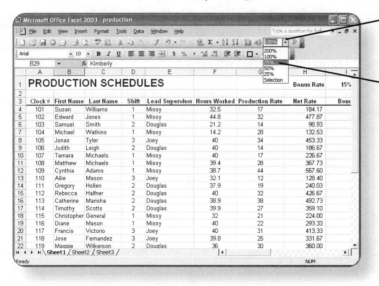

1. Click on the **Zoom button down arrow**. A list of magnifications will display.

2. Click on a magnification **percentage**. The higher the number, the larger the cells will appear on your screen and less of your worksheet will be visible.

TIP
Optionally, type your own magnification percentage.

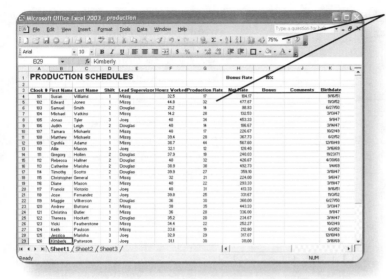

In this example, the zoom was set to 75% which allowed more of the worksheet to display on the screen.

To reset the display to normal, change the zoom to 100%.

Working with Ranges

A *range name* is basically a descriptive name for an area of the worksheet. Range names are much easier to remember than actual cell addresses. You can use range names in formulas or commands such as Go To.

Creating Range Names

Giving cells recognizable range names makes locating data easier. It also can help make formulas more logical and easier to understand.

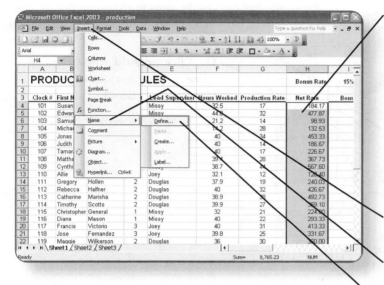

1. Select the **cells** you want to name. The cells will be highlighted.

2. Click on **Insert**. The Insert menu will appear.

3. Click on **Name**. The Name submenu will appear.

4. Click on **Define**. The Define Name dialog box will open.

5. Type the **range name** you want to use. If you have text in the first selected cell, Excel will suggest that as the range name. There are several caveats about creating range names:

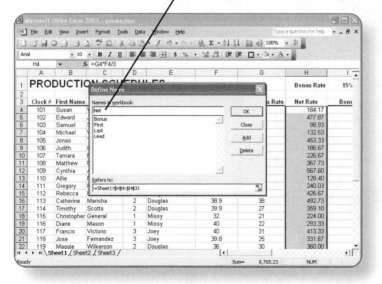

- Range names must begin with a letter or the underscore character.

- Range names cannot include a space or a hyphen.

- Range names are not case sensitive. You can use uppercase or lowercase letters.

- Range names can be up to 255 characters, but shorter is better.

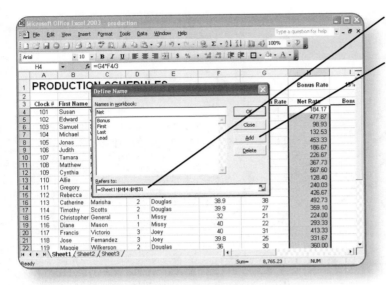

Excel displays the selected cell addresses.

6. Click on **Add**. The range name will appear in the Define Name dialog box.

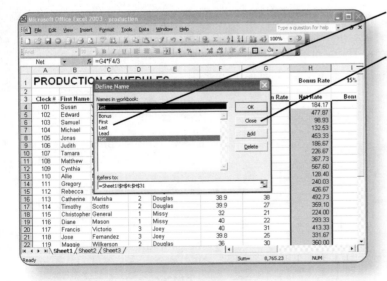

List of range names in the workbook.

7. Click on **Close**. The Define Name dialog box will close.

Using Range Names

Range names can help you jump quickly to specific areas of your worksheet. You can also use range names when creating Excel formulas.

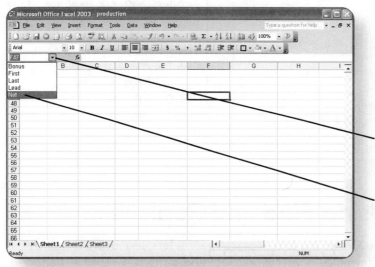

Excel provides a convenient drop-down menu that you can use to quickly move around in your worksheet. Moving to remote areas of your worksheet can be a mouse click away using range names.

1. Click the **Name box drop-down menu**. A list of range names will appear.

2. Click on the **range name** you want to locate.

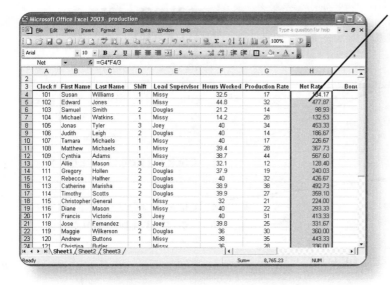

The range will become highlighted.

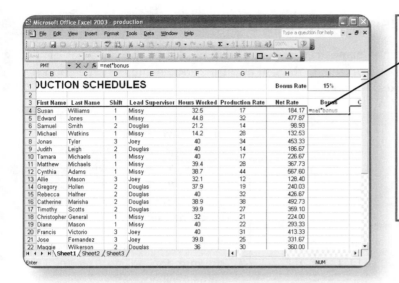

TIP

Using a range name in a formula makes creating formulas much easier to understand. For example, it is easier to identify a formula that is =Income-Expenses than it is to comprehend one that says =SUM(B6:B16)-SUM (B20-B54).

Using Find and Replace

The Excel Find and Replace feature lets you locate specific text or formulas in your worksheet and optionally replace the found data with something different.

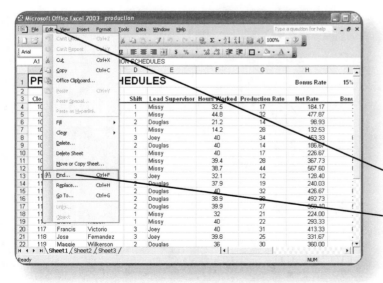

Locating Data with Find

When you have large workbooks, sometimes it's difficult to locate specific entries. You can let Excel locate the data automatically for you.

1. Click on **Edit**. The Edit menu will appear.

2. Click on **Find**. The Find and Replace dialog box will open.

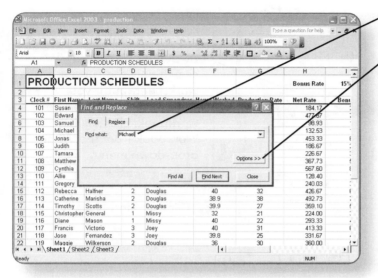

3. Type the **word, phrase, or number** you want to find.

4. Click on the **Options button**. The Find and Replace dialog box will expand to display additional options.

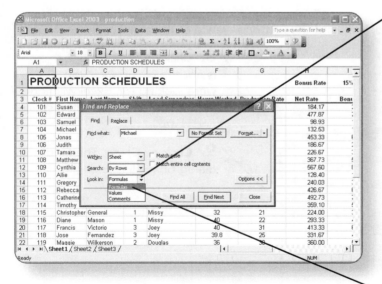

5. Click on the **drop-down menu** next to the Look in list box. A list of options will appear.

The Find feature can search through formulas, values, or comments. If you select formulas, the Find feature will look through both the underlying formulas and the values for the selected data. If you select values, Excel will look only in the results, not in the formulas. If you select comments, Excel will look only in comments.

6. Click on the **type of data** you want to search for. The option will be selected.

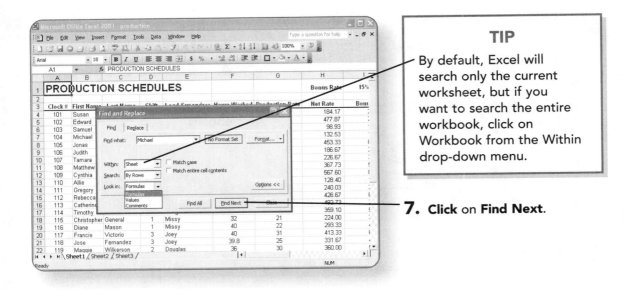

TIP

By default, Excel will search only the current worksheet, but if you want to search the entire workbook, click on Workbook from the Within drop-down menu.

7. Click on **Find Next**.

Excel will find the first occurrence of the word or number.

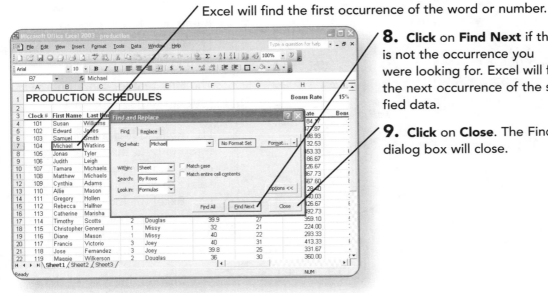

8. Click on **Find Next** if this is not the occurrence you were looking for. Excel will find the next occurrence of the specified data.

9. Click on **Close**. The Find dialog box will close.

Replacing Entries

Excel can locate specific data for you and automatically replace it with different data.

1. Click on **Edit**. The Edit menu will appear.

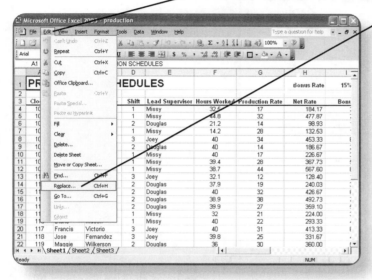

2. Click on **Replace**. The Find and Replace dialog box will open.

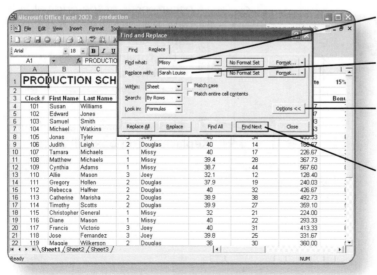

3. Type the **data** you want to replace in the Find what text box.

4. Type the **replacement data** in the Replace with text box.

The Replace box also has options similar to the Find dialog box.

5. Click on **Find Next**. Excel will locate the first occurrence of the selected text.

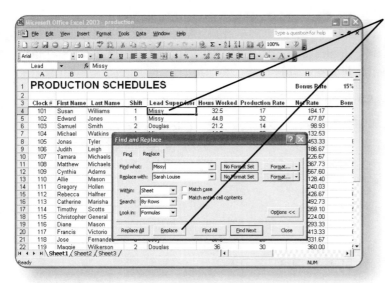

6. Click on **Replace** if you want to replace the found data with the replacement data. Excel will make the replacement and proceed to the next occurrence.

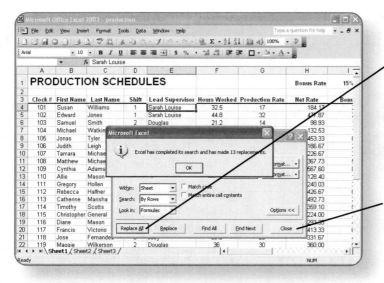

TIP

You can click on Replace All to have Excel replace all occurrences of the original data with the replacement data. Excel will notify you of the total number of occurrences.

7. Click on **Close**. The Find and Replace dialog box will close.

24

Working with Art Images

In a world where everyone is frantically busy, you need to communicate your ideas quickly. Graphic images help you do this. No time or talent to draw? That's not a problem. Excel contains a number of tools to assist you in placing images into your worksheet.

In this chapter, you'll learn how to:

- Insert clip art and other images
- Move and size the art object
- Adjust the contrast and brightness
- Wrap text around an image
- Create WordArt

Inserting Images

There are a number of different types of images, ranging from photographs to drawn art images, to text that takes on artistic shapes. Excel art is considered an *object* which means that you can easily move it, resize it, or modify it.

Inserting Clip Art

Excel comes with a wide variety of clip art. *Clip art* is simply a collection of computer pictures or graphics that are ready to use. You just select an appropriate picture and insert it in your worksheet.

1. Click the **mouse pointer** approximately where you want to insert your image. Don't worry if you choose the wrong area; you will later learn how to move your graphic image.

2. Click on **Insert**. The Insert menu will appear.

3. Click on **Picture**. The Picture menu will appear.

4. Click on **Clip Art**. The Insert Clip Art task pane will open.

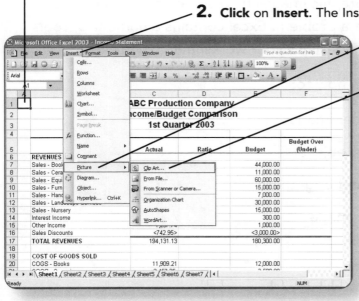

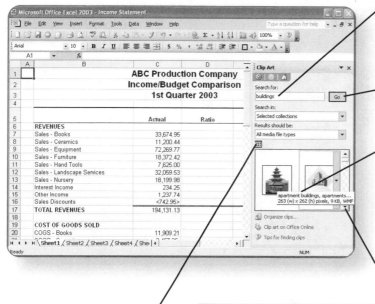

5. Type a **description** of the clip art you want. Excel will look for any clip art matching your description.

6. Click on **Go**. Excel will search for clip art located on your hard drive.

7. Pause the **mouse** over a picture. The selected picture will have a frame around it, an arrow on the right side, and a tip box that will describe the selected image.

8. Use the **scroll arrow** when available to preview more images.

TIP

Click on the Expand Results button to display more images at a time.

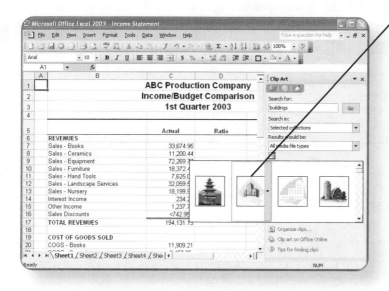

9. Click on the desired **image**. Excel will insert the clip into your worksheet.

You will learn in a later section how to move, resize, and adjust any image you insert into your worksheet.

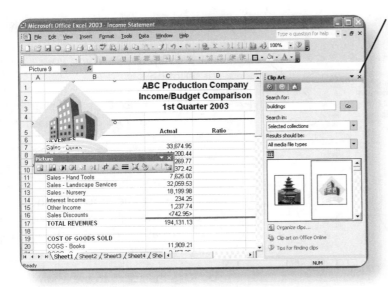

10. Click on the **Close button**. The Clip Art task pane will close.

Inserting Saved Images

You can easily insert your own artwork into an Excel worksheet, whether it's a photograph, scanned image, logo, or other type of artwork.

1. Click the **mouse pointer** approximately where you want to insert your image.

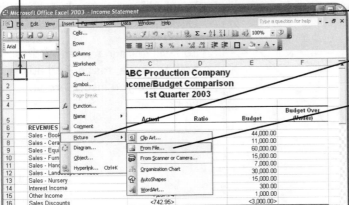

2. Click on **Insert**. The Insert menu will appear.

3. Click on **Picture**. The Picture menu will appear.

4. Click on **From File**. The Insert Picture dialog box will open.

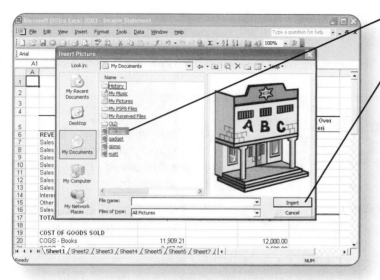

5. **Locate and click** on the **image** you want to insert. The image will be selected.

6. **Click** on **Insert**. The image will be inserted into your current worksheet and the picture toolbar will appear.

You'll learn in a later section how to move, resize, and adjust any image you insert into your worksheet.

Inserting Images from Your Camera

Although you will probably want to use the Windows XP Camera and Scanner Wizard or other software to download a batch of images from your digital camera, you can download images directly from your camera into your Microsoft Excel worksheet. So go ahead, take those pictures of your inventory items and insert them directly into your worksheet.

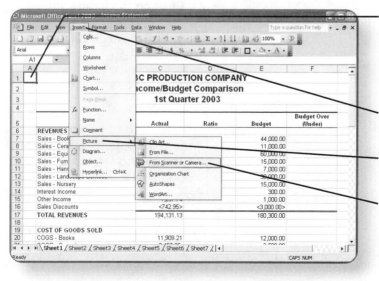

1. **Click** the **mouse pointer** approximately where you want to insert your image. The blinking insertion point will appear.

2. **Click** on **Insert**. The Insert menu will appear.

3. **Click** on **Picture**. The Picture menu will appear.

4. **Click** on **From Scanner or Camera**. A dialog box will open prompting you to specify the device you want to acquire the images from.

NOTE

Your camera must be installed and properly configured with Windows XP.

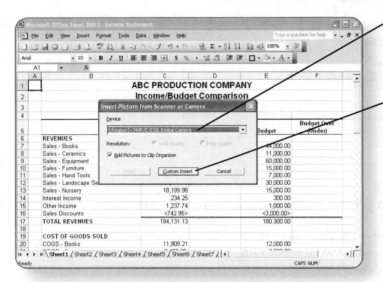

5. Click on the **device** you want to use. Your options will depend on the devices you have installed on your system.

6. Click on **Custom Insert**. The Which pictures do you want to copy? dialog box will open.

The images stored on your camera will appear as thumbnails.

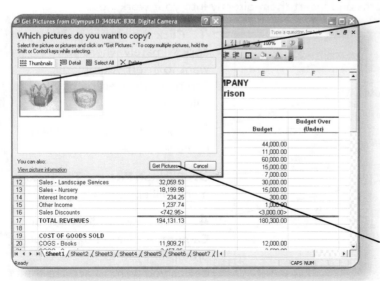

7. Click on the **image** you want to insert into your worksheet. The selected image will have a border around it.

TIP

If you want to insert multiple images, hold down the Ctrl key and select the additional images.

8. Click on **Get Pictures**. Excel will insert the selected images into your worksheet.

You'll learn in the next section how to move, resize, and adjust any image you insert into your worksheet.

Customizing Art

After the image is in your worksheet, you can make adjustments to it so that it blends well with your worksheet. You can move it, change its size, adjust the brightness and contrast, and wrap text around it or over it.

Resizing Images

The image might not fit on the page exactly as you had envisioned it. You can easily make the image smaller or larger.

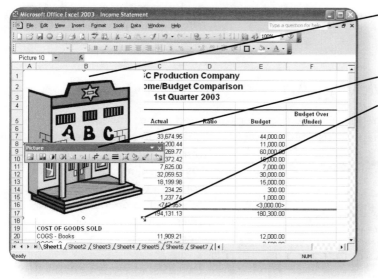

1. Click on the **image**. The image will be selected and eight small handles will appear.

The picture toolbar will appear.

2. Position the **mouse pointer** over one of the handles. The mouse pointer will turn into a double-headed arrow.

3. Press and hold your **mouse button** down on one of the selection handles. The pointer will turn into a plus sign.

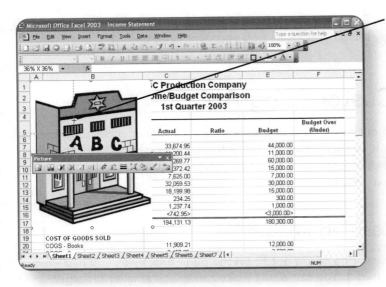

4. **Drag** the **selection handle** out to make the picture larger, or in to make it smaller. A dotted box will indicate the new size.

NOTE

Dragging on any corner handle will resize the height and width of the object at the same time; dragging on any side handle will resize the image in a single direction.

5. **Release** the **mouse button**. The image will remain at the new size.

Moving Art

The picture you choose might need to be moved. As the image is inserted into the worksheet, surrounding text adjusts to make room for it. When you position an image in an Excel worksheet, it automatically aligns (or snaps) to an invisible grid, which helps keep everything lined up.

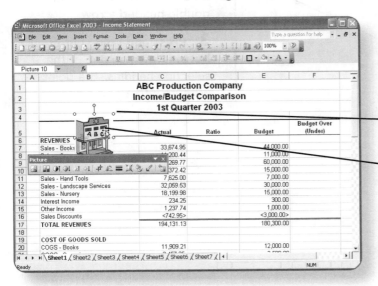

1. **Click** on the **art image**. The image will be selected.

2. **Position** the **mouse pointer** anywhere inside the frame of the graphic. Do not position it over one of the selection handles.

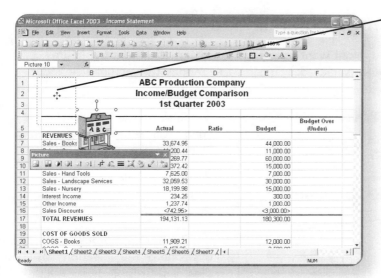

3. Press and hold the **mouse button** and **drag** the insertion point (in the form of a gray dotted line) to the new location. The mouse pointer will be a four-headed arrow.

4. Release the **mouse button**. The graphic will be in the new location.

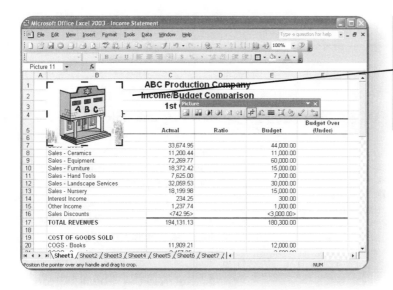

TIP

Click anywhere outside of the image to deselect it. The Picture toolbar will also close.

Cropping an Image

You might want to use just a portion of the entire picture you've selected. You can easily modify the picture size and content by using the Cropping tool.

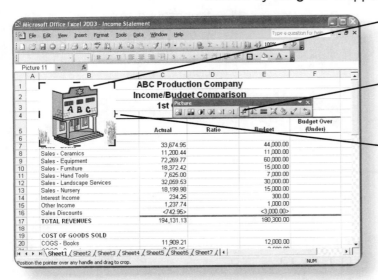

1. Click on the **image**. The image will be selected and the Picture toolbar will display.

2. Click on the **Crop button**. The pointer will change to the Cropping tool.

3. Position the **mouse pointer** over one of the selection handles. The Cropping tool will display over the handle.

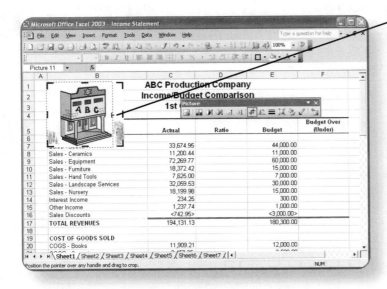

4. Press and hold the **mouse button** and **drag** toward the center of the graphic. The pointer will change to a plus sign, and a dashed line will form a box. The edges of this box form the new edges of the picture, with only the portion inside the box remaining uncropped.

5. Release the **mouse** button. The image will be cropped.

6. **Repeat steps 4 and 5** to crop as many sides as needed until the picture displays only the portion of the image you want.

7. **Click** on the **Crop button** again. The Cropping tool will be turned off.

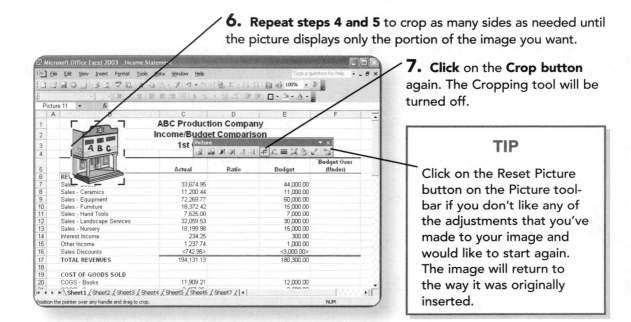

TIP

Click on the Reset Picture button on the Picture tool-bar if you don't like any of the adjustments that you've made to your image and would like to start again. The image will return to the way it was originally inserted.

Adding WordArt

Adding clip art to a worksheet is one way to add visual excitement, but if you're the creative type, you might want to draw your own pictures using Excel's drawing tools. If you want your text to have more impact, WordArt might be your solution. With WordArt, you can take headings or key words and add decorative color schemes, shapes, and special effects.

1. **Click** on **Insert**. The Insert menu will appear.

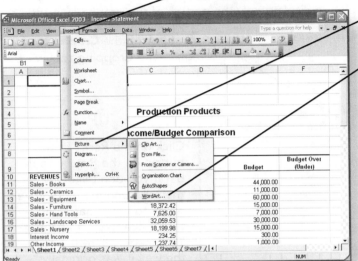

2. **Click** on **Picture**. The Picture submenu will appear.

3. **Click** on **WordArt**. The WordArt Gallery dialog box will open, containing predefined styles in which formats such as shape, color, or shadows are used to enhance text.

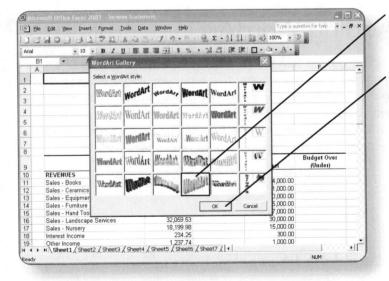

4. **Click** on a WordArt **style**. The selection will have a box around it.

5. **Click** on **OK**. The Edit WordArt Text dialog box will open.

A placeholder in the Text box will say, "Your Text Here."

6. Type the **text** that you want to appear as WordArt. Your text will replace the highlighted text.

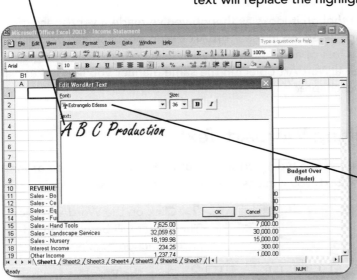

NOTE

Limiting WordArt to a single line of text is a good idea; the elaborate formatting can make lengthier text difficult to read.

7. Select a **font**. The preview box will display your text in the selected font.

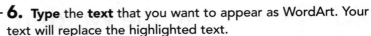
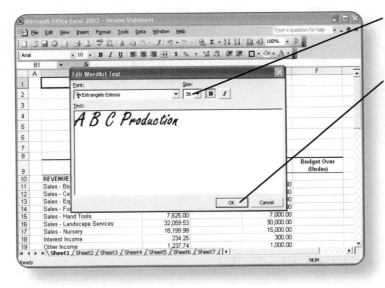

8. Select a **font size**. The preview box will display your text in the selected font size.

9. Click on **OK**. The text that you typed with the WordArt style you selected will be inserted in the worksheet.

Making Adjustments to the WordArt

Even though it looks as though you've made a very specific design selection in the WordArt dialog box, you can actually make lots of adjustments to your selection. You can move and resize a WordArt object in the same manner you learned earlier in this chapter.

Editing WordArt Text

If you made a typing error or you want to adjust the size or font of the text, you can easily open the WordArt feature again.

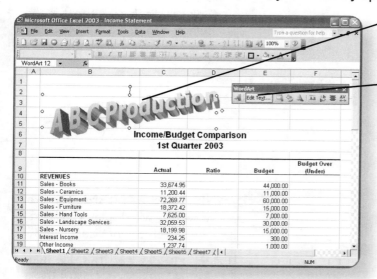

1. **Click** on the WordArt **object**. The object will be highlighted with selection handles.

2. From the WordArt toolbar, **click** on the **Edit Text button**. The Edit WordArt Text dialog box will open.

TIP

Optionally, double-click the WordArt object to display the Edit WordArt Text dialog box.

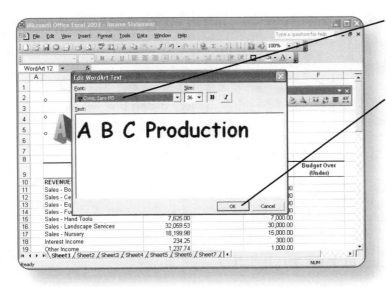

3. Select a new **font, font size, or modify** the **text.** The preview box will display your text in the newly selected settings.

4. Click on **OK.** The WordArt object will reflect your changes.

Changing WordArt Style

When you created the WordArt object, you selected a style from the WordArt Gallery, which contained styles such as shape, color, or shadows that were used to enhance your text. If you want a different WordArt style, you can easily access the WordArt Gallery to select a different style.

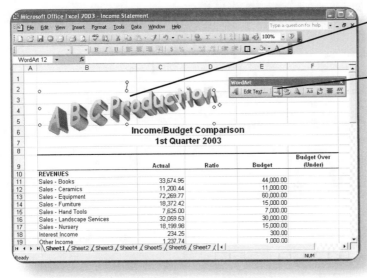

1. Click on the WordArt **object.** The object will be highlighted with selection handles.

2. Click on the **WordArt Gallery button** on the WordArt toolbar. The WordArt Gallery dialog box will open.

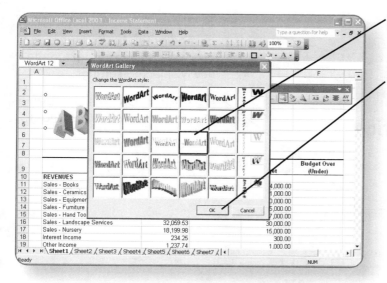

3. **Click** on a WordArt **style**. The selection will have a box around it.

4. **Click** on **OK**. The WordArt Gallery dialog box will close.

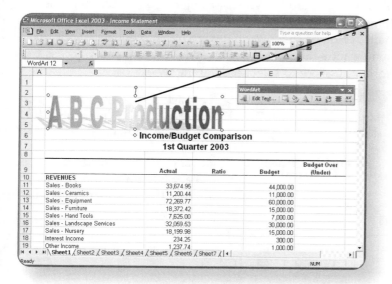

The existing WordArt object will change to the new style.

Reshaping WordArt

In addition to changing the size and style of the WordArt text, you can also change the shape of the WordArt object. The WordArt shape options include placing the WordArt object in a circular or semi-circular pattern, or even waves, triangles, or octagonal shapes.

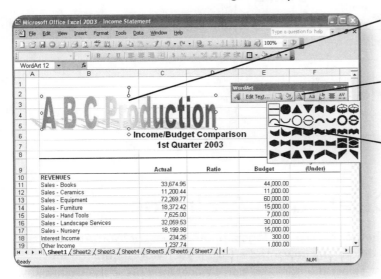

1. **Click** on the **WordArt object**. The object will be highlighted with selection handles.

2. **Click** on the **WordArt Shape button** on the WordArt toolbar. A palette of shapes will appear.

3. **Click** on a **shape**. Your WordArt will change to the shape you selected.

NOTE

Some shapes will make your text hard to read, while others will add an exciting or fun tone to your words. You may have to experiment with the different choices to select the shape to best fit your text.

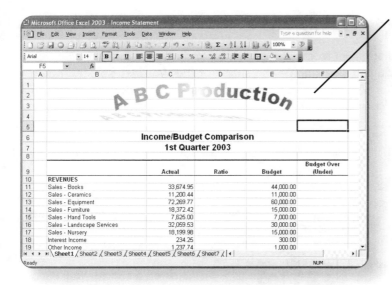

4. Click anywhere in the **worksheet** outside of the WordArt object. The WordArt object will be deselected.

Deleting an Art Image

Whether it's clip art, logos, photographs, or WordArt, it's easy to delete any unwanted art from your worksheet. You must first select the item you don't want, then press the Delete key.

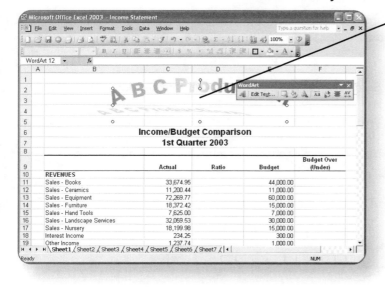

1. Click on the **image**. The image will be selected.

2. Press the **Delete key**. The image will be deleted.

25

Creating Charts from Excel Data

A chart is an effective way to illustrate the data in your worksheet. It can make relationships between numbers easier to see because it turns numbers into shapes, and the shapes can then be compared to one another.

In this chapter, you'll learn how to:

- Create a chart
- Modify a chart
- Delete a chart

Creating a Chart

Creating a chart is a simple process using the Excel Chart Wizard. You first decide what data you want to chart and how you want it to look.

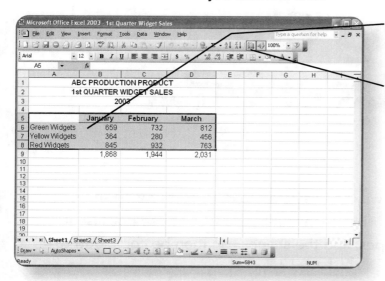

1. **Select** the **range** that you want to chart. The range will be highlighted.

2. **Click** on the **Chart Wizard button**. Step 1 of the Chart wizard will display on-screen.

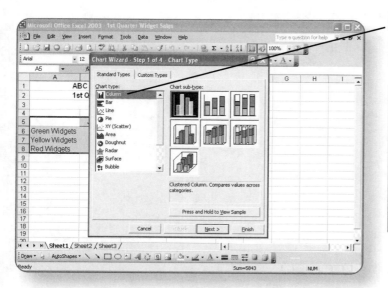

3. **Click** on a **Chart type**. A selection of chart subtypes will be displayed.

NOTE

Traditionally, bar charts compare item to item, pie charts compare parts of a whole item, and line charts show a trend over a period of time.

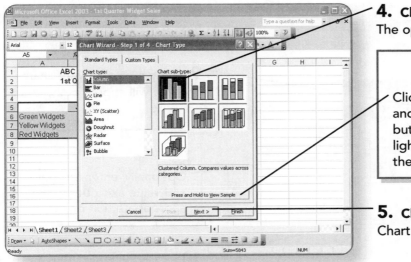

4. Click on a **Chart subtype**. The option will be selected.

5. Click on **Next**. Step 2 of the Chart Wizard will display.

Next, Excel will try to determine the direction of the data—whether the values to be plotted are in rows or columns.

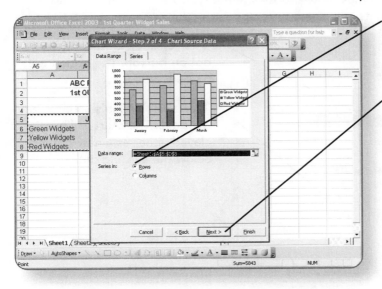

6. Click on **Rows or Columns** to display the data series in rows or columns. Your data will appear in the preview box.

7. Click on **Next**. Step 3 of the Chart Wizard will display.

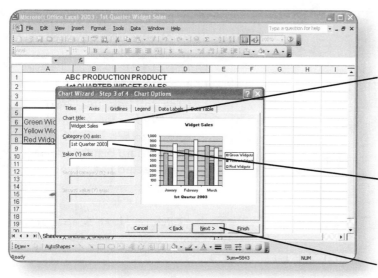

8. **Click** in the **Chart Title text box**. A blinking insertion point will appear.

9. **Type** a **title** for your chart. The title will appear in the chart preview.

TIP

Optionally, enter category and value axis titles in the appropriate text boxes.

---

10. **Click** on **Next**. Step 4 of the Chart Wizard will display.

You must now choose whether you want the chart to display on its own sheet or to appear on the same sheet as the data.

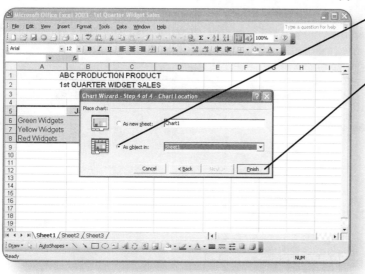

11. **Click** on a **Place Chart option button**. The option will be selected.

12. **Click** on **Finish**. The Wizard will close. The chart will be displayed either as a new sheet or below the existing data.

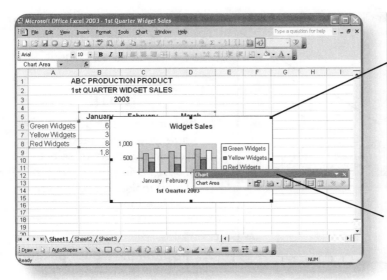

The Chart toolbar also appears.

The data from the selected cells of the worksheet is plotted in a chart. If the data in the worksheet changes, the chart will also change automatically.

In the next section, you'll learn how to change the size and look of your chart.

Modifying a Chart

Creating a chart is so simple that it probably made you want to enhance the chart to improve its appearance. Items you can change include the size, style, color, and placement.

Resizing a Chart

When a chart is inserted on the worksheet page, it will probably be too small for you to read the data correctly. You can use your mouse to resize it.

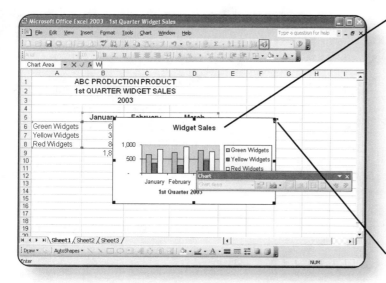

1. If necessary, **click** on the **chart** to select it. The chart will have eight small handles around it.

NOTE

If your chart is on its own page, you don't need to click on the chart to select it. Just having the chart displayed makes it eligible for modification.

2. Position the **mouse pointer** over one of the handles. The mouse pointer will change to a double-headed arrow.

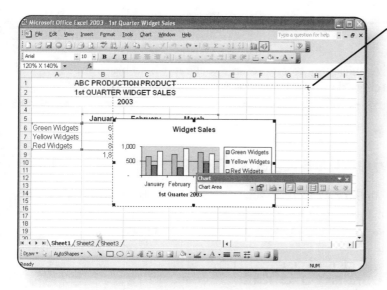

3. Press the **mouse button** and **drag** the **black handle**. A dotted line will indicate the new chart size.

4. Release the **mouse button**. The chart will be resized.

Moving a Chart

When a chart is inserted on the worksheet page, you can easily move it to any location on the page.

1. If necessary, **click** on the **chart** to select it. The chart will have eight small handles around it.

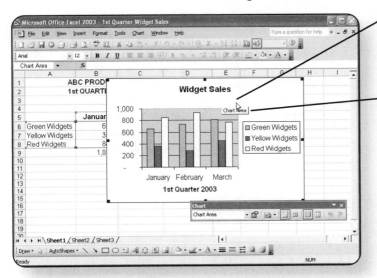

2. Position the **mouse pointer** anywhere over a blank area of the chart. The mouse pointer will be a left-pointing, white arrow.

You will also see a yellow tooltip indicating that you're pointing to the chart area.

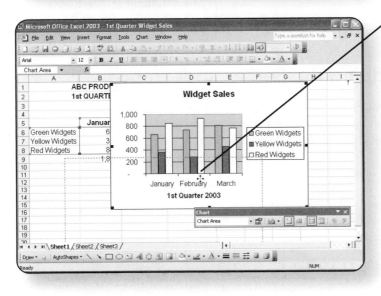

3. Press the **mouse button** and **drag** the **chart** to the new location. The mouse will turn into a four-headed arrow and a dotted-line box will indicate the new position.

4. Release the **mouse button**. The chart will move to the new position.

Changing a Chart Style

If you want to change the style of the chart, you can select a bar, area, pie, line, or a number of other style charts. Most of these charts can also be 3-D.

1. If necessary, **click** on the **chart**. The chart will be selected.

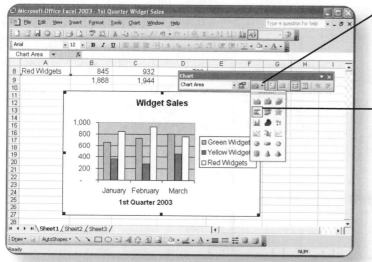

2. Click on the **drop-down menu** to the right of the Chart Type button on the Chart toolbar. A list of chart types will display.

3. Click on a **chart type**. The chart will change to the selected type.

TIP

Use 3-D charts lightly. Adding the extra dimension might make the chart look nice, but can also make the data difficult to read.

Editing the Series Appearance

If you do not like the default colors or patterns assigned to a chart, you can change them for any series.

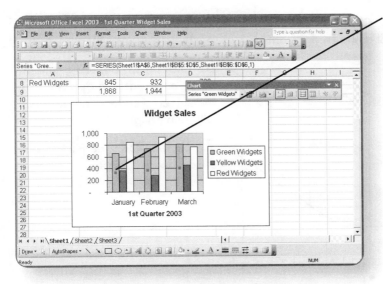

1. Double-click on any colored **bar, line, or series item**. A small black square will appear in all items in the selected series and the Format Data Series dialog box will open.

2. Click on **Patterns**. The Patterns tab will come to the front.

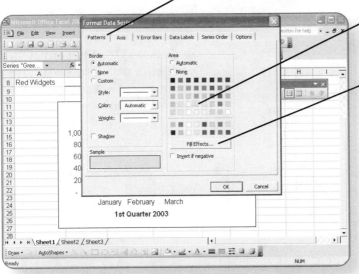

3. Click on a **color** for the selected series. The color will be highlighted.

4. Click on **Fill Effects**. The Fill Effects dialog box will open.

5. Click on the **Gradient, Texture, or Pattern tab**. The tab will come to the front with its available options.

6. Click on any desired **gradient, texture, or pattern options** for the selected series. The pattern will be highlighted.

7. Click on **OK**. The Fill Effects dialog box will close.

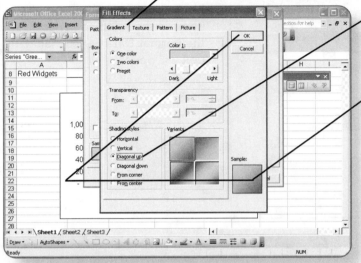

8. Click on **OK**. The Format Data Series dialog box will close and the series will change to the selected options.

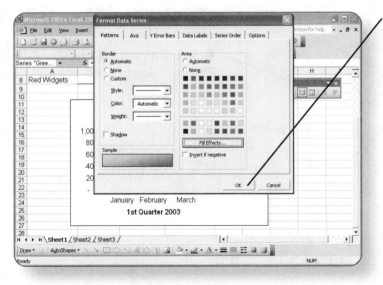

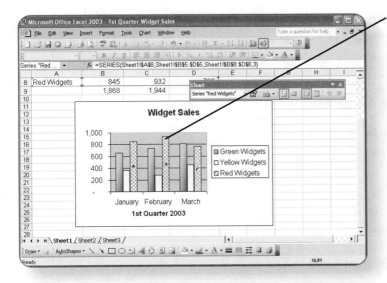

9. Repeat the previous **steps** for each series to be modified.

Modifying Chart Text

You can add or modify any text font, size, color, or border by double-clicking on the text.

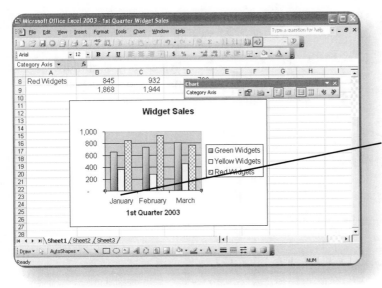

Working with Labels

Labels are the descriptive text you add, including the chart title or labels for the x or y axis of the chart. The legend is also made of labels.

1. Double-click on the **text** you want to modify. The Format dialog box for that section will open.

For example, here the Format Axis dialog box appeared, because the axis text was selected.

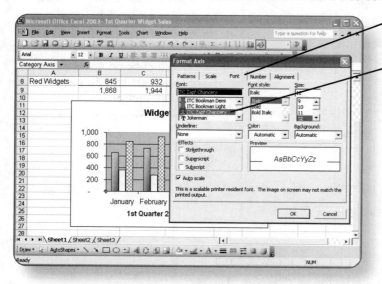

2. Click on the **Font tab**. The Font tab will be on top.

3. Click on any desired **font changes**. The options will be selected.

You can modify the alignment of your labels, including rotating them.

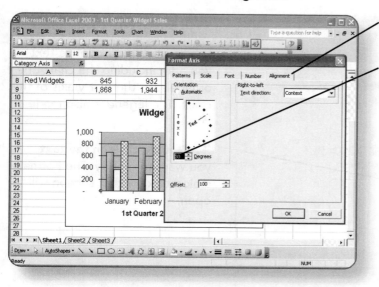

4. Click on the **Alignment tab**. The Alignment tab will be on top.

5. Click on any alignment **options**. The options will be selected.

You also might want to apply a number format to your y axis, which displays the values in your chart. The same number formats available in an Excel worksheet are available for an Excel chart.

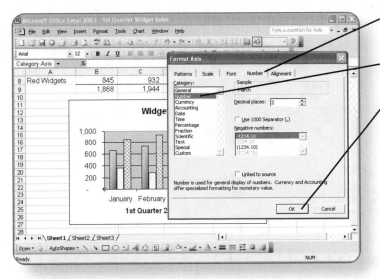

6. **Click** on the **Number tab**. The Number tab will be on top.

7. **Click** a number **format** including decimal point options.

8. **Click** on **OK**. The dialog box will close and the font changes will take effect.

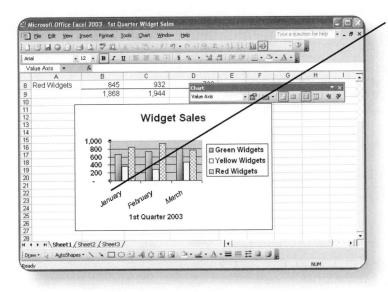

9. **Repeat** for any text you want to modify. The chart will display the changes you selected.

Placing the Legend

You can move the legend box, which is the key describing your y axis data, anywhere on the chart. Additionally, you can modify the legend box color and style. You cannot, however, modify the legend data since the legend is tied to the data series.

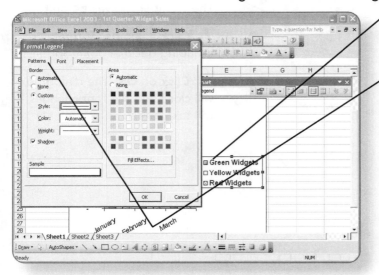

1. Double-click anywhere on the **legend**. The Format Legend dialog box will open.

The Patterns tab allows you to select a border and fill color for the legend box.

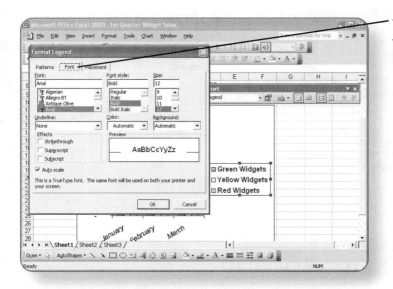

The Font tab allows you to select font, font size, and color for the legend text.

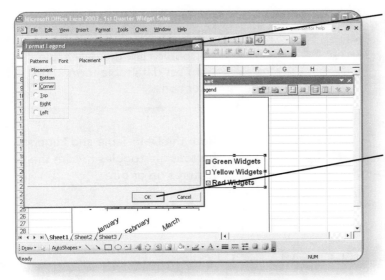

The Placement tab allows you to select a position for the legend, which is by default on the right side of the chart.

2. Make any desired **selections**. The options will be selected.

3. Click on **OK**. The Format Legend dialog box will close.

TIP

You can also click and drag the legend to any desired location.

Displaying the Data Table

A data table is a grid that contains the numeric data used to create the chart. You can add a data table to your chart; it is usually attached to the category axis of the chart. The data table will also display the legend for your chart.

1. Click the **Data Table button** on the Chart toolbar. The chart will display a data table.

Since the data table will contain a legend, you should turn off the legend display.

2. Click the **Legend button**. The Legend will be hidden.

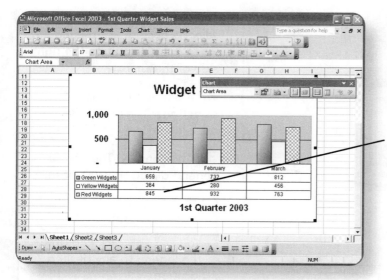

TIP

Double-click the data table to set data table formatting options.

Both the Data Table and Legend buttons are toggles to turn the features on or off.

Deleting a Chart

If you no longer want the chart created from your worksheet, you can delete it. The method you'll use to delete the chart depends on whether the chart is on the same sheet as the data or on a separate sheet.

Removing a Chart from a Data Sheet

If the chart is on the same sheet as the data, you'll delete it with the Delete key.

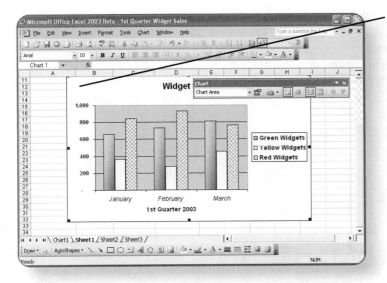

1. Click on the **chart**. The chart will be selected.

2. Press the **Delete key**. The chart will be deleted.

Deleting a Chart on Its Own Sheet

If the chart is on a separate sheet, you'll need to delete the entire sheet to delete the chart.

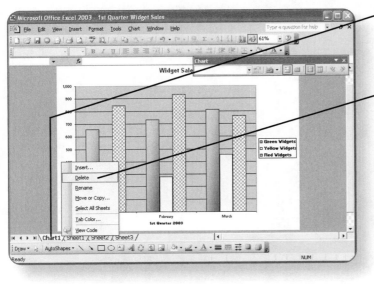

1. Right-click on the **sheet tab**. This tab is usually marked Chart1, Chart2, and so forth. A shortcut menu will appear.

2. Click on **Delete**. A confirmation message will appear.

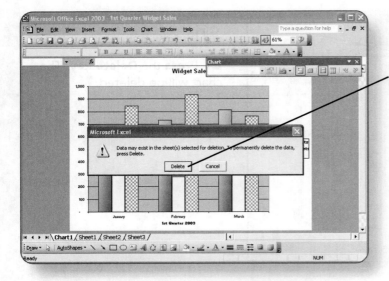

Note that deleting a chart sheet does *not* delete *any data* from the originating worksheet.

3. **Click** on **Delete**. The chart sheet will be deleted.

26

Using the Drawing Toolbar

Excel contains a complete set of drawing tools to help you create drawings, annotations, or diagrams. Also included for the less artistic is a set of predefined shapes called AutoShapes, which make the drawing process easier and faster. After creating your drawings, you can enhance them with special effects such as adding text or shadows.

In this chapter, you'll learn how to:

- Display the Drawing toolbar
- Draw AutoShapes
- Add text to a drawing
- Give shapes a shadow effect
- Make a shape 3-dimensional

Drawing Shapes

You don't have to be a gifted artist to draw lines, circles, squares, or any of a number of different shapes. Excel provides tools to assist you with all your drawing needs.

Displaying the Drawing Toolbar

Excel provides the drawing tools through the Drawing toolbar. You will find the drawing tools useful in many ways. Each button on the Drawing toolbar performs a specific function. Some tools draw lines or shapes; some tools help position the drawn objects on the screen; and you can use some drawing tools to change the color or appearance of a drawn shape or line.

1. **Click** on **View**. The View menu will appear.

2. **Click** on **Toolbars**. A list of available toolbars will display.

3. **Click** on **Drawing**. The Drawing toolbar will display at the bottom of your screen.

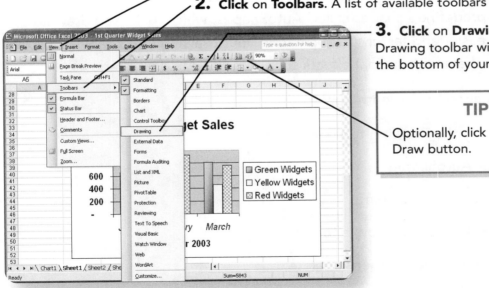

TIP

Optionally, click on the Draw button.

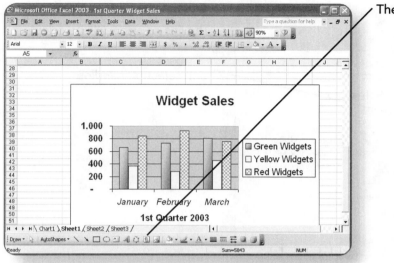

The Drawing toolbar

Creating Lines and Arrows

Two of the most commonly used drawing tools in an Excel worksheet are the line tools and arrow tools. With these tools, you can draw straight lines or angled lines, either of which can have an arrow head. The arrow tool is predefined with an arrow head that will appear at the end of your line. If you use the line tool, you can add the arrow head later.

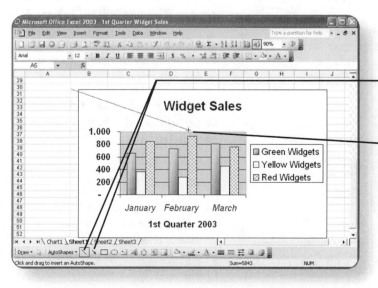

1. Click on the **Line tool or the Arrow tool**. The mouse pointer will become a small black cross.

2. Click and drag in the direction you want the line to go. A line will appear as you drag in the worksheet.

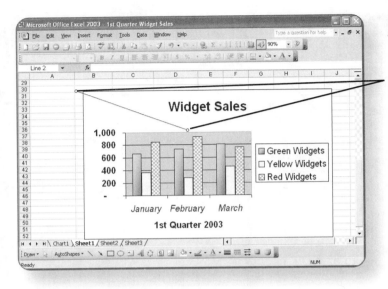

3. **Release** the **mouse button**. The line or arrow will be selected.

Line selection handles.

Choosing a Line Style

After you draw the line, you can make a number of changes to it, including adjusting the thickness of the line and choosing whether the line is a single line or a double line.

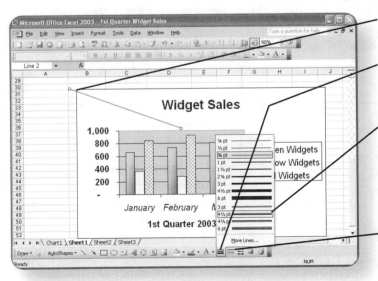

1. **Click** on the **line** you want to modify. The line will be selected.

2. **Click** on the **Line Style button**. A display of available line styles will appear.

3. **Click** on any line **style**. The selected line will change to the new style.

TIP

If you want the line to be a dashed or dotted line, select the line and make a selection from the Dash Style button.

Setting Arrow Heads

If you created a plain line and later determine you want arrow heads, or even if you want different arrow heads than you originally drew, Excel contains a tool to let you select from a variety of arrow heads.

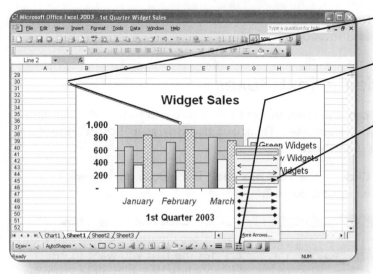

1. **Click** on the **line** you want to modify. The line will be selected.

2. **Click** on the **Arrow Style button**. A display of available arrow styles will appear.

3. **Click** on an arrow **style**. The selected line will change to the new arrow style.

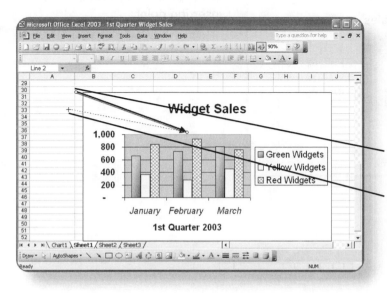

Rotating and Resizing Lines

After you draw the line, if you move your chart or data, you may need to move the line or arrow as well.

1. **Click** on the **line** you want to modify. The line will be selected.

2. **Click and drag** a selection **handle**. As you move the handle around, Excel will resize and rotate the line.

TIP

Position the mouse pointer over the center of a selected line to drag it to a new position.

---

3. Release the **mouse button**. The line will remain at the new size and rotation.

Adding Text Boxes

You can draw text boxes to annotate and further explain data on your worksheet. Think of a text box as a "Post-it" note for your worksheet.

1. Click on the **Text box tool**. The mouse pointer will look like an upside down T.

2. Click and draw a **box** approximately the size you want for the text you want to insert. A white box with a black border will appear along with a blinking insertion point.

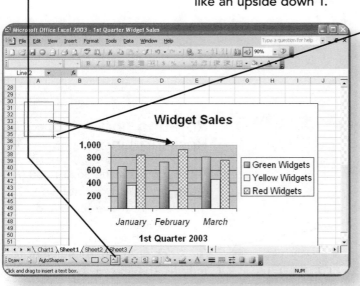

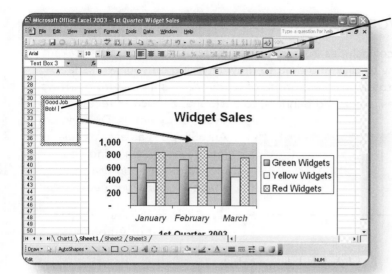

3. Type your **text**. The text will appear in the box.

TIP

Highlight and format the text as you would any text.

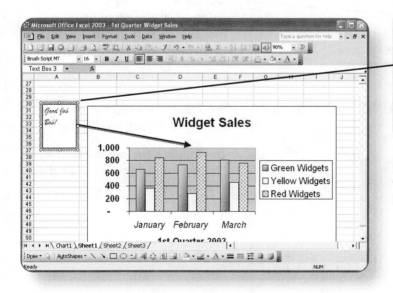

TIP

A text box, like other objects, can be resized by dragging any of the selection handles.

4. Click anywhere **outside** of the **text box**. The text box will be deselected.

Working with AutoShapes

Excel includes built-in images called *AutoShapes* that make it easy to click and drag to draw anything on your worksheet. AutoShapes are a group of ready-made shapes—from arrows, lines, stars, and banners, to basic shapes such as rectangles, ovals, or pyramids. Drawing an AutoShape is as easy as selecting a shape, then using your mouse to click and draw the shape in your worksheet.

1. Click on the **AutoShapes button**. A list of AutoShapes categories will appear.

2. Click on a **category**. A selection of shapes will appear.

3. Click on a **shape**. The palette will close and your mouse pointer will turn into a small black cross.

4. Click and drag the **mouse**. A shaped object will appear.

5. Release the **mouse button**. The new drawing shape will display with selection handles surrounding it.

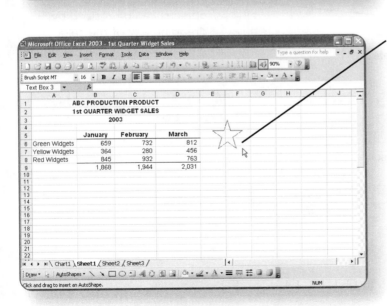

TIP

To insert the same drawing object several times in your worksheet, double-click the Drawing Object button. The button stays selected or "sticky." When you're finished inserting the objects, click the Drawing Object button again, or press the Esc key.

Editing the Drawing Object

The same techniques you learned in Chapter 24, "Working with Art Images"—how to move, resize, and delete art images—are also used for objects you draw with the Drawing toolbar. Sometimes, however, you might want to change the color, line style, or other attributes of your drawing object.

NOTE

Some of the following features are not available with some types of objects.

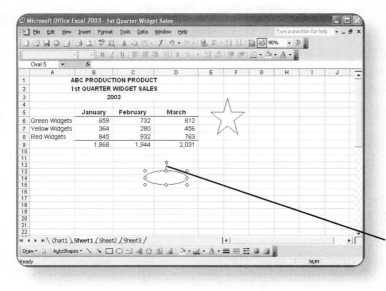

Changing the Object Color and Fill

By default, when you draw an oval, rectangle, or other shape, the interior of the object is filled with solid white. You can change the fill color or you can make the fill area transparent so you can see your Excel data under it. Text boxes do not provide for object fill.

1. Double-click the **object** you want to change. The Format AutoShape dialog box will open.

NOTE

Even if you drew the selected oval or rectangle from the tools on the Drawing toolbar, Excel considers it an AutoShape.

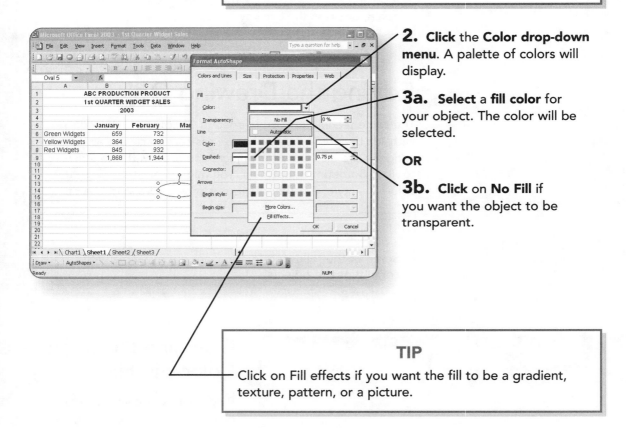

2. **Click** the **Color drop-down menu**. A palette of colors will display.

3a. **Select** a **fill color** for your object. The color will be selected.

OR

3b. **Click** on **No Fill** if you want the object to be transparent.

TIP

Click on Fill effects if you want the fill to be a gradient, texture, pattern, or a picture.

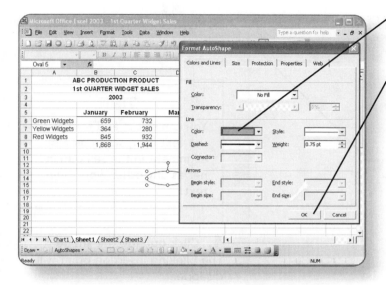

4. Select a **color** for the object border. The color will be selected.

5. Click on **OK**. The selected shape will take the new color attributes.

Adding Text to AutoShapes

When you create an AutoShape object, you can add text to it making it more informative and useful.

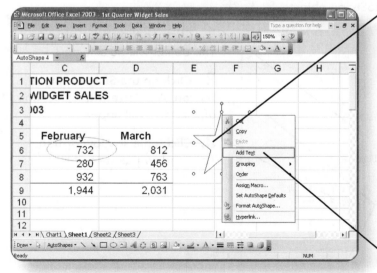

1. Right-click on the **drawn shape**. A shortcut menu will appear.

NOTE

If you selected an AutoShape from the Callouts category, the shape will be ready for text to be entered. You can skip steps 1 and 2.

---

2. Click on **Add Text**. The blinking insertion point will appear inside the AutoShape.

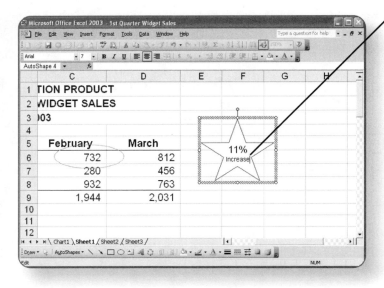

3. Type some **text**. The text will appear in the AutoShape object.

> **TIP**
>
> You can select and format the text font, size, color, or alignment in the same manner as any other worksheet text.

4. Click outside the **shape**. The blinking insertion point will disappear.

Creating Shadows

Shadows can add depth and visual interest to your AutoShape objects.

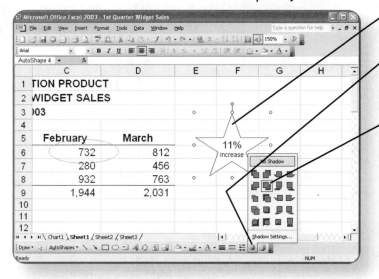

1. Click on the shape **object**. The object will be selected.

2. Click on the **Shadow Style button**. A palette with selections of shadows will appear.

3. Click on a shadow **option**. The shadow palette will close.

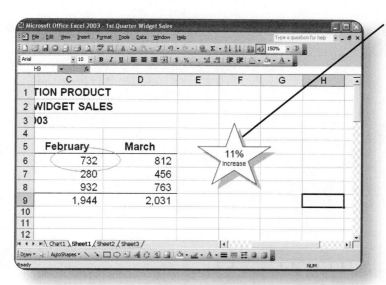

The shadow will appear around the shape.

Making Shapes 3-Dimensional

Make objects come alive by adding 3-dimensional effects! Some objects won't work with 3-dimensional shapes, so in those instances, the feature will not be available.

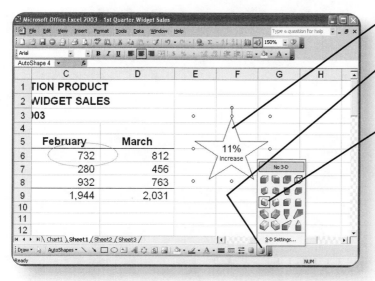

1. Click on the shape **object**. The object will be selected.

2. Click on the **3-D Style button**. A palette with selections of 3-D settings will appear.

3. Click on a 3-D **option**. The object will take on the added dimension.

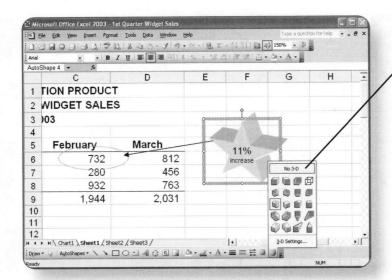

TIP

Remove 3-D settings by choosing No 3-D from the 3-D palette.

27
Working with Data

Excel can store data that can be used in logical conditions such as sorting or filtering to locate specific pieces of information. This is called a *database*, and each row of related information is called a *record*. After you enter data into a worksheet, you may find it easier to locate particular pieces of information if the data were sorted. You can also create filters that specify to display only the data that meets certain criteria, and if you want, you can also stipulate that any data that meets the certain criteria be formatted in a specified pattern.

In this chapter, you'll learn how to:

- Sort data by rows and columns
- Filter your data for specific data
- Work with data subtotals
- Apply conditional formatting

Sorting

You can sort Excel data in ascending or descending order. In an ascending sort, Microsoft Excel sorts numbers first, then alphanumeric data. Ascending will sort alphabetically A through Z or numerically smallest to largest. Sorting descending will do just the opposite; it will sort alphabetically Z through A and numerically largest to smallest. Blank cells are always placed last, whether sorting in ascending or descending order.

Sorting with the Toolbar Buttons

Excel provides two buttons on the Standard toolbar to perform a simple sort, which is data sorted by a single column. If your data is in an inclusive arrangement, you can use the toolbar buttons to quickly sort by a specified column. One button, the AZ button, sorts the data in ascending order, and the other button, the ZA button, sorts in descending order.

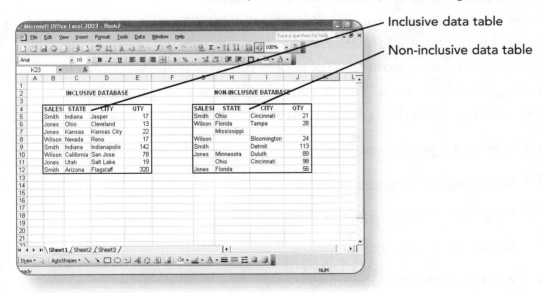

Inclusive data table

Non-inclusive data table

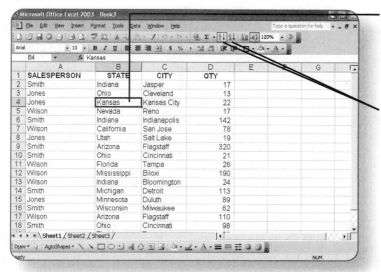

1. **Click** anywhere **in the column** you want to use to sort. Be sure only one cell is selected and not multiple cells—which can result in scrambled data.

2. **Click** on a **Sort button**. The table will be sorted.

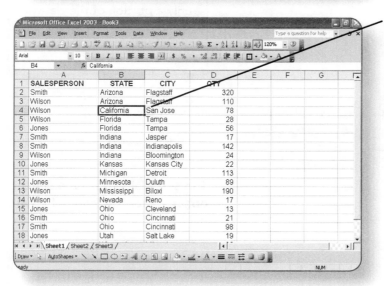

By sorting data in an inclusive arrangement, Excel knows to sort by the selected column, but also keep related data attached to the sorted data.

Sorting with the Sort Dialog Box

If you need to sort your data by more than a single column, you can use the Excel Sort dialog box. With the Sort dialog box, you can specify a column for a secondary or even a third sort. The most common sort is to sort the individual rows in a particular column. You create a secondary sort if two items in the first column are the same.

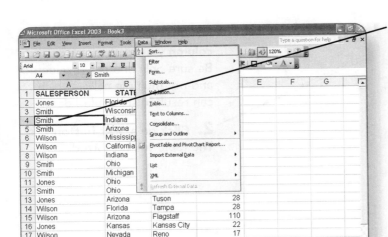

1. Click anywhere in the **data table or,** if the data is in a non-inclusive arrangement, **click and drag** to highlight all the **cells** you want to sort. Be sure to include any cells pertaining to the column you want to sort by. Any cell outside the selected area will not be included in the sort. If your data has a header row, select that data also.

TIP

If there is data in adjacent columns and you highlight only a portion of the data table, Excel will inquire if you meant to include the adjacent columns.

---

2. Click on **Data**. The Data menu will appear.

3. Click on **Sort**. The Sort dialog box will open.

The Sort dialog box provides the option to sort by three different fields.

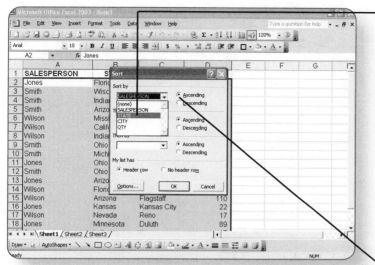

4. Select the **first column** you want to sort by. The column name will appear in the Sort by box.

> ## NOTE
>
> If your data has a header row, Excel will indicate the columns by the header explanation. If there is no header row, Excel will reference the columns by the column letter.

5. Click on **Ascending or Descending**. The option will be selected.

6. Select the **second field** you want to sort by if two or more items in the first column are the same.

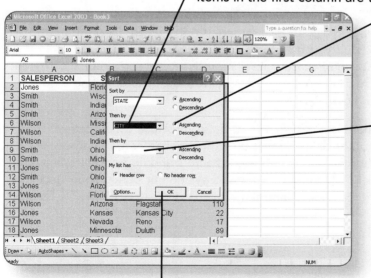

7. Click on **Ascending or Descending**. The option will be selected.

> ## TIP
>
> Optionally, you can specify a third method to sort by if two or more items are the same in both the first field and the second field. To sort by more than three fields, sort the list twice beginning with the least important field.

8. Click on **OK**. Excel will sort the data by the fields you specified.

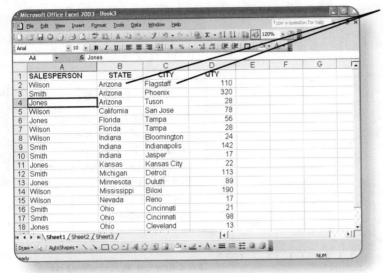

In this example, the data was first sorted by state, then by city.

Sorting by Dates

If you sort by a column of months, Excel will attempt to put them in alphabetical order—April, August, December, February, and so forth. You can, however, prompt Excel to recognize these cells as months and to sort them accordingly. You can also apply these same principles to sorting by days of the week.

There is a certain format dates must use when sorting. The months or days must be either spelled in their entirety or abbreviated with three characters and no period (such as Jan or Fri). Using any other abbreviation or punctuation will make the data sort incorrectly.

1. Select the **data table** you want to sort. The cells will be highlighted.

2. Click on **Data**. The Data menu will appear.

3. Click on **Sort**. The Sort dialog box will appear.

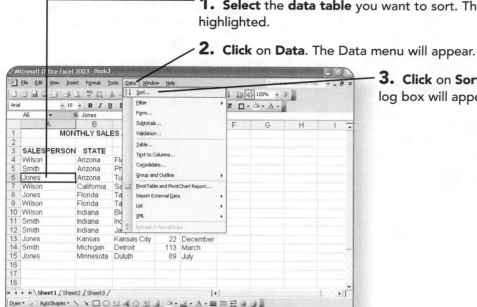

4. Select the **months column** as your primary sort field.

5. Select Ascending or Descending. The option will be selected.

6. Indicate whether your selection includes a **header row**. Header rows are not included in a sort.

7. Click on **Options**. The Sort Options dialog box will open.

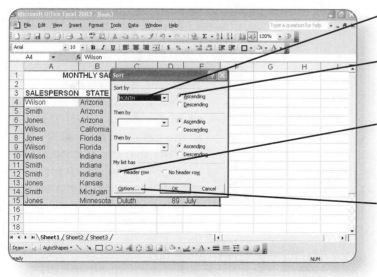

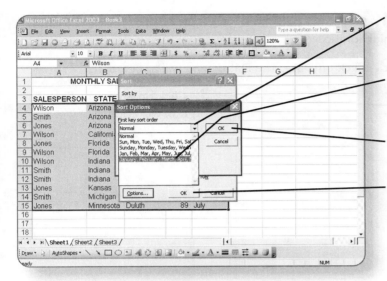

8. Click the **First key sort order drop-down menu**. A list of options will appear.

9. Click on the **pattern** you used for your data. The option will be selected.

10. Click on **OK**. The Sort Options dialog box will close.

11. Click on **OK**. The Sort dialog box will close.

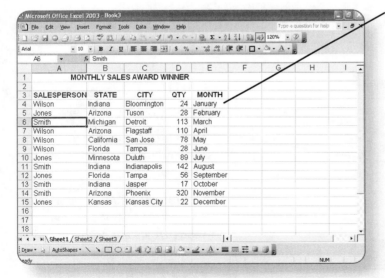

Excel will sort the data by month or day.

Using Filters

When you have a database of information, there are times when you do not want to see all the data you entered, only the data that meets criteria you specify. You can search for entries that match the criteria exactly or data that matches other operators, such as greater than, less than, begins with, or does not equal.

Working with AutoFilter

A very useful tool included with Excel is the *AutoFilter*, which can help you search and extract specific data from your worksheet.

1. **Click** on any **cell** of your database. The cell will be selected.

2. **Click** on **Data**. The Data menu will appear.

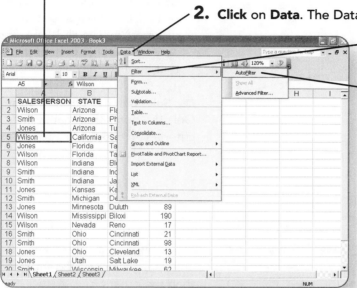

3. **Click** on **Filter**. The Filter submenu will appear.

4. **Click** on **AutoFilter**. Excel will display an AutoFilter arrow at the top of each column in your database.

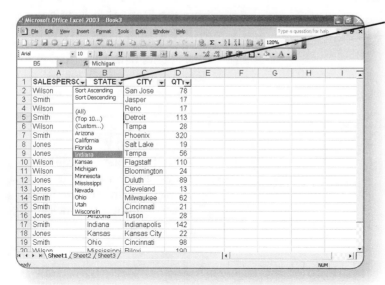

5. **Click** an **arrow**. Excel will display a list of options for that column.

The AutoFilter arrows at the top of each column allow you to select records from the following options:

* **All**. Displays all line items.

* **Top 10**. Displays the 10 most repeated or highest values in a field.

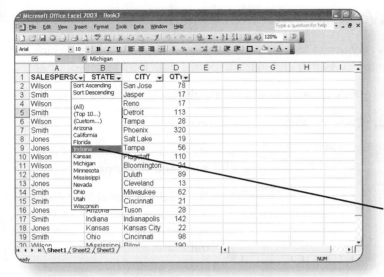

- **Custom**. Displays items that meet your specific requirements. You'll learn about custom filters in the next section.

- **Exact items**. Displays a complete list of the items in the column. You can click one, and only the records that contain that item will display.

6. **Select** an **item** from the list. Only the items that match the criteria you chose will appear.

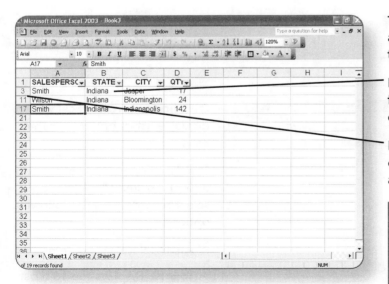

The arrows on a filtered column are displayed in a different color than the others.

In this example, only records from the State of Indiana are displayed.

Rows containing data that does not match your criteria are hidden.

TIP

To further isolate specific items, click the AutoFilter arrow in another column and select an item from the list.

You may want to redisplay all rows and perform a different filter.

7. Click on **Data**. The Data menu will appear.

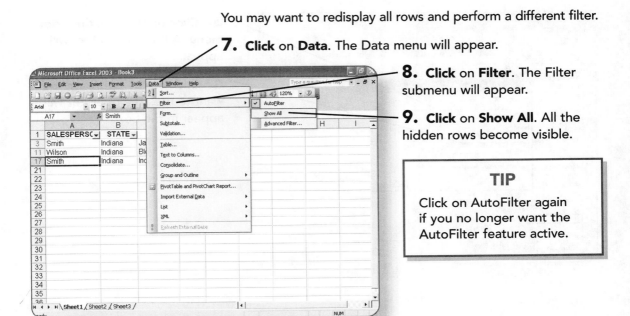

8. Click on **Filter**. The Filter submenu will appear.

9. Click on **Show All**. All the hidden rows become visible.

TIP

Click on AutoFilter again if you no longer want the AutoFilter feature active.

Creating Custom Filters

Using the AutoFilter Custom filter allows you to perform searches on your database for items with a range, or for items that meet a specific set of requirements.

You need the AutoFilter feature to be active to create the custom filter. If the AutoFilter is not active, follow the steps you learned in the previous section.

1. Click on the **AutoFilter arrow** at the top of the column you want to search. A list of options will appear.

2. Click on **Custom**. The Custom AutoFilter dialog box will open.

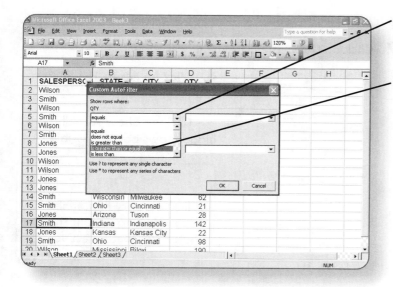

3. Click on the **first drop-down menu**. A list of operators will appear.

4. Click on the **operator** you want to use. The operator will appear in the box.

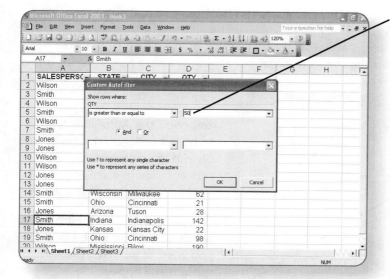

5. Enter the **value** you want to match the operator. The value will appear in the text box.

NOTE

Filter searches are not case sensitive and you can use a wildcard in the value box. Use a question mark (?) to represent a single character or the asterisk (*) to represent a group of characters. For example, entering I* in a box would find INDIANA, IOWA, ICE CREAM, and IDEA. If you typed D?N, Excel would find DAN, DON, or DEN.

If you specify a second filter, you need to specify the request with an AND or an OR option. If you select the AND option, the data must match both requirements you specify. If you select the OR option, the data must match one set or the other, but not necessarily both requirements.

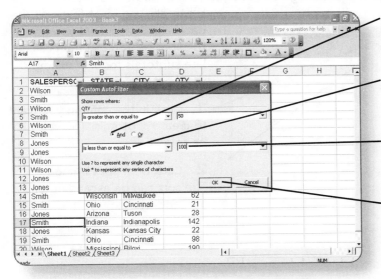

6. **Select** the **AND or** the **OR option**. The option will be selected.

7. Optionally, **select** a second filter **operator**. The operator will appear in the second box.

8. **Enter** the **value** you want to match the second operator. The value will appear in the text box.

9. **Click** on **OK**. Excel will filter the data according to your specifications.

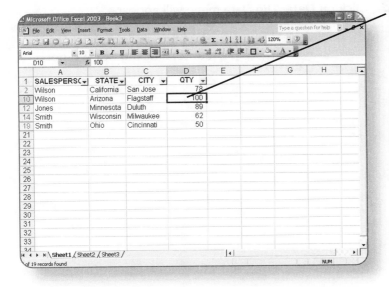

In this example, only those records with sales values between 50 and 100, inclusively, are displayed.

TIP

You can use the sort feature to sort any filtered list.

Data Subtotals

If your database contains numerical data, Excel can look at your database and create subtotals and grand totals, which can help you manage and analyze your data. Before creating subtotals, you must first sort the database by the field you want to subtotal. You can then calculate subtotals for any column that contains numbers.

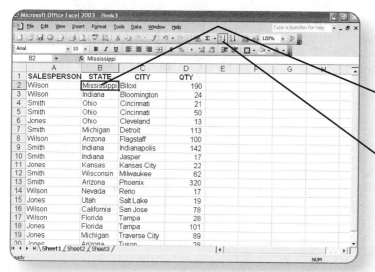

1. **Click** in the **column** you want to create subtotals. The cell will be selected.

2. **Click** on a **Sort button**. The sort can be ascending or descending.

3. **Click** on **Data**. The Data menu will appear.

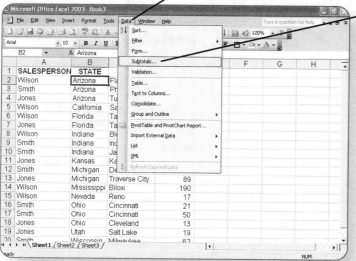

4. **Click** on **Subtotals**. The Subtotal dialog box will open.

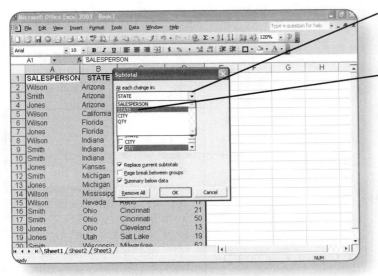

5. **Click** on the **At each change in drop-down menu.** A list of columns will appear.

6. **Click** on the **field** by which you want to create the subtotal break. This must be the field you sorted your data by.

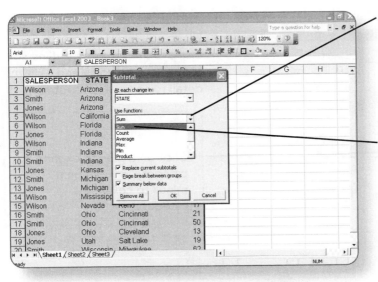

7. **Click** the **Use function drop-down menu.** A list of functions will appear.

You can create subtotals with a summary function, such as Sum, Average, Max, or Min.

8. **Select** the **summary function** you want to use.

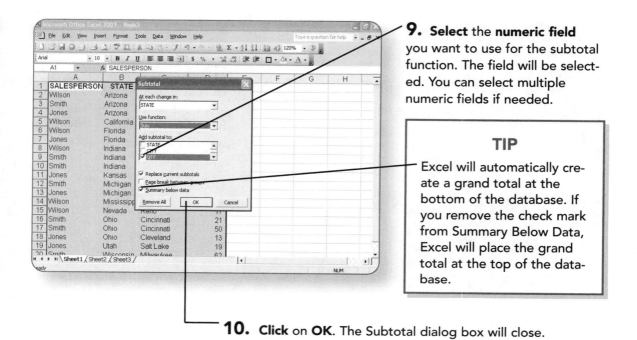

9. **Select** the **numeric field** you want to use for the subtotal function. The field will be selected. You can select multiple numeric fields if needed.

TIP

Excel will automatically create a grand total at the bottom of the database. If you remove the check mark from Summary Below Data, Excel will place the grand total at the top of the database.

10. **Click** on **OK**. The Subtotal dialog box will close.

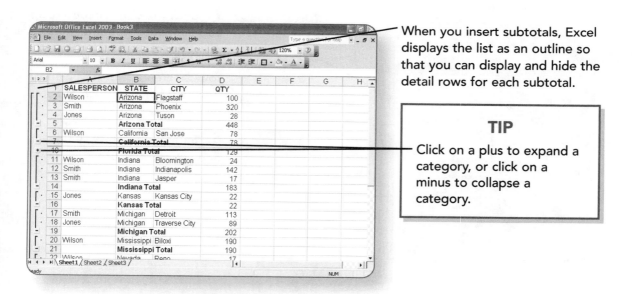

When you insert subtotals, Excel displays the list as an outline so that you can display and hide the detail rows for each subtotal.

TIP

Click on a plus to expand a category, or click on a minus to collapse a category.

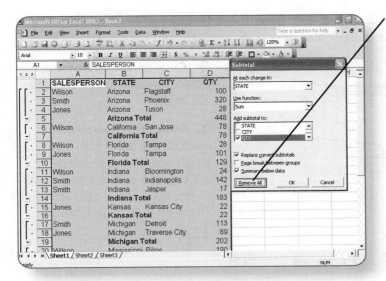

To remove the subtotals, click on the Remove All button from the Subtotal dialog box.

Conditional Formatting

When you use conditional formatting, you can instruct Excel to change the formatting for a cell if the cell's value meets a certain criteria. For example, if the sales for a particular salesperson meets a quota, you could have Excel add blue shading and a border to the cell.

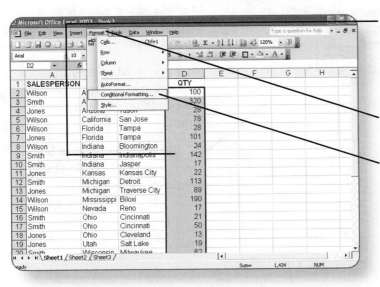

1. **Select** the **cell or multiple cells** with the contents you want to format with conditional formatting. The cell will be selected.

2. **Click** on **Format**. The Format menu will appear.

3. **Click** on **Conditional Formatting**. The Conditional Formatting dialog box will appear.

The second drop-down menu provides a list of operators such as greater than, less than, equal to, and between.

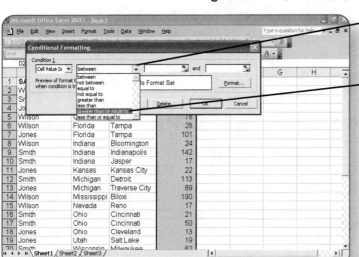

4. **Click** on the **operator drop-down menu**. A list of operators will appear.

5. **Select** the **operator** you want to use. Depending on which operator you select, you will see one or two more boxes to the right of the operator box. These are the value boxes.

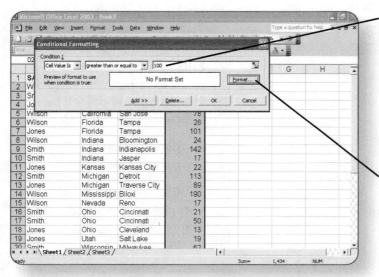

6. **Enter** the **value** you want to check in the value box. If there is a second box, enter a second value.

Now you must specify the formatting you want applied if the condition you just specified is met.

7. **Click** on the **Format button**. The Format Cells dialog box will open.

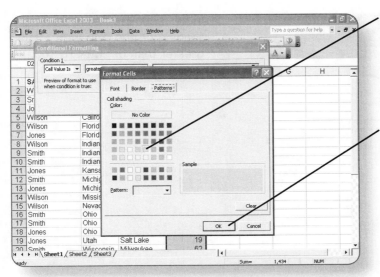

8. Specify the **formatting** you want Excel to apply if the condition is met. You can apply as many available attributes as you need. Font and font size changes are not permitted.

9. Click on **OK**. The Format Cells dialog box will close.

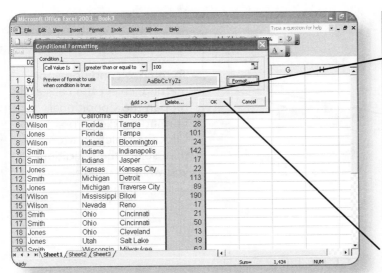

TIP

You can also specify a second or third condition. For example, if the sales quota is reached, the cell becomes yellow, but if the value reaches 125 percent of quota, the cell values become bold. Click on the Add button to add additional conditions.

10. Click on **OK**. Excel will check the cell for the conditions you specified.

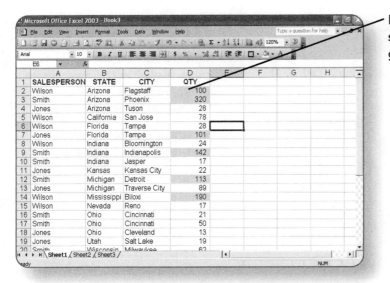

In this example, Excel placed shading on the cells with a value greater than or equal to 100.

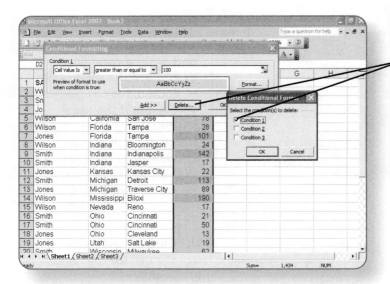

TIP

To remove conditional formatting, select the cells and reopen the Conditional Formatting dialog box. Click the Delete button, then select the conditions you want to delete.

PART III

PowerPoint

28

Understanding the Basics

Every project needs a starting point, and if you're using PowerPoint for the first time, you'll want to start with a quick exploration of the program. Start up the application, look around the program window, and open a few menus. If you're upgrading from a previous version of PowerPoint, a quick look around will reveal some new features that you may find useful. In this chapter, you'll learn how to:

● Start and exit PowerPoint

● Switch between PowerPoint views

● Work with the task pane

● Display and hide toolbars

● Turn off the Personalized Menus feature

Starting PowerPoint

One easy way to start PowerPoint is to select it from the Start menu. Depending on your Windows version and the way Windows is set up, PowerPoint may appear at the top of the Start menu, or it may require you to open the All Programs (or Programs) menu to find it.

1. **Click** on **Start**. The Start menu will appear.

2. **Click** on **Microsoft Office PowerPoint 2003** if it appears on the Start menu's top level. PowerPoint will open, and you can skip the rest of these steps. Otherwise, continue to step 3.

3. **Move** the **mouse pointer** to **All Programs** (or **Programs**). The Programs menu will appear.

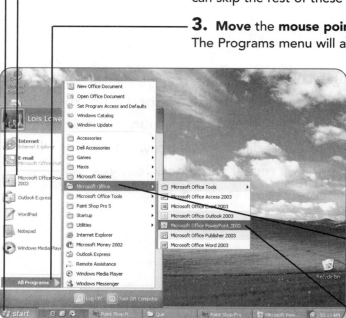

NOTE

The difference in wording in step 3 is due to the Windows version. Windows XP uses All Programs; all other versions use Programs.

4. **Move** the **mouse pointer** to **Microsoft Office**. A menu of Microsoft Office applications will appear.

5. **Click** on **Microsoft Office PowerPoint 2003**. PowerPoint will open and will display a new, blank presentation.

TIP

You can force PowerPoint to always appear at the top of the Start menu by "pinning" it there. In step 4, instead of clicking on Microsoft PowerPoint, right-click it and choose Pin to Start menu. From then on, a shortcut to PowerPoint will appear at the top of the Start menu, and you'll never have to open the All Programs menu again to locate it.

Creating a Desktop Shortcut for PowerPoint

If you use PowerPoint often, you might want to put a shortcut to it on the desktop. You can double-click it to start PowerPoint instead of going through the Start menu each time.

1. **Click** on **Start**. The Start menu will appear.

2. **Move** the **mouse pointer** to **All Programs** (or **Programs**). The Programs menu will appear.

3. **Move** the **mouse pointer** to **Microsoft Office**. A menu of Office applications will appear.

4. **Move** the **mouse pointer** to **Microsoft Office PowerPoint 2003**. PowerPoint will be highlighted.

5. **Hold** down the **Ctrl key** and drag **Microsoft Office PowerPoint 2003** to the desktop. A shortcut to Microsoft PowerPoint will appear on the desktop.

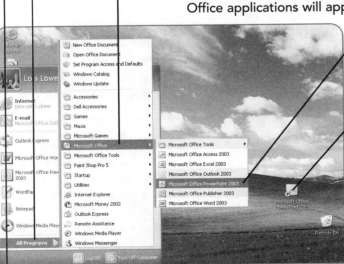

TIP

You can use these steps to create a desktop shortcut for any program that is installed on the computer.

Starting PowerPoint and Opening a Saved File

If you already have a PowerPoint presentation started, you can start PowerPoint by opening that file. PowerPoint files have a .ppt extension, and the icon matches the PowerPoint 2003 icon (orange).

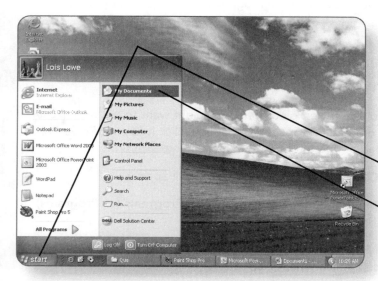

The following steps are for Windows XP, and they assume that your existing file is stored in the My Documents folder. If you have an earlier version of Windows, or if your file is located somewhere else, see the notes following the steps.

1. **Click** on **Start**. The Start menu will appear.

2. **Click** on **My Documents**. The My Documents folder will appear.

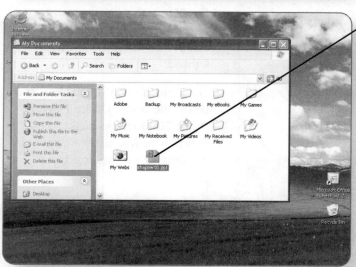

3. **Double-click** on the **presentation file**. PowerPoint will start, and that presentation will open within PowerPoint.

NOTE

Don't have Windows XP? Then double-click the My Documents icon on the desktop instead of performing steps 1 and 2.

Exiting PowerPoint

When you're finished working with PowerPoint, you'll want to exit the program to free up the system for other tasks, and to make your screen more tidy.

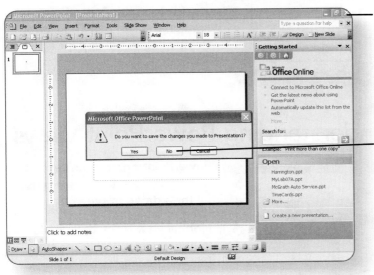

1. Click on **Close** in the upper-right corner of the PowerPoint window. If there are no unsaved changes, PowerPoint will close immediately. If there are changes, a Save dialog box will appear.

2. Click on **No** to discard your changes. PowerPoint will close.

Minimizing and Restoring PowerPoint

If you don't want to close PowerPoint but simply want to move it out of the way temporarily, minimize it. Minimizing a window shrinks it down to an icon on the Taskbar. You can then click that icon to reopen—restore—the window when you're ready to use it again.

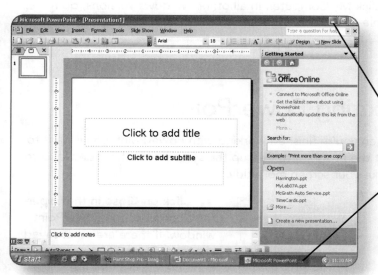

1. **Click** on the **Minimize button** in the upper-right corner of the PowerPoint window. PowerPoint will disappear except for its icon in the Taskbar.

2. **Click** on the **PowerPoint icon** on the Taskbar. The PowerPoint window will appear again.

Understanding PowerPoint Views

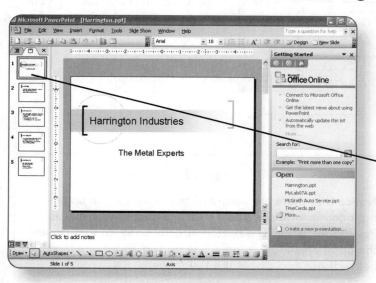

PowerPoint operates in several different views. Each view is useful for a different type of activity.

Normal view is the default view. In Normal view, you'll see the following panes:

- **Slides pane**. Thumbnail images of the slides in the presentation appear here. The other tab at the top of this pane is for the Outline pane, discussed in Chapter 31, "Organizing the Presentation Outline."

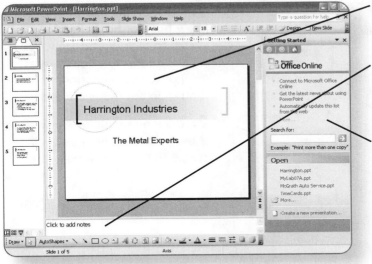

- **Current slide**. A single slide at a time appears here. It's enlarged so you can work on it.

- **Notes pane**. Any speaker notes you type for the slide appear here. These notes aren't visible to the audience.

- **Task pane**. This pane changes depending on what you're doing. You can also **click** its **Close (X) button** to give you more room.

NOTE

A presentation file containing several slides is shown here for example purposes. You'll learn how to open and create presentations of your own starting with Chapter 30, "Learning About Presentations."

Changing to a Different View

There are two other views: Slide Sorter and Slide Show. Slide Sorter view shows thumbnail images of all the presentation slides at once. Slide Show view shows full-screen images of each slide.

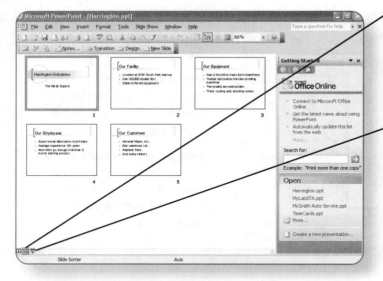

1. **Click** on the **Slide Sorter View button**. PowerPoint will switch to Slide Sorter view. You might use this for a bird's-eye view of the presentation, or to rearrange the slides more easily.

2. **Click** on the **Slide Show View button**. PowerPoint will switch to Slide Show view.

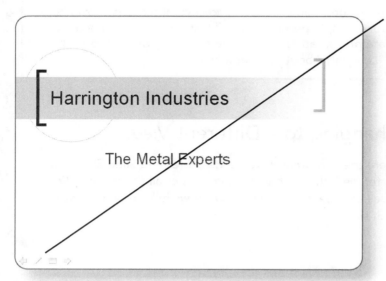

In Slide Show view, there is nothing you can edit. You can only view the slides. You would use this view for giving a presentation. Navigation buttons appear in the corner.

3. **Press** the **Esc key**. Slide Show view will close and the screen will return to Slide Sorter view.

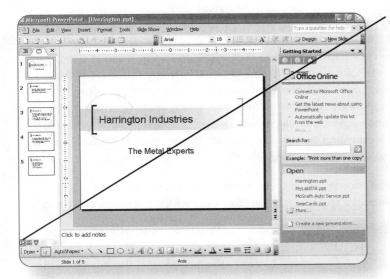

4. Click on the **Normal View button**. PowerPoint will switch back to Normal view.

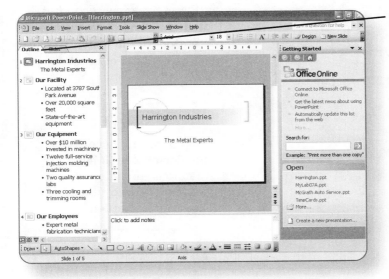

5. Click on the **Outline tab**. The presentation outline will come to the front.

> ### NOTE
>
> You'll learn how to create an outline in Chapter 31, and you'll learn how to rearrange the slides in Chapter 32, "Organizing and Improving the Presentation."

Working with the Task Pane

The task pane is an area that appears to the right of the other PowerPoint panes. There are actually many different task panes, each one containing tools and options appropriate for a certain activity. Most of the time, the correct task pane will appear automatically when needed. For example, if you select the command to change a slide's layout, the Slide Layout task pane will appear automatically.

Many people prefer to work with the task pane hidden so they have more space onscreen. You can redisplay it when you need it.

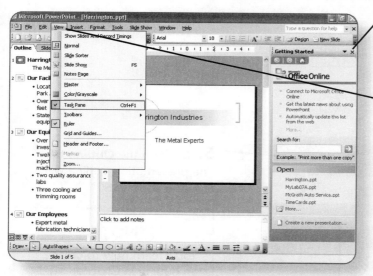

1. **Click** on the **Close button** on the task pane. The task pane will disappear, and the current slide will have more space available.

2. **Click** on the **View menu**. The View menu will appear.

3. Pause for a few seconds if there is a down-pointing arrow at the bottom of the menu. The full menu will appear after a brief delay.

NOTE

Step 3 may be necessary if the Personalized Menus feature is turned on. You will learn how to turn it off later in this chapter.

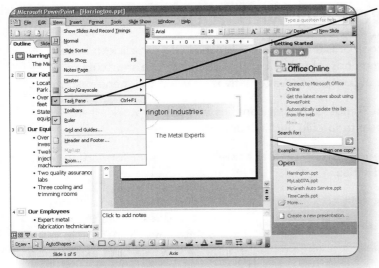

4. Click on **Task Pane**. The task pane will reappear.

TIP

Instead of steps 2 through 4, you can press Ctrl+F1.

5. Move the **mouse pointer** over the border between the current slide's pane and the task pane. The mouse will become a two-headed arrow. Then **drag** to the left or right to resize the task pane.

Choosing a Different Task Pane

PowerPoint will often display a certain task pane based on what you're doing. You can also choose which task pane you want to see at any given moment.

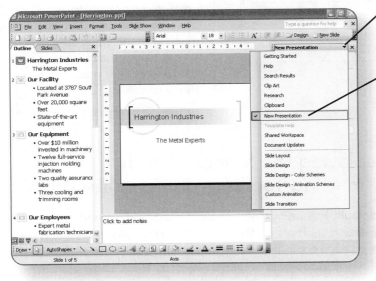

1. Click on the **Task Pane down arrow**. A list of available task panes will appear.

2. Click on a **task pane**. The selected task pane will appear.

TIP

The task pane has its own Back and Forward arrows, just like a Web browser window. You can click the Back (left) arrow to return to a previously used task pane.

Working with Toolbars

A toolbar is a collection of buttons you can click to issue commands. Nearly all of these buttons are shortcuts to menu commands—alternatives to using the menu system.

The Standard toolbar contains buttons for working with the presentation file and its content.

The Formatting toolbar contains buttons for formatting text and slides.

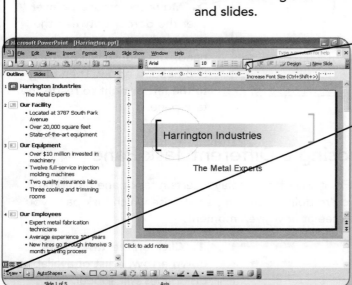

To find out what a particular button does, **move** the **mouse pointer** over it. A ToolTip will appear with a brief explanation.

The Drawing toolbar contains buttons for creating or inserting artwork.

TIP

When you open a menu, you'll see icons to the left of some of the menu commands. These icons correspond to the buttons on the toolbar that match those commands.

Displaying the Standard and Formatting Toolbars on Separate Rows

By default, PowerPoint shows both the Standard and Formatting toolbars on the same row. This causes some buttons on each toolbar to be obscured. Most people prefer to display these toolbars on separate rows. (That's how they're shown in most of the figures in this book.)

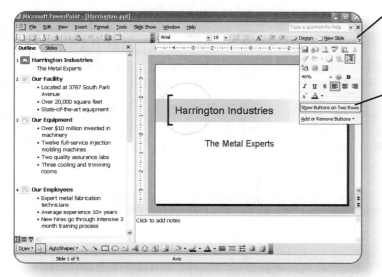

1. Click on the **down-pointing arrow** at the end of the Standard or Formatting toolbar. A menu will appear.

2. Click on **Show Buttons on Two Rows**. The Formatting toolbar will move to a new row below the Standard toolbar.

Moving a Toolbar

You may find that the location of toolbars is inconvenient for the way you work. Toolbars can be moved to any location on the screen that's convenient for you. A toolbar may be docked (attached to other toolbars), or it may float all by itself.

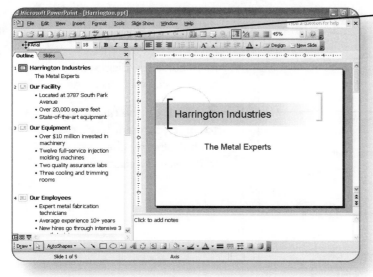

1. Move the **mouse pointer** over the toolbar handle (the set of dots at its left edge). The mouse pointer will change to a four-pointed arrow.

2. Drag the **toolbar handle** to another location on the PowerPoint window. The toolbar will move with the mouse.

If you **drag** the **toolbar** into the middle of the window, it will become a floating toolbar. **Drag** it back to an edge of the screen to dock it again.

Hiding or Displaying a Toolbar

There are many toolbars available in PowerPoint. Some of them appear automatically when needed; others must be displayed manually.

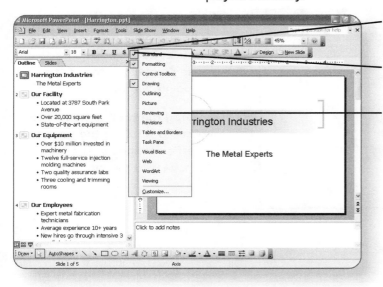

1. Right-click on a **toolbar**. A shortcut menu appears.

Each currently displayed toolbar has a check next to its name.

2. Click on the **name of the toolbar** you want to display (if it's not already checked) or hide (if it's already checked).

> **NOTE**
> What if no toolbars are displayed? In that case, open the View menu, point to Toolbars, and then click the name of the toolbar you want.

Turning Off the Personalized Menus Feature

By default, the Personalized Menus feature is turned on in PowerPoint. When you open a menu, only a few of the available commands appear. PowerPoint monitors your usage, and if you've used a certain command before, it's on that short, initial list. The rest of the commands appear after a few seconds, or when you click the down arrow at the bottom of the menu.

The figures in this book have this personalized menu feature turned off to avoid inconsistency between the book's pictures and your screen. To follow along more closely with the figures in this book, we recommend that you turn this feature off, too.

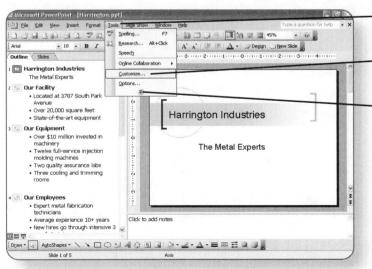

1. Click on **Tools**. The Tools menu will appear.

2. Click on **Customize**. The Customize dialog box will open.

Notice the down-pointing arrow at the bottom of the menu. This indicates that more commands are available than are currently shown.

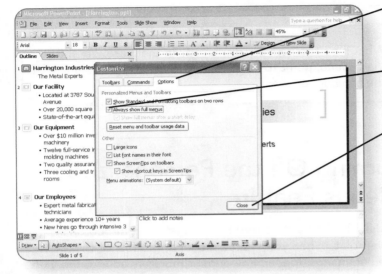

3. **Click** on the **Options tab**. The Options tab will come to the front.

4. **Click** on the **Always show full menus check box**. A check will be placed in the check box.

5. **Click** on **Close**. Your new setting will be applied.

29
Asking for Help

As you work on a presentation, you may find that every now and then you need a quick reminder on how to perform a task or some help learning an unfamiliar program feature. You have several choices. You can refer back to books that you've read, you can get on the Internet and do some research, or you can use the built-in PowerPoint help system. In this chapter, you'll learn how to:

- Use the Ask a Question feature
- View and print Help topics
- Find help on the Internet
- Get program updates

Asking a Question

The Ask a Question box, in the top-right corner of the screen, provides quick access to the Help system.

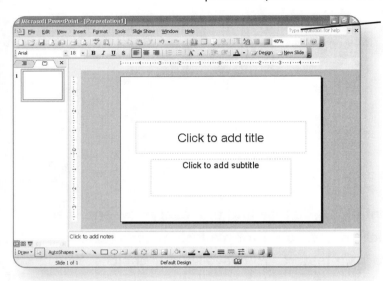

1. **Click** in the **Ask a Question text box**. The cursor will appear in the box.

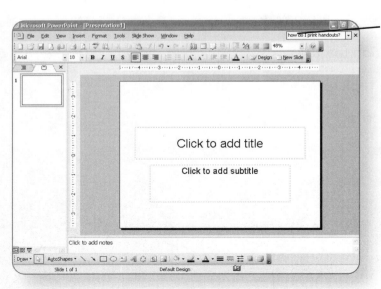

2. **Type** a **question** and **press Enter**. The Help task pane will appear, and the help system will be searched.

NOTE

If you are connected to the Internet, the search for Help topics will include topics available through Microsoft's Web site.

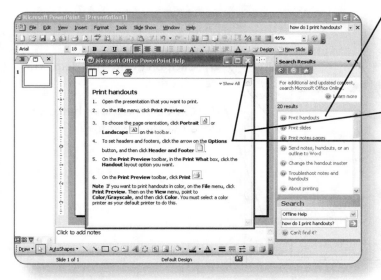

3. Click on the **topic** that most closely answers your question. The Help topic will appear in the Microsoft PowerPoint Help window.

4. Read the **Help topic**.

5a. Click on the **Close button** to close the Help window

OR

5b. See the following steps to print it.

Printing a Help Topic

Printing a Help topic enables you to refer to it easily after you have closed its window onscreen.

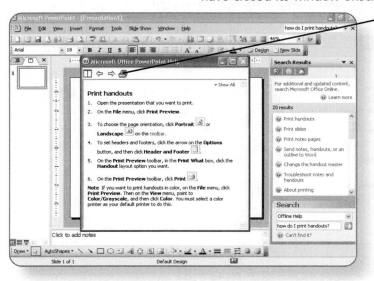

1. Click on the **Print button** in the Help window. The Print dialog box will open.

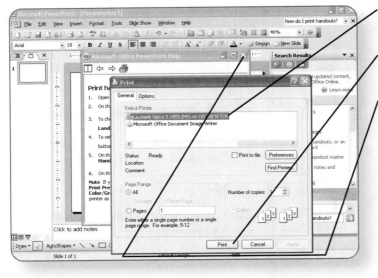

2. Click on the **desired printer**. It will be selected.

3. Click on **Print**. The Help article will print.

4. Click on the **Close button** to close the Help window.

Getting Help on the Internet

When you use PowerPoint while connected to the Internet, PowerPoint automatically integrates online help into its own Help system. You can also visit the Office Online site to browse for additional downloads and information not related to a specific question.

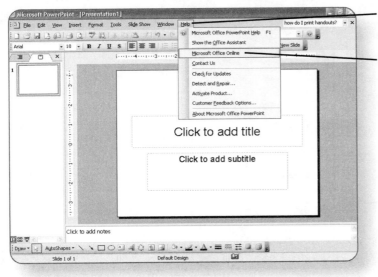

1. Click on **Help**. The Help menu will appear.

2. Click on **Microsoft Office Online**. Your default Web browser will start and you will be connected to the Internet.

3. Explore the **Office Online** site.

Getting Program Updates

Microsoft periodically releases fixes and enhancements for PowerPoint and other Office products. You can download them through the Internet.

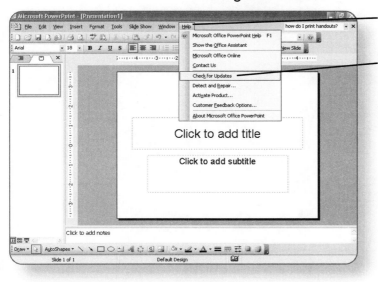

1. Click on **Help**. The Help menu will appear.

2. Click on **Check for Updates**. Your default Web browser will start and you will be connected to the Internet.

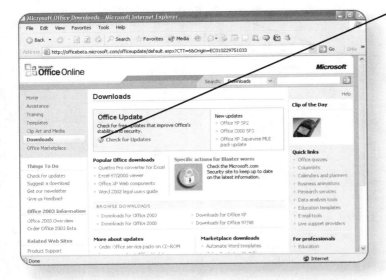

3. **Click** on **Check for Updates**.

4. **Follow the onscreen prompts** to download and install any needed updates.

30

Learning About Presentations

It's time to get started on your first presentation, but you don't know where to begin. Don't worry, PowerPoint contains a number of tools to help you take that first step. You'll find wizards and templates that help you design professional-looking presentations. You can use these wizards and templates as a learning tool or as a start for your presentation. In this chapter, you'll learn how to:

- Start a fast and easy presentation with the AutoContent Wizard
- Use templates to develop a uniform design
- Save a presentation
- Print a presentation

Using the AutoContent Wizard

PowerPoint contains many sample presentations that can give you a quick start. You can use these samples to learn how an effective presentation is built or as a starting place for your own. All of them can be changed to suit your needs.

1. **Click** on the **File menu**. The File menu will appear.

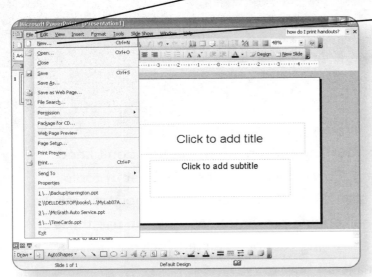

2. **Click** on the **New command**. The New Presentation task pane will appear.

NOTE

The New button on the toolbar starts a new, blank presentation, which is not what we want right now.

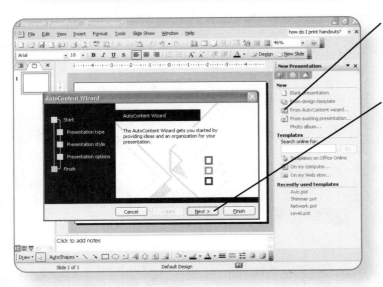

3. **Click** on **From AutoContent wizard** in the New Presentation task pane. The AutoContent wizard will start.

4. **Click** on **Next**. The Presentation type page of the wizard will appear.

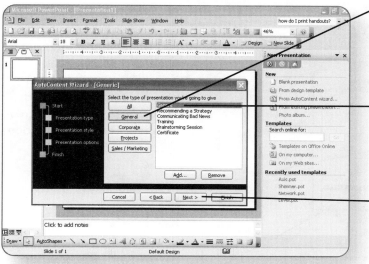

5. **Click** on the **button** for the category of presentation that you want to create. A list of presentation types will appear on the right side of the dialog box.

6. **Click** on a **presentation type** that closely matches the information that you want to use in your presentation. The presentation type will be selected.

7. **Click** on **Next**. The Presentation style page of the wizard will appear.

8. **Click** on the **option button** for the method you will use to display the presentation. The option will be selected. Select from one of these options:

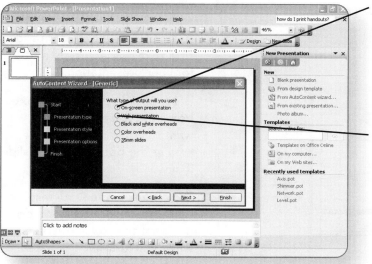

- An **On-screen presentation** is displayed on a computer monitor or on a projector connected to a computer. The computer must have either the PowerPoint program or the PowerPoint viewer installed.

- A **Web presentation** is one that is formatted in HTML and can contain hyperlinks and other Web page elements. This type of presentation can be viewed on the Internet or on a corporate intranet.

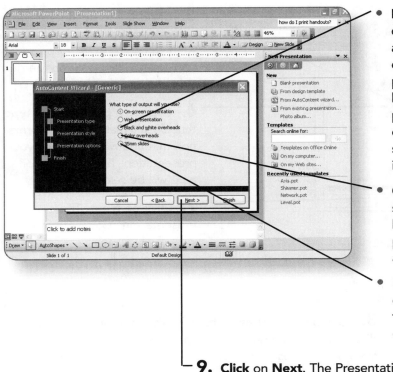

- **Black and white overheads** can be printed from a black-and-white laser printer on either transparencies or paper. Transparencies can be used with an overhead projector to deliver the presentation. These presentation slides are 8.5 x 11 inches in size.

- **Color overheads** are the same as black-and-white overheads, except this type of presentation is printed from a color inkjet printer.

- If you want to deliver a presentation using a slide projector, select the **35mm slides** option.

9. **Click** on **Next**. The Presentation options page of the wizard will appear.

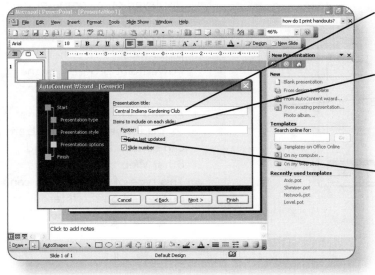

10. **Click** in the **Presentation title text box** and **type** a **title** for your presentation.

11. **Click** in the **Footer text box** and **type** the **text** that you want to appear in the footer area at the bottom of each slide, if any.

12. **Click** in the **Date last updated check box** if you do not want to display the date when you last made updates to the presentation. (This information is found in the footer area of a slide.) The check box will be cleared.

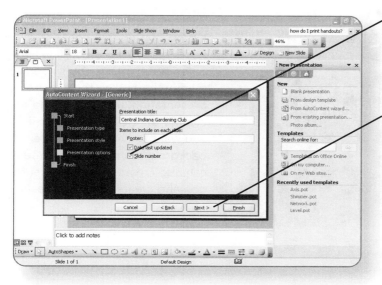

13. **Click** in the **Slide number check box** if you do not want to show the slide number in the footer area. The check box will be cleared.

14. **Click** on **Next**. The Finish page of the wizard will appear.

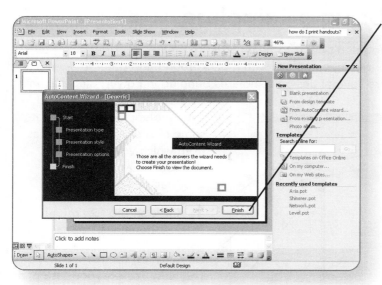

15. **Click** on **Finish**. The presentation will appear in the PowerPoint window.

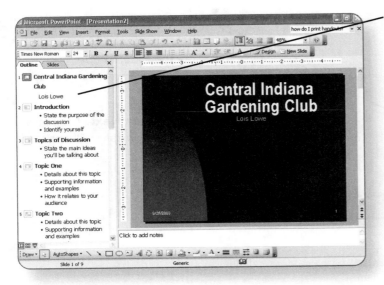

The AutoContent wizard creates a presentation that contains a starting point for an outline and a design template. You'll need to modify the outline to fit your presentation, and you'll need to change the design template if you want to change the slide background and text font. You can also create a blank presentation and create your own design template.

Starting a New Presentation Using a Template

You don't need to be an artist to create a good-looking presentation, complete with a background and other images. There are several design templates bundled in PowerPoint that will be pleasing to both you and your audience. Take a look at some of the design templates from which you can choose, and see if any of them suit your needs.

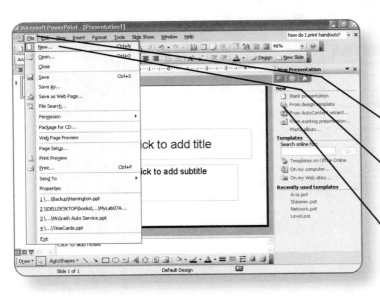

1. Click on the **File menu**. The File menu will appear.

2. Click on the **New command**. The New Presentation task pane will appear.

3. Click on the **From design template hyperlink**. The Slide Design task pane will appear.

4. **Click** on a **design**. It will be applied to the slide, so you can see what it looks like.

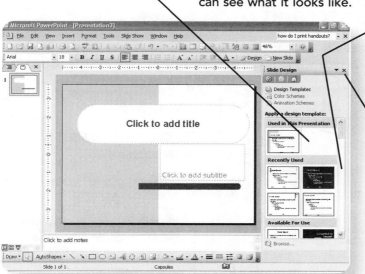

Scroll through the list with the scroll bar.

5. **Repeat step 4** until you find the design you want.

6. **Click** on the **Close button** for the task pane. The task pane will close.

Starting a Blank Presentation

If you are not sure what design or content you want, you might wish to start with a completely blank presentation with no text and no formatting.

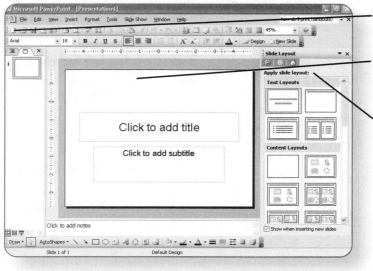

1. **Click** on the **New button** on the toolbar.

A new presentation will appear. It will have a single slide with a Title layout.

The Slide Layout task pane will appear, so you can specify a different layout for the slide, if desired.

Previewing the Presentation Onscreen

As you're working on a presentation, you may want to see how each slide will look when displayed onscreen in Slide Show view.

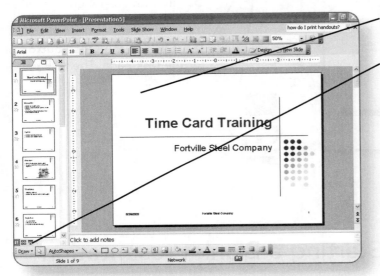

1. Display the **slide** you want to preview.

2. Click on the **Slide Show View button**.

NOTE

In step 2, you can also use the View, Slide Show View command or the Slide Show, View Show command, or you can just press F5. The only difference is that they all start with the first slide rather than the currently displayed one.

The current slide will appear full-screen, as it will look during a show.

3a. Click the **left mouse button** to move to the next slide. Continue through the presentation.

OR

3b. Press the **Esc key** to return to PowerPoint.

Time Card Training

Fortville Steel Company

8/26/2003   Fortville Steel Company   1

Printing the Presentation

When you want a paper copy of a presentation, send the file to a printer. Later in the book, especially in Chapter 44, "Creating Audience Handouts," you will learn more about printing. For now, let's just print a single copy of the presentation with each slide on a separate page.

1. Click on **File**. The File menu will appear.

2. Click on **Print**. The Print dialog box will open.

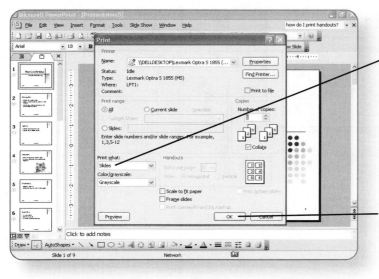

NOTE

For a new presentation, the default view to print is Slides. If you have previously printed handouts or notes pages, that might be the default and you might need to **change** the **Print what setting**.

3. Click on **OK**. The presentation file will be sent to the printer using the default print settings.

Working with Presentation Files

Before you get too involved in developing a presentation, you'll need to save the presentation file. Remember to save the file often so that you don't lose your valuable efforts. Then, once you've started on the presentation, you'll want to see how you are progressing. You can easily preview the presentation or print it.

Saving Your Presentation

It can never be stressed enough that you must save your work often while you are working on a presentation. Also, you may want to back up the presentation file to a floppy disk, a Zip disk, or a recordable CD, in case you run into a computer problem.

1. **Click** on the **Save button** on the Standard toolbar. The Save As dialog box will open.

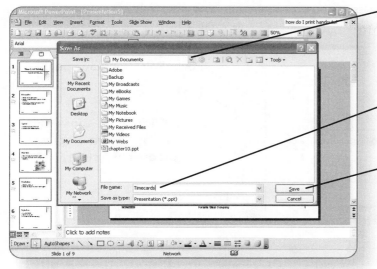

2. Click on the **Save in drop-down list arrow** and **select** the **folder** in which you want to store the file. The folder will be selected.

3. Click in the **File name text box** and **type** a **name** for the presentation.

4. Click on **Save**. The presentation file will be stored in the designated folder, and the file name will appear in the title bar of the PowerPoint window.

NOTE

After you've saved the presentation file the first time, you can save your changes by clicking on the Save button.

Closing the Presentation

When you've finished working on a presentation, close the presentation file. You can close a presentation file without closing the PowerPoint program, or you can close both at once.

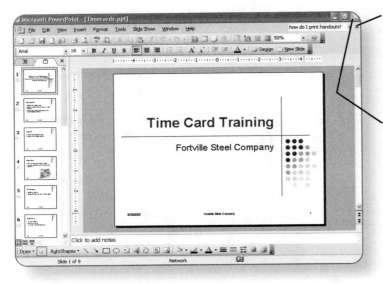

1a. Click on the **Close button** for the presentation. The presentation file will close and PowerPoint will stay open.

OR

1b. Click on the **Close button** for the PowerPoint program. The program will close.

Opening a Recently Used Presentation

PowerPoint keeps a list of the saved files you've worked with recently. This list is found at the bottom of the File menu.

1. Click on **File**. The File menu will appear.

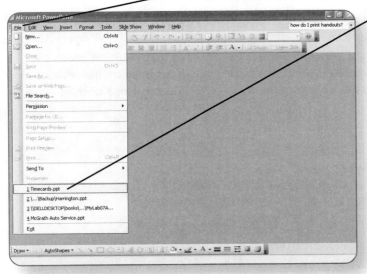

2. Click on the **presentation file** in the recently used file list. The presentation will appear in the PowerPoint window.

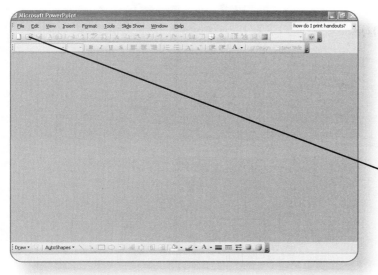

Opening Any Saved Presentation

If the presentation you want to open does not appear at the bottom of the File menu, you can use the Open dialog box to select and open it.

1. **Click** on the **Open button** on the toolbar. The Open dialog box will appear.

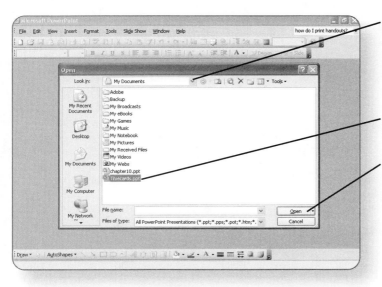

2. **Click** on the **Look in drop-down list arrow** and **select** the **folder** in which you want to look for the file. The folder will be selected.

3. **Click** on the **file name** for the presentation.

4. **Click** on **Open**. The presentation file will open in the PowerPoint window.

NOTE

You can also open a presentation file and start PowerPoint at the same time by double-clicking the presentation file in a Windows file management window.

31

Organizing the Presentation Outline

In the first part of this book, you learned how presentations work by looking at the presentation and design templates. You also learned how to use some of PowerPoint's features to design a presentation. Now it's time for you to fly on your own and start a presentation from scratch. In this chapter, you'll learn how to:

- Develop a presentation outline
- Insert slides from another presentation
- Use a Microsoft Word outline in PowerPoint
- Edit slide text
- Print the outline

Displaying Outline View

Much of the activity in this chapter takes place in the Outline pane. If it does not appear in Normal view already, you can display it easily.

1. **Click** the **Normal View button**. If any other view is in use, it will be replaced by Normal.

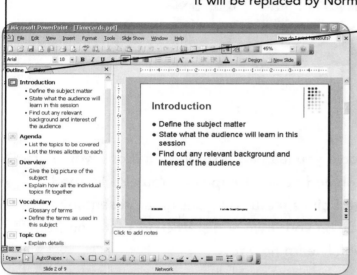

2. **Click** on the **Outline tab**. The presentation outline will appear.

NOTE

If the Outline tab is not already showing, it will not have the word "Outline" on it. Instead, it will have some horizontal lines representing text.

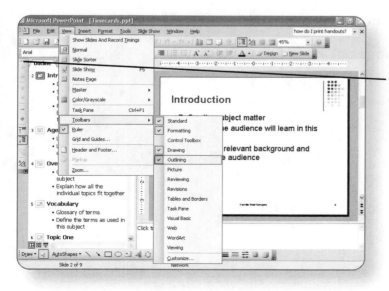

Displaying the Outlining Toolbar

The Outlining toolbar can be useful when you're working with outlines. If it does not appear automatically, you can enable it.

1. Click on **View**. The View menu will appear.

2. Move the **mouse pointer** to **Toolbars**. A list of available toolbars will appear.

3. Click on **Outlining**. The Outlining toolbar will appear along the left side of the PowerPoint window.

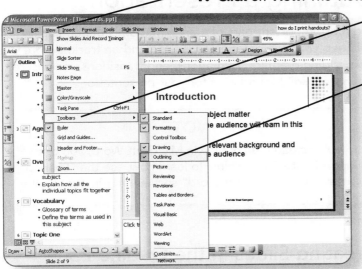

The Outlining toolbar can be used to:

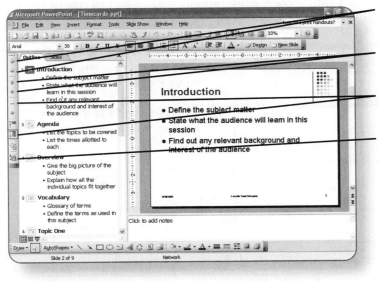

- Promote and demote text within the outline

- Change the order of slides within the presentation

- Collapse and expand the outline

- Display the same text formatting on the outline that is used on the slides

Outlining a Presentation

The most important part of a presentation is the outline, which will keep your presentation organized and on track. Before you start adding graphics, animations, and transitions, make sure you have a solid foundation for your presentation.

NOTE

If you've created an outline in Microsoft Word, you can import it into PowerPoint. To learn how, see the "Sharing Outlines with Microsoft Word" section later in this chapter.

Creating Slides in the Outline Pane

If you used the AutoContent Wizard to start your presentation, an outline has already been started for you (as shown in the preceding figures). It is a simple matter of editing the outline by changing a few words or adding a few new slides. If you started with a blank presentation, you'll need to create each new slide by adding text to the outline.

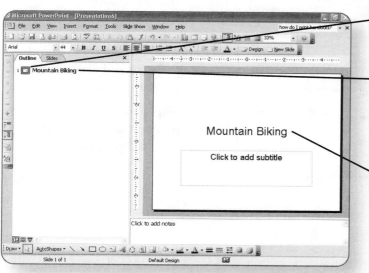

1. **Click** to the **right of the slide icon**. The cursor will move there.

2. **Type** the **text** that you want to appear as the title of the first slide.

NOTE

Notice that the text also appears on the slide in the Title area.

---

3. **Press** the **Enter key**. A new slide icon will appear on a new line.

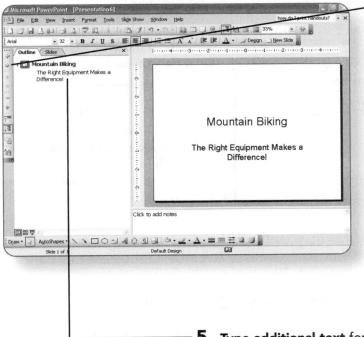

4. **Click** on the **Demote button** on the Outlining toolbar, or **press Tab**. The new line will be demoted in importance so that it represents text on the preceding slide.

NOTE

Each time you press Enter, a new line appears at the same outline level as the previous line. Since you were typing title text in step 2, pressing Enter in step 3 started a new slide. Demoting the line makes it part of the preceding slide.

5. **Type additional text** for the slide.

6. **Press** the **Enter key**. Another line on the same slide will appear for typing.

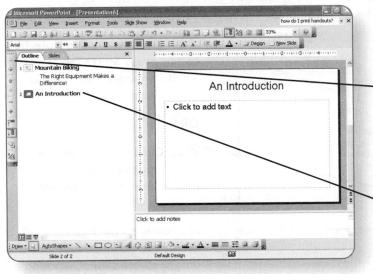

7a. **Return** to **step 5** to type additional text.

OR

7b. **Click** on the **Promote button** on the Outlining toolbar, or **press Shift+Tab**. The new line will be promoted in importance so that it represents a new slide title.

8. **Type** the **text** for the title of the second slide and **press Enter**.

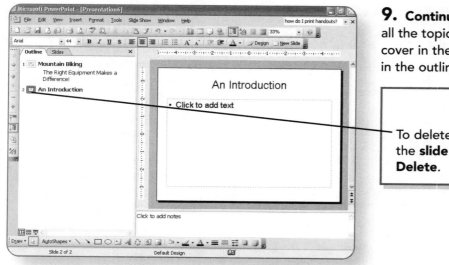

9. Continue adding text until all the topics that you want to cover in the presentation appear in the outline.

NOTE

To delete a slide, **click** on the **slide icon** and **press Delete**.

Promoting and Demoting Lines

Once you've added the topics that you want to cover in the presentation, you may want to change the level at which some outline items appear.

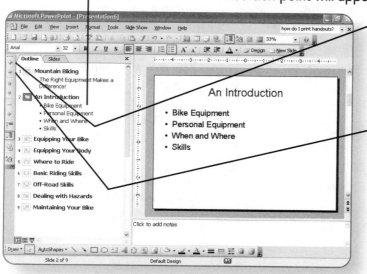

1. Click on the **line** that you want to promote or demote. The insertion point will appear in it.

2a. Click on the **Promote button** or **press Shift+Tab**. The text will be promoted to a higher outline level.

OR

2b. Click on the **Demote button** or **press Tab**. The text will be demoted to the next outline level.

Promoting to the highest level makes the text into slide title text on a separate slide. Demoting a slide title makes it a bullet point on the previous slide.

Rearranging Outline Text

Each paragraph in the outline is either a slide title or a bullet point on the body of a slide. You can move individual paragraphs or groups of them up or down in the outline.

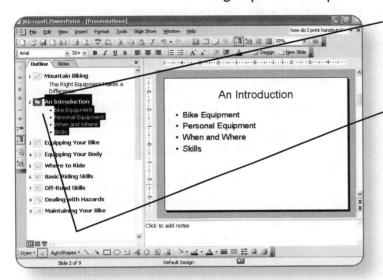

1a. **Click** on a **slide icon**. The entire slide and all its subordinate text will be selected.

OR

1b. **Click** to the **left of an individual paragraph**. Only that paragraph will be selected.

NOTE

To select multiple slide icons or multiple paragraphs, hold down Shift as you click on additional ones.

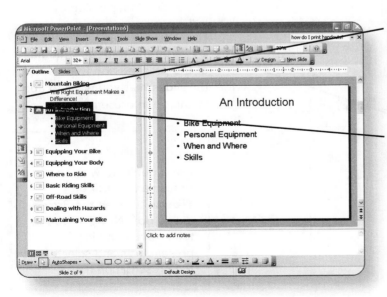

2a. **Click** on the **Move Up button** or **drag** the selection **upward**. The selection will move higher in the outline.

OR

2b. **Click** on the **Move Down button** or **drag** the selection **downward**. The selection will move lower in the outline.

Inserting Slides from Another Presentation

If you want to add an existing presentation to a presentation you're working on right now, just insert the slides from the existing presentation. You can insert the entire presentation or just a group of slides.

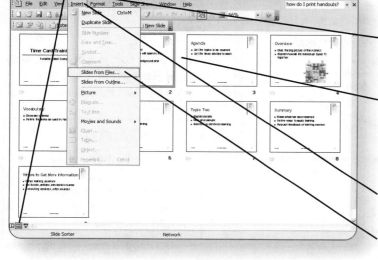

1. Click on the **Slide Sorter View button**. The display will change to Slide Sorter view.

2. Click in the **space** where you want the slides from the other presentation to appear. The insertion bar will appear in the selected location.

3. Click on **Insert**. The Insert menu will appear.

4. Click on **Slides from Files**. The Slide Finder dialog box will open.

5. Type the **path and file name** of the presentation that contains the slides that you want to add to the open presentation.

NOTE

If you don't know the path or file name, **click** on **Browse** to open the Browse dialog box. Navigate to the folder that contains the presentation and select the presentation file.

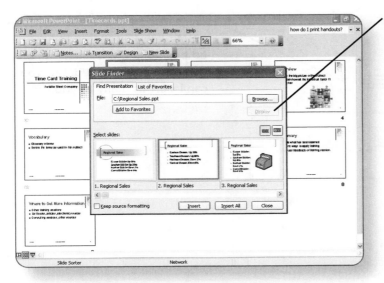

6. Click on **Display** if the slides do not appear automatically. A preview of the presentation slides will appear in the Select slides area.

7. Click on the **slides** that you want to insert into the presentation. The slides will be selected.

8. Click on **Insert**. The selected slides will be inserted into the open presentation.

NOTE

If you want the slides to retain the original slide design, **click** on the **Keep source formatting check box**.

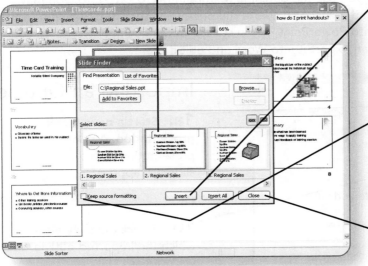

9. Click on **Close**. The Slide Finder dialog box will close.

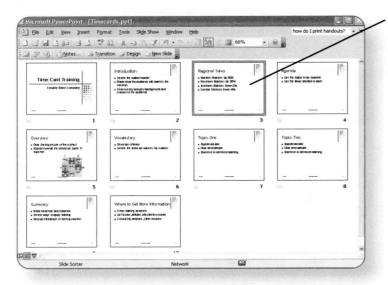

The slides from the existing presentation will appear in the selected position. In this example, only one slide was inserted, but you can insert as many as you like.

Sharing Outlines with Microsoft Word

If you use the outlining feature in Microsoft Word, you may find it easier to create the outline in Word and then import it into PowerPoint. If you started an outline in PowerPoint, you can export it into Word and edit it there.

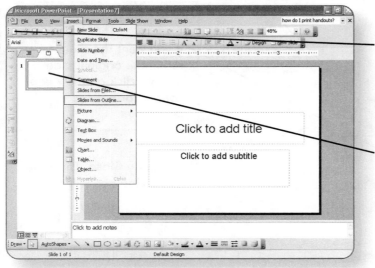

Importing an Outline

1a. **Start** a **new, blank presentation**. A new presentation with a single Title slide will appear.

OR

1b. **Select** the **slide** after which the imported outline text will appear.

2. Click on **Insert**. The Insert menu will appear.

3. Click on **Slides from Outline**. The Insert Outline dialog box will appear.

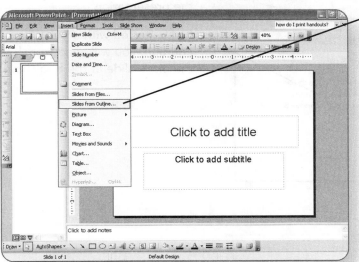

4. Display the **folder** in which you've stored the Word outline file. The folder will appear in the Look in list box.

5. Click on the **file** that contains the outline that you want to add to the presentation. The file will be selected.

6. Click on **Insert**.

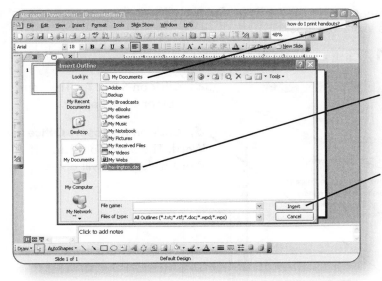

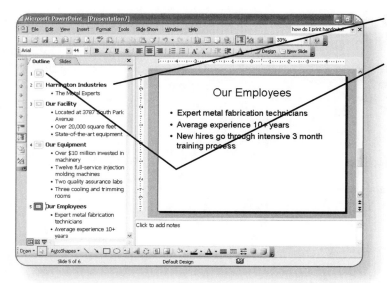

The outline will be inserted into the presentation.

If you started with a blank presentation, you will need to delete the blank slide at the beginning.

Exporting an Outline

You can also send a PowerPoint outline to Word and save it as a Word document.

1. Click on **File**. The File menu will appear.

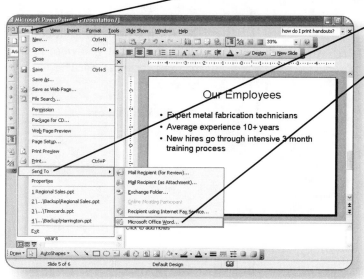

2. Click on **Send To**. The Send To submenu will appear.

3. Click on **Microsoft Office Word**. The Send To Microsoft Word dialog box will open.

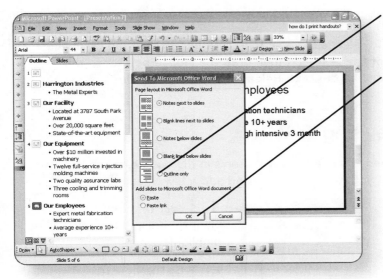

4. Click on the **Outline only option**, if it is not selected already.

5. Click on **OK**. The outline will open in Microsoft Word.

From Word, you can edit or save the outline normally.

Editing Text

Once the basic outline structure is in place, you can make any changes you want to the outline. You may need to change a few words or add a few new words.

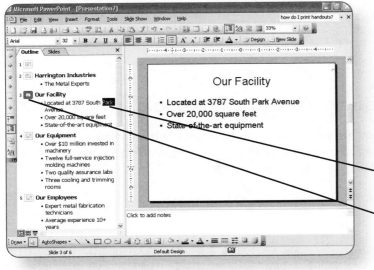

Selecting Text

Before you can edit or format text, you'll need to select the text. Selected text appears inside a boxed background. The selected text can be a single letter or word, or several words. Here are a few tips for selecting text.

- To select a word, **double-click** on the **word**.

- To select an entire slide, **click** the **slide icon**.

- To select a paragraph, **triple-click** it.

- To select the entire outline, **press Ctrl+A**.

- To select a block of text, **click and hold** at the **beginning of the text**, and then **drag** the **mouse pointer** to the **end of the text**. **Release** the **mouse button**.

Revising Text

When you need to revise items in the outline, select the words that you want to replace and add a few of your own.

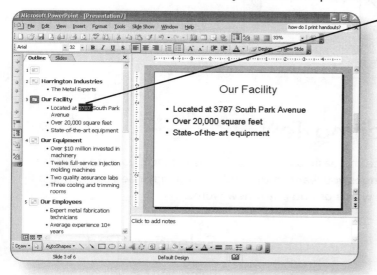

1. **Select** the **text** that you want to replace. The text will be highlighted.

2. **Type** the **new text**. The selected text will be deleted and replaced with the new text.

Adding Text to a Placeholder

If you have created some slide titles in the outline with no subordinate text beneath them, you'll notice that on the slide is a "Click to add text" placeholder.

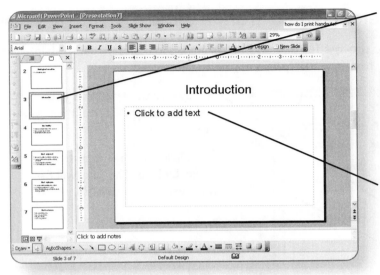

1. Display a **slide** that contains a text placeholder. The slide will appear in Normal view.

NOTE

Click the slide you want in the Slides or Outline pane.

2. Click on the **text** in the placeholder. The placeholder text will disappear, and the cursor will appear in the text box.

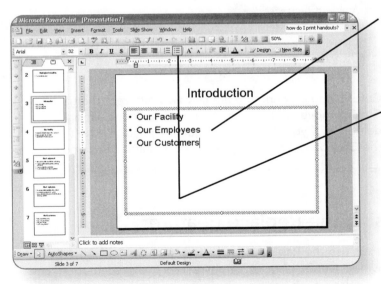

3. Type the **text** that you want in the placeholder.

TIP

The bullets can be removed. **Select** the **bulleted items** and **click** on the **Bullets button** on the Formatting toolbar.

Deleting Text from a Slide

The process for deleting text from a slide is identical to deleting text from the presentation outline.

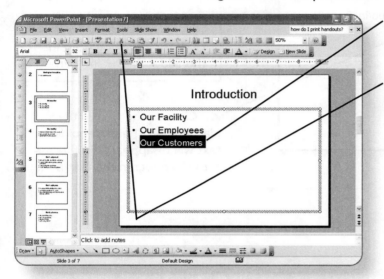

1. **Select** the **text** that you want to delete. The text will be highlighted.

2. **Click** on the **Cut button** or **press Delete**. The text will be removed from the slide.

NOTE

Cutting and deleting are actually two different things. Cutting moves text to the Clipboard; deleting simply deletes it. If you do not subsequently paste the text from the Clipboard, however, the overall result is the same.

Using the Replace Feature

You can use the Replace feature to search for text, such as individual words, phrases, or characters in a presentation, and then replace it with some other text.

1. Click on **Edit**. The Edit menu will appear.

2. Click on **Replace**. The Replace dialog box will open.

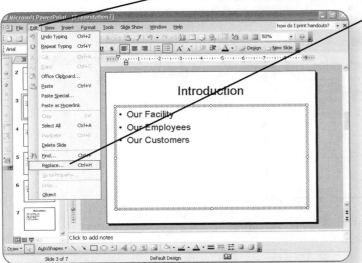

3. Type the **text** that you want to locate in the Find what text box.

4. Type the **text** to be used as the replacement in the Replace with text box.

The **Match case check box** allows you to limit the replacement to certain capitalization.

The **Find whole words only** check box allows you to limit the replacement to whole words.

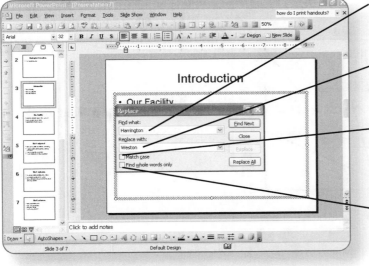

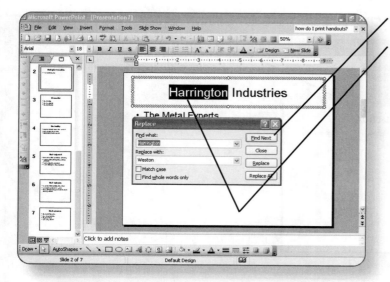

5. **Click** on **Find Next**.

The first occurrence of the word(s) for which you are searching will be highlighted on the slide.

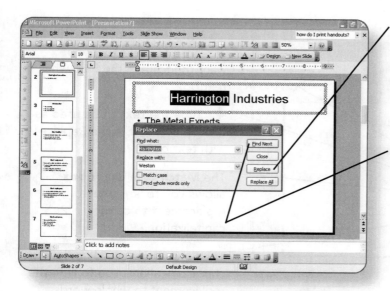

6a. **Click** on **Replace**. The text that is highlighted on the slide will be replaced with the text specified in the Replace with text box.

OR

6b. **Click** on **Find Next** to skip that occurrence.

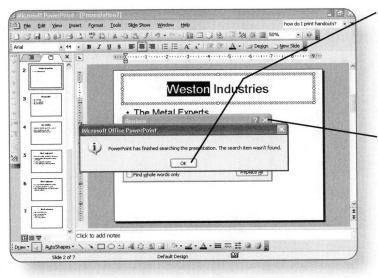

7a. **Repeat steps 5 and 6** until all instances have been found. A dialog box will appear stating that it is finished. Then **click** the **OK button**.

OR

7b. **Click** on **Close** to end the search early.

Printing the Outline

Before you print a presentation outline, display the items in the Outline tab that you want to print. If an item is collapsed (that is, hidden), it will not print. Use the Outlining toolbar to expand and collapse the outline.

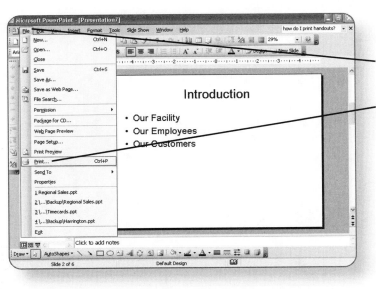

1. **Click** on **File**. The File menu will appear.

2. **Click** on **Print**. The Print dialog box will open.

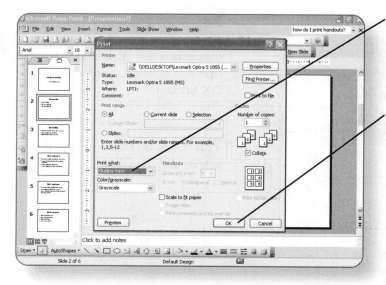

3. **Click** on the **Print what drop-down list arrow** and **select Outline View** from the list. The option will appear in the list box.

4. **Click** on **OK**. The outline will be sent to the printer.

32

Organizing and Improving the Presentation

Creating and editing the text is a good start, but for professional-quality materials, you must polish your work until it shines. This may include running a spelling check, using the thesaurus and other research tools in PowerPoint, and rearranging the order in which your slides appear. In this chapter, you will learn how to:

- Check a presentation for spelling errors
- Look up synonyms in the thesaurus
- Use the research tools for fact-finding
- Rearrange, copy, and delete slides in Slide Sorter view

Spell Checking the Presentation

Before your presentation makes its debut, run the spell checker. Not only will the spell checker help you spot misspelled words, but it will tell you when you repeat yourself.

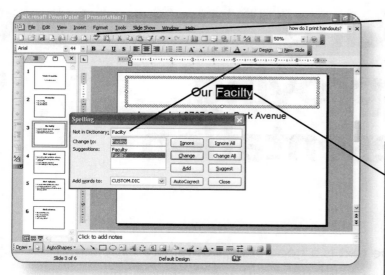

1. Click on the **Spelling button**.

The Spelling dialog box will open with the first misspelled word displayed in the Not in Dictionary text box.

TIP

Look for a red, wavy line while you are adding text to your presentation. Instead of running the full spell check, you can right-click on the word and select the correct spelling from the menu that appears.

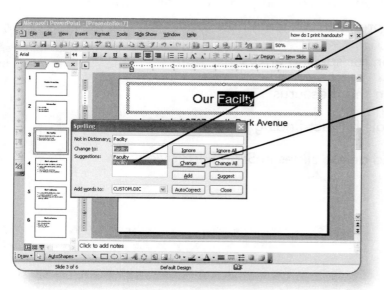

2. Click on the **correct spelling** in the Suggestions text box. The word will be selected and will appear in the Change to text box.

3a. Click on **Change**. The misspelled word will be corrected, and the next misspelled word will appear.

OR

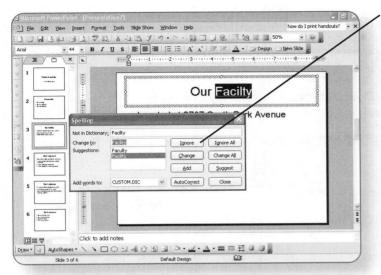

3b. **Click** on **Ignore**. The word will be left as is, and the next misspelled word will appear. When PowerPoint has checked the last word in the presentation, a confirmation dialog box will appear.

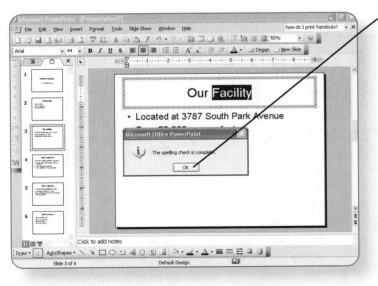

4. **Click** on **OK**. The presentation will be spell checked. You should save the file so that the corrections are preserved.

Using the Research Tools

The research tools, new in PowerPoint 2003, work best when you are connected to the Internet. They rely on Internet databases, such as encyclopedias and news services.

Using the Thesaurus

The thesaurus enables you to find synonyms or antonyms for a word.

1. Double-click on the **word** you want to look up. It will be selected.

2. Click on **Tools**. The menu will appear.

3. Click on **Thesaurus**. The Research task pane will open.

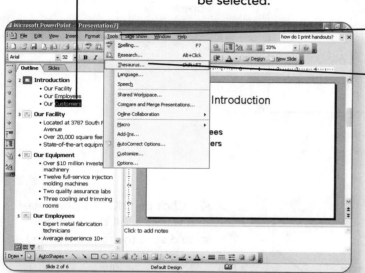

4. Point to the **desired replacement**. A drop-down arrow will appear beside it.

5. Click on the **down arrow**. A menu will appear.

6. Click on **Insert**. The selected word will be replaced by the new one.

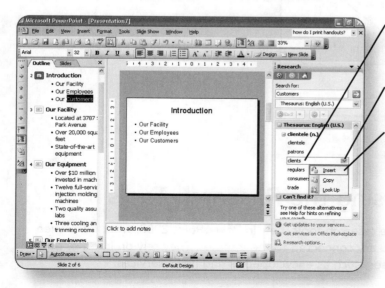

Using Other Research Tools

The thesaurus is only one of Office 2003's research tools. To find extended information about a topic, use the Research command.

1. **Click** on **Tools**. The menu will appear.

2. **Click** on **Research**. The Research pane will appear if it is not displayed already.

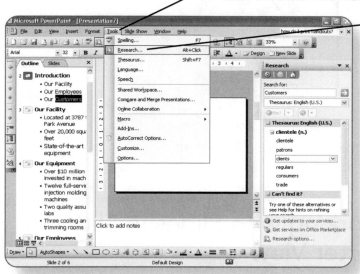

3. **Type** the **word or phrase** to research in the Search for box. The word or phrase will appear there.

4. **Choose a source** from the list of online reference sources.

TIP
Choose All Research Sites to search multiple sources.

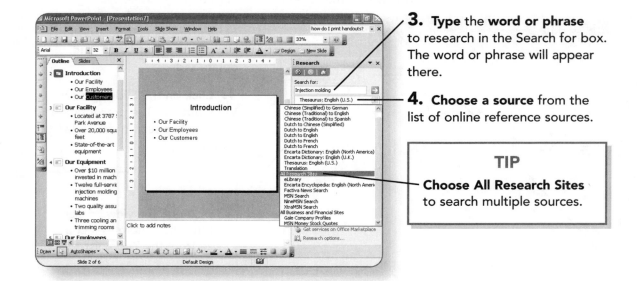

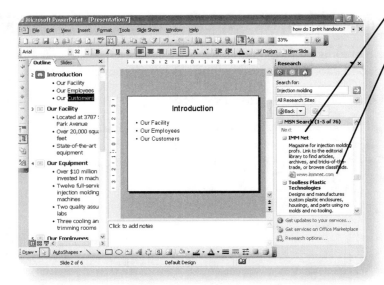

PowerPoint will look up the text in its online research libraries.

5. Click on the **article** you want to read. A Web browser window will display the article.

Working with Slides in Slide Sorter View

You don't have to work with just one slide at a time. The Slide Sorter view displays all the slides as miniatures in neat rows across the screen. This is a good way to see the big picture and view the progress of your presentation. Use this view to rearrange, add, and delete slides.

1. Click on the **Slide Sorter View button**. The presentation slides will appear in the Slide Sorter view.

TIP

To change the viewing size of the slides here, select a size from the Zoom list.

Selecting Slides

Before you can perform certain functions with slides (such as deleting or moving), you'll need to select the slides with which you want to work. You can select a single slide, a contiguous group of slides, or random slides.

Here are a few tips for selecting slides:

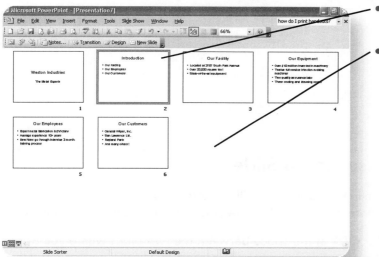

- To select a single slide, **click** on the **slide**.

- To deselect a slide, **click** on a **blank area** of the Slide Sorter view.

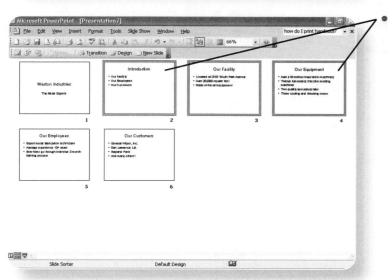

- To select a contiguous group of slides, **click** on the **first slide**, and then **press** and **hold** the **Shift key** while clicking on the last slide in the group.

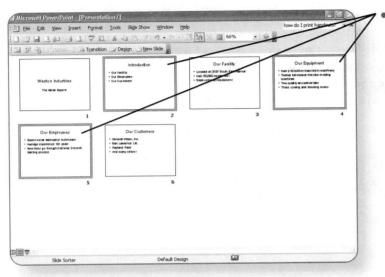

• To select random slides, **click** on the **first slide**, then **press** and **hold** the **Ctrl key** while clicking on the other slides you want to select.

Inserting a Slide

While browsing in the Slide Sorter view, you may find a place where an extra slide is needed. You can easily add a new slide.

1. **Click** in the **space** between the two slides where you want the new slide to appear. The insertion bar will appear between the two slides.

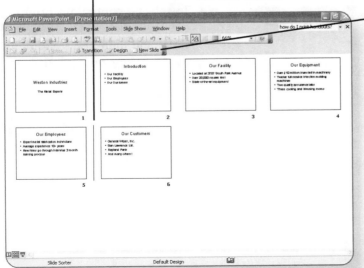

2. **Click** on **New Slide** on the Slide Sorter toolbar.

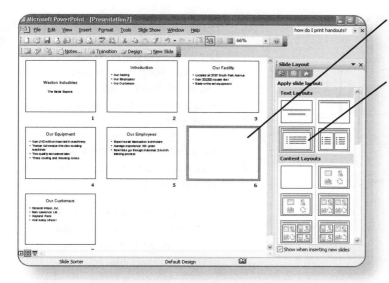

A new slide (using the default slide layout) will appear in the selected place.

The Slide Layout task pane will appear so you can select a layout. The default layout for new slides is Title and Text.

NOTE

To add text to the new slide, double-click on the slide to display it in Normal view.

Duplicating a Slide

When you want to make an exact copy of a slide, use the duplicate command.

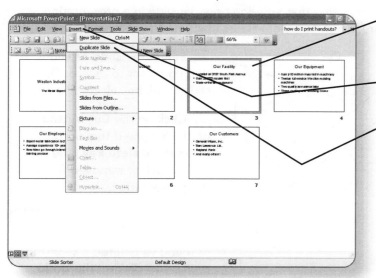

1. **Click** on the **slide** that you want to copy. The slide will be selected.

2. **Click** on **Insert**. The Insert menu will appear.

3. **Click** on **Duplicate Slide**. An identical slide will appear just after the original slide. The duplicate slide will be selected.

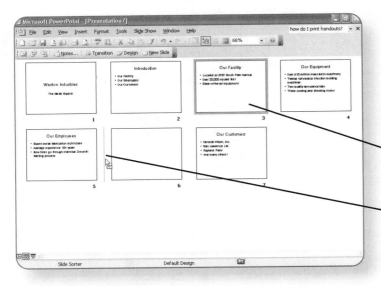

Moving a Slide

The Slide Sorter view can also be used to reorganize slides. Slides can be moved around to better present information with a simple drag and drop.

1. **Click** and **hold** on the **slide** that you want to move. The slide will be selected.

2. **Drag** the **mouse** to where you want to move the slide. The insertion bar will appear in the selected place.

3. **Release** the **mouse button**. The slide will appear in the new position.

Deleting Slides

You may find that you don't need a slide in a presentation. Here is how to delete slides that you do not want.

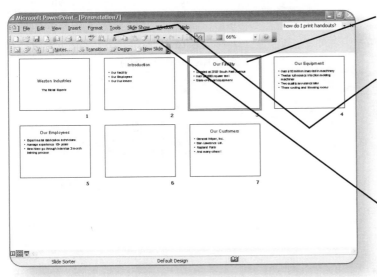

1. **Select** the **slide or slides** that you want to delete. The slide(s) will be selected.

2. **Click** on the **Cut button** on the Standard toolbar or **press** the **Delete key**. The slide(s) will be removed from the presentation.

NOTE

If you've deleted a slide in error, **click** on the **Undo button**. The slide will reappear.

33

Changing the Presentation's Look

In the last few chapters, we have been working with plain presentations —no design, no color. They've been pretty drab! But now it's time to change all that. In this chapter, you'll learn how to:

- Apply a design template
- Select an alternate color scheme
- Apply consistent formatting with slide masters

Changing the Design Template

A design template applies a preset font, color, background, and placeholder arrangement to every slide in the presentation. You learned how to start a new presentation using a design template in Chapter 3, "Learning About Presentations." You can change to a different design template at any time.

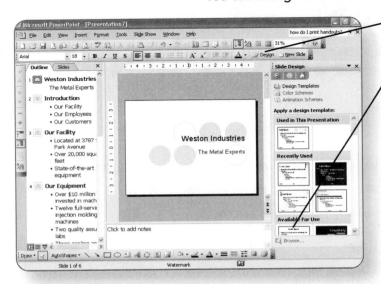

1. **Click** on the **Design button** on the toolbar. The Slide Design task pane will appear.

2. **Click** on the **design template** that you want to change to. The template will be applied.

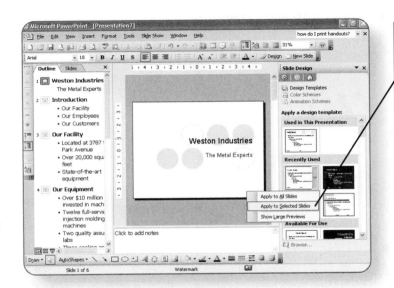

NOTE

You can also apply a template to only the selected slides. Point at the template, and a down arrow appears. Click the down arrow to bring up a menu, and then click on Apply to Selected Slides.

Changing the Color Scheme

Each design template comes with several different color schemes. You can switch to one of its alternate schemes, or you can start with one of those schemes and customize it to make your own color scheme.

Because the color schemes are associated with design templates, you should make your design template choice first, and then choose the color scheme.

Selecting an Alternate Color Scheme

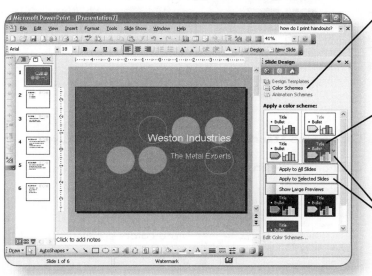

1. **Click** on the **Color Schemes hyperlink** in the Slide Design task pane. The color schemes will appear for the chosen design template.

2. **Click** on the **desired color scheme**. The presentation will change to that scheme.

NOTE

You can also apply a color scheme to the selected slides only, just like you did when applying the design template.

Customizing a Color Scheme

After selecting a color scheme, you may decide to change one or more of its colors.

1. Click on the **Edit Color Schemes hyperlink**. The Edit Color Scheme dialog box will open.

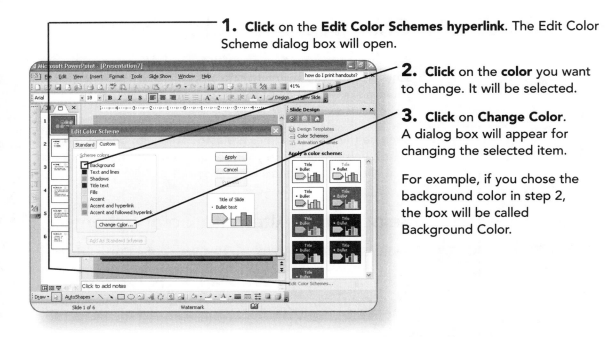

2. Click on the **color** you want to change. It will be selected.

3. Click on **Change Color**. A dialog box will appear for changing the selected item.

For example, if you chose the background color in step 2, the box will be called Background Color.

4. Click on the **Standard tab** if it is not already displayed.

5. Click on the **desired color**. It will be outlined.

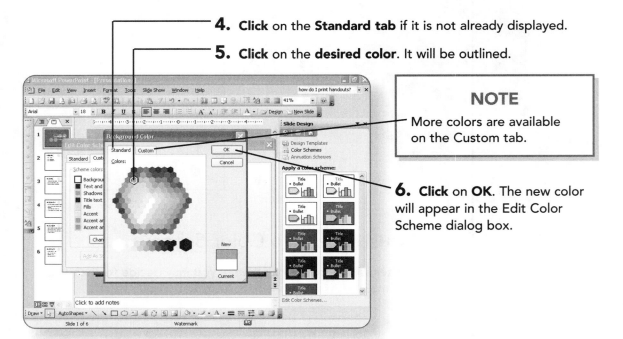

NOTE

More colors are available on the Custom tab.

6. Click on **OK**. The new color will appear in the Edit Color Scheme dialog box.

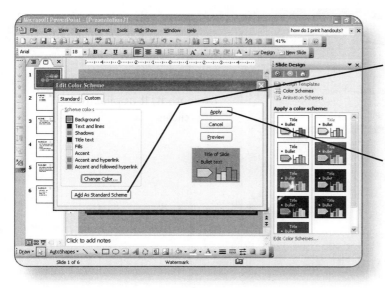

7. Repeat steps 2 through 6 for additional colors, if desired.

8. Click on **Add As Standard Scheme** if you want to save this color scheme. It will be added as a new color scheme on the Slide Design task pane.

9. Click on **Apply**. The dialog box will close and the new color scheme will be applied.

Working with Masters

The *Slide Master* is a template that applies to every slide in the presentation (except slides that use the Title Slide layout, because those take their design from the *Title Master* template).

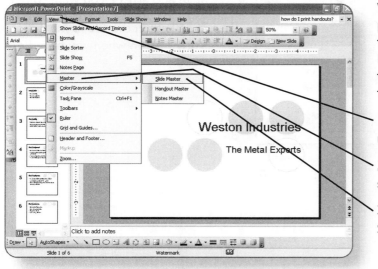

When you apply a design template, you are making changes to the Slide Master and Title Master. You can also change those Masters manually to customize the design.

1. Click on **View**. The View menu will appear.

2. Point to **Master**. The Master submenu will appear.

3. Click on **Slide Master**. The Slide Master view will appear.

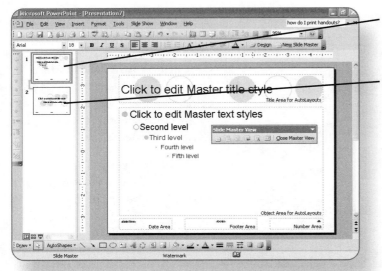

The Slide Master is the top template. It applies to all slides except title slides.

The Title Master is the one beneath it. It applies to title slides.

4. **Click** on the **Slide Master** or **Title Master** to select the one you want to edit.

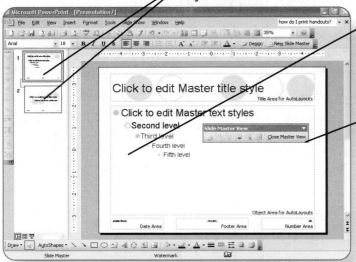

5. **Make changes** as desired. Keep reading to find out some of the changes you can make. You are limited only by how creative and artistic you want to be.

6. **Click** on the **Close Master View button** when you have finished.

Changing Text Formatting

In Chapter 34, "Formatting Slides," you will learn how to format slide text on a single slide, such as adding bold or italic, choosing a different font, or changing the size. You can do the same formatting to the text on the Slide Master or Title Master to change all the slides at once.

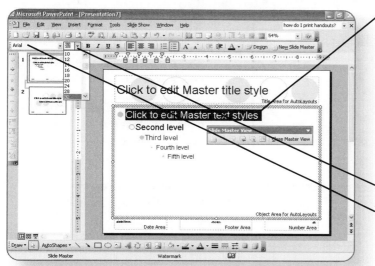

1. Select the **text** that you want to format. The text will be highlighted.

2. Apply text formatting to the text. See Chapter 34 for help, if needed.

Some of the formatting you can apply includes:

- Selecting a different font size
- Selecting a different font

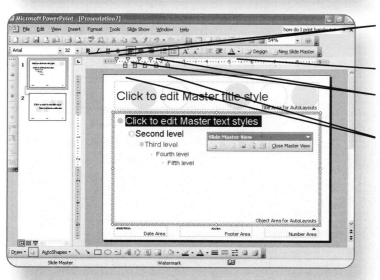

- Choosing bold, italic, underline, and/or shadow
- Selecting a different font color
- Choosing left, right, or center alignment
- Dragging the tab markers to change the indentation

Moving and Resizing Text Placeholders

You can change the size of the Title Area, Object Area, Footer Area, Date Area, and Number Area placeholders.

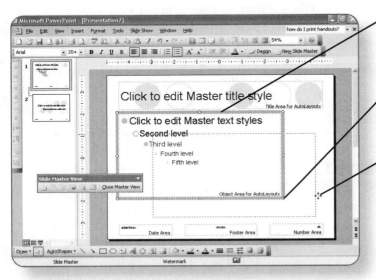

1. Click on a **placeholder**. A border will appear around the placeholder that contains resize handles.

2. Click and **drag** a **resize handle**. A dotted line will show the new size of the placeholder.

3. Position the **mouse pointer** over the placeholder. The mouse pointer will become a four-headed arrow.

4. Click and **drag** the **placeholder** to a new location.

Working with Footers and Special Placeholders

The Slide Master contains placeholder boxes for date/time, slide number, and footer. These can be moved around or resized (see the preceding steps). You can also turn them on or off.

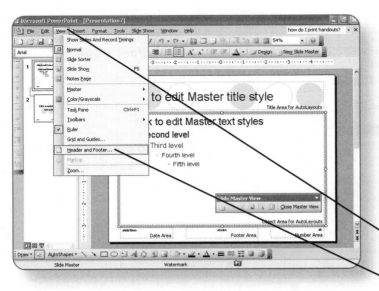

1. Click on **View**. The View menu will appear.

2. Click on **Header and Footer**. The Header and Footer dialog box will open.

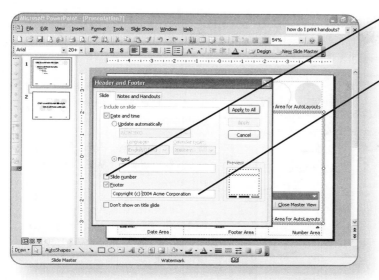

3. **Click** in the **Slide number check box** if you want the slides to be numbered.

4. **Type text** in the **Footer box** if you want footer text on each slide.

NOTE

You can deselect the Footer check box to turn off the footer temporarily, without deleting the footer text that you entered in step 4.

5. **Click** in the **Don't show on title slide check box** if you want to omit all placeholders from title slides.

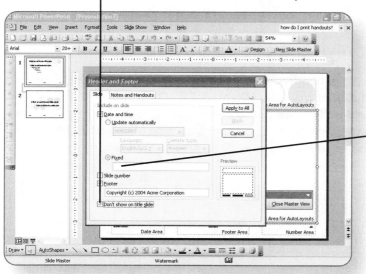

By default, the date/time does not appear, even though the placeholder is turned on. That's because Fixed is the default setting, and the Fixed box is blank.

6a. **Type today's date** in the Fixed box to make it appear on each slide. Then skip to step 9.

OR

6b. **Click** on **Update automatically** to set up an automatic date/time on each slide. Today's date will appear in the box beneath it.

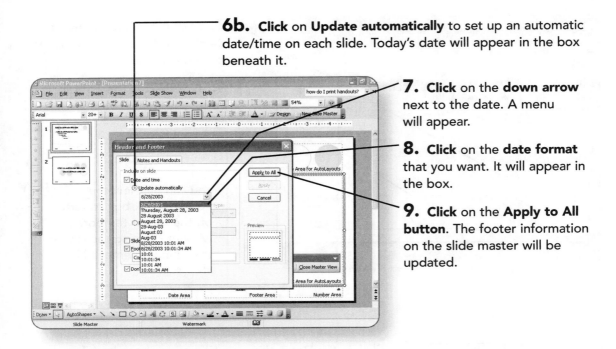

7. Click on the **down arrow** next to the date. A menu will appear.

8. Click on the **date format** that you want. It will appear in the box.

9. Click on the **Apply to All button**. The footer information on the slide master will be updated.

Applying a Slide Background

You have hundreds of choices for a slide background. You can use clip art from the Microsoft Clip Organizer or that you've found on the Internet, scanned photographs, or images you've created in a graphics program, such as Microsoft Photo Editor. Explore your options.

1. **Click** on **Format.** The Format menu will appear.

2. **Click** on **Background.** The Background dialog box will open.

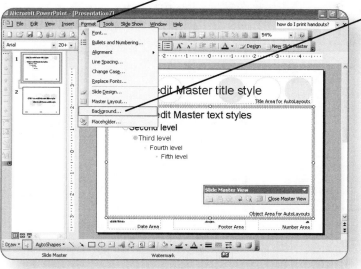

3. **Click** on the **down arrow next to Background fill.** A list of color options will appear.

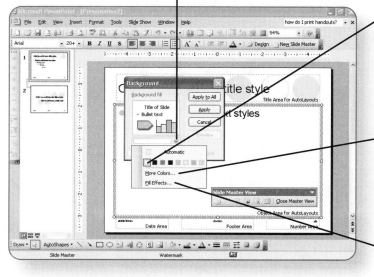

4a. **Click** on a **placeholder color.** A color will be used from the current color scheme. If you change color schemes, the background color will change.

OR

4b. **Click** on **More Colors** and then select a color from the Background Color box. A specific solid color will be used.

OR

4c. **Click** on **Fill Effects** and then select a gradient, texture, pattern, or picture as the background.

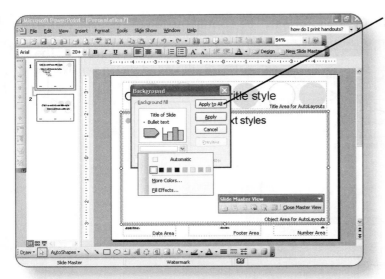

5. Click on **Apply to All** after selecting a background. The background will be applied to the Slide Master.

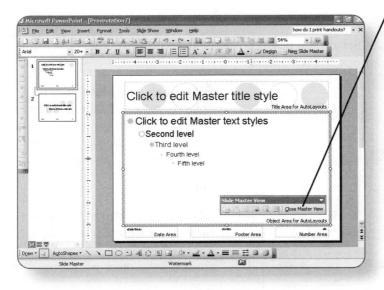

When you are finished working with the Slide Master, you can return to Normal view by clicking Close Master View.

34

Formatting Slides

So far in this book, you have been working mostly with the presentation as a whole. In this chapter, you'll learn how to change the appearance of individual slides by modifying various layout and appearance characteristics. In this chapter, you'll learn how to:

- Apply text formatting
- Change the look of bullets
- Choose different slide layouts
- Insert non-text content with layout placeholders

Formatting Slide Text

Generally speaking, it's a good idea to maintain formatting consistency on all slides. However, sometimes you may want to emphasize a word or group of words by using boldface, italics, color, a larger or smaller size, or a different font.

Working with the Formatting Toolbar

1. Select the **text** that you want to format. The text will be highlighted.

2. Click on a **Formatting toolbar button**. The text will be formatted in the style you've selected.

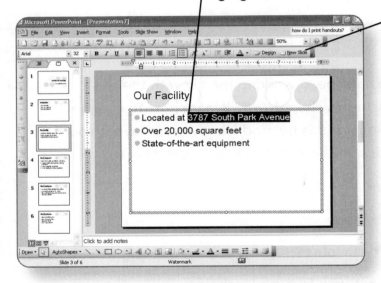

Here are a few formatting styles that you may want to apply to text:

- The **Font list** changes the typeface used for the text.

- The **Font Size list** makes the text larger or smaller.

- Emphasize text so that it stands out from other text by using the **Bold**, **Italic**, **Underline**, and **Shadow buttons**.

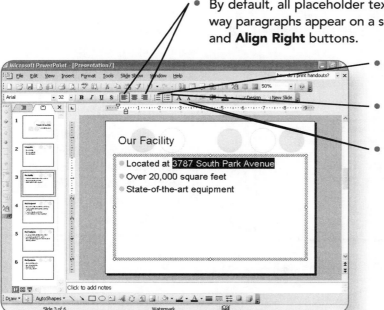

- By default, all placeholder text is left-aligned. To change the way paragraphs appear on a slide, use the **Align Left**, **Center**, and **Align Right** buttons.

- To make a numbered list, use the **Numbering button.**

- You can turn the bullets on or off with the **Bullets button.**

- The **Grow Text button** increases the font size, and the **Shrink Text button** decreases it.

Copying Text Formatting

You can also copy the formatting of text and apply it to other text in a presentation slide:

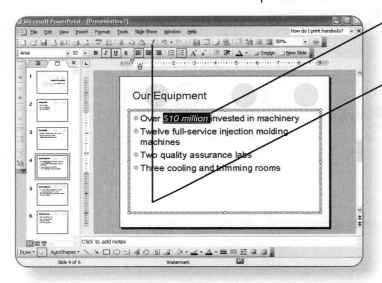

1. Select the **text** that is formatted in the style you want to apply to the other text.

2. Click on the **Format Painter button** on the Standard toolbar. The mouse pointer will turn into a paintbrush.

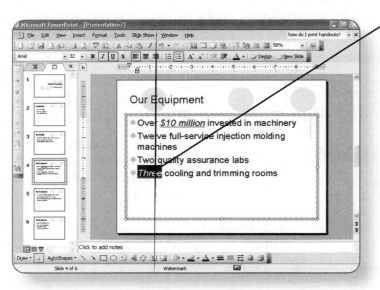

3. Select the **text** to which you want to apply the formatting. The formatting will be copied.

TIP

To apply the copied formatting to more than one text element, double-click in step 2. Then press Esc after step 3 to return to normal mode.

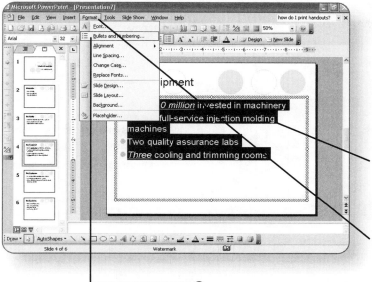

Selecting a Different Bullet Character

The default bullet character depends on the design template you've chosen. You can select a different bullet character without changing the design template.

1. Select the **paragraphs** to which you want to apply a different bullet character. The paragraphs will be selected.

2. Click on **Format**. The Format menu will appear.

3. Click on **Bullets and Numbering**. The Bullets and Numbering dialog box will open.

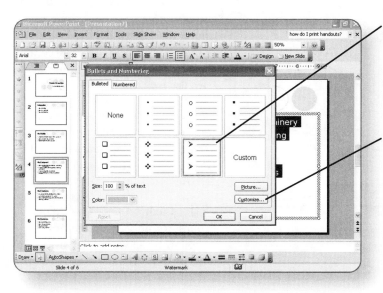

4a. Click on the **bullet character** that you want to use for the bullet list. The bullet will be selected. Then skip to step 10.

OR

4b. Click on **Customize**. The Symbol dialog box will open.

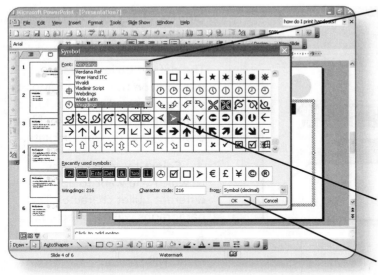

5. **Click** on the **Font box's down arrow** and choose a different font if desired. The characters in the font will appear.

TIP

Wingdings is a good font for selecting bullet characters.

---

6. **Click** on the **character you want** for the bullets. It will be selected.

7. **Click** on **OK**. The Symbol dialog box will close.

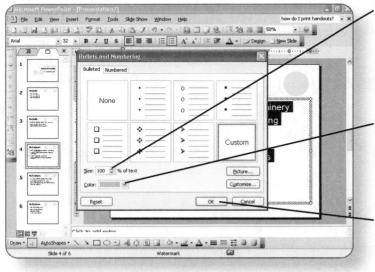

8. **Click** the **Size up and down arrows** to select how large or small the bullet will be, compared to the text. The percentage you choose will appear in the list box.

9. **Click** the **Color down arrow** and **select** a color from the list. The color that appears in the list box will be applied to the bullet character.

10. **Click** on **OK**. The bullet character and color will be applied to all the bullet points in the placeholder.

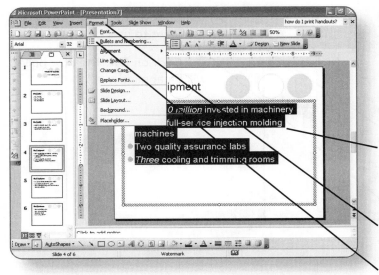

Selecting a Picture Bullet

In addition to the standard bullet types in the preceding steps, you can choose from a variety of pictures for bullets.

1. Select the **paragraphs** to which you want to apply a different bullet character. The paragraphs will be selected.

2. Click on **Format**. The Format menu will appear.

3. Click on **Bullets and Numbering**. The Bullets and Numbering dialog box will open.

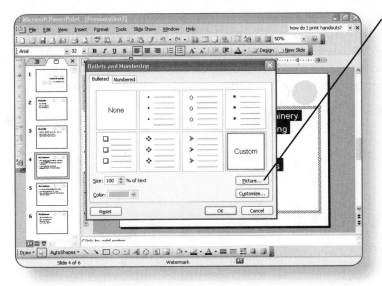

4. Click on **Picture**. The Picture Bullet dialog box will open.

NOTE

You will have many more bullet choices if you are connected to the Internet.

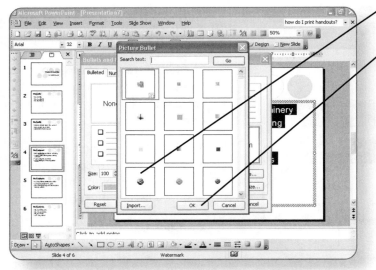

5. **Click** on the **bullet character** you want to use.

6. **Click** on **OK**. The new bullet will be applied.

Selecting a Slide Layout

The first slide in the presentation has a Title layout by default, and other slides have a Title and Text layout. Other layouts may be useful when you have other content besides text to display, such as pictures, graphs, or diagrams. You can add such items to a slide manually, but it is easier to do so by changing the layout and then using the layout placeholders.

1. **Click** on the **slide** that you want to change. The slide will be selected.

2. **Click** on **Format**. The Format menu will appear.

3. **Click** on **Slide Layout**. The Slide Layout task pane will open and the list of available slide layouts will be displayed.

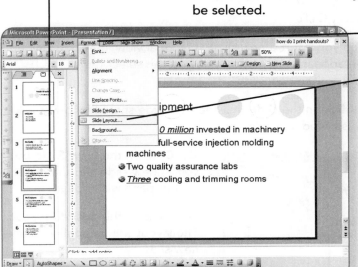

4. **Click** on the **layout** you want to apply to the slide.

NOTE

Hold the **mouse pointer** over a **slide layout** in the Task Pane to see a description of the layout.

The slide will change to the new layout format.

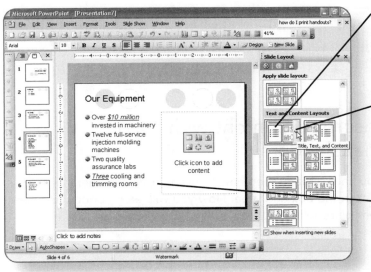

Inserting a New Slide Based on a Layout

When you insert a new slide in Normal view, the Slide Layout pane appears automatically so you can select the desired layout for the new slide.

1. **Click** on the **slide** that the new slide should follow. It will be displayed and selected.

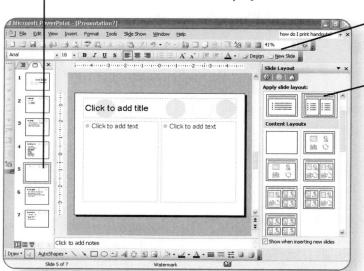

2. **Click** on the **New Slide button**. A new slide and the Slide Layout pane will appear.

3. **Click** on the **desired layout.** The layout will be applied to the new slide.

Inserting Content with Layout Placeholders

You have already seen how to use text placeholders: Simply click in the box and type. Now you will learn about other content placeholders.

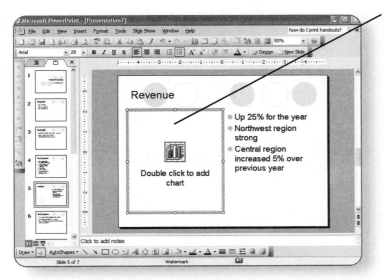

Some slide layouts have a place-holder for a single type of non-text content. Double-click the placeholder to insert that content.

Other slide layouts have a multi-purpose placeholder with icons for six types of content. Double-click on the appropriate icon for the content type you want. Future chapters will address these content types in more detail.

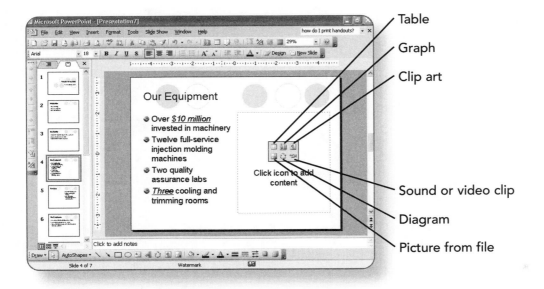

Table

Graph

Clip art

Sound or video clip

Diagram

Picture from file

35
Inserting Graphics

You don't need to be a great illustrator to create slides with good-looking pictures. You just need to know how to work with the tools provided by PowerPoint. Myriad clip art images are at your disposal so that you can vary the design of your presentation. Change the color and size of clip art images to fit on the slide. Delete parts of an image if you want. Let your imagination have fun. You'll also find an arsenal of ready-made shapes and text effects that you can fill, color, and position anywhere. In this chapter, you'll learn how to:

- Select clip art from the Clip Organizer
- Use WordArt to enhance text on a slide
- Create line art images with AutoShapes

Working with Clip Art

The Microsoft Office programs use the clip art in the Clip Organizer. You can find a clip by entering a topic keyword.

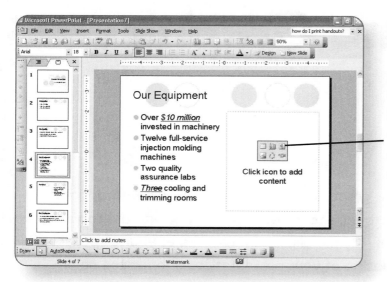

Using a Clip Art Placeholder

One way to open the Clip Organizer is with a Clip Art placeholder on a slide layout.

1. Click on the **Clip Art icon** on a slide layout. The Select Picture dialog box will appear.

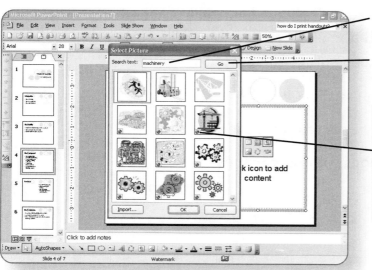

2. Type a **word** in the Search text box.

3. Click on **Go**. Clips matching that keyword will appear.

NOTE

A clip with a globe icon in the corner is from the Internet. If you choose it, it will be downloaded.

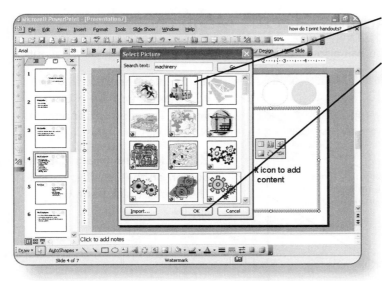

4. Click on the **desired clip**. The clip will be selected.

5. Click on **OK**.

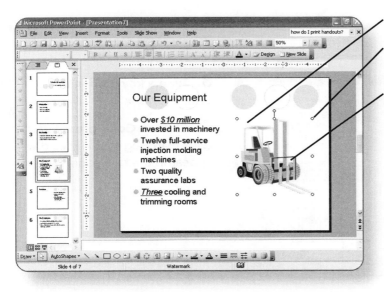

The clip will appear on the slide.

Drag one of the selection handles to resize it.

Drag it by its center to move it.

Adding Clip Art Manually

You can also add clip art to any slide, regardless of its layout.

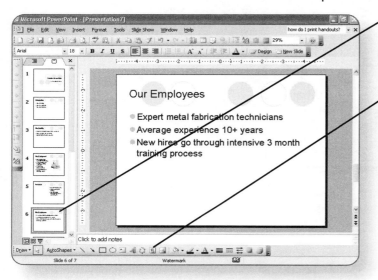

1. Display the **slide** to which you want to add the clip art image. The slide will appear in Normal view.

2. Click on the **Insert Clip Art button** on the Drawing toolbar. The Clip Art task pane will appear.

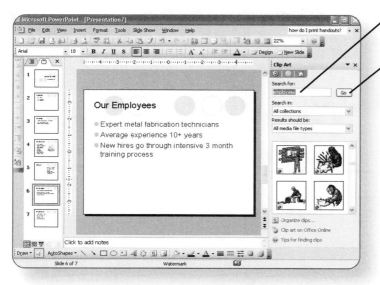

3. Type a **keyword** in the Search for box.

4. Click on **Go** or **press Enter**. Clips matching that keyword will appear in the task pane.

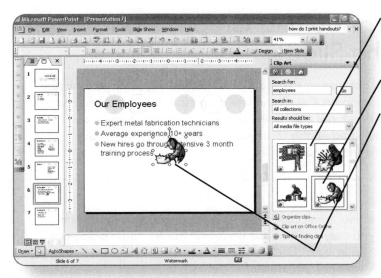

5. **Browse** through the **images** until you find one that fits your needs.

6. **Click** on the **clip**.

It will appear on the slide.

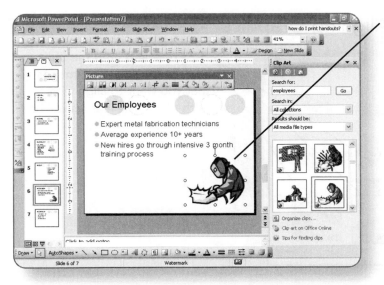

7. **Move** and **resize the clip** as needed.

Positioning Graphics on the Slide

It's not always easy to look at something (such as a picture hanging on a wall) and line it up straight. That's when you need to break out the tools, such as a T-square, a level, or a ruler. You'll find all the tools you need to do the job in the PowerPoint toolbox.

TIP

If you are accustomed to using page layout programs, you may want to use grids and guides to help you position images. Click on the View menu and select Grid and Guides to get started.

Aligning Graphics

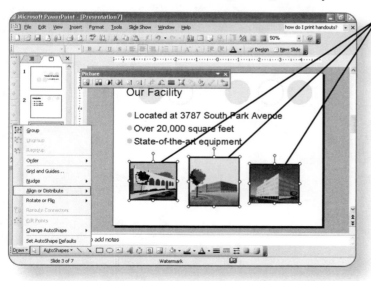

1. Press and hold the **Shift key**, and **click** on the **images** that you want to align with each other. The images will be selected.

2. Click on the **Draw button** on the **Drawing toolbar.** A menu will appear.

3. Move the mouse pointer to **Align or Distribute.** A second menu will appear.

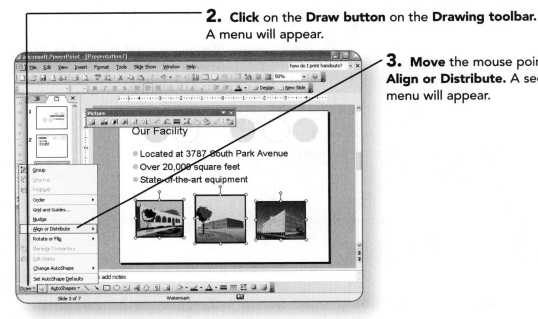

4. Click on the **method** that you want to use to align the objects. The icon to the left of each menu command illustrates the type of alignment. The objects will be aligned relative to each other using the method you've specified.

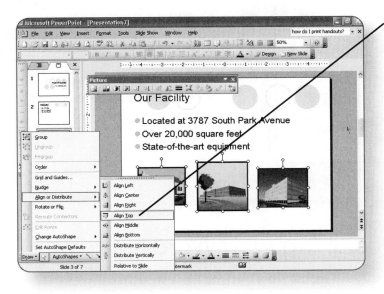

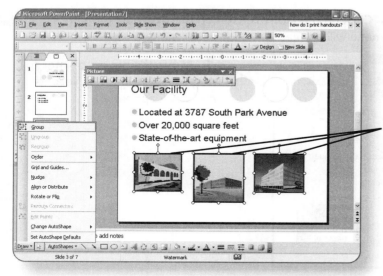

Grouping Graphics

Grouping items is useful when you want to be able to work with several of them as a single item (move, resize, etc.).

1. Press and hold the **Shift key**, and **click** on the **images** that you want to combine to create a single image. The images will be selected.

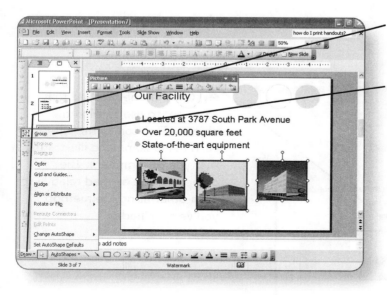

2. Click on the **Draw button** on the Drawing toolbar. A menu will appear.

3. Click on **Group**. The grouped images can now be treated as a single image.

To ungroup, select the grouped object, click on the Draw button, and select Ungroup.

Designing with WordArt

WordArt is another tool that you'll find in all Microsoft Office applications. It's an easy way to create wavy and 3-D text effects. Here's another chance for you to play, but don't get too carried away. Overdone text effects can be a distraction, and you don't want to lose a good audience.

Creating the WordArt Object

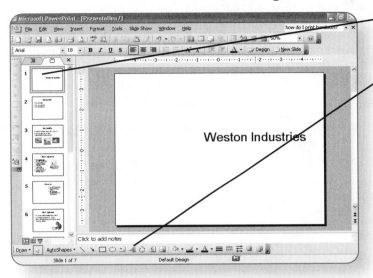

1. **Display** the **slide** that will contain the WordArt object. The slide will appear in Normal view.

2. **Click** on the **Insert WordArt button** on the Drawing toolbar. The WordArt Gallery dialog box will open.

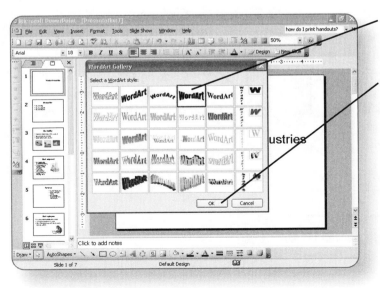

3. **Click** on the **WordArt style** that you want to use. The style will be selected.

4. **Click** on **OK**. The Edit WordArt Text dialog box will open.

5. **Select** the **text** in the Text list box, if necessary, and **type** the **text** you want to appear in the WordArt object.

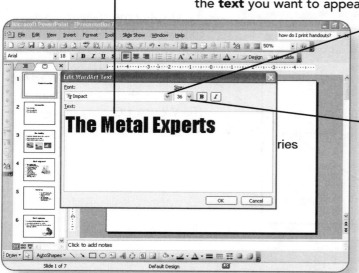

6. **Click** the **Font list box arrow** and select the font that you want to use in the WordArt object. The font name will appear in the Font list box.

7. **Click** the **Size list box arrow** and select the font size for the WordArt object. The font size will appear in the Size list box.

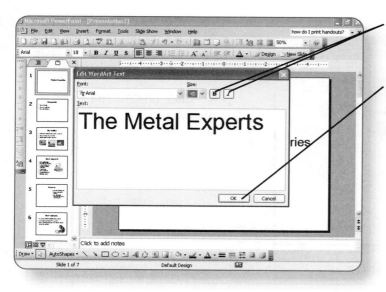

8. **Click** on the **Bold** or **Italic buttons** to apply these styles to the text.

9. **Click** on **OK**. The dialog box will close and the WordArt object will appear on the slide.

Formatting WordArt

After the WordArt has been placed, you can format it in several ways:

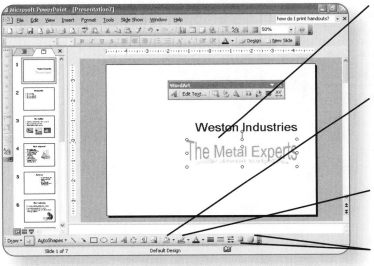

- Double-click the WordArt to reopen the Edit WordArt Text dialog box at any time. Edit the text as needed and click OK to close it when done.

- Change the color of the WordArt with the Fill Color button. You can also apply fill effects such as gradients and textures.

- Change the line color outlining each letter with the Line Color button.

- Apply a shadow or 3-D effect with the Shadow or 3D button. See "Adding a Shadow or 3-D Effect" later in this chapter.

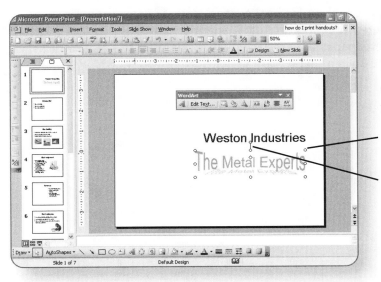

Resizing and Rotating WordArt

In addition to changing the WordArt's color, you can also resize and rotate it.

- Click and drag a handle to resize it.

- Click and drag the Rotate handle to rotate it.

Changing the WordArt's Shape

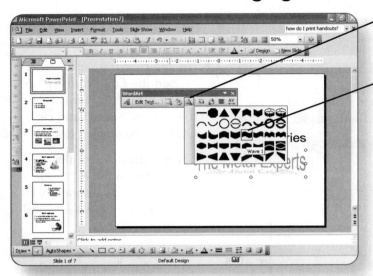

1. Click on the **WordArt Shape button** on the WordArt toolbar. A list of shapes will appear.

2. Click on a **shape**. The shape of the WordArt object will change.

Adding Line Art

When you need a box, a circle, arrows, or callouts, you'll find a variety of ready-made styles from which to choose. When you're looking for banners and stars, or some irregular shapes, there's probably an AutoShape that can do the job. AutoShapes are easy to create. With just a few mouse clicks, you have a shape you can adjust to fit your needs.

Drawing a Line

1. Click on the **Line button**. The mouse pointer will turn into a crosshair.

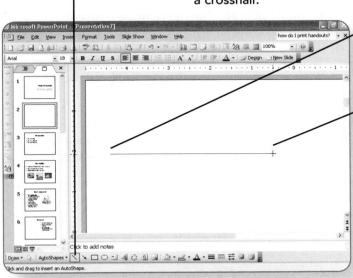

2. Position the **mouse pointer** where the line should begin, and **press and hold** the **left mouse button**.

3. Drag to where the line should end and **release** the **mouse button**. The line will appear.

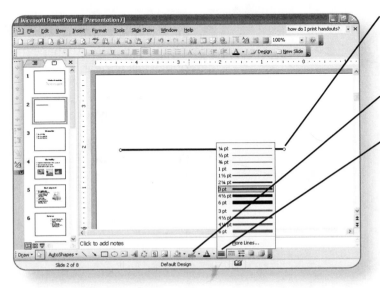

After drawing a line, you can move it by dragging it, or you can resize it by dragging one of its handles.

You can also change its color with the Line Color button

You can adjust its thickness with the Line Style button.

Drawing a Rectangle or Oval

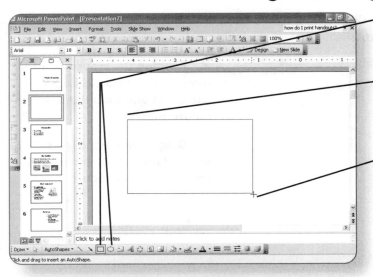

1. Click on the **Rectangle** or **Oval button**. The mouse pointer will turn into a crosshair.

2. Position the **mouse pointer** where the shape should begin, and **press and hold** the **left mouse button**.

3. Drag to where the shape should end and **release** the **mouse button**. The shape will appear.

Drawing an AutoShape

AutoShapes offer a wider variety of drawing options than just ovals, rectangles, and lines.

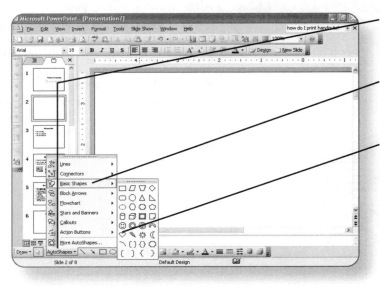

1. Click on the **AutoShapes button**. A menu of AutoShape categories will appear.

2. Move the mouse pointer to a **category**. A list of shapes will appear.

3. Click on a **shape.** The mouse pointer will turn into a crosshair.

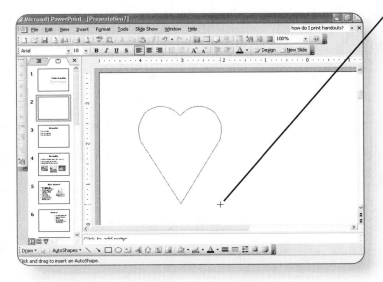

4. Click and drag the **mouse pointer** across the area on the slide where you want the **AutoShape** to appear. An outline will appear on the slide.

5. Release the **mouse button** when the shape is the desired size. The shape will appear on the slide, filled in with the default fill color.

Recoloring the AutoShape

You can change the color with which an AutoShape is filled and/or the color of its border.

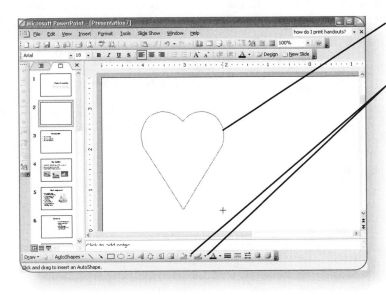

1. Click on the **AutoShape** that you want to change. The AutoShape will be selected.

2. Click on the **down arrow** next to the Fill Color or Line Color buttons. A menu of colors will appear.

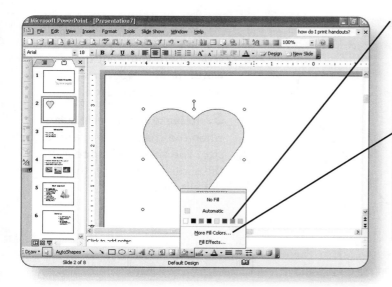

3. Select a **color** from the menu. The color will be applied to the shape.

NOTE

As with other objects, you can choose a placeholder color, you can choose More Fill Colors for a specific solid color, or you can choose Fill Effects for gradients, textures, etc.

Adding a Shadow or 3-D Effect

Sometimes, adding a shadow or 3-D effect to a shape makes it appear to stand out from the slide. This is an easy way to make subtle enhancements that will attract the audience's eye.

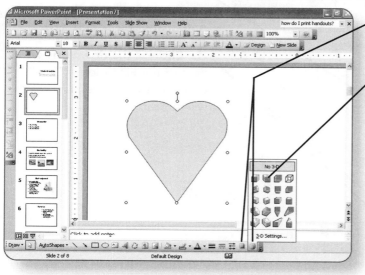

1. Click on the **Shadow Style button** or **3-D Style button**. A list of styles will appear.

2. Click on a **style**. The effect will be applied to the shape.

36

Using Digital Photographs

If you enjoy taking pictures and have a scanner attached to your computer, consider using your own photographs in your presentation. Before you begin scanning photos, set up the scanner and install all the software and drivers necessary to operate it. The scanner software may also come with photo-editing software. Since each scanner comes with its own software, read the user manual carefully so that you can operate the scanner efficiently. Once this is accomplished, it's time to sort through the photo album and select a few pictures to scan. In this chapter, you'll learn how to:

- Scan photographs and place the images directly on a presentation slide
- Resize and crop images after they are inserted on a slide
- Do minor photo touch-ups, such as adjusting the brightness and contrast

Scanning Photographs

Windows XP has built-in support for a number of scanners. If you have a supported scanner and Windows XP, you can scan directly into PowerPoint using the Windows-based scanner interface. You can do it with other Windows versions too, but the interface may vary from the one shown here.

1. **Position** the **photograph** in the scanner.

2. **Display** the **slide** on which you want to insert the scanned photograph.

3. **Click** on **Insert**. The Insert menu will appear.

4. **Move** the mouse pointer to **Picture**. The Picture menu will appear.

5. **Click** on **From Scanner or Camera**. The Insert Picture from Scanner or Camera dialog box will open.

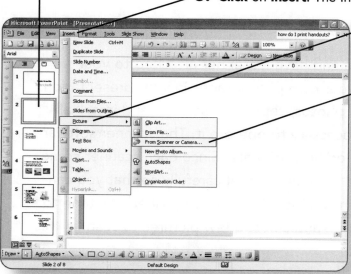

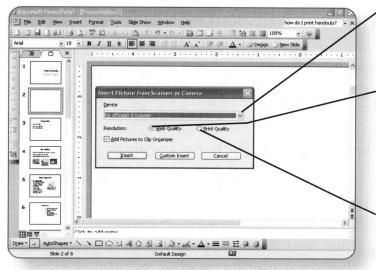

6. **Click** on the **Device drop-down list** and select the scanner from the list. The scanner name will appear in the list box.

7a. **Click** on the **Web Quality option button** if the presentation will be viewed over the Internet or on a computer screen. The option will be selected.

OR

7b. **Click** on the **Print Quality option button** if the presentation will be printed. The option will be selected.

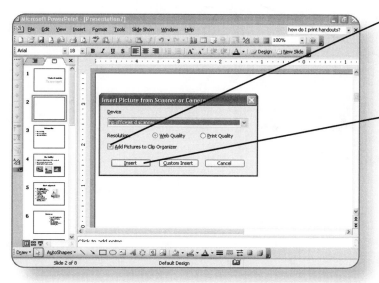

8. **Click** the **Add Pictures to Clip Organizer check box** if you want to keep a copy of the photo in the Clip Organizer. A check will appear in the check box.

9. **Click** on the **Insert button**. The scanner will scan the picture, and it will appear on the slide.

Enhancing Digital Photographs

After you've inserted a picture into a presentation slide, you may want the picture to look different. If you have simple image enhancements to make, you'll find a number of tools on the Picture toolbar.

Displaying the Picture Toolbar

The Picture toolbar should be displayed automatically when a picture is selected. If it doesn't, you can force it to appear.

1. Click on **View**. The View menu will appear.

2. Move the mouse pointer to **Toolbars**. The Toolbars menu will appear.

3. Click on **Picture**. The Picture toolbar will appear.

Cropping Pictures

You can remove unwanted parts of an image easily with the Crop button.

1. **Click** on the **Crop button** to display the crop marks.

2. **Click** and **drag** the **crop handles** until the part of the picture that you want to keep is inside the crop marks.

The crop handles are the black lines in the corners and sides of the image.

TIP

To reset cropping, drag the crop handles back out again.

3. **Click** on the **Crop button** again or **press Esc** to apply the changes to the image.

Rotating the Picture

There are several ways to rotate a picture.

- **Click** and **drag** the **rotate handle** to the right or left. The picture will turn as you move the mouse.

- **Click** on the **Rotate Left button**. The picture will turn counterclockwise by 90 degrees.

- **Click** on **Draw**, **click** on **Rotate or Flip**, and then **click** on a **rotation**.

Adjusting Brightness and Contrast

Sometimes all you need to make a picture look better is a little image enhancement. When an adjustment to the brightness or contrast is in order:

- **Click** on the **More Contrast button** to add definition between the light and dark colors in the image.

- **Click** on the **Less Contrast button** to soften images that are too harsh.

- **Click** on the **Less Brightness button** to make an image appear darker.

- **Click** on the **More Brightness button** to lighten the colors in an image.

Changing the Image Mode

The default mode for an image is Automatic. It shows in color. To convert the image to grayscale, black-and-white, or a watermark, select one of those modes instead.

1. **Click** on the **Color button** on the Picture toolbar. A menu will appear.

2. **Click** on the **desired mode**.

• To give images an elegant, old-fashioned look, use the Grayscale command.

• Give images a faded look by selecting Washout. This command creates a light-colored, almost transparent version of the image. The washout effect works well when you don't want an image to stand out on a page, or if you want to place text over the image.

37

Incorporating Tables

You've probably seen tables used in spreadsheets and word processing documents. Tables are a great way to organize information into neat rows and columns. They can be simple, or you can make them fashionable with designer lines and colors. In this chapter, you'll learn how to:

- Insert a table on a slide and add text to the table cells
- Change the size of the table and the size of rows and columns within the table
- Create borders around the table and around individual cells in the table

Creating a Table

Before you begin building a table, you should have an approximate idea of the size you want. If you aren't exactly sure, you can always add and delete rows and columns later.

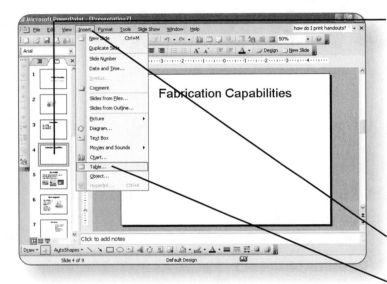

1. Open the **slide** on which you want to insert a table. The slide will appear in Normal view.

TIP

Place the table on a slide that has plenty of room for it. You might want to switch to a different slide layout first.

2. Click on **Insert**. The Insert menu will appear.

3. Click on **Table**. The Insert Table dialog box will appear.

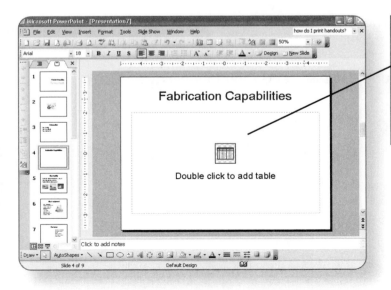

NOTE

Instead of steps 1-3, you can display a slide that has a Table placeholder layout, and then double-click the placeholder icon.

4. **Click** in the **Number of columns text box** and **type** the **number of columns** that should be contained in the table.

5. **Click** in the **Number of rows text box** and **type** the **number of rows** in the table.

6. **Click** on **OK**.

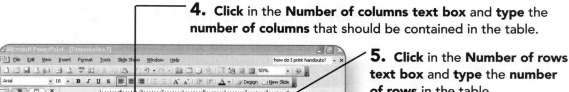

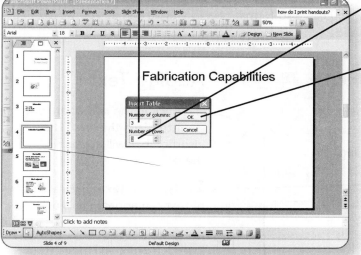

The table will appear on the slide.

TIP

Click and drag the resize handles to change the width and height of the table.

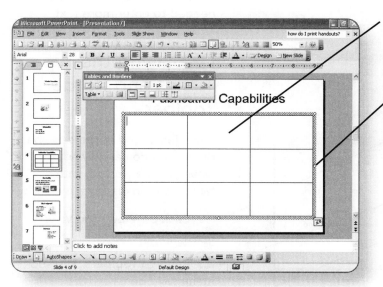

Inserting Text into the Table

After creating the table, you can add words to the different cells. You can also format text in a table just as you would on a slide.

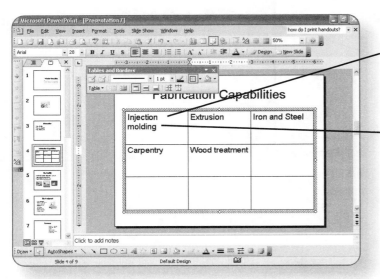

Adding Text

1. **Click** in the **cell** where you want to place the text. The insertion bar will appear in the cell.

2. **Type** the **text**. Several lines of text can appear in a single cell.

3. **Press** the **Tab key**. The insertion point will move to the next cell.

4. **Repeat steps 2 and 3** as needed to enter more text.

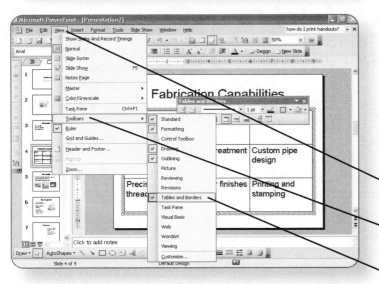

Displaying the Tables and Borders Toolbar

If the Tables and Borders toolbar does not automatically appear when you are working with a table, you can display it manually.

1. **Click** on **View**. The View menu will open.

2. **Point** to **Toolbars**. The submenu will open.

3. **Click** on **Tables and Borders**. The Tables and Borders toolbar will appear.

Aligning Text in a Cell

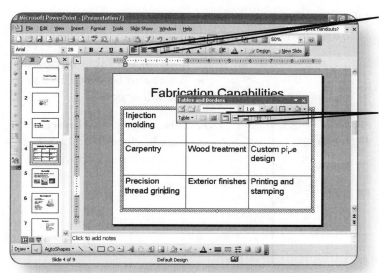

Use the **Align Left**, **Center**, and **Align Right** alignment buttons on the Formatting toolbar for horizontal alignment within cells.

Use the **Align Top, Center Vertically**, and **Align Bottom** alignment buttons on the Tables and Borders toolbar for vertical alignment within cells.

Modifying the Table

If you find that a table doesn't contain enough cells, you may need to add a few rows or columns. Or, if you got carried away and have more table space than you need, start deleting extra cells.

Adding Rows and Columns

1. Click in the **row or column** that will be adjacent to the new row. The insertion bar will appear in a cell.

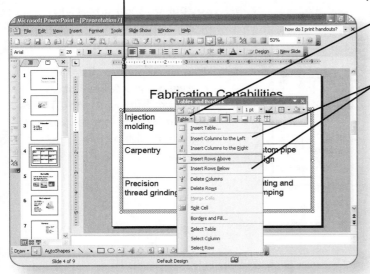

2. Click on the **Table button** on the Tables and Borders toolbar. A menu will appear.

3. Select one of the **Insert commands**, depending on what you want to insert and where.

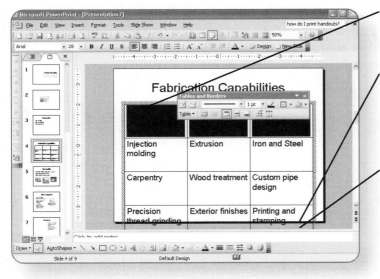

The new row or column will appear in your table. It will be highlighted.

The table might hang over the edge of the slide after the insertion. If it does, drag a handle to resize it. See "Resizing the Table" later in this chapter.

To add a new row at the bottom, click in the last cell and press Tab.

Deleting Rows and Columns

1. **Click** in a **cell** that is contained in the row or column that you want to delete. The cursor will appear in the cell.

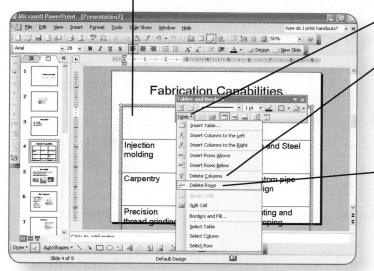

2. **Click** on the **Table button**. A menu will appear.

3a. **Click** on **Delete Columns**. The column in which the insertion point was positioned will be deleted.

OR

3b. **Click** on **Delete Rows**. The row in which the insertion point was positioned will be deleted.

Merging Cells

If you want to create a row across the top of the table in which to make a heading, you can combine several cells into a single cell.

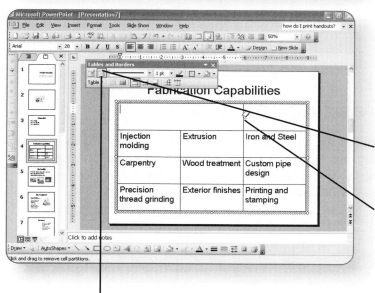

1. **Click** on the **Eraser button**. The mouse pointer will turn into an eraser.

2. **Click** on the **cell border** between the two cells that you want to merge. The border between the two cells will be deleted.

3. **Click** on the **Eraser button** again when you are finished merging cells.

Splitting Cells

You can also split a cell into several cells to make space for additional information.

1. Click in the **cell** that you want to split into two cells. The insertion bar will appear in the cell.

2. Click on the **Split Cell button**. A new cell will be added to the table.

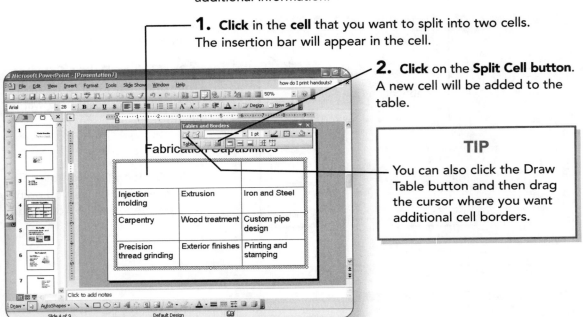

TIP

You can also click the Draw Table button and then drag the cursor where you want additional cell borders.

Resizing the Table

Sometimes tables need to be resized to fit on a slide or to display information in a neat and tidy format. Not only can you change the outer dimensions of a table, but you can make rows wider and cells taller.

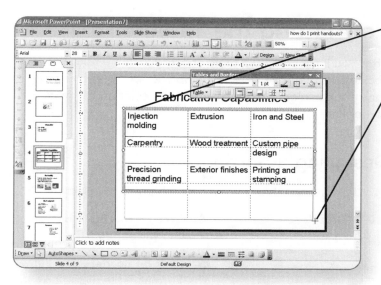

1. Click on the **table**. The table placeholder and the resize handles will appear around the outside border of the table.

2. Click and **drag** a **resize handle**. An outline will show the new size of the table.

3. Release the **mouse button**. The table and all of the cells will be resized proportionately.

You can also resize individual rows and columns. To resize rows:

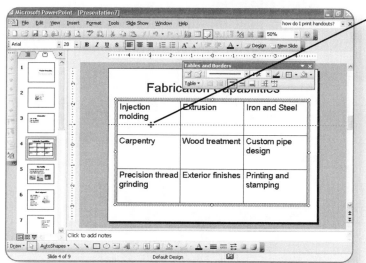

4. Click and **drag** on the **border** between two rows. The border will turn to an outline to show how the two rows will be resized.

5. Release the **mouse button**. The two rows will be different heights.

Columns work the same way, except you drag the vertical lines between them.

Formatting the Table

After you have created a table and added some text, you may decide that the table lacks color. Spruce up tables by adding background colors and by changing the color and style of the border lines.

Designing a Border

1. **Click** on the **table border**. The table will be selected.

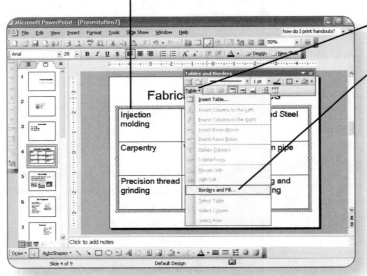

2. **Click** on the **Table button**. A menu will appear.

3. **Click** on **Borders and Fill**. The Format Table dialog box will open, and the Borders tab will be displayed.

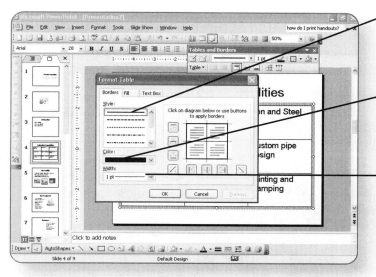

4. **Click** on the **line** in the Style list box that you want to apply to a border. The line style will be selected.

5. **Select** a **color** from the Color list box to apply to the line style. The color will appear in the list box.

6. **Select** a **line width** from the Width list box. The width will appear in the list box.

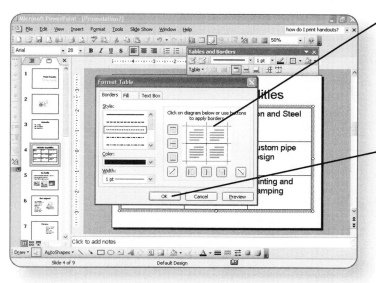

7. **Click** on the **border** in the diagram to which you want to apply the line style. The diagram will be updated with the new border line style. You will need to click once for each border you want to affect.

8. **Click** on **OK** when you are done. The table border will be updated with the new line style format.

Adding Color to Cells

1. **Select** the **cells** to which you want to add a background fill color. The cells will be highlighted.

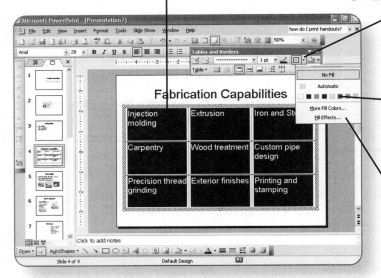

2. **Click** on the **down arrow** next to the Fill Color button. A list of colors from which you can choose will appear.

3. **Click** on a **Color**. The selected cells will be filled with the new color.

TIP

Use Fill Effects for gradient and pattern fills.

38

Producing Charts and Graphs

Charts and graphs are the visual representation of a relationship between two or more items. They can show a trend over a period of time or an item's size in relation to the total. All these relationships can be displayed with bars, pies, lines, and scattered dots. Your charts can be flat or 3-D. PowerPoint can create some complex charts, but keep your audience in mind. Ease of understanding should be your major goal. In this chapter, you'll learn how to:

- Use a datasheet to enter information for a graph

- Display datasheet information using different chart and graph formats

- Create a graphical representation of the hierarchy within a group

Entering Data for the Chart

Before building a chart, organize the data you'll be depicting. Most charts compare two types of data, such as a budget where the amount spent on certain items is listed for a range of dates. PowerPoint provides a small example to get you started. Just replace the sample data with your own information.

1. Display the **slide** on which you want to insert the chart. The slide will appear in Normal view.

2. Click on **Insert**. The Insert menu will appear.

3. Click on **Chart**. The sample chart and chart datasheet will appear on the slide.

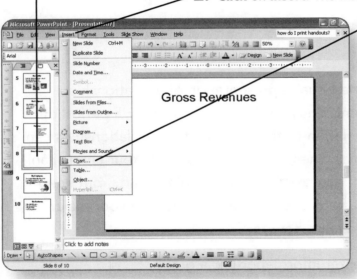

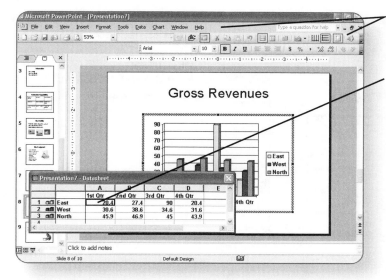

Notice that the toolbars and menus are different while you're working with a chart.

4. Click in a **cell** on the datasheet. The cell's contents will be selected.

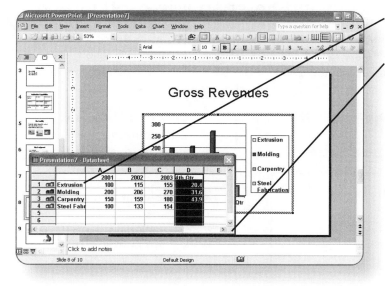

5. Type the **data** that you want to appear in the chart.

You can resize the datasheet to display more rows and columns.

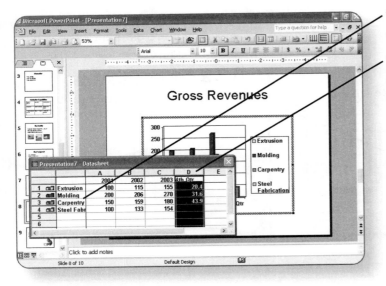

Type in additional rows and columns as needed.

To clear unused rows or columns, click on the row or column heading and press the Delete key.

Exiting and Entering Microsoft Graph

The tools you use to create the chart, as in the preceding section, are called *Microsoft Graph*. You enter Microsoft Graph by starting a new chart or double-clicking an existing one. You exit it by clicking on the slide area outside the chart.

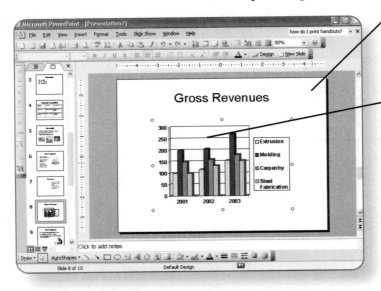

1. Click on a **blank area** of the slide. The datasheet will close and your information will appear in the chart.

2. Double-click on the **chart**. The Microsoft Graph tools will reopen, including the different menus and toolbar buttons.

Changing How the Data Is Plotted

You can change the meaning of a chart by changing how the data is plotted in the worksheet grid—either by rows or by columns.

1. Double-click on the **chart**. The chart will be selected and the charting tools will appear in the toolbar.

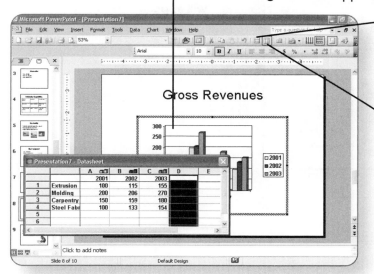

2a. **Click** on the **By Rows button**. The data will be plotted by rows.

OR

2b. **Click** on the **By Columns button**. The data will be plotted by columns.

Formatting the Chart

After you have entered all the data into the datasheet, it's time to create charts that will most effectively display the relationship between the two types of data you are comparing.

Selecting a Chart Type

The default chart type is the column chart. You'll also find an assortment of bar charts, pie charts, line charts, scatter charts, and many more. After you select a chart type, customize the chart to make it look the way you want.

1. Double-click on the **chart**. The datasheet will open and the Microsoft Graph tools will appear.

2. Click on **Chart**. The Chart menu will appear.

3. Click on **Chart Type**. The Chart Type dialog box will open, and the list of standard charts will appear.

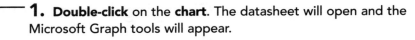

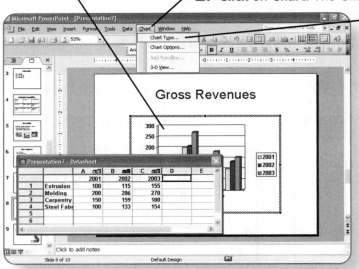

4. Click on the **category** of chart in the Chart type list. The category will be selected, and the variations of the chart type will appear in the Chart sub-type area.

5. Click on a **style** of chart in the Chart sub-type area. The chart will be selected, and you can read a description of it.

6. Click on **OK** when you have selected a chart type. The chart will be updated to display the selected chart type.

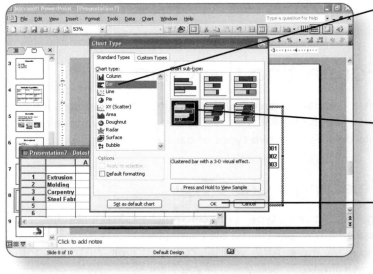

Including Text Labels

If the chart appears on a slide that already has a title, you might not need a title on the chart itself. It is available if you want it. Labels for the vertical and horizontal axes are also available.

1. **Double-click** on the **chart**. The chart will be selected.

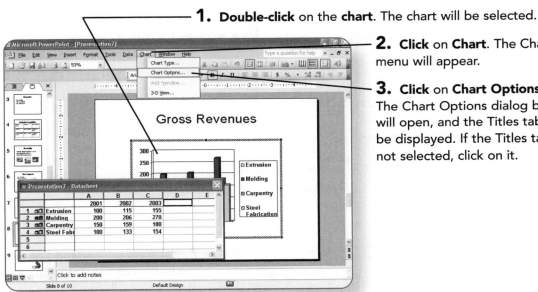

2. **Click** on **Chart**. The Chart menu will appear.

3. **Click** on **Chart Options**. The Chart Options dialog box will open, and the Titles tab will be displayed. If the Titles tab is not selected, click on it.

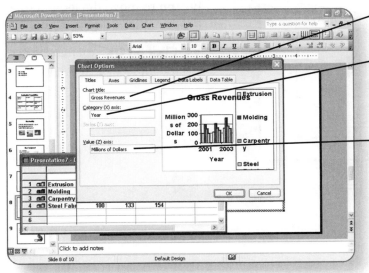

4. **Click** in the **Chart title text box** and **type** a **title** for the chart.

5. **Click** in the **Category (X) axis text box** and **type** a **label** for the information displayed on the X (horizontal) axis.

6. **Click** in the **Value (Z) axis text box** and **type** a **label** for the information displayed on the Z (vertical) axis. This box is available only for 3-D charts.

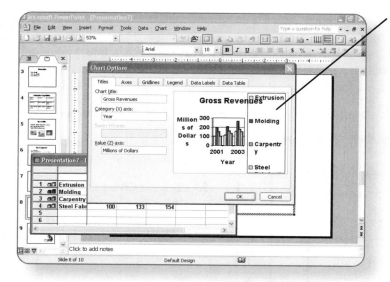

Don't worry if the sample doesn't look right. The fonts and sizing may be off, but it will appear correctly on the actual slide.

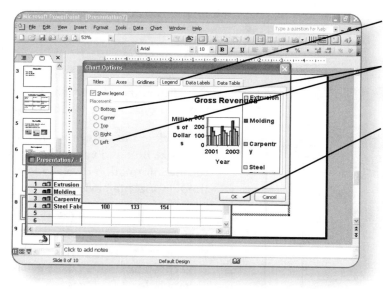

7. **Click** on the **Legend tab**. The legend options will appear.

8. **Click** on a **Placement option button** to move the legend to a different place on the slide.

9. **Click** on **OK**. Your changes will be applied to the chart.

Changing a Font

You can change the fonts and font sizes used in various elements of the chart.

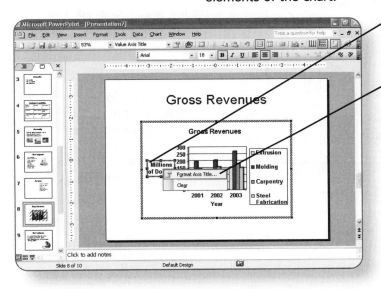

1. Click on some **text** on the chart that you want to change. It will be selected.

2. Right-click the **text** and choose **Format [*the type of text you've chosen*]**. A Format dialog box will appear.

3. Click on the **font** you want on the Font tab. If the Font tab does not appear automatically, click it.

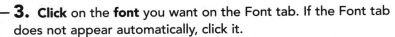

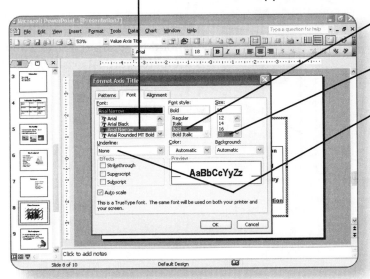

4. Click on the desired **text attributes**, such as bold or italic.

5. Click on the **font size** you want.

6. Select an **underline style**, if desired.

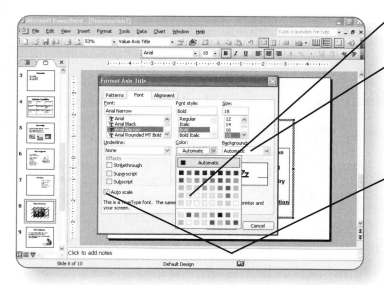

7. **Select** a **specific text color**, if desired.

8. **Select** a **background style** for the text, if desired. The default is Automatic.

NOTE

Auto scale allows PowerPoint to resize the text if you resize the chart later. Leave it on in most cases.

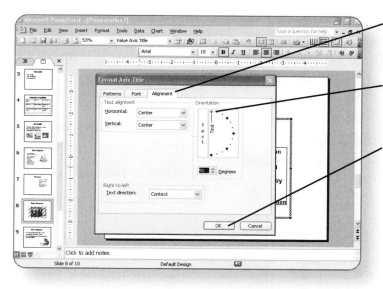

9. **Click** on the **Alignment tab**. The Alignment controls will appear.

10. If desired, **drag** the **red diamond** to rotate the text. This is useful for vertical axis labels.

11. **Click** on **OK**. Your changes will be applied.

39
Creating Diagrams

The Diagrams feature in PowerPoint offers several graphical ways of presenting information to an audience. One of the most common is an organization chart, a type of diagram that shows the people in an organization and their relationships to one another. Other types of graphics include pyramids and circle diagrams. In this chapter, you'll learn how to:

- Insert a diagram
- Add text to a diagram
- Add and remove boxes from an organization chart
- Format a diagram

Inserting a Diagram

PowerPoint contains several types of diagrams, and they all can be customized to fit your needs. They're all inserted the same way.

1. Select the **slide** on which you want to place the diagram. The slide will appear.

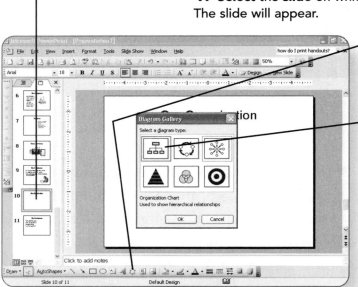

2. Click on the **Insert Diagram or Organization Chart** button. The Diagram Gallery dialog box will open.

3. Double-click on a **diagram type**. The diagram will appear on the selected slide.

Adding Text to a Diagram

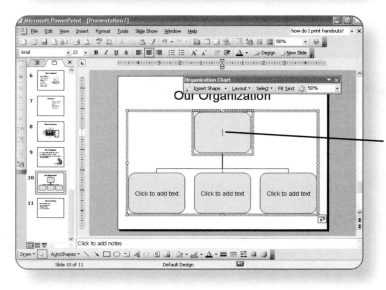

After placing the diagram, you can click inside any part of it and type text.

1. Click on the text placeholder for the **shape** to which you want to add a text caption. The text placeholder will disappear, and the cursor will appear in the middle of the shape.

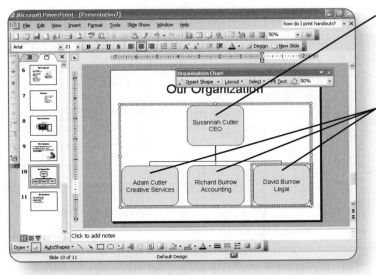

2. **Type** the **text**. To add multiple lines of text to a shape, press Enter at the end of each line. The text will appear inside the shape.

3. **Add text** to the other shapes in the diagram.

Changing the Diagram Structure

In many respects, all of the diagram types are the same. However, when it comes to changing the structure (that is, adding and removing text boxes), the organization chart is somewhat different from the others. Let's address it separately.

Adding Organization Chart Boxes

In an organization chart, each box has a relationship to another box. It is either subordinate to it or a peer (at the same level).

1. Click on an **existing box** that the new box will be related to.

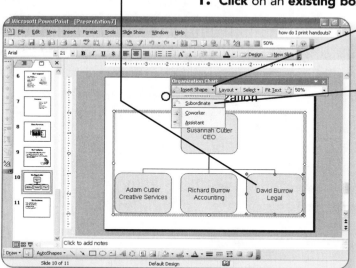

2. Click on the **down arrow** next to the Insert Shape button. A menu will open.

3. Click on the **relationship** of the new box to the existing one. The new box will appear.

TIP

Subordinate is the default. If you want Subordinate, you can click the Insert Shape button instead of opening its menu.

Adding Boxes on Other Diagrams

To add a box:

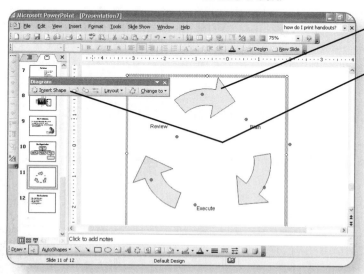

1. Click on the **diagram**. The Diagram toolbar will appear.

2. Click on the **Insert Shape button**. A new shape and accompanying text box will appear.

Deleting Boxes

This works for any diagram type.

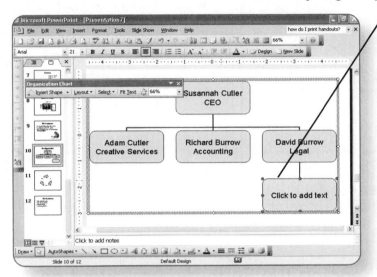

1. Click on the **border around the box** you want to delete. Gray circles will appear as its selection handles, with Xs inside the circles.

TIP

Don't click inside the box, or you'll just be deleting the text.

2. Press the **Delete** key. The box will be deleted.

Changing Reporting on an Organization Chart

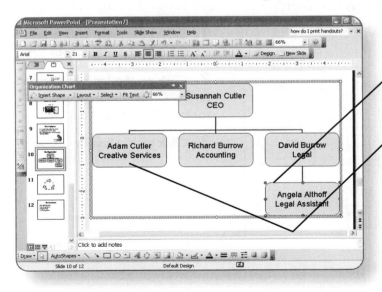

You can move a subordinate box so that the person it represents reports to some other supervisor.

1. Click on the **border of the box** to be moved. Gray circles will appear as its selection handles.

2. Drag and **drop** it on top of a **different supervisor**.

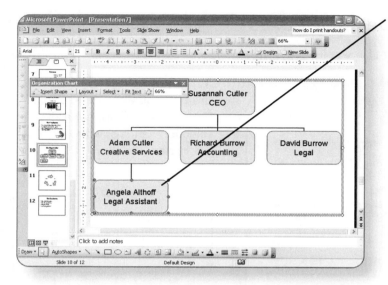

It will be moved so that it is subordinate to the new supervisor.

You must drag it *on top of* the other box. Dragging it below the box, where it will appear after it's connected, will not work.

Changing the Subordinate Layout on an Organization Chart

When there are multiple subordinates, it may be useful to change the way the subordinates' boxes hang off their supervisor's box.

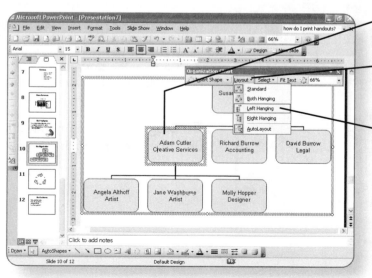

1. **Select** the **supervisor's box**. An outline will appear around it.

2. **Click** on the **Layout button** on the Organization Chart toolbar. A menu will appear.

3. **Click** on the **layout** you want.

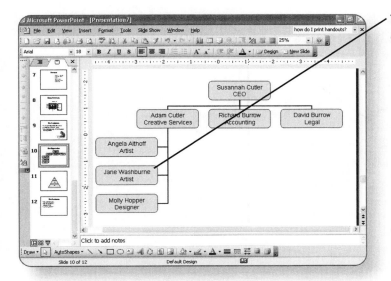

The subordinate boxes will change to that layout.

Reversing the Order on Diagrams

Some diagram types can be reversed. For example, the text on a pyramid that goes from top to bottom can be reversed so that the label that was previously on the bottom of the pyramid is now on the top. Or for diagrams that go in a circle, the labels can be changed from clockwise to counterclockwise.

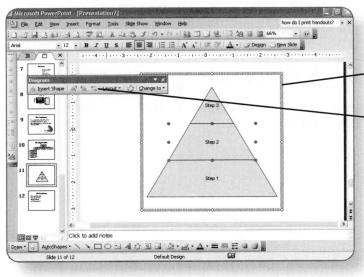

1. Select the **diagram**. Its outer border will be selected.

2. Click on the **Reverse button**.

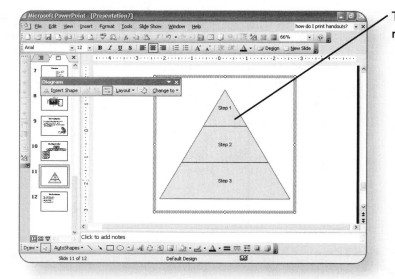

The order of the text will be reversed.

Applying Formatting to the Diagram

There are several ways to give the diagram a different look. If you'd like a quick and easy way to stylize a diagram, use one of the AutoFormats. You can also apply a unique color and line style to each shape and add a background to the diagram area.

Using AutoFormats

This works on all diagram types, although the choices of style are different for each type.

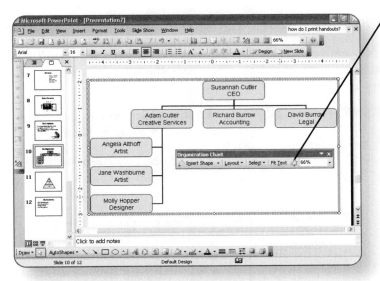

1. Click on the **AutoFormat button**. The Style Gallery dialog box for the diagram will open.

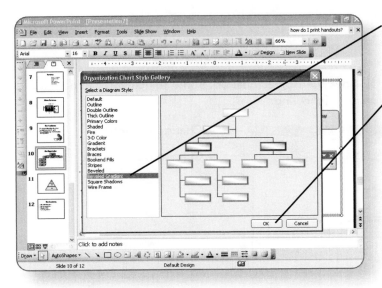

2. Click on a **style** from the Select a Diagram Style list. A preview of the selected style will appear in the Preview pane.

3. Click on **OK** when you have made your selection. The diagram style will be updated.

Manually Formatting the Diagram

If you want to override the AutoFormat settings, you must turn AutoFormat off. Then you can apply different colors, lines, fonts, and so on.

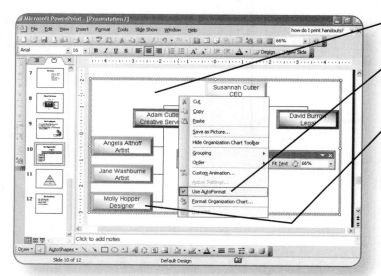

1. Right-click on any part of the diagram. A menu will appear.

2. Click on **Use AutoFormat**. The menu will close, and AutoFormat will be turned off.

3. Click on a **box** of the diagram. That box will be selected.

4. Format the **box** as desired. Some things you can do include the following:

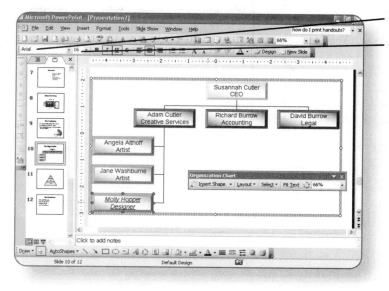

• Change the font

• Change the font size

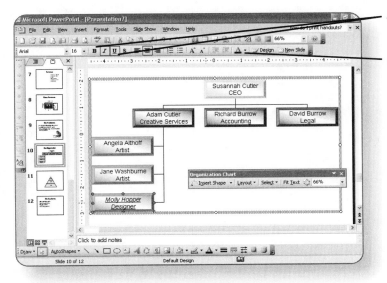

- Apply font attributes such as bold, italic, and underline
- Change the font color

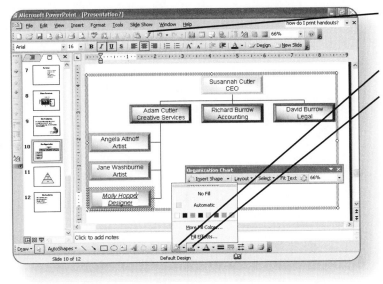

- Copy formatting from one box to another with Format Painter
- Choose a different fill color
- Choose a different border color

40

Animating the Slide Show

It's time to wake up your audience and roll a few objects across the screen during your slide show. How about a cool transition effect as each slide fades into the next slide? Or you could make bullet points fall from the sky as you introduce each point. The possibilities are endless. In this chapter, you'll learn how to:

- Use animation schemes to apply quick and easy slide transitions and animations
- Make slide elements march onto the slide in order
- Add cool effects so that one slide fades into the next slide

Using Slide Transitions

Moving from one slide to another is called a *slide transition*. It can be a simple replacement of one slide for the next, or you can set up fancier transitions that move between them.

1. **Select** the **slide(s)** to which you want to apply the transition effect. The slide(s) will be selected.

If you want to apply it to all slides, it does not matter which slide(s) you select.

2. **Click** on **Slide Show**. The Slide Show menu will appear.

3. **Click** on **Slide Transition**. The Slide Transition task pane will appear.

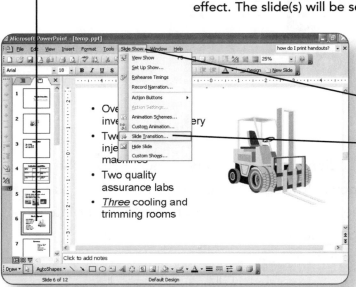

4. **Click** on a **slide transition**. The transition will be selected, and a preview of the transition will appear if the AutoPreview check box is selected.

5. **Click** the **Speed list box arrow** and select the speed at which you want the transition to play. The speed will appear in the list box.

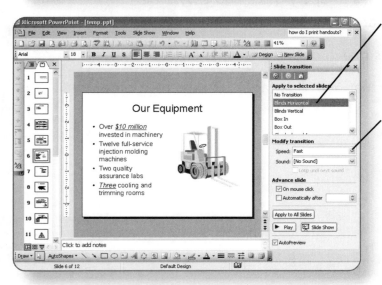

6. Click the **Sound list box arrow** and **select** a sound to play during a slide transition, if desired. The sound will appear in the list box.

TIP

If you want to play a sound that you have stored on your computer, select Other Sound from the bottom of the list.

NOTE

The first time you select a sound, a box may appear prompting you to install the Sound Effects feature. Click OK to do so.

7. Specify when the transition will occur:

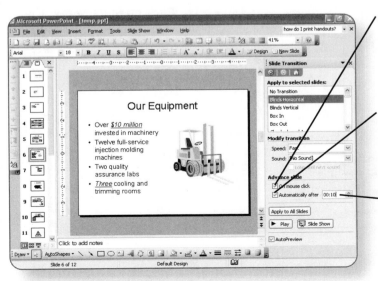

Mark the **On mouse click check box** if you want the transition to occur when you click the left mouse button. It is marked by default.

Mark the **Automatically after check box** if you want the transition to occur automatically after a specified time.

Enter a **number of seconds** in the text box to specify the amount of time for the Automatically after setting.

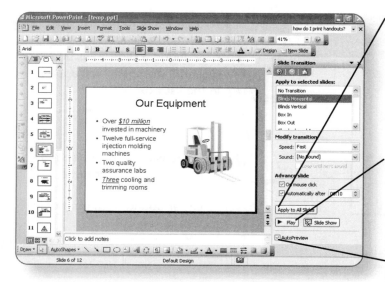

8. Click on **Apply to All Slides** if you want all slides to use this transition. It will be applied to all slides.

If you don't do this, it will apply only to the slides you selected in step 1.

9a. Click on **Play**. The transition effect will play in Normal view.

TIP

If you mark the AutoPreview check box, the transition will play without your having to click the Play button.

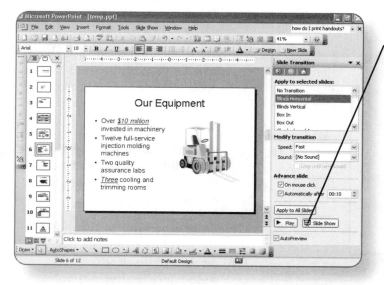

OR

9b. Click on **Slide Show**. The transition effect will play in Slide Show view.

Applying an Animation Scheme

Whereas a transition moves from one slide to another, an *animation* moves an individual object onto or off of the screen within a slide. PowerPoint comes with many preset animation schemes that are designed for ease of use. You can also create custom animations, as covered later in this chapter.

1. Display the **slide** to which you want to apply the animation. The slide will appear in Normal view. If you want to apply the animation to several slides, select the slides in Slide Sorter view.

2. Click on **Slide Show**. The Slide Show menu will appear.

3. Click on **Animation Schemes**. The Slide Design task pane will appear, and the available slide animations will be listed.

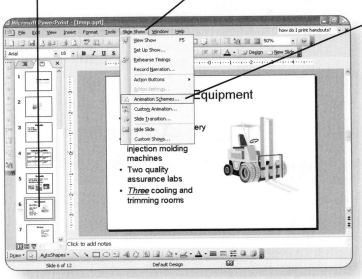

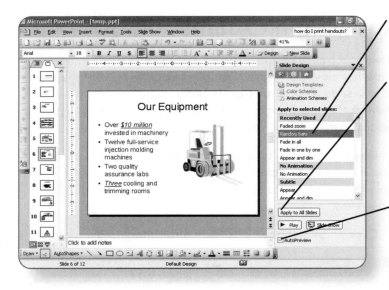

4. **Click** on an **animation scheme**. The animation will be applied to the selected slides.

5. **Click** on **Apply to All Slides** if you want every slide in the presentation to use the same animation scheme.

NOTE

Place a check mark in the AutoPreview check box if you want to watch the animation in action when you select the animation scheme.

Creating Custom Animation

Custom animation allows you to specify exactly what you want to animate and how it should be done.

TIP

You can start with an animation scheme from the preceding set of steps, and then customize it.

1. Open the **slide** that contains the element that you want to animate. The slide will appear in Normal view.

2. Click on **Slide Show**. The Slide Show menu will appear.

3. Click on **Custom Animation**. The Custom Animation task pane will appear.

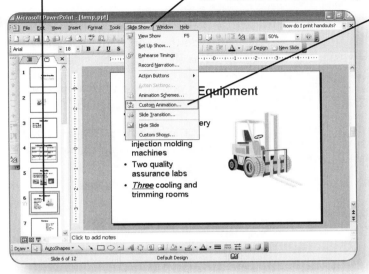

If you applied an animation scheme previously, the animation for it will be shown.

Each animated item has a number representing the order in which it will execute.

Each animated item appears in the Custom Animation list.

Groups of related items, such as individual bullet points in a list, are shown as a single item. Click the down arrow to display them.

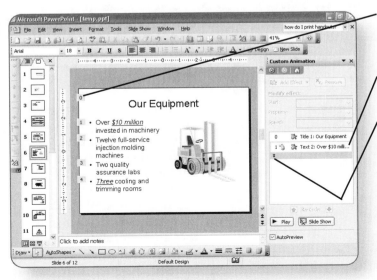

Adding an Animation Effect

Start with a slide that does not already have any animation effects for this procedure.

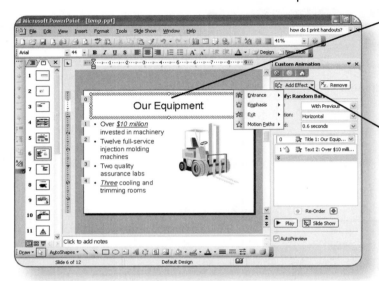

1. Click on the **element** on the slide that you want to animate. The element will be selected.

This could be a title, a bulleted list, or a graphic object.

2. Click on **Add Effect** on the task pane. A menu will appear.

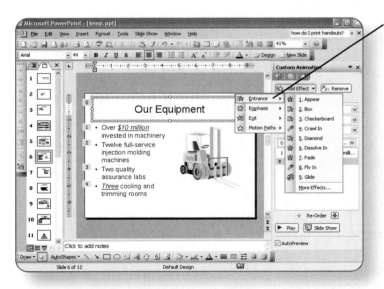

3. Point to a **category** of effects. A second menu will appear.

NOTE

Entrance effects control how the object enters the slide. *Emphasis effects* make it do something after its entrance. *Exit effects* control how it leaves the slide. A *motion path* is an advanced feature that enables you to specify exactly where the object travels.

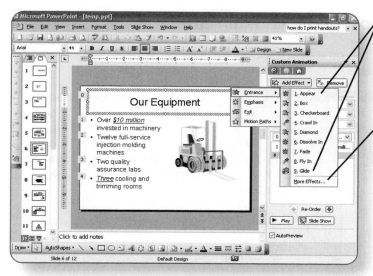

4a. **Click** on one of the **effects** shown on the menu. It will be applied to the object, and you are done.

OR

4b. **Click** on **More Effects**. A dialog box with a list of special effects will open.

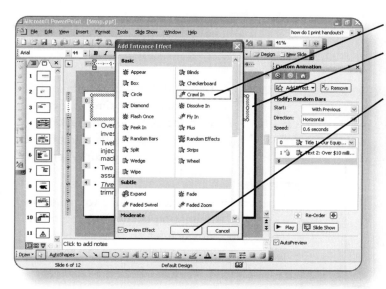

5. **Click** on an **effect**.

A preview of the effect will play in the Normal view.

6. **Click** on **OK** when you have selected an animation effect. The animation will be applied to the slide elements. You can now modify the animation.

Modifying an Animation

Do this on a slide that already has one or more animated objects.

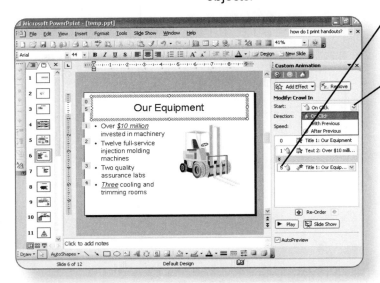

1. Click on the **animation effect** in the task pane. It will be selected.

2. Select an **event trigger** from the Start list. On Click is the most common.

Use With Previous to make the animation occur simultaneously with the previous animation. If there is no previous animation on this slide, it will occur when the slide itself appears.

Use After Previous to make the animation occur after the previous animation. You can also enter a delay between them.

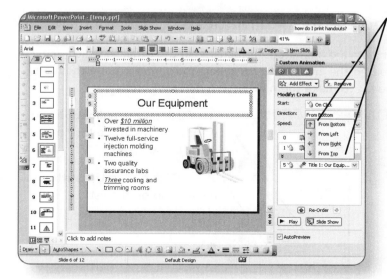

3. Select a **direction** from the Direction list.

The significance of Direction depends on the animation type. For example, if it is an entrance effect, the object will enter the slide from the chosen direction.

4. Select a **speed** from the Speed list.

TIP

You can also right-click the animation on the task pane and choose Effect Options to open a dialog box containing more choices. For example, you can enter a delay to be used with the After Previous event trigger, and you can specify a sound that should play with the animation.

Reordering Animations

Objects are animated on the slide in the order in which you created the animations for them. You can rearrange them on the list to make them occur in a different order.

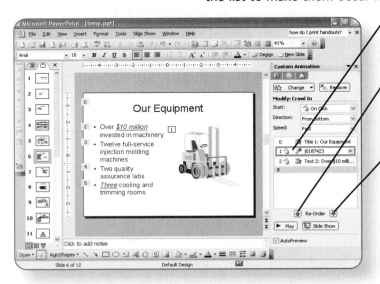

1. **Click** on the **animation** you want to move in the task pane. It will be selected.

2a. **Click** on the **Up button** to move it up on the list.

OR

2b. **Click** on the **Down button** to move it down on the list.

Removing an Animation

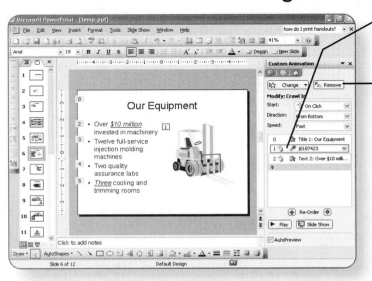

1. **Click** on the **animation** you want to remove. It will be selected.

2. **Click** on **Remove**. The animation will be removed.

41

Moving Along with Multimedia

Another way to make a slide show interesting and keep your audience's attention is to add music and video. You may have music that you've created using your computer's MIDI equipment and software, or you may have a music CD that you'd like to play. Also, if you have digital video files, it's easy to show videos during a slide show. In this chapter, you'll learn how to:

- Play a sound file as background music
- Listen to a CD while playing a slide show
- Watch movies during a slide show presentation

Adding Sound Clips to a Slide

PowerPoint lets you play a sound clip while a certain slide is displayed during a slide show. This could be a music clip, a sound effect, or any other sound recording in a common audio format such as WAV, WMA, or MP3.

These steps do *not* apply to using audio from a CD-ROM or using voiceover narration. See the specific sections on those topics later in this chapter.

1. Display the **slide** in Normal view that should receive the sound clip.

2. Click on **Insert**. The Insert menu will appear.

3. Point to Movies and Sounds. A second menu will appear.

4. Click on **Sound from File**. The Insert Sound dialog box will open.

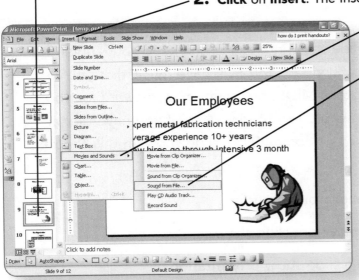

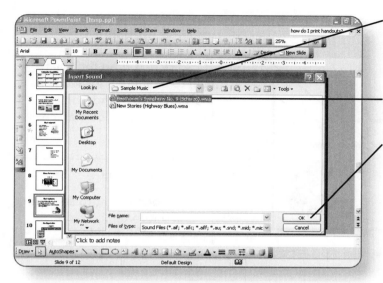

5. Navigate to the **folder** that contains the sound file. The folder's name will appear in the Look in list box.

6. Click on the **sound file**. The file will be selected.

7. Click on **OK**. A confirmation dialog box will open.

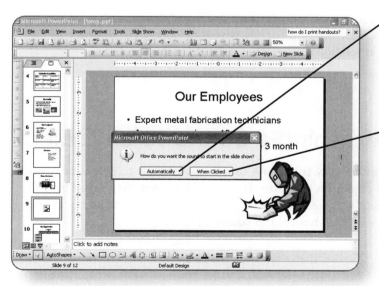

8a. Click on **Automatically** if you want the sound to play when the slide appears during the slide show.

OR

8b. Click on **When Clicked** if you want the sound to play only when its icon is clicked during the slide show.

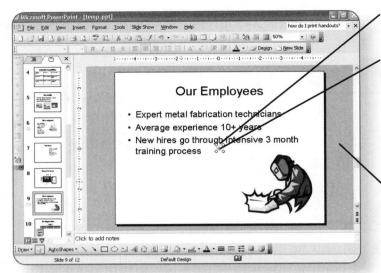

The sound icon appears in the center of the slide.

9. Click and **drag** the **sound icon** to a different location on the slide. The sound icon can be moved to any location on the slide.

TIP

If you don't want to see the sound icon on the slide, drag it off the slide.

TIP

You can use the Custom Animation task pane, as in Chapter 40, to specify when the sound will execute in relation to the other animations on the slide.

Attaching a Sound to an Object

Another way to place a sound on a slide is to associate it with an object on the slide. This could be a graphic, a text box, or anything else. Then, whenever that object is clicked or pointed to with the mouse, the sound will play.

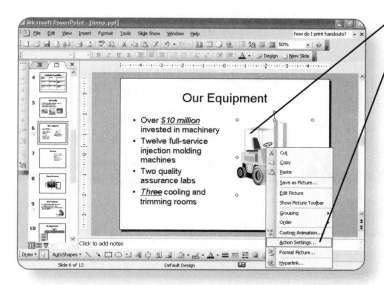

1. **Right-click** on the **object**. A menu will appear.

2. **Click** on **Action Settings**. The Action Settings dialog box will open.

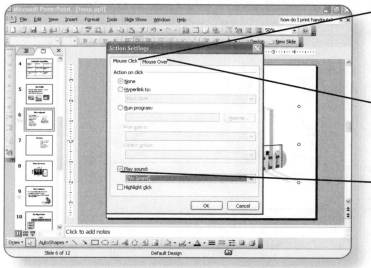

3a. **Click** on the **Mouse Click tab** if you want the sound to occur when the object is clicked.

OR

3b. **Click** on the **Mouse Over tab** if you want the sound to occur when the mouse touches the object.

4. **Click** on the **Play sound check box**. The drop-down list will become available.

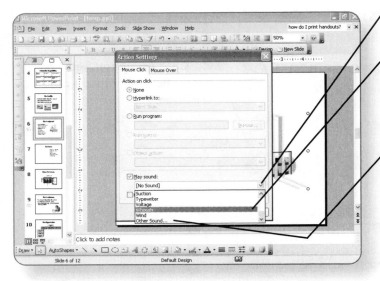

5. **Click** on the **down arrow**. The drop-down list will open.

6a. **Click** on the **sound** you want. It will appear in the Play sound box.

OR

6b. **Click** on **Other Sound** and browse for the sound you want.

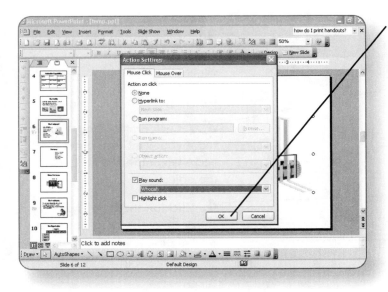

7. **Click** on **OK**. The dialog box will close, and the sound will be associated with that object.

Playing Audio CDs

Another way to play music while a slide is displayed during a slide show is to pop a music CD into the computer and let PowerPoint play the CD tracks that you specify.

NOTE

When you deliver the presentation, the same music CD will need to be in the computer's CD-ROM drive.

---

1. **Place** the **CD** that you want to play into the CD-ROM drive.

2. **Display** the **slide** for which you want to play the CD track. The slide will appear in Normal view.

3. **Click** on **Insert**. The Insert menu will appear.

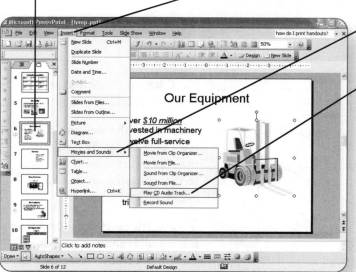

4. **Point to Movies and Sounds**. A second menu will appear.

5. **Click** on **Play CD Audio Track**. The Insert CD Audio dialog box will open.

6. **Click** in the **Start at track text box** and **type** the **track number** for the first track on the CD that you want to play.

7. **Click** in the **End at track text box** and **type** the **track number** for the last track on the CD that you want to play.

You can select not only the starting and ending track, but also the number of seconds into them that you want to start.

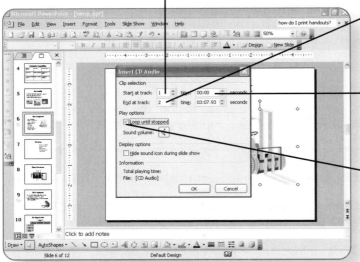

8. **Click** on **Loop until stopped** if you want this same set of tracks to repeat until the presentation is over.

9. **Click** on the **Speaker icon**. A volume control will appear.

10. **Drag** the **volume slider bar** up or down. The volume of the clip will change (in relation to the system sound volume in general).

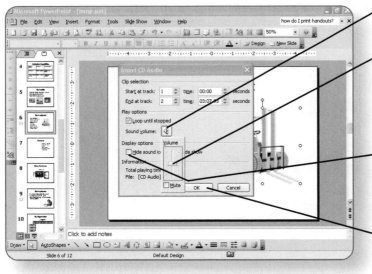

11. **Click** on **Hide sound icon during slideshow** if you do not want the CD icon to appear on the slide.

12. **Click** on **OK**. A confirmation dialog box will open.

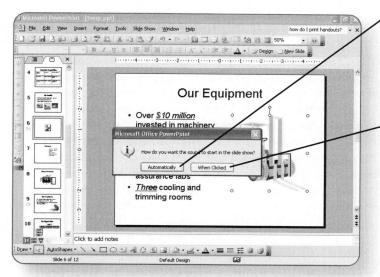

13a. **Click** on **Automatically**. The CD clip(s) will play automatically when the slide appears during the slide show.

OR

13b. **Click** on **When Clicked**. The CD clip(s) will play only when the CD icon is clicked during the slide show.

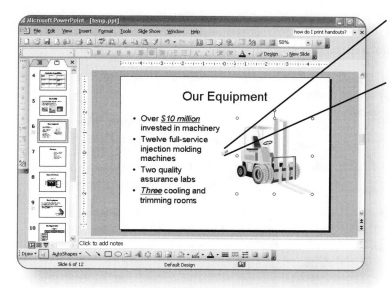

Unless you chose not to display the CD icon on the slide, it appears in the center of the slide.

14. **Click** and **drag** the **CD icon**. The CD icon will be moved to a different location on the slide.

NOTE

The CD clip will play only as long as that individual slide is onscreen. If you want the CD clip to play across multiple slides, you must do a bit of extra work. After adding the CD clip to the slide (as in the previous steps), go to Custom Animation and display the Effect Options for the CD clip, as described in Chapter 40. Then set Stop Playing After ____ Slides to 999. It will continue to play until the end of the presentation, or until it receives another instruction to play a CD clip on a later slide.

Adding Video Clips to a Slide

Digitized video files can also be used on PowerPoint slides to play a video during the slide show. For instance, you may have a product demonstration video that may be interesting to your slide show audience. Instead of playing the video on a separate display, just insert the video onto the slide.

1. Open the **slide** in which the video will appear. The slide will appear in Normal view.

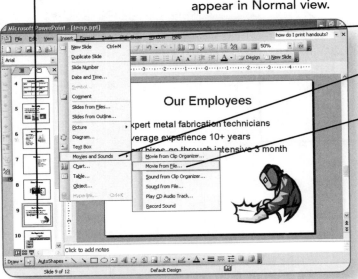

2. Click on **Insert**. The Insert menu will appear.

3. Point to Movies and Sounds. A second menu will appear.

4. Click on **Movie from File**. The Insert Movie dialog box will open.

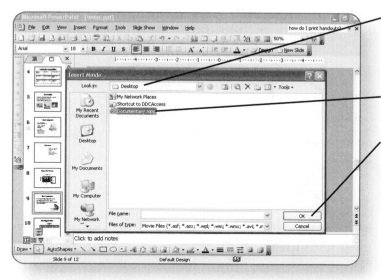

5. Navigate to the **folder** that contains the movie file. The folder's name will appear in the Look in list box.

6. Click on the **movie file**. The file will be selected.

7. Click on OK. A confirmation dialog box will open.

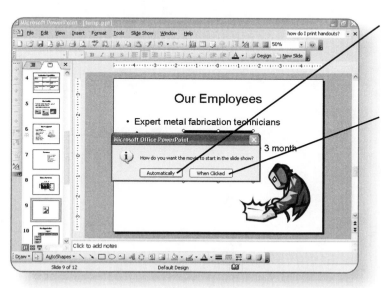

8a. Click on **Automatically** if you want the movie to play when the slide appears.

OR

8b. Click on **When Clicked** if you want the movie to start when you click on the movie icon.

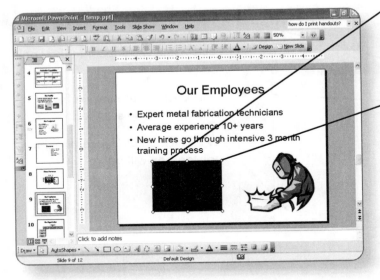

The first frame of the movie appears on the slide. In this case, the first frame is black because the movie starts by fading in.

9. Click and **drag** the **resize handles**. The movie clip window will be resized.

NOTE

You can fine-tune the way the movie plays by right-clicking it and choosing Edit Movie Object.

42

Working with Other Office Applications

One of the nice parts about Microsoft Office is how seamless it is to transfer content between its various applications. For example, it's easy to use an Excel chart in PowerPoint, a PowerPoint outline in Word, or any other combination. There are several ways of getting content from place to place, depending on how you want it to behave. It can stand alone in its destination location, or it can retain a link either to its original data file (linking) or to the application that created it (embedding). In this chapter, you'll learn how to:

- Copy items using the Office Clipboard
- Use Smart Tags to specify how items are copied
- Drag and drop items between Office applications
- Link and embed items

Using the Office Clipboard

The Office Clipboard is an enhanced version of the Windows Clipboard. Instead of being able to store only one item at a time, the Office Clipboard can store up to 24 items that you can copy between all Office programs (not just within PowerPoint).

Displaying the Clipboard

1. Click on **View**. The View menu will appear.

2. Click on **Task Pane** if there is not already a checkmark beside it. The Task Pane will appear.

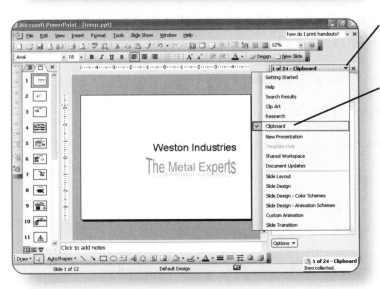

3. Click on the **Task Pane down arrow**. A list of available task panes will appear.

4. Click on **Clipboard**. The Clipboard task pane will appear.

Copying and Pasting with the Clipboard

You can copy and paste between applications or within the same one. The application you copy from is the *source application*; the one you copy to is the *destination application.*

1. **Select** the **data** that you want to add to the Clipboard. It may be in PowerPoint or some other application.

> ### NOTE
>
> You can select any amount of text, an object, or more than one object. To select multiple objects, hold down Ctrl as you click on each one.

2. **Click** on the **Copy button** or press Ctrl+C. The item will be copied to the Office Clipboard.

3. **Minimize** the **source application window** if you are copying between applications.

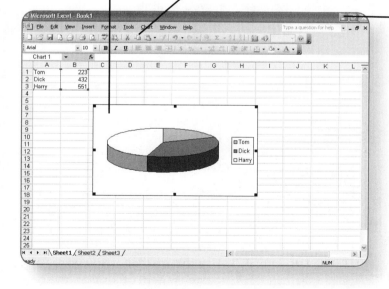

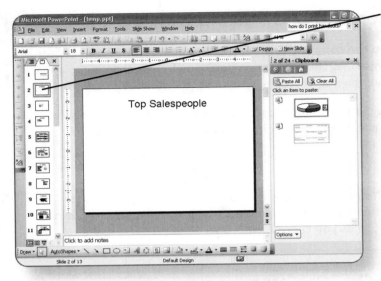

4. Display the **slide** (in PowerPoint) on which you want to paste. The slide will appear in Normal view.

5. If you're pasting text, **click** in the **text box** where you want to paste. The insertion point will appear there.

> ### NOTE
>
> Step 5 is necessary only when you're pasting text. If you're pasting a graphical object, it will appear on the center of the slide, and you can then drag it where you want it.

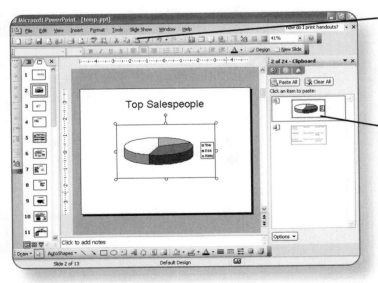

6a. Click on the **Paste button**. The most recently copied item will be pasted from the Clipboard.

OR

6b. Click on the **item** in the Clipboard task pane that you want to insert. A copy of the item will appear on the slide. Use this method if you want to paste an item other than the one you most recently copied.

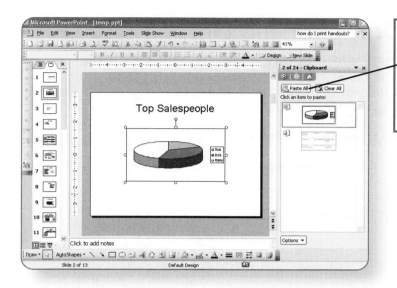

Keeping the Source Formatting When Pasting

If you are pasting text, it takes on the formatting of the desti-nation by default. A Smart Tag icon appears next to the pasted text. You can use that icon to return the pasted text to its orig-inal formatting, if needed.

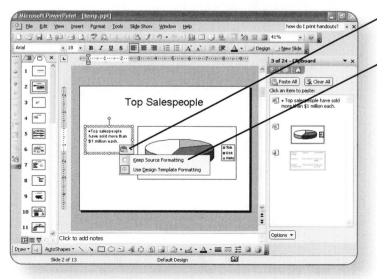

1. **Click** on the **Smart Tag icon**. A menu will appear.

2. **Click** on **Keep Source Formatting** if you want to retain the original formatting of the text. The text format will change back to the way it appeared in the Office application from which it was copied.

Dragging and Dropping Between Applications

A fast way to move items between two programs is to use the drag-and-drop method.

1. **Open both applications**.

2. **Resize** and **arrange** the **application windows** so that both are visible at once.

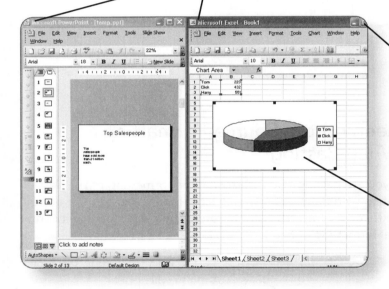

> ## NOTE
>
> To accomplish step 2, click the Restore button in a window so that it is no longer maximized, and then drag its border to resize it or drag its title bar to move it.

3. **Select** the **item(s)** that you want to copy. The items will be selected.

4. Press and **hold** the **Ctrl key**. This will cause whatever is dragged to be copied, rather than moved.

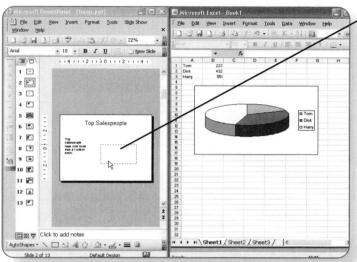

5. Drag the **object** from the source application to the destination application. The mouse pointer will show a box on it as you drag.

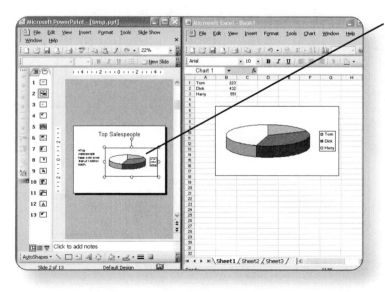

6. Release the **mouse button** at the desired location in PowerPoint. The object will be copied.

Linking Content

Linking is a way of retaining a connection between the copied material and its source file, such that when the source changes, the copied material will change too. For example, you could link to an Excel chart. Then, whenever that chart changed in Excel, it would change in PowerPoint too.

NOTE

The link will be updated when the PowerPoint file is opened *only* if the file to which it is linked is available. Otherwise, the last update will appear.

Linking Part of a File

You can link just a part of another file, such as the chart from an Excel workbook, or you can link an entire file.

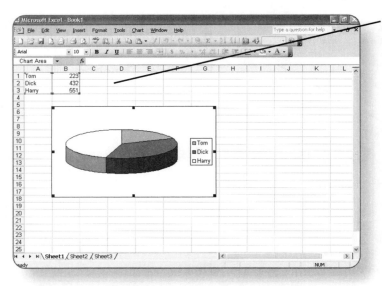

1. **Open** the **file** containing the object to be linked. It can be in any application that supports linking. (That includes all Microsoft Office applications.)

NOTE

The file in step 1 must have been saved. That is, it must have a name. Otherwise, there will be no file name to link to.

---

2. Select the **portion of the file to be copied**. This could be a single object, a range of text or cells, or any other amount of data.

3. Click on the **Copy button**, or press **Ctrl+C**. The data will be copied to the Clipboard.

4. Minimize the **source application**.

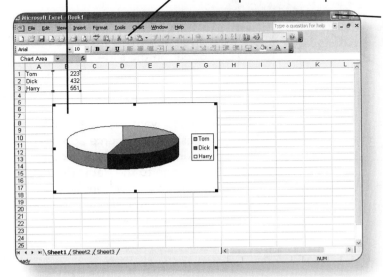

5. Display, in PowerPoint, the **slide** on which the linked object should appear.

6. Click on **Edit**. The Edit menu will appear.

7. Click on **Paste Special**. The Paste Special dialog box will open.

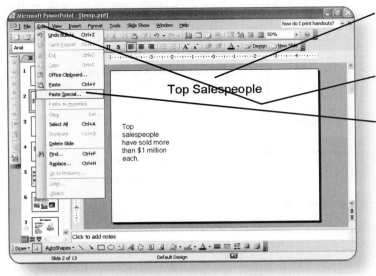

8. **Click** on **Paste Link**. The As list will change to show only linkable object types.

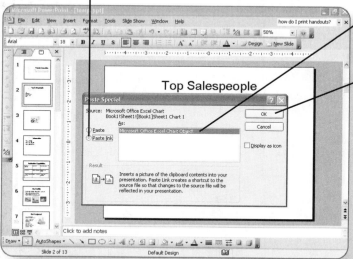

9. **Click** on the **desired object type**. In most cases, there will be only one choice.

10. **Click** on **OK**. The link will be pasted, and the object will appear on the slide.

NOTE

If you want to test the link, restore the source application's window and make a change to the data. Then restore PowerPoint and observe that the change has been made in PowerPoint too.

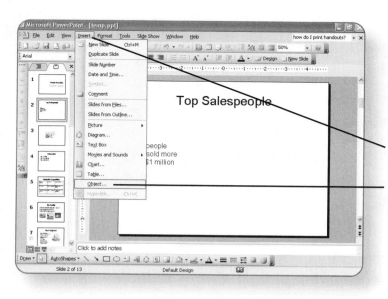

Linking an Entire File

This method is useful if the content you want to link to is an entire file by itself, such as a graphic file.

1. **Click** on **Insert**. The Insert menu will appear.

2. **Click** on **Object**. The Insert Object dialog box will open.

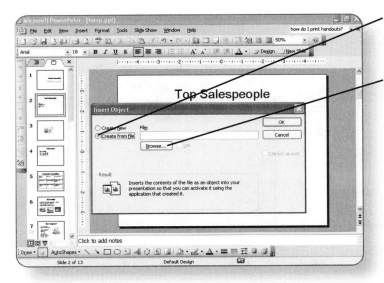

3. Click on **Create from file**. The File text box and Browse button will appear.

4. Click on **Browse**. The Browse dialog box will open.

5. Choose the **folder** in the Look in box. The folder's contents will appear.

6. Click on the **file** you want. A preview of it will appear.

7. Click on **OK**. The file's name and path will appear in the Insert Object dialog box.

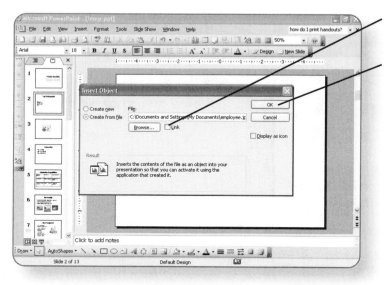

8. Click on the **Link check box**. A check will be placed in it.

9. Click on **OK**. The file will appear as slide content, and a link to the original will be maintained.

Changing the Link Update Method

You can change a link's properties so it can be updated either manually or automatically. Updating manually is a good choice when the source file is not always available.

1. Click on **Edit**. The Edit menu will appear.

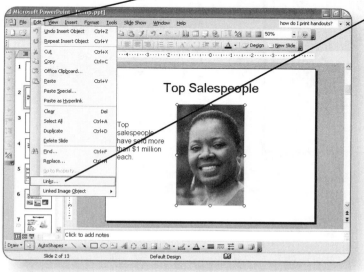

2. Click on **Links**. The Links dialog box will open.

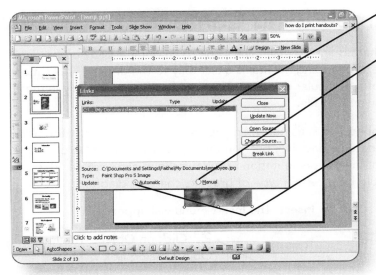

3. Click on the **link** you want to change. It will be highlighted.

4a. Click on **Manual** to set it to manual updating.

OR

4b. Click on **Automatic** to set it to automatic updating.

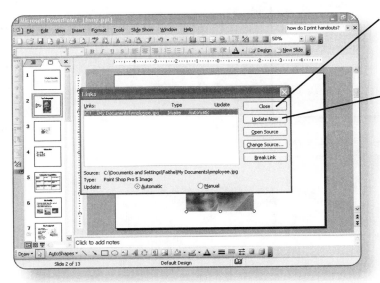

5. Click on **Close**.

NOTE

With manual updating, you must initiate the update. To do so, return to the Links dialog box, select the link, and click Update Now.

Embedding Content

Whereas linking maintains a link to an original copy of the data file, embedding maintains a link only to the original application (not a particular data file). The data itself is stored only in the PowerPoint file.

Embedding is useful when you have no need for an externally updatable data file, but you want to place some type of content in your presentation that PowerPoint can't create. This could be a certain type of graphic, chart, or diagram.

1. **Click** on **Insert**. The Insert menu will appear.

2. **Click** on **Object**. The Insert Object dialog box will open.

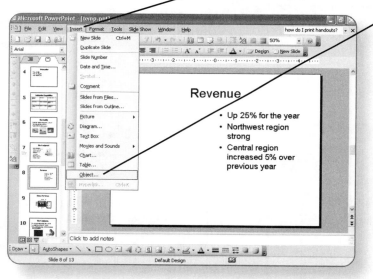

3. Click on the **object type** you want to create. It will be selected.

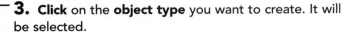
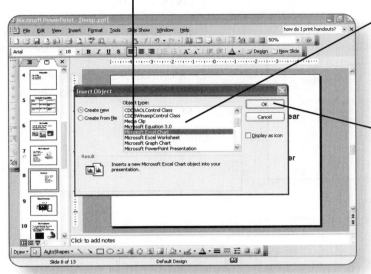

The object types listed here represent the OLE-compliant applications installed on your computer. Your list may be different than the one shown here.

4. Click on **OK**. The controls for creating that object will appear.

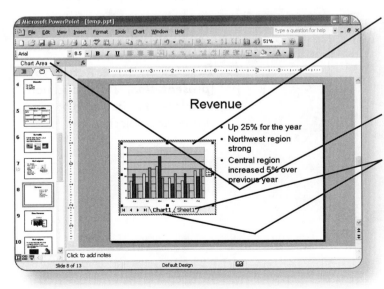

Depending on the object type chosen, a separate window may appear, or the controls may appear within the PowerPoint window.

5. Use the **controls that appear** to create the content.

For example, here an Excel chart and worksheet appears. Click the Sheet1 tab to edit the data, and use the Chart menu to change the chart's features.

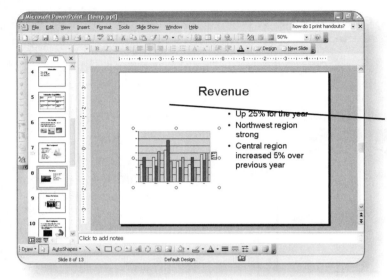

Returning to PowerPoint

If you're using an application from within the PowerPoint window:

Click on the **slide's background**. PowerPoint will return to normal operation.

OR

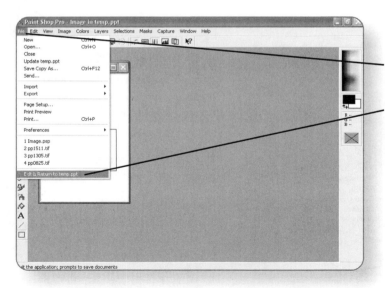

If you're using an application that appears as a separate window:

1. Click on **File.** The File menu will appear.

2. Click on **Exit & Return to [*presentation*].** The application will close, and PowerPoint will display the object.

Editing an Embedded Object

1. Double-click on the **object** on the PowerPoint slide. Its application's controls will appear so you can edit it.

2. Make changes to the object.

3. Return to **PowerPoint**, as in the preceding steps.

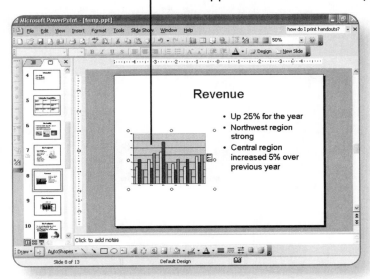

43

Adding the Final Touches to Your Presentation

You've finished creating your presentation. Now it's time to add a few items that will help you when you deliver it. If you'll be delivering it in front of an audience, you'll want to use notes. You'll also need to practice. To prepare for potential questions from the audience, you may want to hide a few slides up your sleeve. Self-running presentations (such as kiosks) that use voice-over narration are more effective than those without accompanying sounds. In this chapter, you'll learn how to:

- Create speaker notes
- Customize the Notes Master
- Use hidden slides
- Rehearse and set timings

Using Notes

When you're giving a presentation, cue cards are a handy item. Not only do they help relieve anxiety caused by stage fright, but they also enhance a presentation. You can develop notes and print them with a copy of the slide to help keep your presentation on course. To provide your audience with more information, print a notes page that they can take home.

Adding Notes to a Slide

1. Click on the **Normal View button**. Your slide will appear in Normal view.

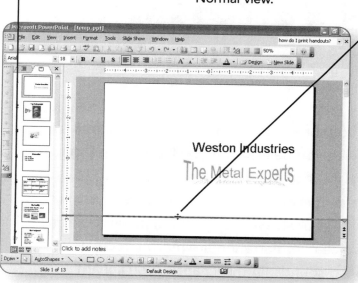

2. Click and **drag** the **bar** up to the middle between the Slide pane and the Notes pane. The mouse pointer will turn into a double arrow, and an outline of the bar will show how the pane size will be changed.

3. Release the **mouse button**. The two panes will be resized, and you'll have more room to work in the Notes pane.

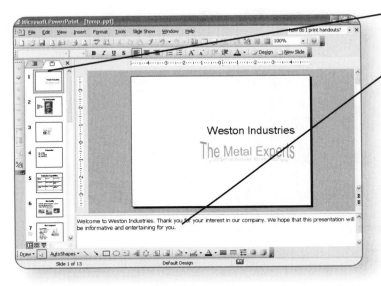

4. Display the **slide** to which you want to add the notes. The slide will appear in the Slide pane.

5. Click inside the **Notes pane** and **type notes** as desired. These notes can be anything that will help you remember what you need to say, or that will provide additional background as needed during the presentation.

TIP

When a presentation is displayed as Web pages, notes can be shown on a page along with the corresponding slide.

Working in Notes Page View

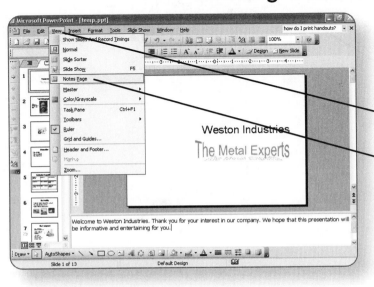

Notes Page view is a special view designed specifically for typing and editing notes. It displays each slide as it will appear when you print Speaker Notes.

1. Click on **View**. The View menu will appear.

2. Click on **Notes Page**. The Notes page for the slide will appear. This is actually a preview of what the Notes page will look like when printed.

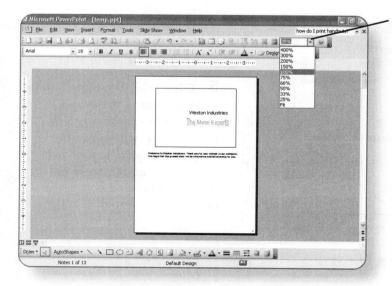

3. **Click** on the **down arrow** next to the Zoom button and select a magnification level.

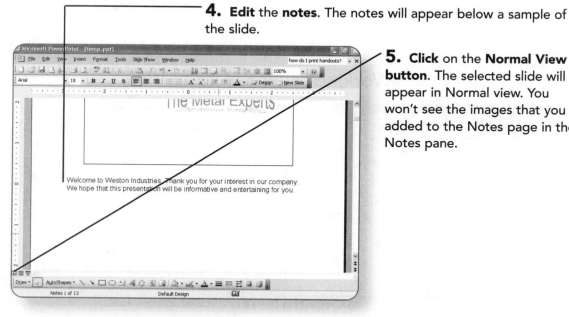

4. **Edit** the **notes**. The notes will appear below a sample of the slide.

5. **Click** on the **Normal View button**. The selected slide will appear in Normal view. You won't see the images that you added to the Notes page in the Notes pane.

Working with the Notes Master

You worked with the Slide Master in Chapter 33, "Changing the Presentation's Look." Like the Slide Master, the Notes Master is where you can set the basic format and look for all the Notes pages in your presentation.

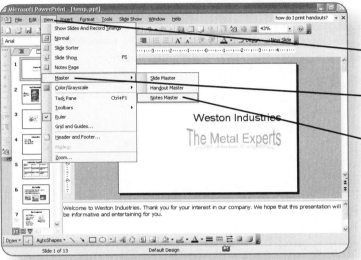

1. **Click** on **View**. The View menu will appear.

2. **Point to Master**. A submenu will appear.

3. **Click** on **Notes Master**. The Notes Master page will appear.

Removing a Placeholder

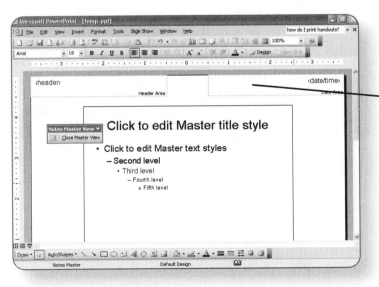

The Notes Master has several placeholder boxes. You can delete any placeholders that you do not want.

1. **Click** on the **placeholder to remove**. The placeholder will be selected.

2. **Press** the **Delete** key. The placeholder will disappear.

Moving a Placeholder

1. **Click** on a **placeholder's border**. It will be selected.

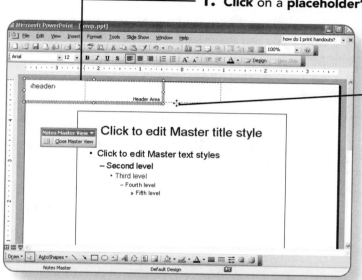

2. **Point** the **mouse pointer** at the border, but not on a selection handle.

3. **Drag** the **placeholder** to a different location.

Resizing a Placeholder

1. **Click** on the **placeholder's border**. It will be selected.

2. **Point** the **mouse pointer** at a selection handle. The mouse pointer will become a double-headed arrow.

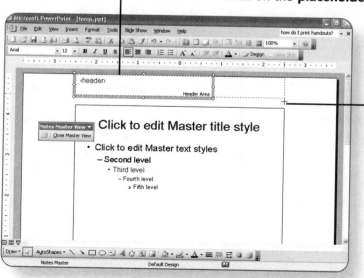

3. **Drag** the **selection handle** to change the size of the placeholder box.

Restoring Deleted Placeholders

1. Click on the **Notes Master Layout button**. The Notes Master Layout dialog box will open. Any placeholders that have been deleted will appear as empty check boxes.

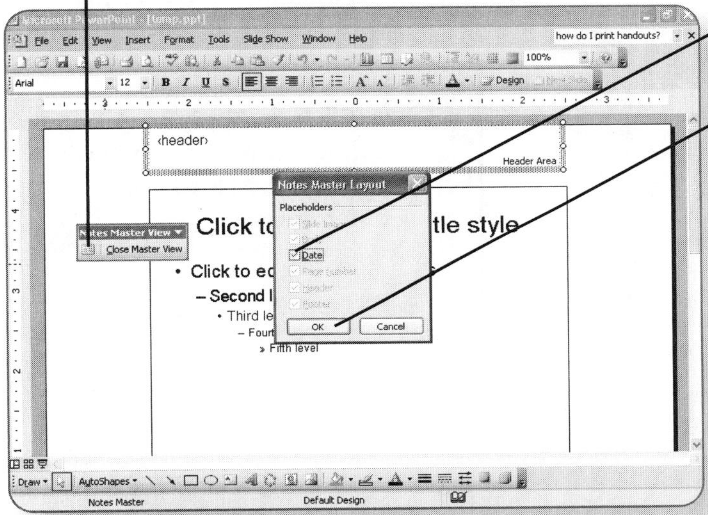

2. Click in a **check box** for a placeholder you want to restore.

3. Click on **OK**. The placeholder will be restored on the Notes Master.

Editing Headers and Footers

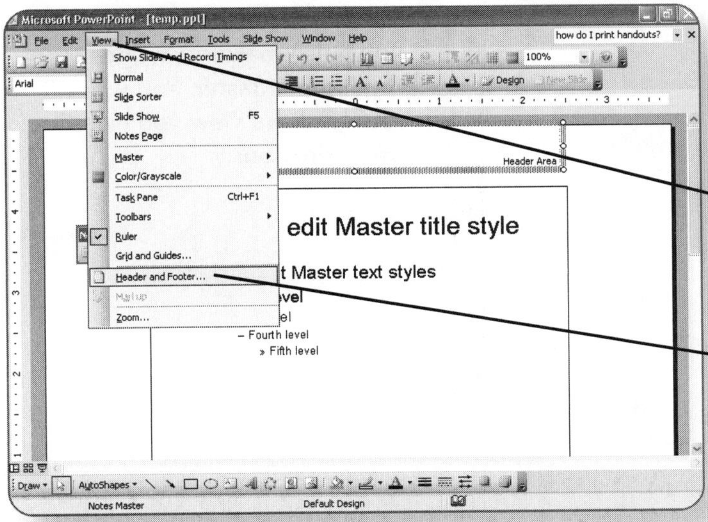

The preceding procedures worked with the placeholders for the header and footer elements. Now you will specify what text should appear in them.

1. Click on **View** to add information to the Header and Footer areas. The View menu will appear.

2. Click on **Header and Footer**. The Header and Footer dialog box will open, and the Notes and Handouts tab will be on top.

3. Mark the **check boxes** for the placeholder items you want to appear, and **clear** the **check boxes** for the placeholders you don't want to appear.

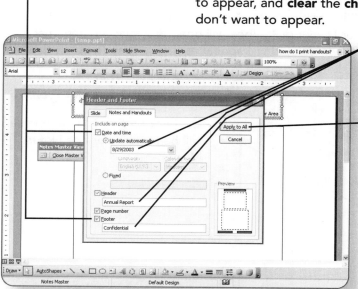

4. Type any **text** that you want to appear in those areas, or specify automatic entry (as with Date and time).

5. Click on **Apply to All**. The information you've typed will appear in the Header and Footer areas.

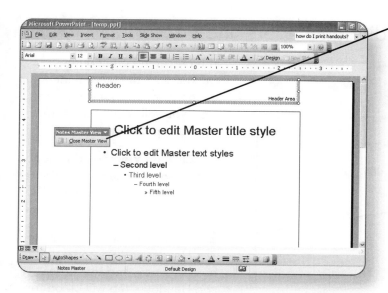

6. Click on the **Close Master View button** on the Notes Master View toolbar when you finish making changes to the Notes Master. You will return to the view you were using previously.

Printing Your Notes

1. Click on **File**. The File menu will appear.

2. Click on **Print**. The Print dialog box will open.

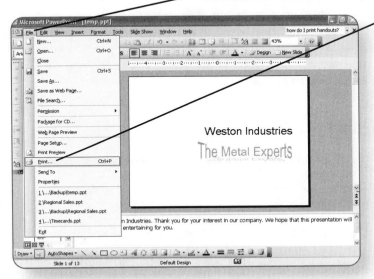

3. Click on the **down arrow** next to the Print what list box, and **click** on **Notes Pages**. The option will appear in the list box.

4. Change any other **options** as needed.

5. Click on **OK**. The Notes pages will be printed.

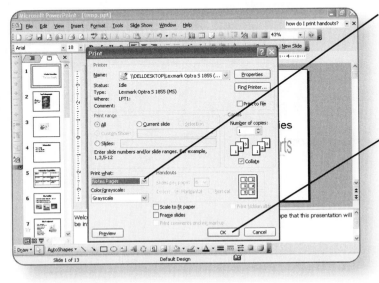

Using Hidden Slides

At some point during a presentation, you'll probably receive questions from your audience. Before you deliver your presentation, try to anticipate some of the questions you'll be asked. Make slides that will answer the questions, or provide additional background information in the notes. Your audience will think that you're brilliant!

Hiding a Slide

This same procedure both hides and unhides slides.

1. Display the **slide** that you want hidden. The slide will appear in Normal view.

2. Click on **Slide Show**. The Slide Show menu will appear.

3. Click on **Hide Slide**. The slide will be hidden until you ask for it during your slide show.

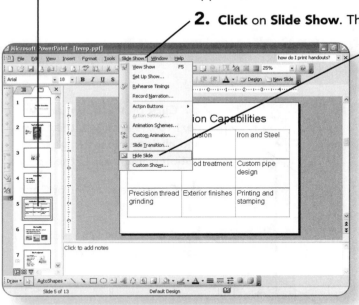

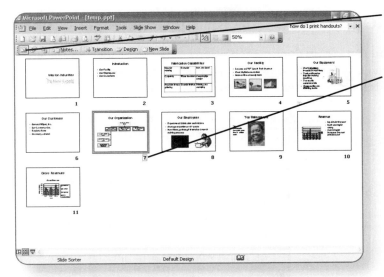

There is a Hide Slide button on the toolbar in Slide Sorter view that hides and unhides slides.

A hidden slide has a Hidden indicator around its slide number.

Using Hidden Slides During a Slide Show

Start in the slide show (in Slide Show view). See Chapter 44, "Creating Audience Handouts," for help.

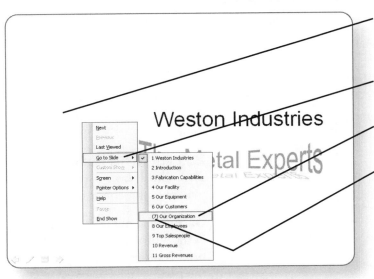

1. Right-click on the **slide** that is showing in Slide Show view. A shortcut menu will appear.

2. Point to Go to Slide. A submenu will appear.

3. Click on the **slide to display**. The slide will appear.

A hidden slide has parentheses around its slide number.

Recording Slide Timings

You can set up your presentation so that the slides advance manually (on a mouse click), and/or so that they advance automatically after a certain amount of time.

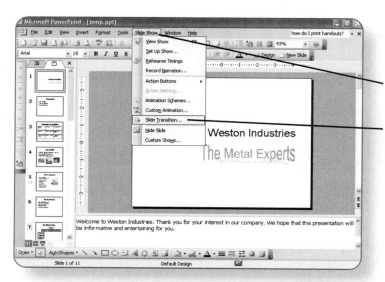

Most of the timing settings are assigned from the Slide Transition task pane.

1. Click on **Slide Show**. The Slide Show menu will open.

2. Click on **Slide Transition**. The Slide Transition task pane will appear.

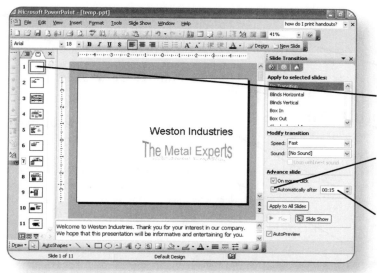

Setting the Timing for an Individual Slide

1. Display the **slide** for which you want to set the transition timing.

2. Click on the **Automatically after check box**. A check will be placed in the check box.

3. Enter a **number of seconds** in the Automatically after text box. The number will appear in the box.

Setting the Same Timing for All Slides

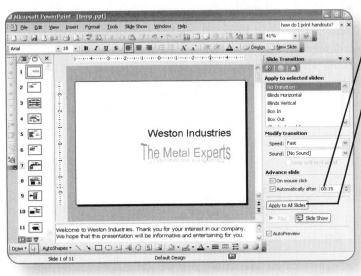

1. **Set** the **timing** for one slide, as in the preceding steps.

2. **Click** on **Apply to All Slides**. The same timing will be assigned to every slide in the presentation.

Recording Custom Timings for Each Slide

If you are not sure how much time to allocate for each slide, you can play the slide show and rehearse your speech as it runs. PowerPoint will record the amount of time you spend on each slide.

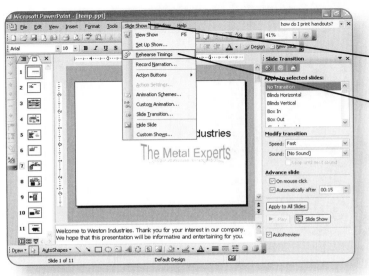

1. **Click** on **Slide Show**. The Slide Show menu will open.

2. **Click** on **Rehearse Timings**. The presentation will open in Slide Show view with a Rehearsal toolbar.

3. Speak, or do whatever it is you are going to do during the actual show, to help gauge when to move to the next slide.

4. Click on the **Next button**, or **click the mouse**. The next slide will appear. The Rehearsal toolbar will keep a count of the seconds spent on each slide.

5. Repeat steps 3 and 4 until you reach the end of the slide show.

6. Click on **Yes** to keep the slide timings. Slide Show view will exit.

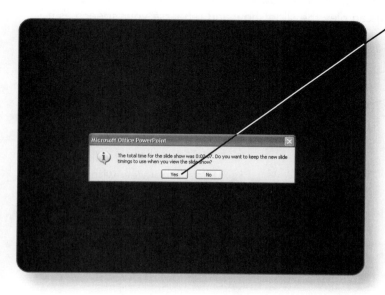

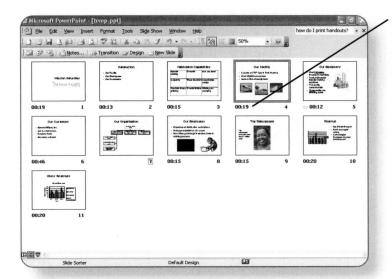

PowerPoint will reappear in Slide Sorter view, and the transition time for each slide will appear beneath it.

44

Creating Audience Handouts

Most presentations are designed primarily for display on some type of screen, whether it's a computer screen, a slide projector screen, or some other large format. However, you may also want to print a hard copy of the presentation slides for your audience to refer to. In this chapter, you will learn how to:

- Print audience handouts

- Format handouts with the Handout Master

- Export audience handouts to Word

Printing Handouts

PowerPoint can print handouts in a variety of styles, from one to nine slides per page. These layouts are ready to go from the Print dialog box.

1. **Click** on **File**. The File menu will appear.

2. **Click** on **Print**. The Print dialog box will open.

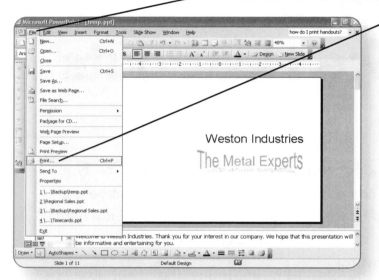

3. **Click** the **down arrow** next to the Print what list box and **click** on **Handouts**. The option will appear in the list box.

4. **Click** on the **Frame slides check box** to check or clear it as desired. If checked, it will place a black border around each slide image on the printout. This can be useful for slides with a white background.

5. **Click** on the **Print hidden slides check box** to check or clear it as desired.

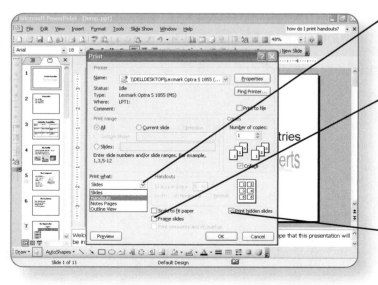

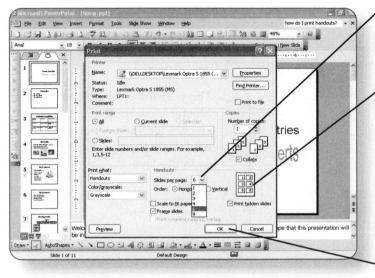

6. Click the **down arrow** next to Slides per page, and **click** the **number of slides** you want on each handout page.

The sample next to the box will change to show the chosen layout.

7. Select any **other options** as needed. For example, choose a page range or a number of copies, as you learned in Chapter 30, "Learning About Presentations."

8. Click on **OK**. The handouts will be printed.

Formatting Handouts with the Handout Master

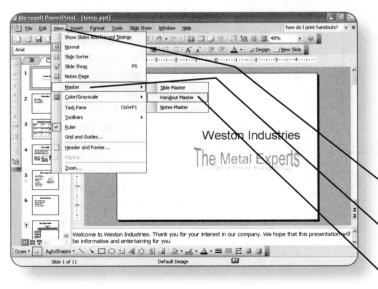

The handouts that are printed with certain numbers of slides per page are controlled by the Handout Master. It works much like the Slide Master (Chapter 33, "Changing the Presentation's Look") and the Notes Master (Chapter 43, "Adding the Final Touches to Your Presentation").

1. Click on **View**. The View menu will appear.

2. Click on **Master**. A submenu will appear.

3. Click on **Handout Master**. The Handout Master will appear.

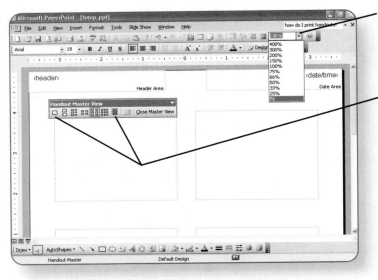

4. Click on the **down arrow** next to the Zoom list box, and **click** on **Fit**. The entire page will appear.

The buttons on the Handout Master View toolbar represent layouts for various numbers of slides per page. Each is a separate layout.

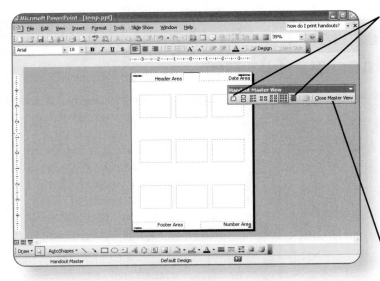

5. Click on a **button** on the Handout Master View toolbar. The display will change to show the layout for the chosen number of slides per page.

6. Make any **changes** to the layout. For example, you can change the font used in placeholder boxes, delete the placeholders, or move them. You cannot change the size or positioning of the slide boxes.

7. Click on the **Close Master View button**. The presentation will appear in the previous view in which you were working.

Exporting Handouts to Microsoft Word

As you saw in the preceding section, PowerPoint doesn't have many options for customizing the handout layout. You can get more freedom to change the layout by exporting the handouts for a particular presentation to Word and working with them there.

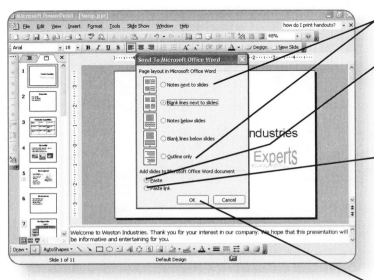

1. Click on **File**. The File menu will appear.

2. Point to **Send to**. A submenu will appear.

3. Click on **Microsoft Office Word**. The Send To Microsoft Office Word dialog box will open.

4. Click on one of the **layouts**. It will be selected.

5a. Click on **Paste**. Copies of the slides will be exported to Word.

OR

5b. Click on **Paste link**. The material exported into Word will retain a link with the PowerPoint presentation. This is useful if you want to reprint the handouts from Word after making more changes in PowerPoint.

6. Click on **OK**. The handouts will be displayed in Word.

7. **Make any changes** in Word as needed. You can edit text, change the fonts, resize the slide images, and so on.

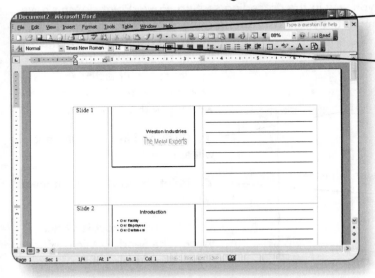

8. **Click** on the **Print button** to print the handouts from Word.

9. **Save** your **work** in Word if you want to save the file for later reprinting. The procedure is the same as saving in PowerPoint. See Chapter 30.

45

Delivering the Presentation

You're ready to give your presentation in front of a live audience. Each slide contains just the right content and is formatted so that your audience can see it clearly. You've rehearsed and rehearsed until your voice is hoarse. Your handouts are printed and stashed away in your briefcase. Now it's time to give the presentation in front of a live audience! In this chapter, you will learn how to:

- Present the show with Slide Show view
- Navigate between slides
- Use the pen in Slide Show view

Presenting a Live Slide Show

To start your live show, simply enter Slide Show view.

1. **Click** on **View**. The View menu will appear.

2. **Click** on **Slide Show**. The slide show will begin.

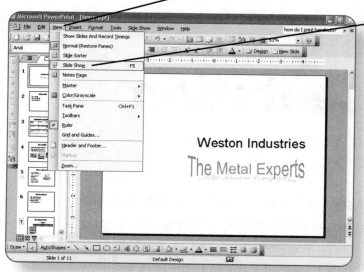

You can also open the **Slide Show** menu and choose **View Show**, or **press F5**.

You can also click the **Slide Show View button**. This starts the show at the selected slide, not necessarily at the beginning.

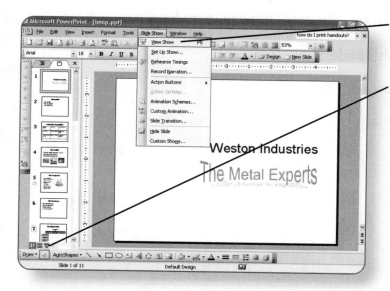

Moving Between Slides

To move between slides with the keyboard or mouse:

- Click the **left mouse button**, or press **Enter** or the **right arrow**, to move forward.

- Press the **Backspace key** or the **left arrow** to move backward.

You can also use an on-screen menu system.

1. **Right-click** anywhere in Slide Show view. A menu will appear.

2a. **Click** on **Next** or **Previous**.

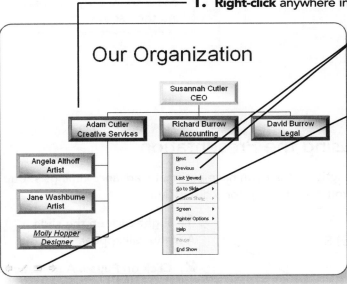

Our Organization

Susannah Cutler
CEO

Adam Cutler
Creative Services

Richard Burrow
Accounting

David Burrow
Legal

Angela Althoff
Artist

Jane Washburne
Artist

Molly Hopper
Designer

Next
Previous
Last Viewed
Go to Slide   ▶
                   ▶
Screen   ▶
Pointer Options   ▶
Help

End Show

NOTE

When you move the mouse, the icons in the bottom-left corner appear. Clicking this one opens the same menu as right-clicking.

OR

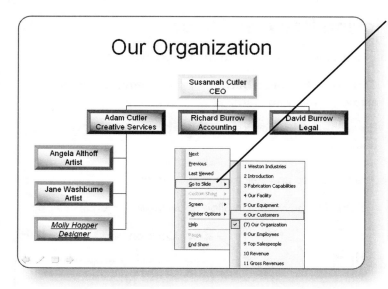

2b. **Point** to **Go to Slide** and then **click the slide** to display.

NOTE

When you reach the last slide, a black screen will appear with a message prompting you to press any key to return to PowerPoint. You can also end a show early by pressing the Esc key.

Pausing the Presentation

Pausing is useful if you have automatic advance timings set up and you need to stop for a discussion.

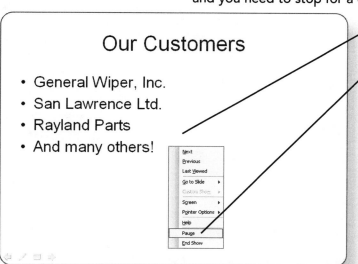

1. **Right-click** on the **slide**. A menu will appear.

2. **Click** on **Pause**. Automatic advance will be stopped.

NOTE

There is no shortcut key for the Pause command. The natural choice would be P, but P is used for "Previous" and takes you to the previous slide.

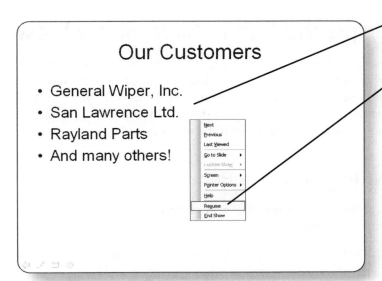

3. **Right-click** on the **slide** again when you are ready to resume. A menu will appear.

4. **Click** on **Resume**. Automatic slide advance will resume.

Blanking the Screen

You can blank out the screen temporarily during the presentation. This might be useful if you want to pause for an extended discussion but don't want to turn off the projector.

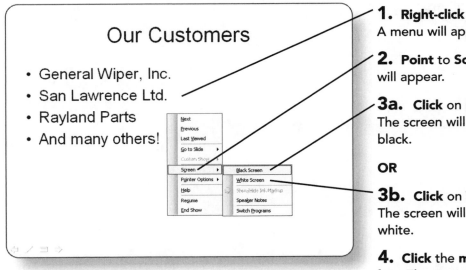

1. **Right-click** on the **slide**. A menu will appear.

2. **Point** to **Screen**. A submenu will appear.

3a. **Click** on **Black Screen**. The screen will become solid black.

OR

3b. **Click** on **White Screen**. The screen will become solid white.

4. **Click** the **mouse** or **press** a **key**. The presentation will resume.

Using the Pen in Slide Show View

The pen feature enables you to annotate the slides—that is, to write on them. If you have a tablet and stylus for computer use, you can use it for the annotation. Otherwise, you can click and drag to create lines and writing (although many people find it awkward to write with the mouse).

Writing with the Pen Tool

1. **Move** the **mouse**. The menu buttons in the bottom-left corner will appear.

2. **Click** on the **Pen** button. A menu will appear.

3. **Click** on the **type of pen** you want. The menu will close and the pointer will change to a colored dot.

Ballpoint and Felt Tip are two thicknesses of solid ink. Highlighter is semitransparent ink.

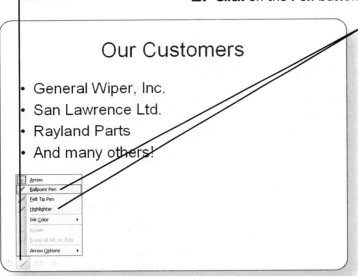

Our Customers

- General Wiper, Inc.
- San Lawrence Ltd.
- Rayland Parts
- And many others!

Arrow
Ballpoint Pen
Felt Tip Pen
Highlighter
Ink Color
Eraser
Erase All Ink on Slide
Arrow Options

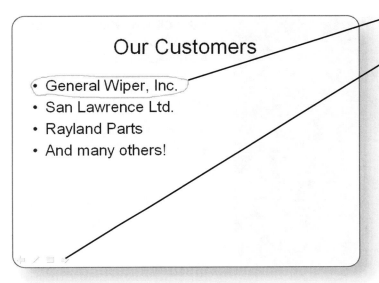

4. Drag on the **slide** to draw or write your annotations.

5. Click on the **Next button**, or press **Enter** or the **right arrow key**, to advance to the next slide.

The pen will stay active when you're moving between slides.

6. Click on the **Pen button**. The menu will appear.

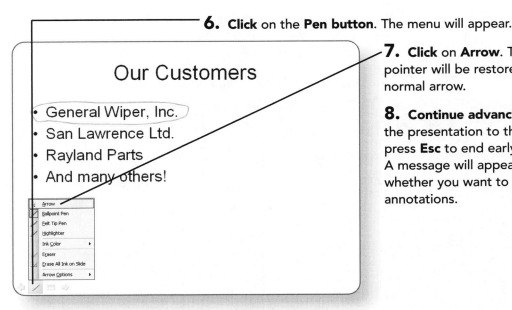

7. Click on **Arrow**. The mouse pointer will be restored to a normal arrow.

8. Continue advancing through the presentation to the end, or press **Esc** to end early. A message will appear, asking whether you want to save your annotations.

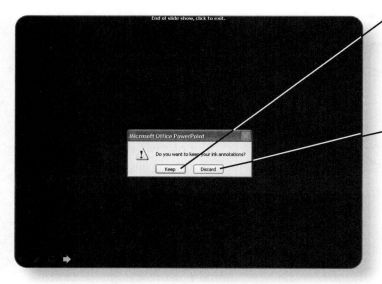

9a. **Click** on **Keep**. The drawings will be converted to AutoShapes and transferred to the slides. See the next section.

OR

9b. **Click** on **Discard**. The annotations will not be kept.

Working with Saved Annotations

Saved annotations appear as free-form AutoShape drawings on the slides. You can delete them, move them, and so on, just like ordinary AutoShape objects.

1. **Display** a **slide** containing annotations.

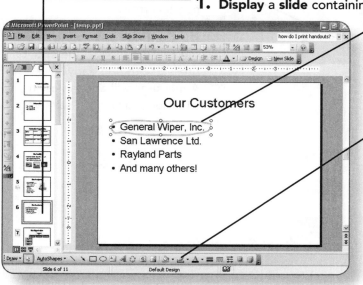

2. **Click** on the **annotation line**. It will be selected.

3. **Modify it** as desired. You can:

- Press Delete to delete it.

- Change its color with the Line Color button.

- Drag it to a different spot on the slide.

Changing the Pen Color

You can select any color for the pen during the presentation, and you can change it to a different one at any time.

1. **Move** the **mouse**. The buttons in the bottom-left corner of the screen will appear.

2. **Click** on the **Pen button**. A menu will appear.

3. **Point** to **Ink Color**. A submenu will appear.

4. **Click** on a **color**. Future pen usage will be in that color.

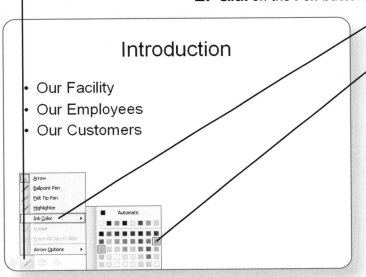

46

Creating a Self-Running Presentation

Some presentations must be delivered remotely, either because the people you want to reach aren't available to sit through a live lecture, or because you want to use the presentation on the Web or some other widely distributed medium. There are some special considerations when you're preparing such a show, and this chapter will deal with them. In this chapter, you will learn how to:

- Create hyperlinks
- Create action buttons for navigation
- Add voice-over narration recordings

Creating Hyperlinks

A *hyperlink* is a link from one location or document to another. When the user clicks a hyperlink, the destination document appears. You are probably familiar with hyperlinks on Web pages from using the Internet. You can also create hyperlinks on PowerPoint slides. These hyperlinks can point to other slides in the presentation, to e-mail addresses, or to other files stored anywhere on a network or on the Internet.

A hyperlink can be attached to any object, including any amount of text or a graphic object. For example, the user could click on underlined text as a hyperlink, or click on a graphic that is a hyperlink.

Hyperlinking to Another Slide in the Presentation

You would not normally hyperlink from one slide to the next one, because simply clicking the mouse will move to the next slide. However, you might hyperlink in order to jump around in the order (for example, to skip a certain set of slides), or to jump to a hidden slide.

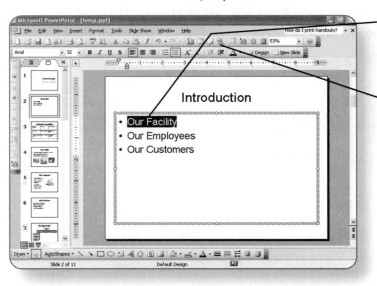

1. **Select** the **text** or **graphic** that you want to use as the hyperlink. The text or graphic will be selected.

2. **Click** on the **Insert Hyperlink button**. The Insert Hyperlink dialog box will open.

CREATING HYPERLINKS **711**

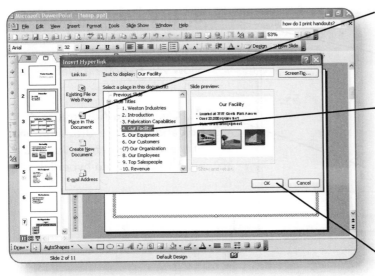

3. **Click** on **Place in This Document** in the Link to list. A list of slides found in the presentation will appear in the center of the dialog box.

4. **Click** on the **slide** in the Select a place in this document list box that you want to appear when a visitor clicks on the hyperlink. The slide will be selected, and a preview of the slide will appear in the Slide preview box.

5. **Click** on **OK**. The hyperlink will be created.

Creating Hyperlinks to Web Sites

A hyperlink to a Web site will open a Web browser when the user clicks on it, taking the user away from your PowerPoint presentation.

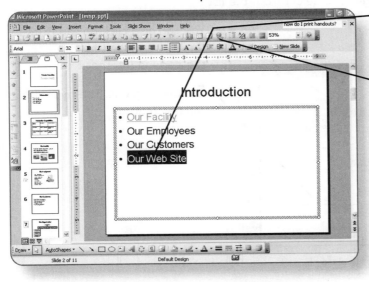

1. **Select** the **text** or **image** that will be used as the hyperlink. The text will be selected.

2. **Click** on the **Insert Hyperlink button**. The Insert Hyperlink dialog box will open.

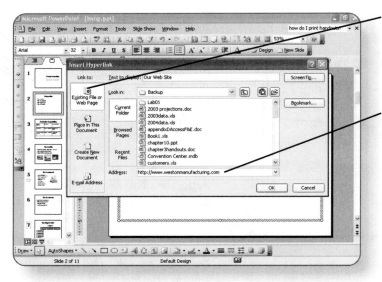

3. **Click** on **Existing File or Web Page** in the Link to list. The dialog box will change to allow you to enter a Web page's URL address.

4. **Click** in the **Address text box** and **type** the **URL address** of the Web page to which you want to create the hyperlink.

If you don't know the URL address, and if it's a page you've visited recently using your Web browser, click on Browsed Pages and select from the list.

You can also click on the Browse the Web button to browse for the page in Internet Explorer.

5. **Click** on **OK**. The hyperlink will be created.

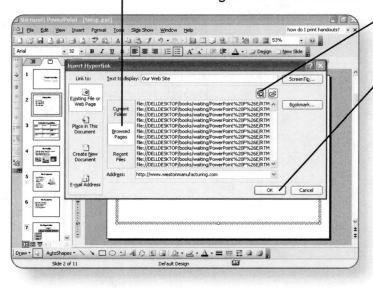

Creating an E-Mail Hyperlink

To give your audience an easy way to contact you, place an e-mail hyperlink on one of the slides. When people click on the e-mail hyperlink, a new message window will open from their default e-mail program. Your e-mail address (or any other address you specify) will appear in the To field. They just need to type a message and send it to you.

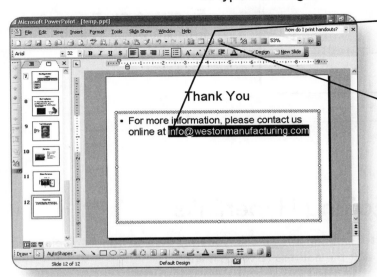

1. **Select** the **text** or **image** that you want to use as the e-mail hyperlink. The item will be selected.

2. **Click** on the **Insert Hyperlink button**. The Insert Hyperlink dialog box will open.

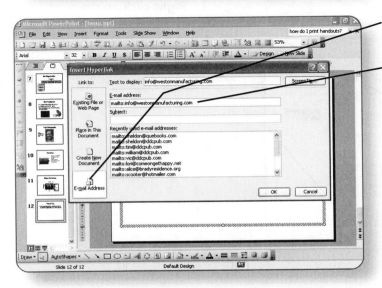

3. **Click** on **E-mail Address** in the Link to list.

4. **Click** in the **E-mail address text box** and **type** the **e-mail address** to which you want to create the link.

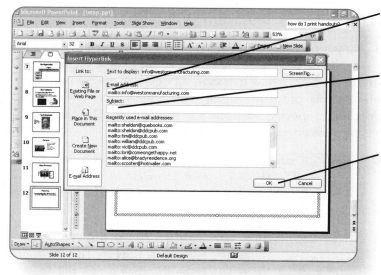

You do not have to type mailto: at the beginning; PowerPoint adds this automatically.

If you want e-mail sent from this link to contain a specific message header, type it in the Subject text box.

5. **Click** on **OK**. The e-mail hyperlink will be created.

Editing Hyperlinks

After creating a hyperlink, you may want to edit its display text or edit the address to which it links.

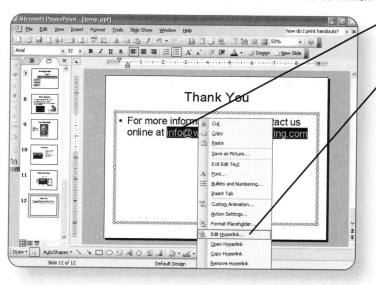

1. **Right-click** on the **hyperlinked text** or **object**. A menu will appear.

2. **Click** on **Edit Hyperlink**. The Edit Hyperlink dialog box will open.

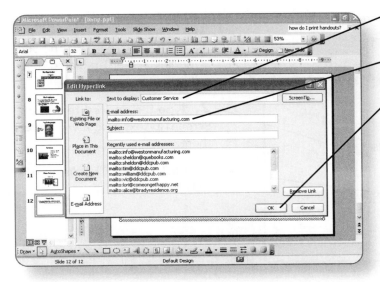

3. **Edit** the **text to display** in PowerPoint, if desired.

4. **Edit** the **address of the hyperlink,** if desired.

5. **Click** on **OK**. The dialog box will close and your changes will be made.

Thank You

- For more information, please contact us online at Customer Service

Click here to send e-mail

Using a ScreenTip

A *ScreenTip* is a box that pops up when the user points at the hyperlink. It can contain any text you like. Some people use it to show the URL if the display text shows something different.

From the Insert Hyperlink or Edit Hyperlink dialog box:

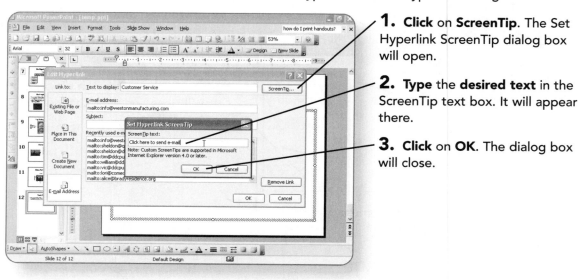

1. Click on **ScreenTip**. The Set Hyperlink ScreenTip dialog box will open.

2. Type the **desired text** in the ScreenTip text box. It will appear there.

3. Click on **OK**. The dialog box will close.

Creating Action Buttons

An *action button* is a graphic that is specifically designed for use as a hyperlink. Action buttons enable the person watching the presentation to move between slides by clicking on graphical buttons onscreen.

You can place an action button on an individual slide (for example, as a jump point to a hidden slide), or you can place it on the Slide Master so that the same button appears on all slides.

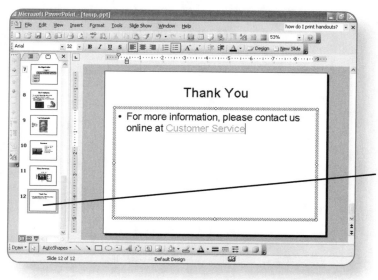

1. Open the **slide** on which you want to place the action buttons. The slide will appear in Normal view.

NOTE

If you want to place the button on all slides, display the Slide Master in step 1.

2. Click on **Slide Show**. The Slide Show menu will appear.

3. Point to Action Buttons. A submenu will appear.

4. Click on the **button** that you want to insert into the slide. The mouse pointer will turn into crosshairs.

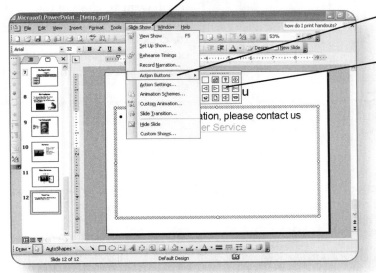

5a. Click on the **mouse pointer** where you want to place the navigation button. The button will appear in a predefined size, and the Action Settings dialog box will open.

OR

5b. Click and drag the **mouse pointer** to the exact size and shape you want for the button. When you release the mouse, the button will appear, and the Action Settings dialog box will open.

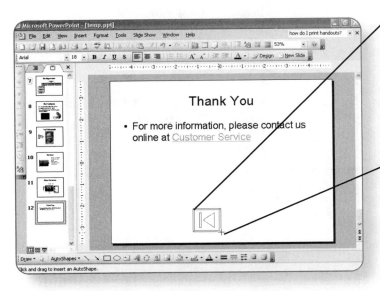

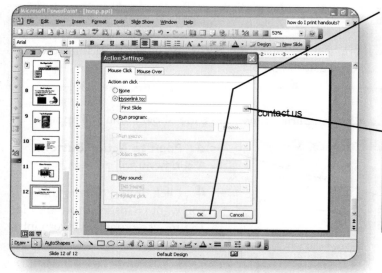

6. Click on **OK** to accept the default hyperlink. The button will be used as a hyperlink to the specified page.

TIP

If you want to change the slide that the button links to, click the down arrow next to the Hyperlink to list box and select a different slide.

Action buttons are treated just like AutoShapes for the purposes of formatting.

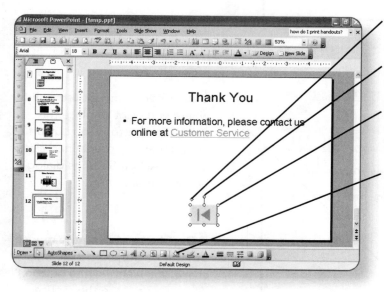

Change its bevel width by dragging the yellow diamond.

Rotate the button by dragging the green circle.

Change the button's size and shape by dragging a selection handle.

Change the fill color with the Fill Color button.

Adding Voice-Over Narration

Voice-over narration works great in presentations for which a live speaker will not be present.

1. **Click** on **Slide Show**. The Slide Show menu will appear.

2. **Click** on **Record Narration**. The Record Narration dialog box will open.

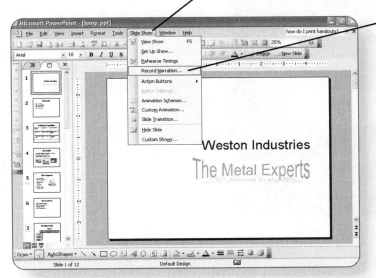

NOTE

If this is the first time you're using this feature, click on the Set Microphone Level button and follow the wizard.

TIP

Linking the narration to the presentation file places the recording in a separate file from the PowerPoint presentation.

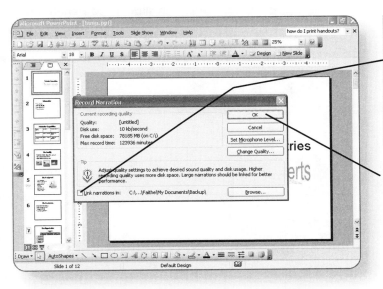

3. **Click** on **OK**. The slide show will start and you can begin recording.

4. Work your way through the presentation until you come to the end. The screen will go black, and a confirmation dialog box will appear.

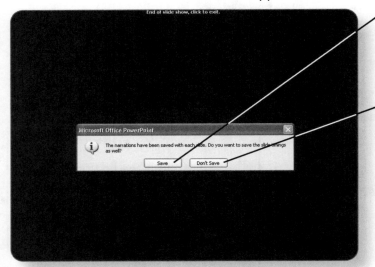

5a. Click on **Save**. The timing of the slide show will be saved along with the narration.

OR

5b. Click on **Don't Save**. Only the narration will be saved.

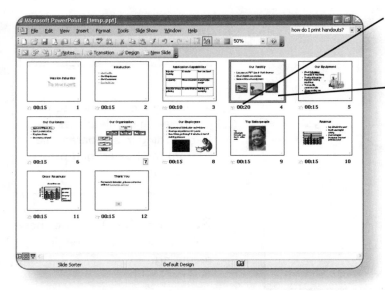

The presentation will appear in Slide Sorter view with the timing for each slide listed beneath it.

Double-click a slide to display it in Normal view.

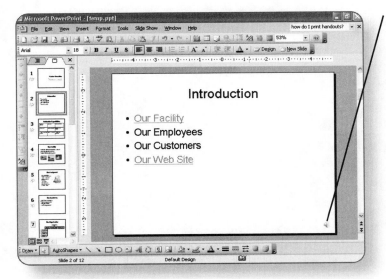

In Normal view, you will see a sound icon in the corner of each slide. You can double-click that sound icon to hear the recorded narration.

47

Publishing to the Web or CD

PowerPoint includes some features that make it easy for you to share a self-running or user-interactive presentation with others. You can save a presentation in Web format and make it available on any Web site, or you can copy it to a writeable CD and then duplicate and distribute the CD. In this chapter, you will learn how to:

- Save a presentation in Web format
- Create a self-running presentation on a CD

Publishing the Presentation in Web Format

Publishing in Web format is useful when you are trying to reach an audience over a network. This can include the Internet or an internal corporate intranet. The main advantage of this distribution method is that the people viewing it do not need PowerPoint installed on their PCs—or even a Windows-based operating system.

1. Click on **File**. The File menu will appear.

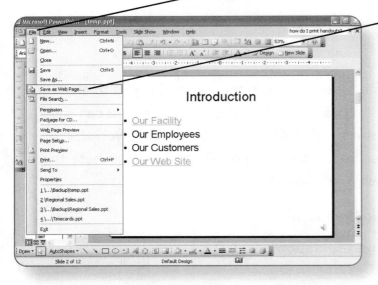

2. Click on **Save as Web Page**. A special version of the Save As dialog box will open.

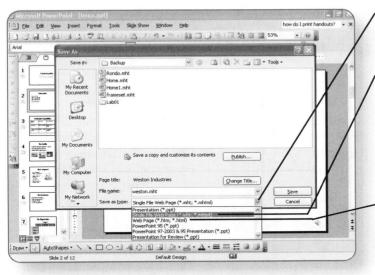

3. Click on the **down arrow** next to Save as type and **select** the **type of file** you want.

The default file format, Single File Web Page, puts the entire presentation into a single file. This is convenient, especially for attaching to e-mails. However, some older Web browsers may not be able to display such a file.

Web Page creates a single Web page as a starting point and a folder of support files containing the graphics. This is the "traditional" way of storing Web pages and is universally accepted.

4. Click on **Change Title**. The Set Page Title dialog box will open.

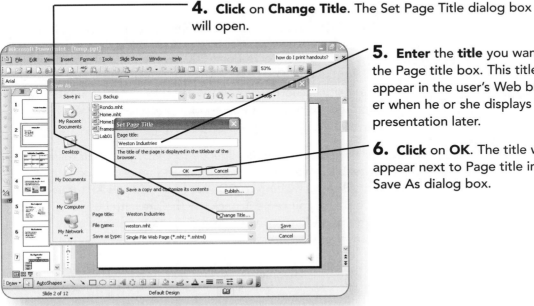

5. Enter the **title** you want in the Page title box. This title will appear in the user's Web browser when he or she displays the presentation later.

6. Click on **OK**. The title will appear next to Page title in the Save As dialog box.

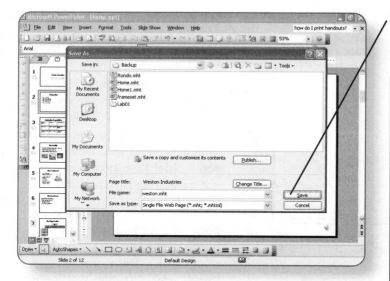

7. **Click** on **Save**. The presentation will be saved in Web format.

> **NOTE**
>
> You can save the file in any location (as you learned in Chapter 30, "Learning About Presentations"). You can also save it directly to a Web server by entering the URL for the Web address in the File name box, or by going through My Network Places. That is beyond the scope of this book, however.

Publishing a Presentation to CD

A new feature in PowerPoint 2003 is the ability to create a self-contained CD that contains the presentation and a copy of a utility called PowerPoint Viewer. This utility enables any computer to display a PowerPoint presentation even if PowerPoint isn't installed.

For this feature to write directly to a CD, you must have a writeable or rewriteable CD drive and an operating system that supports writing to CD (such as Windows XP). If you don't have them, you can still package the presentation for CD and save the package to your hard disk. You can then copy the files to another disk later.

1. **Click** on **File**. The File menu will appear.

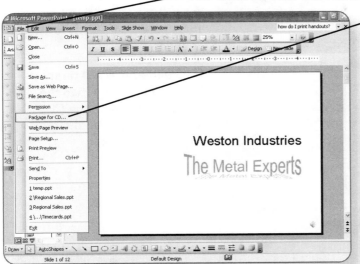

2. **Click** on **Package for CD**. The Package for CD dialog box will open.

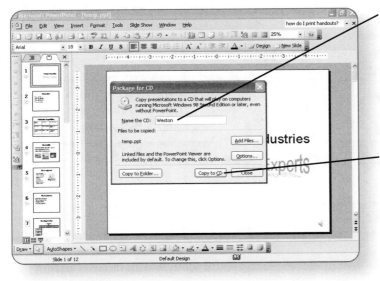

3. **Type** a **name** for the CD in the Name the CD box. This name will appear beneath the CD icon in My Computer when the disc is inserted into a computer.

4. **Insert** a **blank writeable CD** into your CD-R or CD-RW drive.

5. **Click** on **Copy to CD**.

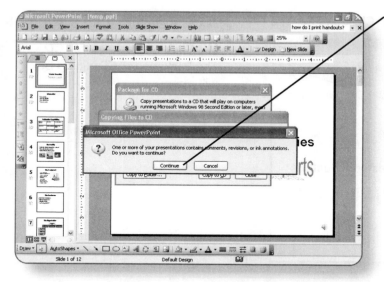

6. Click on **Continue,** if needed. You will see this dialog box only if you have comments, revisions, or annotations.

The needed files will be transferred to the CD. When the process is finished, the CD will be ejected from the drive (on most systems).

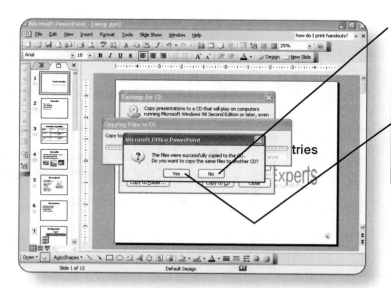

7. Click on **No**. The Package for CD dialog box will reappear.

NOTE

You can click on Yes in step 7 if you need to make extra copies, and then follow the prompts that appear.

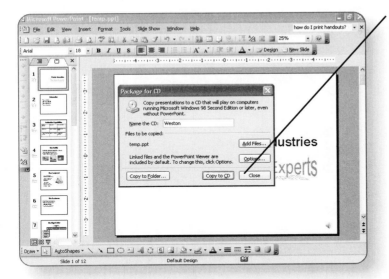

8. Click on **Close**. The Package for CD dialog box will close.

A
Word Shortcut Keys

Keyboard shortcuts are keys or key combinations that you can press instead of selecting menu commands. You may have noticed the keyboard shortcuts listed on the right side of several of the menus. You can use these shortcuts to execute commands without using the mouse to activate menus. You may want to memorize these keyboard shortcuts—not only will they speed your productivity, but they will also help decrease wrist strain caused by excessive mouse usage.

When several keys are listed together, you hold down the first key while tapping the second key. For example, if you see Ctrl+N, you first press and hold down the Ctrl key, tap the N, then release the Ctrl key. In this appendix, you'll learn how to:

- Get up to speed with frequently used keyboard shortcuts
- Use keyboard combinations to edit text
- Use the speech shortcut keys

Learning the Basic Shortcuts

Trying to memorize all of these keyboard shortcuts isn't as hard as you may think. Windows applications all share the same keyboard combinations to execute common commands. Once you get accustomed to using some of these keyboard shortcuts in Word, try them out on some of the other Office programs.

Working with Menus

You can make selections from Word menus without using the mouse. Perhaps you've noticed the underlined letters on menus and commands. Those are *selection letters*; they allow you to work with menus and commands by using the following shortcuts.

To execute this command	Do this
Open a menu	Press Alt then the menu's selection letter
Select a menu command	Press the menu item's selection letter
Close a menu or dialog box	Press Esc
Show a shortcut menu	Press Shift+F10

Getting Help

You don't need to wade through menus to get some help using a program. Try these useful keyboard shortcuts.

To execute this command	Do this
Use Help	Press the F1 key
Use the What's This? button	Press Shift+F1

Working with Documents

The following table shows you a few of the more common keyboard shortcuts that you may want to use when working with documents.

To execute this command	Do this
Create a new document	Press Ctrl+N
Open a different document	Press Ctrl+O
Switch between open documents	Press Ctrl+F6
Save a document	Press Ctrl+S
Use the Save As command	Press F12
Print preview a document	Press Ctrl+F2
Print a document	Press Ctrl+P
Close a document	Press Ctrl+W
Exit Word	Press Alt+F4

Working with Text

The easiest keyboard shortcuts to learn are those that manipulate text. Try your hand at selecting, editing, and formatting text using some of the commonly used text combinations.

Selecting Text

Before you can perform any editing and formatting task on the text in your document, you must select the text. This table shows you how to use keyboard combinations to select text. Before you begin, you need to move the cursor to the beginning of the text that you want to select.

To execute this command	Do this
Highlight the character to the right of the cursor	Press Shift+Right Arrow
Highlight the character to the left of the cursor	Press Shift+Left Arrow
Highlight an entire word	Press Ctrl+Shift+Right Arrow
Highlight an entire line	Press Shift+End
Highlight a paragraph	Press Ctrl+Shift+Down Arrow
Select an entire document	Press Ctrl+A
Go to a specific page	Press Ctrl+G

Editing Text

Once you have selected the text to which you want to make the editing changes, apply one of the combinations in the following table.

To execute this command	Do this
Delete the character to the left of the cursor	Press Backspace
Delete the character to the right of the cursor	Press Delete
Delete the word to the left of the cursor	Press Ctrl+Backspace
Delete the word to the right of the cursor	Press Ctrl+Delete
Cut selected text	Press Ctrl+X
Make a copy of selected text	Press Ctrl+C
Paste the copied text	Press Ctrl+V
Spell check a document	Press F7
Find text in a document	Press Ctrl+F
Repeat Find command	Press Shift+F4
Replace text in a document	Press Ctrl+H
Undo an action	Press Ctrl+Z
Redo an action	Press Ctrl+Y
Move text	Press F2
Add a date field	Press Alt+Shift+D
Add a hyperlink	Press Ctrl+K
Insert a manual page break	Press Ctrl+Enter

Formatting Text

To make your text look good, you may want to change the font, font style, or one of the many standardized paragraph styles.

To execute this command	Do this
Change font attributes	Press Ctrl+D
Make text bold	Press Ctrl+B
Make text italic	Press Ctrl+I
Make text underlined	Press Ctrl+U
Make text double underlined	Press Ctrl+Shift+D
Remove character formatting	Press Ctrl+Spacebar
Single space a paragraph	Press Ctrl+1
Double space a paragraph	Press Ctrl+2
Set 1.5 line spacing	Press Ctrl+5
Center a paragraph	Press Ctrl+E
Left align a paragraph	Press Ctrl+L
Right align a paragraph	Press Ctrl+R
Justify a paragraph	Press Ctrl+J
Left indent a paragraph	Press Ctrl+M
Create a hanging indent	Press Ctrl+T
Right indent a paragraph	Press Ctrl+Shift+M
Remove paragraph formatting	Press Ctrl+Q
Change text case	Press Shift+F3
Change style	Press Ctrl+Shift+S

Speech Commands

Here are a few commands that help when working with speech. These keyboard shortcuts work with the Windows key, which is located on the bottom row of your keyboard and features a flying Windows logo.

To execute this command	Do this
Turn the microphone on and off	Press the Windows key+V
Toggle between Dictation and Voice Command mode	Press the Windows key+T

B
Excel Shortcut Keys

Keyboard shortcuts are keys or key combinations you can press as alternatives to selecting menu commands. You may have noticed the keyboard shortcuts listed on the right side of several of the menus. You can use these shortcuts to execute commands without using the mouse to activate menus. You may want to memorize these keyboard shortcuts. Not only will they speed your productivity, but they will also help decrease wrist strain caused by excessive mouse usage.

When several keys are listed together, you hold down the first key while tapping the second key. For example, if you see Ctrl+N, you first press and hold down the Ctrl key, tap the N, then release the Ctrl key.

In this appendix, you'll learn how to:

- Get up to speed with frequently used keyboard shortcuts
- Use keyboard combinations to edit text
- Use the speech shortcut keys

Learning the Basic Shortcuts

Trying to memorize all these keyboard shortcuts isn't as hard as you may think. Windows applications all share the same keyboard combinations to execute common commands. Once you get accustomed to using some of these keyboard shortcuts in Excel, try them out on some of the other Office programs.

Working with Menus

You can make selections from the Excel menu without using the mouse. Perhaps you noticed the underlined letters on menus and commands. Those are *selection letters* and they allow you to work with menus and commands by using the following shortcuts.

To execute this command	Do this
Open a menu	Press Alt then the menu's selection letter
Select a menu command	Press the menu item's selection letter.
Close a menu or dialog box	Press Esc
Show a shortcut menu	Press Shift+F10

Getting Help

You don't need to wade through menus to get some help using the program. Try these useful keyboard shortcuts.

To execute this command	Do this
Use Help	Press the F1 key
Use the What's This? Button	Press Shift+F1

Working with Workbook Files

The following table shows you a few of the more common keyboard shortcuts that you may want to use when working with any type of Office file.

To execute this command	Do this
Create a new workbook	Press Ctrl+N
Open a different workbook	Press Ctrl+O
Switch between open workbooks	Press Ctrl+F6
Save a workbook	Press Ctrl+S
Use the Save As command	Press F12
Print a file	Press Ctrl+P
Close a file	Press Ctrl+W
Exit Excel	Press Alt+F4

Working inside Workbooks

While working with a workbook, Excel provides a plethora of shortcut key strokes to speed up your data entry or worksheet movement.

Moving around a Workbook

To quickly move around in a workbook, use these shortcut keys:

To move	Do this
One cell in any direction	Press an arrow key
To the next cell on the right	Press Tab
To the next cell on the left	Press Shift+Tab
One screen page in any direction	Press Alt+ an arrow key
One screen up or down	Page Up or Page Down
One screen left or one screen right	Alt+Page Up or Page Down
To the beginning of the current row	Press Home
To cell A1	Press Ctrl+Home
To the last used cell in the worksheet	Press Ctrl+End
To the next worksheet	Press Ctrl+Page Down
To the previous worksheet	Press Ctrl+Page Up
To specfiy an exact cell	Press F5

Typing and Editing Cell Data

When you are typing data, you can save time with these short-cut keys:

To execute this command	Do this
Edit the current cell	Press F2
Start a new formula	Press = (equal sign)
Start an AutoSum formula	Press Alt+=(equal sign)
Start a new line in the same cell	Press Alt+Enter
Insert today's date	Press Ctrl+' (apostrophe)
Insert the current time	Press Ctrl+Shift+: (colon)
Cancel typing entry	Press Esc
Undo the last action	Press Ctrl+Z
Repeat last action	Press Ctrl+Y
Cut	Press Ctrl+X
Copy	Press Ctrl+C
Paste	Press Ctrl+V
Clear cell contents	Press Delete
Delete the selected cells	Press Ctrl+- (hyphen)
Insert blank cells	Press Ctrl+Shift++ (plus sign)
Insert a hyperlink	Press Ctrl+K
Fill down	Press Ctrl+D
Fill right	Press Ctrl+R
Insert a new worksheet	Press Shift+F11

Selecting Ranges of Cells

You can use your mouse to select a range of cells for editing, or you can use these keyboard shortcuts.

To select this	Do this
The entire worksheet	Press Ctrl+A
The current selection by one cell	Press Shift+arrow key
The current selection to the end of a row	Press Ctrl+Shift+right arrow
The current selection to the end of a column	Press Ctrl+Shift+down arrow
The current selection to the last used worksheet cell	Press Ctrl+Shift+End
The current selection to cell A1	Press Ctrl+Shift+Home
An entire column	Press Ctrl+Spacebar
An entire row	Press Shift+Spacebar
The current selection to the beginning of a row	Press Shift+Home

Formatting Data

Many formatting commands have a toolbar button, but you can also access the commands with keyboard shortcuts. Both common character formatting and number formatting commands have shortcuts.

To apply this format	Do this
Bold	Press Ctrl+B
Italics	Press Ctrl+I
Underline	Press Ctrl+U
Open the Format dialog box	Press Ctrl+1
Number	Press Ctrl+Shift+! (exclamation point)
Date	Press Ctrl+Shift+# (number sign)
Currency	Press Ctrl+Shift+$ (dollar sign)
Percentage	Press Ctrl+Shift+% (percent symbol)
Time	Press Ctrl+Shift+@ (at symbol)
General	Press Ctrl+Shift+~ (tilde)
Apply the outline border	Press Ctrl+Shift+& (ampersand)
Remove the outline border	Press Ctrl+Shift+_ (underscore)

Miscellaneous Commands

These keyboard shortcut commands don't seem to fit in any of the standard categories, but are very useful when working with Excel.

To do this	Do this
Create a chart	Press F11
Hide the selected rows	Press Ctrl+9
Unhide any hidden rows within the selection	Press Ctrl+Shift+((opening parenthesis)
Hide the selected columns	Press Ctrl+0 (zero)
Unhide any hidden columns within the selection	Press Ctrl+Shift+) (closing parenthesis)
Check Spelling	Press F7

C

PowerPoint Shortcut Keys

Shortcut keys are a quick and efficient way to execute commands. They increase productivity and decrease the strain caused by excessive mouse usage. Shortcut keys are common to all Microsoft Windows and Office applications, and many of them are common between applications.

This appendix introduces many commonly used shortcut keys. Keep this guide close at hand and practice using the shortcut keys. You'll find that with a little time and patience, you'll be using the keyboard as naturally as you once used the mouse. In this appendix, you'll learn how to:

- Display shortcut keys in the ScreenTips

- Work with presentations

- Navigate the Help system

- Edit text

- Organize an outline

- Move around in a table or presentation

Showing Shortcut Keys in ScreenTips

The menu system lists the shortcut key for a command on the right side of the menu. Shortcut keys can also be displayed in the ScreenTips. When you enable this option, you'll see the shortcut key for a command when you hold the mouse pointer over a toolbar button.

1. **Click** on **Tools**. The Tools menu will appear.

2. **Click** on **Customize**. The Customize dialog box will open.

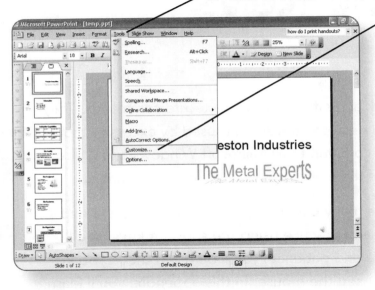

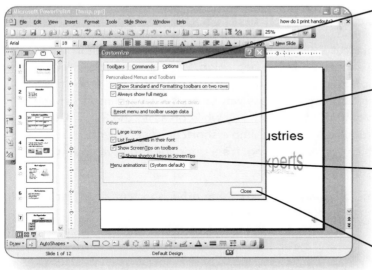

3. **Click** on the **Options tab** if it is not selected when the dialog box opens. The Options tab will come to the front.

4. **Click** in the **Show ScreenTips on toolbars check box**, if it is not selected. A check will be placed in the check box.

5. **Click** in the **Show shortcut keys in ScreenTips check box**. A check will be placed in the check box.

6. **Click** on **Close**. The dialog box will close.

7. **Hold** the **mouse pointer** over a toolbar button. If a shortcut key is assigned to the command, it will appear in the ScreenTip.

Basic Shortcuts

Shortcut keys are easy to remember if you just start with a few shortcuts in the beginning. When you start using these few shortcuts without reverting to the mouse, add a few new shortcut keys. An easy way to start is to get into the habit of holding down the Ctrl key while pressing the S key (Ctrl+S) on a regular basis. This simple shortcut saves the document on which you are working. It's a good idea to save your work every few minutes.

The following table lists some other shortcut keys that will help you get your job done faster.

To execute this command...	Use this shortcut key
Start a new, blank presentation	Ctrl+N
Save a presentation	Ctrl+S
Close a presentation	Ctrl+W
Open a presentation	Ctrl+O
Spell check a presentation	F7
Print a presentation	Ctrl+P
Run a slideshow	F5

Working with the Help System

To display the Help task pane, press F1.

Working with the Outline Pane

In Chapter 31, "Organizing the Presentation Outline," you learned how to edit a presentation outline using the Outlining toolbar. The following table lists the shortcut keys you can use to make this job easier.

To execute this command...	Use this shortcut key
Insert a new slide	Ctrl+M
Demote an outline item	Tab
Promote an outline item	Shift+Tab
Move a paragraph down in the outline	Alt+Shift+Down Arrow
Move a paragraph up in the outline	Alt+Shift+Up Arrow
Show only the title for a selected slide	Alt+Shift+minus sign
Show all of the text for a selected slide	Alt+Shift+plus sign
Collapse an outline to show only the slide titles	Alt+Shift+1
Expand an outline to show all the text on all slides	Alt+Shift+9

Editing Text

As you are adding text to a presentation outline or to the slides, you'll want to try your hand at a few shortcut keys that will make it quicker to select and edit text.

To execute this command...	Use this shortcut key
Select one character to the right	Shift+Right Arrow
Select one character to the left	Shift+Left Arrow
Select from cursor to end of word	Ctrl+Shift+Right Arrow
Select from cursor to beginning of word	Ctrl+Shift+Left Arrow
Select from cursor to next line	Shift+Down Arrow
Select from cursor to previous line	Shift+Up Arrow
Delete selected text	Ctrl+X
Copy selected text	Ctrl+C
Paste text from the clipboard	Ctrl+V
Delete one character to the left	Backspace
Delete one word to the left	Ctrl+Backspace
Delete one character to the right	Delete
Delete one word to the right	Ctrl+Delete
Find text on a slide	Ctrl+F
Replace text on a slide	Ctrl+H
Undo editing changes	Ctrl+Z
Redo editing changes	Ctrl+Y

Formatting Text

Formatting text using shortcut keys is easy, and most of these shortcut keys are easy to remember. To format text, select the text and then use the appropriate shortcut keys. The following table lists the most common formatting shortcut keys.

To execute this command...	Use this shortcut key
Change the font of the selected text	Ctrl+Shift+F
Make the font larger	Ctrl+Shift+>
Make the font smaller	Ctrl+Shift+<
Make the text bold	Ctrl+B
Underline the text	Ctrl+U
Italicize the text	Ctrl+I
Center a paragraph	Ctrl+E
Left-align a paragraph	Ctrl+L
Right-align a paragraph	Ctrl+R

Moving Around in a Table or Slide Show

With the mouse, it's a snap to move from cell to cell in a table, or from slide to slide in a slide show. Just one click and you're there! Moving around with the keyboard isn't as intuitive. Use the following table to get around inside tables and slide shows.

To execute this command...	Use this shortcut key
Go to the next cell in a table	Tab
Go to the previous cell in a table	Shift+Tab
Move to the next row in a table	Down Arrow
Move to the previous row in a table	Up Arrow
Move to the next slide in a slide show	Spacebar
Go to the previous slide in a slide show	Backspace
Display a specific slide in a slide show	Type the slide number and press Enter
End the slide show	Esc

Index